What Every Chief Executive Should Know

USING DATA TO MEASURE POLICE PERFORMANCE

D1716698

JON M. SHANE

Foreword by **WILLIAM J. BRATTON**

Looseleaf
Law Publications, Inc.

43-08 162nd Street • Flushing, NY 11358
www.LooseleafLaw.com • 800-647-5547

This publication is not intended to replace nor be a substitute for any official procedural material issued by your agency of employment nor other official source. Looseleaf Law Publications, Inc., the author and any associated advisors have made all possible efforts to ensure the accuracy and thoroughness of the information provided herein but accept no liability whatsoever for injury, legal action or other adverse results following the application or adoption of the information contained in this book.

Library of Congress Cataloging-in-Publication Data

Shane, Jon M.
 What every chief executive should know : using data to measure police performance / Jon M. Shane.
    p. cm.
 Includes bibliographical references and index.
 ISBN-13: 978-1-932777-38-3 (pbk.)
 ISBN-10: 1-932777-38-5 (pbk.)
 1. Police administration--Evaluation--Statistical methods. 2. Police--Personnel management--Evaluation--Statistical methods. 3. Performance--Evaluation--Statistical methods. 4. Police administration--United States--Evaluation--Statistical methods. 5. Police--Research--Statistical methods. I. Title.
   HV7935.S47 2007
   363.2'2--dc22

                                                          2007009779

*To my beautiful, adoring, understanding wife Vincenzina
and the greatest gift she ever gave me,
our son Michael Donovan.
There is nothing more important than a family filled with
love, humor, compassion and understanding.
And that I have!*

Jon M. Shane is completing doctoral studies at Rutgers School of Criminal Justice. He also holds a certification in non-profit management from Rutgers Graduate School of Public Administration. His research interests are social disorganization theory, routine activities theory, opportunity theory, ecology and crime, environmental criminology, performance issues and issues affecting the police. He is also a retired Captain from the Newark Police Department, a graduate of the 193rd session of the FBI National Academy and a graduate of the 25th session of the Police Executive Research Forum's Senior Management Institute for Police at Harvard's John F. Kennedy School of Government. He is an adjunct professor at Fairleigh Dickinson University, Teaneck, New Jersey and a part-time lecturer for Rutgers University, Newark campus, where he teaches courses in policing and criminal justice. Mr. Shane has worked with other law enforcement agencies across the country developing policy, conducting performance audits, research and management studies to measure performance. He is currently a research consultant for the Police Foundation, Washington, D.C. and a subject matter expert for the Center for Problem Oriented Policing. He is also the principal in a consulting practice, Jon M. Shane Associates, specializing in policy development, police management and administration, program evaluation, and strategic planning (jonmshane@ netscape.net).

▶ Acknowledgments

Writing a book takes a great deal of determination. Although most of it comes from within, a great deal also comes from outside through the help and inspiration of friends, family, colleagues and associates. While this book is a culmination of personal experience, most of that personal experience would not have occurred without dedicated police professionals, friends and mentors who guided me throughout my formative years in the police department and throughout my academic career. For that I am eternally grateful.

First, and foremost, to my exceptionally talented and professional wife, Vincenzina, who has dedicated herself to educating and guiding children in the public school system. She was my original principal reviewer and, with great attention to detail, was able to find one too many fragmented sentences that seemed to read just fine to me. I think she also found one upside down period! But, that's why I love her so.

To my friends and colleagues at Rutgers School of Criminal Justice and Rutgers Graduate School of Public Administration who enjoyed hearing that I was putting this book together. Rutgers unquestionably has some of the most talented scholars and some of the brightest students I have ever come across—their persistent encouragement is quite noble. Specifically, thanks go to Dr. Gerald Miller, associate professor, Rutgers Graduate School of Public Administration for lighting my inspirational fire and for showing me how much the public deserves efficient government. Dr. Miller is unmistakably a gentleman and a scholar and deserves every bit of the accolade bestowed here. To Seungmug "Zech" Lee, a friend and fellow student who painstakingly reduced thousands of cases to a comprehensible and useable format for the aoristic crime analysis model presented in this book. I greatly admire his intellect and patience. To Nutan Patel, Patrycja E. Lesniowska, Luis Matos, Bilal J. Mian and Steven Mark for their consultation and technological savvy on data analysis-they have bright futures ahead! And to Dr. Ronald V. Clarke, an internationally recognized criminologist and scholar, for his encouragement and leadership. I first met Dr. Clarke in the fall of 1997 and I instantly became a follower. Dr. Clarke was never beyond making me strive to meet his exacting standards, which is why I have become a perfectionist myself. I accept all of his criticism constructively, which has made me realize that for all our knowledge, we are merely scratching the surface.

To my friends and colleagues at the Newark Police Department and those in the law enforcement community I have come to admire. Little did I realize how much knowledge and life experience I would derive from my early days, working nights, holidays, weekends, in a radio-car in the 5th precinct. It was there that some life-long friendships were forged: Deputy Chief Brian Gaven (ret.), a noted and trusted colleague whom I worked alongside for nearly seventeen years and who is a paragon of police professionalism; Deputy Chief Daniel J. Delorenzi (ret.) who exemplifies integrity and police leadership. I had the unmistakable pleasure of working with Danny for many years and then collaborating on several projects after retirement, especially a revised Compstat model that refines aspiring police leaders' knowledge, skills and abilities. Thanks, Dan, for thinking enough of me to work on it with you; and to retired Deputy Chief John D. Dough, now Chief at the Essex County Sheriff's Office, Newark, who has been a friend, a colleague and a mentor throughout my entire career. Chief Dough is *the* consummate professional in every sense of the word and without whose unrelenting pursuit of excellence and encouragement I would be ten steps behind everyone else today.

To Deputy Chief Gary Brennan, Los Angeles Police Department, whom I had the pleasure to meet in Boston during the 25th session of the Senior Management Institute for Police. A devout professional and exceptional police leader; my only regret is not having befriended Gary earlier in my career. To Lieutenant I Sean Malinowski, Executive Officer, Office of the Chief of Police and Detective III Jeff Godown, Office of the Chief of Police, Los Angeles Police Department, for their assistance and support in reviewing and commenting on the original manuscript. And to Chief William J. Bratton, Los Angeles Police Department, perhaps the most progressive and influential police leader in the last 40 years. As he so fittingly said, police executives are the agents of change who can transform cities across the country into places "fit for all families" to live, work and visit and that cops do matter when it comes to making cities safer. I deeply admire his commitment to public service, his risk-taking persona and his proclivity to reshape police organizations through accountability and performance. Few have accomplished what he has in such prestigious posts.

Finally, to Looseleaf Law Publications, especially Mary Loughrey, Maria Felten and the editorial staff who made the process from manuscript to finished product something special. Thanks to everyone for the opportunity, particularly those anonymous reviewers who offered a great deal of insight on the original drafts.

▶ Table of Contents

PART TWO – Statistics and Data Analysis

Table of Contents

Measuring the things police do is not something new. In the 1920s as the political era of 19th century policing was giving way to the 20th century's professional model, reform leaders like O.W. Wilson and William H. Parker began to experiment with performance measurement, primarily through the FBI Uniform Crime Report-Part I crimes. Another early professional-era measurement was rapid response to calls for service-this was seen as the hallmark of professional-era policing. Part of these leaders' relentless analytic management style was to use the data police routinely capture to demonstrate how they could be effective at reducing crime while simultaneously being efficient. For they understood that which gets measured could be improved!

Among their many accomplishments Wilson's management philosophy sought efficiency over politics. Parker continued in the same fashion with an emphasis on reducing wasteful spending. Both police leaders relied on data to drive department performance. But measurement in the early years was not tactical or strategic, nor was it linked to the priorities or mission of the agency. Analysis was also confounded by the pen and paper since computers had not yet made their way into law enforcement. Early efforts to measure police performance was, however, the impetus for a new generation of police leaders who emerged in the 1970s to take a fresh look at how police departments measure success and affix accountability. Policing was about to undergo another paradigm shift, this time into the community era, where there was a great emphasis on police legitimacy, as well as crime control, which would be measured by the level of respect and compassion as perceived by the community.

A number of hard lessons were learned from the distant, professional model of policing and police leaders sought to capitalize on some of those weaknesses. Among them was the idea that police departments are rich in data that could be used to reorient the agency for success; success would be measured in different ways, not just by reducing crime. From the 1970s through today, policing has made some of its most innovative and successful changes. Foremost among them are the advent of problem-oriented policing (POP) and the incorporation of technology to solve problems. The POP style of policing requires data analysis so the nature, magnitude, distribution, seriousness and rate of change for a given problem can be measured. These components are essential to driving crime downward-and driving crime down through analysis is facilitated with technology such as desktop computers, basic analysis software and crime mapping techniques. The confluence of the POP philosophy and information-technology is the foundation for the Compstat process that was introduced in the New York City Police Department (NYPD) in 1994. This

innovative management technique spawned a diffusion of performance management throughout the policing profession.

In order to be effective and efficient the NYPD had to reorient itself,
beginning with capturing information that was accurate and timely; then
devising effective tactics to counter the problem; then rapidly deploying
resources around the information; finally, conducting relentless follow-up to
ensure the problem did not recur. These four principles are the cornerstone of
performance management, which can only be accomplished by collecting,
analyzing and reporting on streams of data routinely collected by the
department. These core management principles now drive the mission of the
Los Angeles Police Department (LAPD): "to protect and serve," something that
has never been done before, while, at the same time, help shape the priorities
of the department.

Crime is not the only "bottom line" measure of performance in the LAPD
today nor is it the only measure other chiefs use to determine success. In an era
of increasing demands and limited resources, police managers in all jurisdictions are struggling to improve their capacity to prevent terror attacks, to serve
their communities and control crime constitutionally, compassionately and consistently. There are numerous administrative processes that lend themselves to
analysis, which bespeak efficiency, compassion and fairness such as budgeting,
prisoner processing, and use of force. The LAPD, for example, has historically
operated with lean budgets. The police department has also operated with a
force-strength much leaner, per capita, than many other major U.S cities. This
means the LAPD must consistently operate with greater operational and fiscal
accountability to maintain a posture ahead of the crime curve-there is no room
for waste! In order to improve organizational capacity and community
responsiveness, the LAPD relies on a variety of performance indicators that
relate to the department's mission.

This book comes at a time when police departments across the country are
being tasked with doing more with less, which means working smarter within
the confines of a lean budget. One of the efficiency methods Jon Shane identifies
is linking workload to costs, in order to demonstrate the level of effort necessary
to serve the city. Another method he identifies is devising logic models that
support programs worthy of outside funding to supplement basic police service.
Perhaps, most importantly, Jon identifies a method for developing a business
plan that includes performance measures that are logical, which can be applied
to and easily understood by those who are held accountable. Part of the success
of Compstat lies in its value to assess collective performance by evaluating the
performance indicators assigned to each organizational element. Once the
indicators are affixed and data is captured, it is the individual commanders'
responsibility to carry out the strategies necessary to meet the standard. This
can only happen in an environment where performance is measured based on
objective data.

In order to successfully deliver crime control, integrity, general police service and fiscal accountability Jon Shane understands the route is through performance management. The result is his book that describes simply and concisely how to analyze, use, interpret and report on data and how that process can drive accountability and improve performance. I know, as the chief executive of six major police departments, that as the person who is ultimately accountable, I need to measure what matters in order to be successful. Jon Shane's book gets right to the heart of the matter and lays out a thoughtful approach to improving accountability and efficiency in any organization, regardless of size. Police leaders will be well served by reading this book; they will also be well served by having policy advisors and other staff members read the book, then devise performance measures suitable for their department.

The community-era of the 21st century demands performance and accountability from its elected and appointed government officials. To this end police leaders should redouble their efforts and examine how they are assessing performance and what measures they are using. This book provides a level of detail that capitalizes on the innovativeness of the Compstat process, so much so that a new era of police performance management is emerging through that which Jon Shane has crafted. This book shows what to do and how to do it.

William J. Bratton
Chief of Police
Los Angeles Police Department

The concept for this book was developed after years of watching many police executives, elected leaders, command-rank officers and mid-level managers struggle for answers to questions, such as: how many police officers do we need? Is there a relationship between the number of police officers we have and the crime rate? How much can we expect our crime rate to decline if we allocate another 10, 50, 100 or 1,000 hours of overtime? Given the department's historical performance if we hire an additional 2, 5, 20 or 100 officers, then what crime rate can we expect? Do the citizens feel safe? Are the citizens satisfied with the police department? Can we say with a specific degree of certainty that the citizens have confidence in the police department? How do we know if our programs are working as intended? Are we performing better, worse or about the same as last year? Do we need more officers in patrol (or the detective bureau or the traffic division)? If so, then *how many* do we need to handle the work? What is our projected workload for the next two years?

The answers that were offered were rarely, if ever, based on empirical evidence, usually only extemporaneous thought. Sometimes the answers were reasonably formulated based on what a wise executive *believed* was correct given past practice, but none of the conclusions held any statistical significance. This is a significant shortcoming for budget-conscious mayors, city council members, city managers and business administrators. This is also a shortcoming for police executives who demand accountability and performance from their employees. Policy decisions based on answers not supported by empirical information is not sound management; indeed, such decisions are flimsy. Police scholar Kenneth Culp Davis (1974:704) noted that, "police policy is characteristically based on superficial guesswork and hardly at all on systematic studies by staffs of qualified specialists or on investigations like those conducted by our best administrative agencies and legislative committees."[1]

The defining moment for this book came during a meeting with a Police Director who wanted answers from his commanding officer of Fleet Management regarding police vehicle availability. The police department was in the process of purchasing new police cars and developing a performance-based service agreement with an automotive repair vendor. The Police Director asked his Fleet Management commander: *"How many marked vehicles are out of service at any given time?"* The commander replied, *"about 20%."* The Director then asked him, *"how many marked vehicles do we need to ensure that 100% of the marked fleet is operationally ready for service?"* (the marked fleet consisted of 312 police vehicles). The Fleet Management commander replied, *"I'm not sure."* Another commander calculated 20% of 312 and replied, *"We need to buy an additional 62 vehicles, or 120% to keep the fleet at 100%."* This is not accurate.

v

The Fleet Management commander said "*at any given time 20% of the fleet is out of service for repair.*" "At any given time" means the *average* amount of time; actual percentages vary on a daily basis. If the **average** amount of time the fleet is down for repair is 20%, then 20% of *all* marked vehicles must be accounted for. To solve this problem, first, an additional 62 vehicles must be purchased to account for the 20% of the *existing* fleet that is out of service ($312 \times 20\% = 62$). Of the 62 new vehicles purchased, 20% of them will be out of service as well, because, as the Fleet Management commander stated "*at any given time*" 20% of the vehicles are out of service for repairs. Twenty percent of the 62 new vehicles is an additional 12 vehicles ($12 = 62 \times 20\%$). If the department bought an additional 12 vehicles, 20% of those vehicles would also be out of service; 20% of 12 is 2 ($2 = 12 \times 20\%$). Lastly, 20% of the 2 new vehicles will be out of service; 20% of 2 is .4. In this case it is better to err on the side of caution and round up to 1 instead of rounding down, unless the city simply cannot afford the extra vehicle: $312 + 62 + 12 + 2 + 1 = 389$ total vehicles.

Therefore, the correct answer to the question, "*How many marked vehicles do we need to ensure 100% of the marked fleet is ready for operational service?*" is 390. Said differently, the department would have to invest in an additional 78 vehicles ($312 + 78 = 390$), or increase the fleet by 25%, not 20% as the commander suggested. Since the approximate cost of one fully-equipped marked police vehicle is $30,000 there is a significant budget impact by miscalculating the number of cars actually needed.

This deceptively simple problem could prove embarrassing if the Police Director did not properly budget for vehicle purchases. Here is how the slippery slope might go: 20% of the fleet is out of service for repairs → 20% fewer cars means fewer officers will be deployed in cars on patrol → fewer police cars in the field means response time suffers → if response time suffers, then citizen satisfaction declines. A parallel problem is this: → a service agreement is prepared and public bids are developed based upon inaccurate data → if the department does acquire the appropriate number of vehicles, the vendor will not be able to repair all of them because the service agreement that eventually became the contract specified the vendor will repair only "X number" of vehicles for the agreed upon price, and so forth…The data elements existed and were part of that which was routinely captured, it is just that the Fleet Commander did not know how to put them together.

The premise of the book is to encapsulate some of the strategies for conquering these seemingly intractable management issues and make them easy to understand and apply. The book should be used as a reference text that is consulted periodically as performance measures are developed and analysis techniques are contemplated. It is most appealing because for management issues, the spreadsheets with formulae have already been created. This means readers can begin using the material immediately by simply copying the spreadsheets from the enclosed Resource CD and inserting agency-specific data.

The book is intended for the following audiences who often have the ability to influence department policy or who must solve operational or administrative problems within certain constraints:

1. **Police Executives** – The agency's chief executive and his or her command staff need to understand the concepts presented in this book in order to *steer* the agency while the workforce *rows*. Part of steering the ship is successfully navigating the waters: where the department is currently, where it should be or would like to go and how to get there. This is the essence of planning and budgeting. Enduring, surviving and thriving as a chief executive is predicated on the success of well-formulated plans that have the resources to fulfill them (Jurkanin, Hoover, Dowling and Ahmed, 2001:85-96). The material presented in this book will help prepare the navigation chart for the ship's departure.

2. **Crime Analysts and Police Planners** - Crime analysts and police planners are typically those who are tasked with helping develop the navigation chart. They are often well suited to do so because they deal with data all the time. This familiarity with different data sets, software applications and presentation are indispensable for driving organizational movement and helping the chief executive execute his or her strategy according to plan. The methodology and concepts in this book will help crime analysts and police planners take the agency to the next level by arming them with some intermediate-level procedures not often used in police planning.

3. **Consultants** – Consultants are in a unique position to help agencies create efficiencies and improve performance for several reasons: 1) they work closely with the chief executive and the command staff to define the problem or issue, set desired goals and manage expectations; 2) they help develop hypotheses that guide the problem solving process; 3) they immerse themselves in the agency's business logic to understand how it operates. This leaves the workforce to concentrate on daily operations while the consultant devotes quality time to the granular aspects of planning and analysis; 4) they share early findings through interim reports, which helps ensure seamless implementation of recommendations. These lines of regular communication help solidify relationships by developing the trust necessary to act as counselors; 5) they are independent and not beholden to any member of the agency that is under study; and 6) they can validate internal agency processes. This creates legitimacy in the organization because of the consultant's professional advice and expertise. This text will help the consultant shape the police management environment by showing clients precisely what data elements to organize and capture and how they should be presented. The consultant can also use the models on the CD to plug-in their client's actual data to create reports that will confirm or dispel assertions from supporters and critics.[2]

4. **Business Administrators, County Executives and City Managers** –
   At the forefront of service delivery is the person who is responsible for
   conducting the daily affairs of the city (or county or state). The decisions
   they make are quite often driven by economics: *how much will this cost?* And
   rightfully so! The government entity is not a bottomless money pit. The
   services that are delivered should be analyzed for their efficiency and, where
   feasible, alternatives should be considered.[3] This book contains a section on
   efficiency analyses and budgeting that helps government leaders make
   informed choices and shows the value in linking workload to costs with
   objective criteria. This is especially important when resource consolidation
   or resource sharing is being contemplated. Although the models are
   police-specific, they are directly transferable to other elements of the government body (fire department, health and human services, schools etc.).
5. **Students and Instructors of Police Management and Public
   Administration and Police Analysis** – Students will find this book very
   informative because it uses realistic examples; instructors will find it
   especially helpful as an adjunct text to required reading in topic areas such
   as budgeting, crime analysis, and government performance because the
   formulas and examples are already prepared. The concepts in this book are
   presented in models on the accompanying Resource CD. This gives
   instructors quality time to concentrate on lecture preparation instead of
   having to create the statistical models in spreadsheets.

Just as there were skeptics when N.Y.P.D. Commissioner Bill Bratton
introduced Compstat in the early 1990's, those who dismissed his idea of using
data to manage police operations better, so, too, will there be critics who
question the value of the material presented here. That is, until a few forward-
thinking chief executives delve into the examples and compel their command
rank personnel to seize the opportunity presented to them. Early successes from
performance-based management will make believers out of others who will wait
on the sidelines to see how their colleagues did. The approach to that end is
through strategic thinking—conceptualizing an idea, operationalizing its
component parts, designing data collection processes and data analysis—
analyzing, summarizing and drawing conclusions from the data. This text
represents the next level of Compstat by combining the disciplines of criminal
justice, public administration and business management. It also embodies the
principles of strategic and assumption-based planning to help administrators
solve common police management problems and to help develop strategic
management plans. While the examples are drawn from police experience, the
concepts are applicable to any type of government or non-profit entity.

The purpose of this book is to expose police executives to a few basic concepts that can dramatically improve efficiency and analytic capabilities, and
provide administrators with a logical and defensible method for conducting
accurate analyses. In order to improve efficiency it is important to know the

current state of affairs. What follows is the question: *How do we know what "improved" looks like?* If police executives are to review operations intelligently, then they should have a basic premise to guide them. That premise is the systematic structure of performance management. Quite often police departments do not articulate formal performance standards. Very simply, there is no way to determine if individual officers, entire bureaus and divisions or specific programs have performed as expected because no performance standards have been enunciated. This book aims to help institutionalize performance management and analysis by giving police executives the tools necessary to widely adopt the concepts presented here, not just reduce them as part of the historical record on the topic.

By applying the principles in this book chief executives will be able to: 1) provide the public and elected officials with informative data on crime and agency performance, 2) measure the effects of preventive efforts including community-based and police-based programs, 3) uncover patterns and trends in performance that can serve as best practices and facilitate benchmarking exercises, 4) measure overall agency workload, efficiency and effectiveness including the performance of specific divisions, 5) analyze the factors associated with success or failure of various police initiatives, 6) provide comparative norms of performance across divisions and other police agencies, 7) furnish baseline data for research, budget and performance issues, 8) assess budget expenditures directly related to crime control and service delivery, 9) forecast future states for more enlightened police planning and 10) assess what worked, when, where and how as the agency moves toward becoming a "learning organization" (President's Commission of Law Enforcement and Administration of Justice, Task Force Report on Assessment, 1967:123-124).

Wherever efficiency can be gleaned, whether in deployment, budgeting, crime control, staffing, program evaluation, or citizen satisfaction, basic analysis can reveal how well the agency is performing and serve as a comparison to help explain something or make it easier for executives to understand.[4] And in lean fiscal times, proving the agency is conducting business as efficiently as possible is paramount to success. In the words of Peter Drucker (1990): what is the bottom line when there is no "bottom line?" Performance!

▶ Symbols, Abbreviations and Acronyms

a	Intercept
ABB	Activity-based Budgeting
ABC	Activity-based Costing
ABP	Assumption-based Planning
ACSI	American Customer Satisfaction Index
AFIS	Automated Fingerprint Identification System
ANOVA	Analysis of Variance
ARIMA	Autoregressive Integrated Moving Average
AS	Actual Strength
ASC	American Society of Criminology
ASCII	American Standard Code for Information Interchange
ASP	Armament Systems and Procedures (expandable tactical baton)
ATF	(Bureau of) Alcohol, Tobacco and Firearms
AVL	Automatic Vehicle Locator
AWOL	Away Without Leave
b	Slope
BJA	(United States) Bureau of Justice Assistance
BJS	(United States) Bureau of Justice Statistics
CAD	Computer Aided Dispatch (System)
CALEA	Commission on Accreditation for Law Enforcement Agencies
CBA	Cost Benefit Analysis
CBO	Community-based Organization
CCTV	Closed Circuit Television
CEA	Cost Effectiveness Analysis
CFS	Calls for Service
CJ	Criminal Justice
CO	Commanding Officer
CODIS	Combined DNA Index System
CompStat	Computer Statistics
COPS	(United States Department of Justice, Office of) Community Oriented Policing Services
CPH	Calls per Hour
CPTED	Crime Prevention through Environmental Design (pronounced "sep-ted")
CPY	Calls per Year
DARE	Drug Abuse Resistance Education
DEA	(United States) Drug Enforcement Administration
DF	Degrees of Freedom
DNA	Deoxyribonucleic acid
DOC	Department of Corrections

DOJ	(United States) Department of Justice
DV	Domestic Violence
DWI	Driving While Intoxicated
e	Error Term
EDP	Emotionally Disturbed Person
EEOC	Equal Employment Opportunity Commission
ES	Effective Strength
EWS	Early Warning System
F	(F Distribution) Continuous Probability Statistic
FBI	(United States) Federal Bureau of Investigation
FBINA	FBI National Academy
FISS	Firearm Injury Surveillance System
FOIA	Freedom of Information Act
FTE	Full Time Equivalent
GAO	(U.S) Government Accountability Office (formerly Government Accounting Office)
GASB	Government Accounting Standards Board
GIS	Geographic Information Systems
GREAT	Gang Resistance Education and Training
HY	Hours worked per Year
IACP	International Association of Chiefs of Police
ICPSR	Inter-University Consortium for Political and Social Research
ICV	In-car Video
ID	Identification(s)
IRP	(Rampart) Independent Review Panel
IT	Information/Technology
KCMO	Kansas City, Missouri (Police Department)
LAPD	Los Angeles Police Department
LEMAS	Law Enforcement Management and Administrative Statistics
MDC	Mobile Data Computer
MO	Modus Operandi (method of operation)
MS	Mean Sum of Squares
NAPA	National Academy of Public Administration
NAWH	Net Annual Work Hours
NCIC	National Crime Information Center
NCJRS	National Criminal Justice Reference Service
NCMEC	National Center for Missing and Exploited Children
NCOVR	National Consortium for Violence Research
NIBIN	National Integrated Ballistic Information (System)
NIBRS	National Incident-Based Reporting System
NIJ	(United State Department of Justice) National Institute of Justice
NOBLE	National Organization of Black Law Enforcement Executives
NSA	National Sheriffs Association

NYPD	New York (City) Police Department
OLS	Ordinary Least Squares
OR	Operations Research
P	Positions
p-Value	The probability of wrongly rejecting the null hypothesis if it is in fact true
PDA	(Portable) Personal Digital Assistant
PEMDAS	Parentheses, Exponents, Multiplication, Division, Addition, Subtraction
PF	Police Foundation
PERF	Police Executive Research Forum
PEST	Political, Economic, Social and Technological (Analysis)
POP	Problem-oriented Policing
PS	Performance Standard
PSA	Public Service Announcement
PSAP	Public Safety Answering Point (911 call reception and communications center)
R	Required Personnel
R Sqr (R^2)	Coefficient of Multiple Determination
RAND	Research and Development (Corporation)
RF	Relief Factor
RICO	Racketeer Influenced and Corrupt Organization (Act)
RMS	Records Management System
ROI	Return on Investment
SAF	Staff Adjustment Factor
SARA	Scanning, Analysis, Response Assessment (problem-solving model)
SHR	(FBI UCR) Supplemental Homicide Reports
SMART	Specific, Measurable, Accountable, Results-Oriented, Time-Bound
SMIP	(PERF) Senior Management Institute for Police
SPSS	Statistical Package for the Social Sciences
SQL	Structured Query Language
S.S.	Sum of Squares
SWOT	Strengths, Weaknesses, Opportunities and Threats (Analysis)
T	Number of Tours
t Stat(istic)	A measure used to determine whether two means are statistically different
TASER	Thomas A. Swift Electric Rifle (aka/stun gun)
TOT	Turned Over To
TQM	Total Quality Management
TRO	Temporary Restraining Order
TRU	Telephone Reporting Unit
UCR	(FBI) Uniform Crime Report

X	Independent Variable
XO	Executive Officer
Y	Dependent Variable

1

▶ **Introduction**

Background

Virtually everything in policing is subject to measurement and, as such, should be measured. As Moore and colleagues (2002:142-143) poignantly stated, "even if citizens and their representatives do not demand accountability, measuring performance is still ethically and morally the right thing to do. When someone becomes a police executive, he or she explicitly assumes the responsibility for deploying a valuable, collectively owned asset. It is his or her moral and ethical duty not only to use that asset well, but also to give an account of how the asset is being used so that the 'owners' of the enterprise can be satisfied that their purposes are being reliably achieved. These moral and ethical obligations are particularly weighty for public sector enterprises because the 'owners' cannot show their displeasure simply by selling their shares and exiting.[5] Instead they are stuck with the regime that is created, and are forced to use their voice to ensure that their interests are reflected in the way the enterprise operates. For their voice to be effective, they must have accurate information about police performance…" Measuring performance creates public value: "1) it is good management, 2) enhances the quality of services delivered, 3) what gets measured gets done, 4) aids in budget development and review, and 5) answers why public resources are being spent on these activities."[6] (Jankofsky, N.D.)

To that end government agencies are expected to perform their mission with the least amount of money possible while achieving the greatest efficiency. Insofar as possible efficiency can be said to be achieved when input resources are minimized, cycle times are reduced, and costs are reduced along the pathway to ideal firm size.[7] Along that same pathway it is hoped there are economies of scale that improve citizen satisfaction, reporting accuracy and service reliability, which are indicators of effectiveness. Although government is big business, it is not intended to be profitable nor charge consumers more than is necessary to deliver its services. If government is wasting money, then there are probably inefficiencies (Metzenbaum, 2006). In many instances, when asked, a police executive does not have an answer for how much it costs to deliver basic services, such as: the cost to respond to a domestic violence call? The cost to investigate a murder? Or, the cost to respond to a (false) burglar alarm? Moreover, the cost of delivering various programs, such as patrol, criminal investigations and communications are expensive endeavors and executives should be accountable for how they deliver those services. The truth is that these questions are answerable within a reasonable degree of certainty and the right answers can make the difference between receiving funding for a new program or being rejected. The U.S. Department of Justice, Bureau of Justice Assistance (BJA) now requires most grant applications to incorporate an evaluation component to demonstrate efficiency and effectiveness.[8]

These are important and fundamental questions for determining how efficiently the organization is operating, or where adjustments must be made. It is also important for strategic planning purposes: if a police department knows where it is spending its time and resources, then it is able to go after external funds (i.e., government and non-profit grants) to establish programs that directly impact service delivery. For example, if a police department is spending twenty-five percent of its time responding to domestic violence calls, then it is logical to develop a program that addresses domestic violence with the hope of eventually redeploying local assets (material and personnel) to another cause.

There is scant literature on *how* to create efficiency in police departments. Much of the literature is theoretical and does not provide the necessary formulas for administrators to follow. There is a wealth of information on the principles of Total Quality Management (TQM), but little information on "how to" use TQM to create the nexus between workload, processes and budget. One of the best ways to start is through analysis of the responsibilities of each organizational element. By answering the question: *What services does this program deliver?* whether according to function (as in a forensics laboratory), geographical area (as in a precinct station), clientele (as in a domestic violence or youth services program) or by purpose (as in field operations, traffic or detectives) (Iannone, 1987:22), a workload analysis will help solve the first cut at creating an efficient organization. The examples presented here are aimed at reconciling input, output and outcome measures as they relate to efficiency.

Why Collect and Analyze Data?

There are three recognized purposes for collecting and analyzing data: "1) monitoring, 2) agency accountability and 3) research" (Maxfield and Babbie, 2001:129). Monitoring helps agency executives assess various conditions in support of its mission, examine resource allocation and consider alternatives. Agency accountability is a fundamental tenet of democratic government; "government agencies are obliged to keep records that document their actions and areas of responsibility" (Maxfield and Babbie, 2001:131). Lastly, to support internal and external research. Internal research is typically conducted by an administrative element of the agency to improve processes and compare performance, thus becoming more efficient. External research is typically conducted by research organizations such as RAND, The Police Foundation, PERF or public and private universities to improve conditions, identify relationships among various social phenomena and, when possible, identify causes of specific conditions.

Collecting data that supports external research also helps bridge the gap between academics and practitioners, who should be working cooperatively to solve crime and quality of life issues. Although the gulf has been shrinking over the last few decades, practitioners often hold the keys to the kingdom (i.e., access to data and processes). Among the many advantages of partnering with an external research group and making data available to them, are: 1) from a reactive perspective, satisfying the mandates of a consent decree; from a proactive perspective, staving off the imposition of a consent decree, 2) access to (often free) expert data analysis beyond the capabilities of the agency, 3) building an image as a leader in policing innovation, 4) building a reputation as a transparent agency, 5) grant funding and take-aways that would not be available to the agency by itself, 6) data analysis that supports expert testimony in court to defend agency policy and practice, 7) independent validation of program effects, and 8) very importantly, unencumbering agency employees from the time-consuming task of exploratory and explanatory research, thus leaving the employees to devote more quality time to the agency's mission.

Data analysis can also reveal estimates of the cost of crime, including the costs associated with policing and the administration of criminal justice. Several studies have been empaneled to study crime's economic impact:

- According to *Victim Costs and Circumstances: A New Look,* a survey administered for the Justice Department, the estimated cost of crime in the Unites States was $450 billion. "The survey was reported to be the first to try to measure the cost of child abuse and domestic violence along with crimes like murder, robbery and rape" (Law Enforcement News, 1996);
- The University of Pennsylvania Health System (UPHS) placed the cost of crime in the United States in the early 1990's "between $200 billion and $800 billion in federal, state and local government expenditures for the criminal justice system, police and corrections" (UPHS, 2006);
- Cohen and Miller (1997) estimated the mental health care costs for crime victims, which included "...total dollar value of counseling and therapy received by crime victims was $9.7 billion and the median value was $8.3 billion. Assuming 70 percent of the normal fee was paid, the mean estimate of actual expenditures was $6.8 billion and the median estimate was $5.8 billion;"
- The cost of gunshot violence in the United States was estimated at "$20 billion a year and that one-fifth of this cost was in medical expenses—$200 per household" (Headden, 1996:31).
- Miller, Cohen and Wiersema (1996:17) estimated that the aggregate annual victim costs "...amounted to $450 billion between the 1987-1990 time period...this number included both tangible and intangible costs."

- Sara Collins (1994:40) estimated the total cost of crime in the United States was $674 billion...of which $78 billion was spent on the criminal justice system; of the $78 billion, $39 billion was spent on police protection every year.

The point in looking at these studies is that crime exacts a dreadful human toll and providing police service to control it is an expensive, labor-intensive undertaking! How much does it cost to provide police and criminal justice services in your jurisdiction to control crime? Collecting and analyzing data is important if crime control is to be effective and efficient. As the largest segment of a government's budget, the police have a responsibility to deliver efficient services that can help control crime. Also, police departments are inundated with data. Every day police agencies capture tremendous amounts of valuable data from various sources, but invariably the data is archived and little or no analysis is performed. Meanwhile, staffing, deployment and budgets proceed without the scrutiny they deserve, or the logic necessary to engender support.

The police department is the most visible and perhaps the most important segment of local government and usually occupies the top spot in local budget allocation. Therefore, without minimizing the importance of other public agencies, the actions and influence of a police department cannot only have ramifications across the entire public safety spectrum, but may also play a role in the vitality and economic viability of the community. The best decisions that directly impact community wellness are those that result from as much information analysis as possible. Law enforcement agencies that use statistics as part of their decision tree can:

1. "Plan programs and services more efficiently,
2. Assess program's impact on target population,
3. Assess program cost and benefits,
4. Ensure programs are running as effectively as possible,
5. Improve [citizen] satisfaction."[9]

Data that is captured by various sources tells the story of a city (or a county or a state). Police reports tell of the crime picture (www.fbi.gov/ucr/ucr. htm#cius); census data tells of the health and welfare of the community (www.census.gov); school data tells of the level and quality of education;[10] labor data tells of the economic and employment picture (www.bls.gov); county jail incarceration data tells of selective incapacitation and specific deterrence. This means that police executives must analyze the data, as a doctor would analyze a patient's personal data, over a period of time, to measure the success or failure of a particular treatment. In order to properly treat a specific condition, it is necessary to know as much about the condition as possible.[11] Since the police department provides service 24 hours a day, 365 days each year, they are best poised to analyze and measure the things that matter most to elected officials. The idea behind using data models is to allow the data to tell the story about what is going on both inside and outside the organization so management can: 1) intelligently distribute resources when and where they are needed, 2) make better informed decisions about resource appropriation, and 3) adjust policies and programs as necessary. The concept of discerning mathematical models is to ensure that management is operating with the best available information regarding its current or proposed practices.

A police department's success is ultimately in the eyes of the beholder: the community. Elected leaders may examine the crime rate or the number of programs the agency delivers to determine its success. Other components of the criminal justice system may determine success by how many victims are referred for additional service (i.e., victim-witness advocacy; violent crime compensation board), or how many cases are referred for prosecution (i.e., number of cases for grand jury presentment). Most of the measurement standards applied to police departments have been output-based, such as the number of arrests (or summonses or field interrogations) that were delivered. Traditionally there has been little emphasis on the cost per unit, which is critical to efficiency. Granted, output measures are necessary, but outputs do not measure success in the eyes of the true benefactors—the citizens. Citizens will measure success by whether the police department has changed things in the community, such as their quality of life. This is the difference between measuring output and outcome.

Twenty-first century policing in the United States is changing. There is more emphasis today on service consolidation, resource and information sharing and alternatives to creating yet *another* independent law enforcement agency in a nation with more than 17,000 existing police departments.[12] As local elected officials and police leaders search for alternatives to expensive policing, they must first know the service-impact their community is expected to generate, then how much service or resource-sharing will cost before they can determine efficiency. A primary goal of this book is to enable policy makers and chief executives of any police department to create meaningful business or strategic plans that rely on empirical data. This will bolster credibility and support for the department's budget and for the department's organizational plan.

The most common alternative for providing police service to municipalities is purchasing police service from a neighboring municipality. Purchasing services often proves to be less costly when compared to the costs associated with establishing a municipal police department. Also, depending upon the agreement, the level of service and efficiency is often greater because of the resources of a larger police department. As an example, in a one-officer police department, the officer usually works eight hours per day, five days a week for a total of forty hours a week. When not working, the officer is usually "on call" and if called out, the municipality must pay overtime or reimburse the officer.

There is usually no patrol conducted during the sixteen-hour period the officer is off duty. When purchasing service from another department, the forty hours purchased can be distributed throughout the twenty-four hour day whenever the need for patrol exists. In addition, if an emergency or major case develops, the resources of the larger department, including investigators, crime scene specialists and traffic safety personnel are available to the community purchasing police services...Many elected officials in Pennsylvania, for example, have found this method for providing municipal police service to be very beneficial for their communities (Governor's Center for Local Government Services, 1998:3-4).

Another method of providing local police service is developing a program of consolidated police services or resource sharing (Ostrom, Whitaker and Parks, 1978). In this approach several municipalities join together to create a police department which is outside the direct control of any one municipality. The police department is governed by a separate board or commission composed of officials from each community. The board or commission acts in the same capacity as the borough council, board of commissioners or board of supervisors. That is, the board or commission establishes basic policing policy, establishes funding levels and controls finances, handles matters relating to personnel and establishes operational procedure. Each municipality contributes its share of the total cost of operating the department based upon whatever method of distributing costs is agreed upon. The community's representative on the board or commission serves as its liaison and expresses the community's policing needs to the police department through the board or commission. A community without a police department and considering alternatives to creating its own may wish to contact neighboring communities to assess that community's interest in creating a consolidated police department. Municipalities with small police departments may also want to consider this approach as a method of improving police services or reducing cost (Governor's Center for Local Government Services, 1998:4).

A resource sharing model is a mode of operation in which certain resources within one agency may be shared by multiple agencies. This model often incorporates centralized support services, such as dispatching and 911 telecommunications, jail services (Fyfe, 1983) and decentralized patrol. This alternative to providing police services can best be described as simply providing your own police patrol and relying upon other units of government or agencies to provide support. Purchasing support functions such as dispatching/communications services, record-keeping, criminal investigations and personnel service functions can help to keep costs to a minimum and control unnecessary growth in the police department. Before municipal elected officials move to expand an existing police support service or create a new supporting function within their police department they should consider the alternative of purchasing such services from other sources. It may also be appropriate to consider purchasing such services, even when expanding an existing unit or creating a new one is not being considered. Purchasing support services often proves to be much less costly than maintaining the service within the police department and is usually just as efficient (Governor's Center for Local Government Services, 1998:4).

Implementation[13]

"The devil is in the details" is a common term referring to implementation, meaning the difficult part is in the many small details that implementation requires. Aside from conceptualization, implementation is often the most onerous part of any program because of the administrative and operational details that must be worked out. Implementation begins with mid-level management who must answer: *how do we make this plan work?* Mid-level managers must work through the minutiae to bring the plan to life (Geller and Swanger, 1995). There is no single approach to implementation since law enforcement agencies are so varied and differ in their constraints (i.e., collective bargaining and labor agreements, legislation, civil service rules, and labor and employment case law). Implementation failure is a frequent criticism of social intervention programs (Sherman et. al., 1998:156). It is also a frequent criticism of police management. With respect to implementation and how a police department can become a "learning organization" from the programs it implements, Geller (1997:2-3) said this about police administrators:

> *"They watch bewildered and despairing as their organization leaps from one tactic and program to another—rarely bothering to conduct a meaningful feasibility study or figure out what worked and what didn't work and under what conditions the last time a similar problem was tackled...A learning organization learns to measure what really matters, for it understands that what we measure is taken more seriously."*

Making performance measures and efficiency analyses work is a matter of tasking the right people with the right resources to get the right data to the chief executive and his or her staff so that decisions can be made. Author and business scholar Jim Collins (2001:13) conceptualized similar principles in his research on exceptional companies and how these companies were able to engineer "long-term sustained performance." These principles were implemented in the Dallas Police Department under Chief of Police David Kunkle with outstanding results.[14] Smoothing implementation and minimizing implementation failure can be achieved by following these recommendations:

1. **Task the right people...** Who is right for the job of efficiency analysis is highly idiosyncratic; it does not have universal implications because law enforcement agencies in America are so diverse. Who actually carries out the analysis is not as important as where the analysis is carried out. It does not necessarily matter whether the person who

conducts the analysis is a police officer, lieutenant or captain. Although, taking a "talent inventory" of employees' competencies in research, analysis, planning, public speaking, and writing is important. What is more important is that the individual or organizational element reside at the top of the organizational plan. This will reduce the lines of reporting between where the analysis is conducted and the decision makers; quick decisions can be made because the bureaucracy and chain of command are reduced (Iannone, 1987:20).

For example, if the agency is already practicing Compstat, then it might make sense to place at least some of the functions described in this text in the hands of those who routinely collect most of the agency's data. Another suitable place is the administrative element of the organization. Personnel responsible for administrative aspects in a law enforcement agency typically answer directly to the chief executive. Functions such as planning, budgeting, program and policy development, grants development and crime analysis often reside at the top of the organization because these functions have a direct impact on operations: administrative personnel design the plans and operational personnel implement the plans. By following the principles in this text anyone who is tasked with conducting data analysis will be able to replicate what is illustrated here and interpret the results.

2. **...with the right resources...** There is not much beyond basic computer workstations, printers and software to create efficiencies. As with most things in a police department there will be some costs associated with performance development, but the costs will be spread across the agency and they will generally be minimal. Once the data elements are captured and routed to the right people all that is left is to analyze the data. This text purposely relies on Microsoft Office© products, specifically MS Excel,© which is widely available. The requirement for the computer workstations is that they are robust enough to support the software applications and the hard drive is large enough to archive large volumes of data. If the data will not be stored locally (i.e., on the hard drive of a desktop computer), then it is important the workstation have enough processing power to retrieve the information from a data warehouse where it can be temporarily stored on the desktop until it is discarded. For example CAD and RMS data files are enormous and cannot be stored locally; the data must be retrieved from a data warehouse, analyzed locally, then discarded.

If working exclusively with hard-copy reports, then the data must be entered into an electronic format for analysis. This might be a desktop database application such as MS Access,© a spreadsheet application such as MS Excel© or a statistics package such as SPSS. The larger the data file the more rich the data set will be for comprehensive analyses. A large data set will help identify trends and patterns that arise over time; different analysis techniques will help uncover those pattern trends.

After the data is analyzed it must be printed and disseminated. Data is essentially useless unless it is used to guide, train, inform and persuade to make decisions. In this form data must be reduced to comprehensible narrative reports, charts/graphs, tables and maps that are printed or otherwise delivered to those who are in a position to influence policy or make decisions. The printer need not be color except that color crime maps or color graphs are sometimes easier to discern than black and white, which relies on fill-styles (patterns or symbols) to differentiate between data groups.

3. **...to analyze the right data, then...** The right data is also idiosyncratic based upon the agency's priorities. However, with a few variations, law enforcement agencies conduct the same type of work under relatively the same conditions. This means performance measures and accountability are (generally) the same. Therefore, the right data is that which:

   a. Promotes effective resource allocation including making predictions about future states;
   b. Promotes personnel management and increases internal accountability;
   c. Increases external accountability among collaborating agencies (government, private, non-profit);
   d. Promotes fiscal accountability including reducing costs;
   e. Is a logical indicator of success;
   f. Helps specify the problem;
   g. Helps manage finite human and material resources;
   h. Helps assess how citizens feel or what they think about an issue;
   i. Uncovers behavior patterns of individuals or groups;
   j. Reveals the factors or combination of factors that prompt change in behavior to reduce crime and improve quality of life;
   k. Reveals the effect of a particular program or policy;
   l. Reveals how well the agency accomplished what they intended to do, and
   m. Supports decision-making at all levels of the agency.

4. **...devolve decision-making and accountability to get things done, while concurrently...** This practice entails giving commanders and mid-level managers the freedom to execute mission-related processes as they see them within certain constraints. As Michaelson (2001:24) stated, only the tactics change, not the strategy. The strategy is the process as formulated in policy and other written plans; it the art of "doing the right things." The tactics are contact actions, the procedures used to accomplish the strategy; it is the art of "doing things right." The commander is responsible for his or her division and should be given the flexibility to meet the performance standards set by management without being micromanaged; "micromanaging an organization with techni-

cally and emotionally competent employees can result in problems" that stifle creativity and forward motion (Delorenzi, Shane and Amendola, 2006:38). Once the strategy is formulated, the first series of performance reports should be developed privately with those who are to be held accountable before placing them in a public forum, such as Compstat. This will promote a sense of mutual trust and understanding. It will also make those involved in the process reasonably comfortable with the data and illustrate how it will be used (Friedman, 1997:23).

5. **...building expertise by developing knowledge, skills and ability (KSA's).** This is training. In order to become a learning organization, employee KSA's must continuously be developed. This means that commanders must not look upon training as the loss of an employee for the training period; rather they should see it as a long-term investment in the agency as employees strengthen their core competencies, which is a qualitative performance indicator itself. KSA's are enduring and intended to sustain the organization long beyond the chief executive's tenure (see Maguire, 2004 for an excellent discussion about police departments as learning organizations).

One word of caution about performance data: it has its limitations! Without it, police operations would grind to a halt. This is often termed paralysis by analysis. With over reliance on it, police operations will grind to a halt. The right data should be used to confirm or dispel observations, past experiences and to help make decisions. It has been said that the human experience cannot be mathematized, so use data to support experience and judgment, not replace it. Author and performance expert Harry Hatry (1999) identified three limitations of performance measurement:

1. "Performance data do not, by themselves, tell why the outcomes occurred." The process leading to the outcome is often what must be assessed to determine what went right and what went wrong. How programs are carried out, the sequential steps, may reveal the strengths and weaknesses of the process. This is why workflow processing, process evaluation and logic modeling are important to performance (more about logic models ahead).

2. "Some outcomes cannot be measured directly." It is impossible to measure things that did not happen; the absence of crime is one of them. Measuring crime that did not happen is not possible but a good proxy is comparing and analyzing the number of things that **did** happen. Although there are ways to control for other influences that may have contributed to a reduced crime rate, an executive will never know if an individual officer or a specific organizational element directly accounted for the reduction. The best measure in this case is the difference between the baseline measure and subsequent measures. Following imple-

mentation of a particular program or operation, all else being equal, if there is a reduction in crime, then the program is probably the cause.

3. "The information provided by performance measurement is just part of the information managers and elected officials need to make decisions." This is where experience is crucial! Data should guide leadership, managers' judgment and community sentiment when it comes to policy decisions. Data is not flawless so it should be used to reinforce what appears to be logical and sensible in a given situation, and what is sensible is idiosyncratic to the time, location, persons involved and fact-pattern.

This text outlines over two hundred performance indicators in seven critical dimension areas that can help chief executives achieve these goals. The seven critical dimension areas could be reduced even further for more discreet management. Indeed, the approach to performance leadership is to identify, capture and analyze a "large number and wide variety of performance indicators" that lead toward "better practice" (Behn, 2004:21). The performance indicators and critical dimension areas that an agency settles on should "improve societal outcome by 'growing the good'—the health, safety, well-being, and general quality of life...[while concurrently] 'slowing the bad'—harmful or unhealthy events, risk-raising causal factors, unnecessary costs, wasted time, fraud, corruption, and incivility" (Metzenbaum, 2006:6). Remember, the purpose of developing performance measures is to help improve service delivery. Doing so is not an exact science. Therefore, performance measures should be based on the best professional judgment of the chief executive, the command staff and consultants, if any. This is typically accomplished by aligning activities, core processes and resources with four distinct categories, then selecting performance measures for each:

1. **"Fiscal Accountability:** Government spends its money as authorized, with as little waste as possible;
2. **Ethical Accountability:** Agencies operate honestly, without conflict of interest, self-dealing, other forms of fraud, or abuse of the power of governmental authority;
3. **Democratic Accountability:** Government agencies do what their citizens want and need, engaging citizens and their elected representatives in understanding trade-offs and making well-informed choices among competing priorities. Government agencies treat people civilly and courteously, unless there are strong justifications not to, so people do not resent or resist government because it has acted in a rude, slow, or inappropriate manner;
4. **Performance Accountability:** Government agencies and their employees work intelligently and diligently to deliver effective and cost-efficient government programs" (Metzenbaum, 2006:6).

Presumptions

As with any book aimed at executive and upper-level management, there is a presumed level of knowledge on behalf of the readers and users. This book draws a few assumptions:

1. An understanding of basic arithmetic;
2. An understanding of basic police management principles;
3. An 8-hour work tour;
4. "Ability to use a computer and how to manipulate spreadsheets and databases;
5. Ability to use analysis software;
6. Users routinely produce management reports to drive police operations;
7. Users are accustomed to carrying out data analysis;
8. Users may be familiar with pre-post (before-after) evaluations of police operations or social interventions and;
9. Users have basic knowledge of statistics and research methodology" (Clarke and Eck, 2005:v).

Because this book presumes basic mathematics knowledge, it does not provide a pedantic review of intricate mathematical concepts, inasmuch as those concepts are not required.[15] Also, basic police supervision and management principles vary with individual management style. How an executive chooses to manage personnel and processes after being armed with the results from an empirical analysis is not the subject of this book. Finally, the calculations and the formulas in the examples are based on an 8-hour work day. There are a variety of work tours employed in personnel scheduling such as the 4-10 schedule (4, 10-hour days), however many police departments operate on an 8-hour schedule. Different calculations must be used to arrive at the same solution for a schedule devised on 10-hour days.

Subsumed in the knowledge of basic mathematics is an understanding of basic statistics. "Statistics is a mathematical science pertaining to collection, analysis, interpretation and presentation of data."[16] An example of an intermediate statistical concept known as multiple regression analysis will be presented. A complete overview of analysis of variance, correlation, confidence levels and explained variance is beyond the scope of this text. It will be useful to explore these statistical notions beforehand if you are not familiar with them. The concepts are not difficult to learn or understand. Simply put, this book is designed to help create efficiency and improve performance, not to help learn basic mathematical concepts.

Finally, users should have a basic knowledge of MS Excel© and its associated suite of products. The examples in this book use MS Excel© as the primary software application since it is readily available on most desktop computers. MS Excel© is a user-friendly and robust spreadsheet application that can provide analysts and planners with all the necessary tools to create meaningful statistical reports.

Basic Mathematics Review

The concepts presented in this book are not complicated. All of the formulas use basic math procedures that can be performed on a standard calculator. When solving an expression it is possible to arrive at different answers if the mathematic procedures are not followed. The basic math procedures, also known as the order of operations, must follow this sequence: parentheses, exponents, multiplication, division, addition, and subtraction. This is sometimes referred to by the acronym PEMDAS. When solving a math problem the order of operations is as follows:

1. **P:** Solve all parenthetical equations first, beginning with the innermost parentheses and working outward, then
2. **E:** Solve all exponent equations, then
3. **M:** Multiply, then
4. **D:** Divide, then
5. **A:** Add, finally
6. **S:** Subtract

When looking for mathematical accuracy, one important concept that you will frequently use is rounding. For example, when calculating a relief factor (RF) a guiding management principle for handling a portion of the RF (e.g., .58) is to use rounding (e.g., .58 is rounded to1). When rounding, it is best to use a consistent method to ensure accuracy. The best convention for this is to look to the right of the number you are going to keep. If you are rounding to the first decimal place, then look to the second digit; if you are rounding to the second decimal place, then look to the third digit. If the digit to the right of the number you are keeping is greater than 5, then you should round up (e.g., 1.586 becomes 1.59). If the digit is less than 5, then round down (e.g., 1.583 becomes 1.58). The same convention holds true for rounding the nearest whole number. In the case of relief factoring whole numbers represent the number of personnel required; stated differently, it is the number of personnel that must be hired or redeployed in personnel model (remember, hiring personnel is expensive, so knowing just how many you will need is important).

There is another convention that is important in order to maintain consistency. If you are rounding to the second decimal place, and the third digit is a 5, you cannot automatically round up because you will introduce systematic bias to your calculations. You will obviously be consistent, but to consistently round up will overestimate your numbers. Instead, adopt this rule: if the third digit is a 5, then look to the digit immediately *before* the 5. If that digit (the second digit) is an even number, then round up. If the digit is an odd number, then round down. For example, a relief factor 1.585 should become 1.58; a relief factor 1.535 should become 1.54. Following this convention your decision to round up or down will always be the same. If the number preceding the 5 is even (0, 2, 4, 6, 8) or if it is odd (1, 3, 5, 7, 9) is has the same number of chances of occurring, five. Since the same number of occasions exists, and odd and even numbers are given an equal chance of appearing in your calculations, there is no bias (Bachman and Paternoster, 2004)

Upcoming Sections

This book will present some common police management problems and solutions. By solving these niggling problems, a chief executive can create a more efficient workplace. The first section deals with how to organize and measure things that are meaningful to elected officials and police executives, what data to capture to make informed decisions, various data types and where to find data. The following section deals with statistics. Statistics is merely a branch of mathematics that concerns collecting, analyzing, interpreting and presenting large quantities of numerical data. After a discussion on statistics there is a review of the different types of software applications that are available to help analyze the data. Commercially available software is easy to use. In fact, one of the favored software applications is probably already on your desktop—Microsoft Excel©, part of the Microsoft Office© suite. Once you have the data and have analyzed it, it must be presented. After all, the goal is to use data to solve problems and present solutions to those who matter most. This section deals with effective ways to present data so you can easily convey your message. The final section presents six useful examples of problems frequently encountered in police departments. These problems are drawn from experience and discussion with police executives who frequently voice their concern over how to solve some seemingly intractable management issues.

Critical Issue	Solution
Proportional Staffing	Workload Analysis 1. Relief Factoring 2. Patrol Force 3. Communications Center 4. Investigative Division
Creating a Nexus Between Workload and Costs	Activity-based Budgeting
Drawing Inferences and Making Predictions	Intermediate Statistical Analyses 1. Predicting the Crime Rate Based Upon Overtime Allocation 2. Predicting the Crime Rate Based Upon Existing Police Performance Measures 3. Drawing Inferences about Police Response Time Based Upon Demographic Data 4. Drawing Inferences about Police Response Time Based Upon Absenteeism 5. Making Predictions through Forecasting and Moving Average Analysis
Disjointed Management Accountability	Compstat Process
Developing Deployment Plans for Crimes without a Definitive Starting Time	Aoristic Crime Analysis
Measuring the Costs, Benefits and Effectiveness of Police Programs	Efficiency Analysis

Each management issue is presented with an explanation of how to achieve results using existing data. The data files for each example are located on the Resource CD that accompanies this text and are fully replicable. The data files must be saved to your computer, then, simply plug-in your agency's data and format the spreadsheet to suit your needs. Most of the formulas are pre-programmed. The procedures that use intermediate statistical techniques require you to execute the procedure from scratch.

The performance indicators necessary for a meaningful analysis can be easily captured and analyzed. Department goals can be easily translated into a business plan that summarizes the operational and financial objectives of the department, and through detailed plans and budgets, the objectives will show how the end outcomes will be achieved.

On the Resource CD

The best way to learn how to create efficiencies and improve performance is to actually do it! The data files on the Resource CD offer useable Excel© workbooks to construct models that suit your agency. Each of the files directly relates to the material presented in this book, which should make it much more appealing to a broad range of users. To see the actual formula in an Excel© data cell, simply place the cursor in the cell; the formula will display in the formula bar at the top of the page. Alternatively, you can place the cursor in the cell and double click the mouse; the cell will activate and display the formula and the other cells that compose the formula.

Formula Bar   **Activated Cell**

Investigations Workload Analysis and Staffing Plan

Investigative Demands	Hours Per Unit	Units Per Year	Detectives Required	Total Employee Hours Per Modality	Personnel Needed
Arrest (Detectives only)	1	5,945	1	5,945	5
Arson	3	242	1	726	1
Aggravated Assault (shooting, stabbing, blunt force)	3.55	1,365	1	4,846	4
Bomb Threat	3	12	1	36	0
Burglary	6	2,292	1	13,752	11
Carjacking	3	77	1	231	0
Code Enforcement Violations	1.5	207	1	311	0
Court	2.5	245	4	2,450	2
Criminal Mischief/Vandalism	2	2,402	1	4,803	4
Domestic Violence	4	2,604	1	10,416	8
Drug Sales	2.5	3,025	3	22,685	18
Fire (car, house, building)	2	123	1	246	0
Fraud/Forgery	2	313	1	626	1
Gambling Offense	2	468	1	936	1
HazMat Condition/Dangerous Circumstances	2	1,183	1	=B20*C20*D20	2
Juvenile Condition (curfew, truancy and all others)	2	484	1	969	1
Kidnapping	30	11	2	660	1
Liquor/Tavern Violation	1.5	1,419	1	2,129	2
Murder	40	81	4	12,960	10
Open Door Condition	0.75	774	1	580	0
Person with a Weapon	1.5	401	1	602	0
Prisoner Debriefings	0.416	38,957	1	16,206	13
Prostitution	1.5	1,479	1	2,219	2
Public Intoxication/Public Consumption	0.75	664	1	498	0
Rape	5	85	1	425	0

Note to users: Due to the size and complexity of police departments across the country it is not possible to design a standard business model that fits every agency. The data files are customizable to a limited degree and should serve most users well. Their functionality is complete, however, different agencies may not follow the same convention or terminology nor will they have the same level of complexity. The data files on the Resource CD include:

File Type	File Name on Resource CD	Description of File Contents
Activity-base budget with workload analysis, budget recap and graph models	**Activity-base Budget**	A completed and fully replicable ABB that includes: 1) organizational recap, 2) five separate ABB's for patrol, investigations, communications, traffic and prisoner processing, 3) personnel distribution models, 4) FTE requirements and 5) descriptive statistics for each ABB.
Aoristic crime analysis workbook with burglary model	**Aoristic Crime Analysis Workbook**	A completed and fully replicable aoristic crime analysis model that includes: 1) burglary model, 2) modified burglary model (as presented in this text), 3) full aoristic data set with over 1,000 cases, 4) 1 year aoristic data set, 5) 2 year (24 month) aoristic burglary model. Table 45 of the aoristic model is reproduced on the Resource CD and does not appear in the text due to its size.
Regression analysis and crime control workbook with response time analysis	**Regression Analysis and Crime Control Workbook**	A completed and fully replicable regression workbook that includes: 1) regression crime control data and formulas, 2) overtime regression data, formulas and output summary, 3) response time data and formulas, and 4) medical services data with a forecast model.
Analysis workbook with various rates and ratios	**Analysis Workbook**	FBI UCR data from 2004 with associated formulae for crime rate, response time descriptive statistics and a ratio matrix.
Forecasting workbook with various models and graphs	**Forecasting Workbook**	A completed and fully replicable forecasting workbook that includes: 1) calls for service forecast data with weekly, monthly and yearly models, 2) yearly forecast model of workload and arrests, and 3) forecast model and moving average analysis of court overtime.
Efficiency analysis workbook with workload analysis	**Efficiency Analysis Workbook**	A completed and fully replicable efficiency analysis workbook that includes: 1) a cost-benefit analysis and 2) a cost-effectiveness analysis with associated formulae.
Police business plans	**Police Business Plans**	There are 11 .pdf files with police business plans from Australia, Canada and the United Kingdom. Use them to mindmap or outline a business plan for your organization.

PART ONE
Performance Measurement

2

▶ Identifying Meaningful Measures

There has been considerable debate about what to measure in police departments particularly because there is little consensus about what constitutes "good performance" and because measuring it is complex and takes many forms (Alpert and Dunham, 2001; Alpert, Flynn and Piquero, 2001; Langworthy, 1999); Maguire, (2004); Skogan and Hartnett (1997:74) commented that "developing performance indicators that reflect either the activities or the outcomes associated with community policing is a difficult task-one which few departments have successfully faced up to." Most, if not all police officers and police executives consider preventing and controlling crime the primary function of the police department. Yet, in reality, the vast majority of most police officers' time is spent providing service-related activities not associated with crime. However, there is little doubt that crime and quality of life is probably the most important responsibility of the police department and the function that most concerns the citizens of the community. "Citizens more often judge the police department by its ability to handle crime when it does occur than by any other police activity" (Governor's Center for Local Government Services, 1998:15). Consequently, citizens should play an active role in helping shape the performance measures, expectations and end outcomes that the police department will endeavor to meet. A good example of police-community collaboration on setting performance measures is from Scotland. In May 2006 Scotland's Justice Minister Cathy Jamieson announced:

"The way police forces measure their performance is to be reformed with the aim of ensuring it is clearer, more consistent and provides better information to the public about how local services are being delivered...As we strive to further improve the service to the public, we must also look at how best we measure and report performance across forces to support better public accountability...We want to reform the performance measure system—not to provide more management information or set targets for the sake of it—but to avoid the current duplication of effort and ensure we have a more consistent approach to measuring, reporting and managing police performance on what really matters to forces and local communities. One which educates the public and stakeholders about how the service responds to the scale and diversity of the demands placed upon it, and uses performance information to support learning and the sharing of best practice."[17]

The notion of police-community collaboration in setting performance standards is common throughout England and Wales, less so in the United States. Remarking about police performance indicators scholar Paul Collier stated (2006:165) without greater "public discussion about the objectives of policing, efforts to improve public satisfaction with policing are likely to fail." In this sense the community is part of the "authorizing environment" that Moore (2002:84) described, which constitutes "...all those political actors or agents who have the *formal* power to review police department operations, or the *informal* power to *influence* those who do. In short, it is all the people who can, as a practical or legal matter, call the police to account."

Police departments are unique in that their accomplishments are often not as visible as they are in other government, business or industrial enterprises, so evaluating performance is even more important. One thing that matters greatly to tax payers is crime and citizen safety. The amount of crime in a community is not exclusively a police responsibility. There are many factors that contribute to the amount of crime in a given community, many of which are uncontrollable by the police. However, the police department does accept a major responsibility for the amount of crime, since crime and its control directly relate to its primary purpose for existing (Governor's Center for Local Government Services, 1998). Expressing "good performance" typically comes through measures of time, quantity, quality or cost, which are easily captured in police departments[18] (Hoover, 1995). Fortunately, there are ways to measure success, with statistical accuracy, that account for these dimensions and also account for the nebulous social influences of crime. These statistical procedures necessary to produce meaningful results go beyond the simplistic standard measure of "crime rate per 100,000 people,"[19] or "number of police offers per 1,000 residents" to answer complex questions such as how much does poverty, unemployment, residential mobility and other social phenomena explain the total variance in the crime rate? For example, the statistical procedure linear regression has the ability to adjust for other factors influencing whatever may be under examination. Maguire (2004:6) offers the example of how regression analysis can be used to create a "risk adjusted homicide rate" that purges the influence of "poverty, unemployment, race, divorce, and population density." Linear regression is a technique that is profiled later in this book through an example of police response time in which similar social phenomena are controlled.

Unlike the crime rate and the uncertainty of whether or not it is controllable by the police, the number of crimes that are solved or "cleared by arrest" is a definite measure of police effectiveness. Comparing clearance rates to other departments' clearance rates is a reasonable performance measure; the chief may conclude that the department is doing as well as most other police departments. On the other hand, if clearance rates are too low, it may be a reflection of police efficiency and performance. Comparing year-to-year clearance rates of serious crime by a police department is also an appropriate measure of police effectiveness. The success rate of police departments in solving less serious crimes is usually greater than for serious crimes. For example, FBI Part II offenses, by their very nature, are often solved at the moment they are committed. Crimes such as disorderly conduct, driving under the influence, liquor law violations, public intoxication and gambling are in this category, and these crimes are often witnessed by the police.

A police department's success rate in subsequent criminal investigations is also assessed by the rate of conviction for cases brought before the courts. If a police department's conviction rate is above or below average (in comparison to whatever average you are using—a neighboring city; the county; the state; or historical department average), it is often a reflection of the effort that went into the investigation and the preparation of the case for court. If a police department consistently loses criminal prosecutions to poor evidence collection and forensic examination, suppressed confessions, poor crime scene documentation or poor witness preparation, this directly affects its efficiency level in solving crimes and obtaining convictions. Another element of success is the cost for which services are delivered. The highest quality service delivered for the least amount of money, as expressed in terms of per-unit cost, virtually guarantees cost effectiveness (Grabosky, 1988). "Highest quality" service can be expressed by the agency as a ratio of services delivered to complaints received, but quality will always be defined by the public in terms of their perceived satisfaction. "Specifically, efficiency refers to the ratio of the quantity of the service provided [e.g., number of dispatched calls for service—CFS] to the cost, in dollars or labor, required to produce the service. According to [the Government Accounting Standards Board-G.A.S.B], these indicators are defined as indicators that measure the cost (whether in dollars or employee hours) per unit of output or outcome" (National Center for Public Productivity, 2006:4). Examples include cost per call for service and cost per criminal investigation.

The type and number of services provided, other than those normally accepted as police responsibilities, are established by the governing body and the police department's chief executive. Once established, the manner in which they are performed becomes a measure of department efficiency. The inevitable question becomes: *What measuring devices may be used in addition to simply observing what occurs through official police reports and personal observation?* (Alpert and Moore, 1994). One method is to survey those to whom service was provided. Specific questions may be asked through prepared questionnaires and the results analyzed for performance. Fortunately, public perception is an area of performance that is subject to a survey instrument. Where a specific group or clientele receive police services, it is not difficult to assess the level of police efficiency and service provided. Survey distribution may be accomplished through a variety of means: direct mailers; door knockers; attached to the annual tax notice, periodic water or sewer bill; attached to a car's windshield, known as a "windshield survey," or through a regular community newsletter, if one exists. An increasingly popular and inexpensive method of administering a survey is via the Internet. Although the response rate is limited to those who have access to a computer, and the sample will not be random, the Internet is a very useful and efficient way to assess community attitude. As with any community survey, sample size, response rate and methodology for conducting the survey will affect the results, so design, collection and analysis is important.[20] Another method of measuring the public's attitude concerning police service is to maintain copious internal affairs records resulting from contacts with the police. The chief executive should ensure that procedures are established within the department to maintain such records. Periodic review of internal affairs records will assist local officials in assessing citizen satisfaction, at least to some degree.

Identifying meaningful measures will vary between communities based upon local priorities. The most important aspect of identifying such measures is the ability "...to make the connection between lower-level activities and higher-level goals...Whatever the...agency counts, and however good the agency is at counting it, the question of significance remains" (Sparrow, 2000:293). The guiding question should be: *What difference will this make?* The number of felony indictments is meaningless unless a conviction follows; the number of traffic summonses issued is meaningless unless residential speeding is reduced; the number of arrests for disorderly conduct is meaningless unless groups of rowdy juveniles cease congregating in public parks. The idea here is to ensure the activities (outputs) that will be counted are *actually* indicators of success (Maltz, 1990:39).

Creating Performance Measures

Performance measures are created for a variety of reasons, but reciprocal accountability is one of the more important reasons. Reciprocal accountability means top down and bottom up. Most people think of accountability as downward-flowing from superior to subordinate, rarely upward-flowing from the subordinate to the superior (Plunkett, 1994:67; Schroeder, Lombardo, Strollo, 1995:21). Granted, police employees must willingly submit themselves to the obligations of public life, which includes accepting responsibility for, and, when necessary, proffering a statement or explanation of reasons, causes, or motives to account for one's actions. This is the essence of downward accountability. However, the agency has an obligation to its employees as well. If the agency executive intends to hold subordinate personnel accountable for their actions, then the agency must: 1) "clarify what is expected, 2) examine activities and performance measures and compare actual performance with what is expected, 3) act on findings to improve activities and performance measures, and 4) communicate findings in accordance with agency and regulatory policy."[21] Otherwise, how are employees to know what is expected of them? Schroeder,

Lombardo and Strollo (1995:165) noted that one barrier to evaluating performance is the "lack of performance standards." Whatever the agency decides to evaluate must be accompanied by a description of what constitutes acceptable and unacceptable performance. To leave performance dimensions and standards undefined creates a system that does not measure what it is intended to measure and becomes nothing more than a set of subjective interpretations that vary greatly among those doing the interpretation. Performance standards "bring sanity, fairness and consistency to supervisory tasks, enhance performance levels, and make promotions, awards and disciplinary actions fair" (Jones, 1998:109-112).

In an environment where staff executives avoid reciprocal accountability they are inevitably abrogating their responsibility. This is typically the result of a lack of understanding on behalf of the executive who does not know how to lead his or her employees toward genuine targets. Such an environment is often filled with brusque, condescending language and antagonistic behavior toward the subordinates who are directed to fulfill unrealistic, unarticulated, indeed impossible, targets. A democratic management style is substituted for an autocratic, ad hominem style that engenders fear of punishment in the subordinates for missing the target. This inevitably harms the work product; indeed, the work product may be sabotaged by subordinates as a form of retribution for the leaders' failure to create reasonable performance expectations and self-impose accountability. Friedman (2005:87, 144, 89) made some of the best remarks about the association between fear of punishment and performance measures:

> "...In almost everyone's experience, the matter of measurement has been connected at one time or another to punishment...It is no wonder that there is an atmosphere of fear that surrounds this work...There is a long history of setting unrealistic performance targets and then beating people up when they fail to meet them. This practice is based on the misguided belief that such targets coupled with fear of punishment will lead to better performance. In practice, unrealistic targets detract from credibility. And fear turns out to be one of the worst ways for managers to motivate people. People working within this punishment culture will try to pick measures they look good on or set targets they can easily meet. The measures are rarely the most important ones and the targets are meaningless. The organization appears to be practicing performance accountability, but it's a waste of time...We must stop using arbitrary performance targets to punish people, instead move to a fair way to assess and credit progress using baselines...You cannot ask managers to support a system that **deliberately** embarrasses them."

The fundamental advantage of promulgating reasonable performance measures is that employees will have "a better sense of what is expected of them...The objectives are much clearer and less ambiguous" (Wilson, 1970:53). Police scholar Jerome Skolnick (1966:180) found that the employee "always tried to perform *according to his most concrete and specific understanding of the control system"* (italics in original). In other words, the employee first sought the standard by which he or she would be measured then adjusted his or her performance according to what was expected. In creating performance measures the idea is to compare employee-level (individual) or division-level (aggregate) behavior against an unequivocal written standard. In this regard performance measures should be impersonally applied to easily understood and demonstrated examples of work, ideally derived from documented job descriptions, under circumstances such that the norm of equality can be observed (Wilson, 1970:54) (the norm of equality can be derived from empirical baseline observations, not by affixing quotas, which are usually indefensible and may be illegal-see "baseline" in glossary).

Author Vincent Henry (2002:267) made the point about reciprocal accountability when he described the Compstat process. Henry commented that commanders should push back on the administration for shared accountability from the executives:

> *"This is the commander's chance to bring problems and issues (especially those concerning the adequacy of resources and crime patterns that cross precinct boundaries) to the attention of the executive staff-in essence to publicly communicate their needs and, in doing so, **to place some of the responsibility and some of the accountability on the executives."*** (emphasis mine).

In this sense the executive's responsibility is to set policy, then, having done so, secure the resources (funding, staffing, public support, equipment and accoutrements) to see it through by enabling subordinate personnel to perform as expected (Wilson, 1970:57). An executive's failure to meet his or her responsibilities is the point at which autocratic leadership usually begins to reign over a democratic style-this is where the executive's shortcomings reveal themselves, such as berating the employee for not accomplishing the task at hand. The implications of Henry's comment echo those of Wilson and include things like budgeting, scheduling efficiency, workload demands, personnel complement, sick leave rate, and police-fleet availability to name a few. Executives must self-impose performance standards and make the necessary resources available within those constraints to ensure those they will hold accountable can meet the expectations (upward accountability). To do otherwise is to establish a double standard and risk being labeled a hypocrite, where the executive demands accountability and imposes it on subordinate personnel, yet is absolved from it. Thereafter, if the executive takes adverse employment action against a subordinate because he or she failed to meet the agency's expectations, then the executive's behavior is unethical; it will be virtually impossible for managers to legally hold employees accountable for arbitrary or shifting expectations.

Toward that end of shared accountability an important, often overlooked, purpose behind creating performance measures is to insulate the agency against itself. Unguided discretionary power (i.e., the lack of or shifting, arbitrary, inconsistent performance standards) often results in due process violations when the agency fails to confine and structure police managers' discretion. Performance measures serve to correct this and help to avoid formal employee grievances, help reduce the actual and perceived arbitrary denial of contractually conferred benefits and ensure more uniform delivery of police service. Selective accountability that is applied sporadically by managers does not work to improve performance; instead it erodes confidence in management and supervision. Once the agency self-imposes and consistently examines what it wants from its employees, such as through a business plan, and makes it known to them, then mutual accountability will ensue. This is why creating valid performance measures is critical to the agency's mission and employee productivity.

Part of this book is about helping chief executives identify and create better performance measures for their organization, which will engender consistent employee performance and service delivery. Before doing so the executive should observe a few basic principles to minimize resistance and ease the implementation process. A performance model based on these principles tends to ensure the policy is acceptable to the community, attractive to the police, able to be administered by subordinate personnel, sound and legal: 1) claim the ethical high ground, 2) rely on best-practices for appropriate measures, 3) prepare legally defensible business plans, and 4) involve various layers of staff during development.

Claiming the ethical high ground reiterates what Moore and colleagues (2002:142-143) said about measuring performance: the ethical obligations for public sector managers are high. This means the executive should not allow others, such as organized labor (unions), watchdog groups, fraternal groups or opposition leaders to frame the issue of performance measurement as a "quota system" since this has organizational, legal and political implications. Organizationally, the line staff may unite around rumor or union semantics that portray management as "sinister" with the intent to impose unfair labor practices that are contrary to the labor agreement, accepted past practice or arbitrators' decisions. This then "confirms" labor's "suspicions" about management and may undermine the model's legitimacy. Legally, opposition leaders may attempt to use performance measures as the impetus for litigation or an injunction to keep managers from "discriminating against" or "harassing" employees in the interest of organizational goals (see Latham and Wexley, 1981:13). This is why it is important to document empirical baseline measures and set performance standards against them instead of imposing arbitrary measures that have no empirical foundation. Politically, elected leaders may react negatively and hastily if they are uninformed, or worse, if they are fed a steady diet of rumor from critics, since they often receive support and other endorsements from various constituent groups, both inside and outside the police department. Instead management should be frame the issue around what it actually represents: improved service delivery.

The second principle is to rely on best-practices for appropriate measures. If the performance measures do not logically relate to a specific program, or they are shown not work toward a specific goal, then they should be revised or discarded, if possible. There is no reason to continue with a practice that does not support the eventual outcome, whatever that outcome may be. Researching best-practices means looking to credible sources for solutions about what has been done in the past to address a similar issue. Instead of trying to "reinvent government," it is better to rely on ideas and measures that practitioners have already created, which are both reliable and valid. The National Research Council (2004:99-103) identified seven important "drivers of innovation in policing." The drivers summarize "particular institutions and processes" by which innovation is adopted in police agencies. Adapting that same process to creating performance measures reveals some interesting sources police agencies can turn to as they embrace performance management. The approach should be to look internally and externally to the academic and research communities, other law enforcement agencies, court decisions, employee/union grievances, technological developments, community-based organizations (CBO's) and professional affiliation groups for ideas and emerging best practices.

Source	What it Commands	Example	Performance Indicators
Performance Measures by Edict	Court decisions, civil lawsuits, EEOC complaints and employee/union grievances can invalidate old practices and a define new minimum legal standards	Criminal interrogation (Miranda v. Az) Search and seizure (Mapp v. Oh) Consent decrees (U.S. v. Pittsburgh) Police shootings (Tn v. Garner) No quotas (NJS: 40A:14-181.1 et. seq.)	# of adverse suppression hearings Total dollars paid in lawsuits # of officers identified via EWS Incidence of use of (deadly) force Rate of employee/union grievances
Performance Measures through Research	Government, academic and nonprofit research has dispelled long-standing beliefs about police work and confirmed others	Failure of preventive patrol (KCMO) Mandatory arrest for DV (Minneapolis) Rapid police response time (KCMO) SARA model/POP (Newport News, Va) Sequential eyewitness ID's (Illinois)	Rate of recidivism; Rate of arrest Local incarceration rate # of calls expedited via TRU # of successful POP/CPTED plans Rate of false eyewitness ID's
Performance Measures as a Confluence of Problems and Solutions	Research findings, police practices and technology often intersect to foster change and efficiency	Hot-spot policing; GIS/Crime mapping Forensic evidence and fingerprint analysis (CODIS; AFIS; NIBIN) Deception/lie detection analysis Swift information-driven decisions Accountability systems	# of directed patrols # of polygraph/voice-stress exams % of successful forensic exams # of PDA's and MDC's deployed % of fleet ICV and AVL equipped # of officers retrained via EWS

Source	What it Commands	Example	Performance Indicators
Performance Measures Stimulated by Local Governance	The external social and political environment leads to changes in policing, often prompted by disparate treatment, inefficiency, ineffectiveness, and a desire to promote social justice and equatability	Greater employment of minority officers Greater employment of women officers Police-community relations units Civilian review/oversight boards Community policing movement Problem-oriented policing movement	% of multilingual officers; signing % of agency diversity % of minority recruiting goals met % of personnel vacancies filled # of crime watch groups formed Overall citizen satisfaction rating
Performance Measures through Professional, Accrediting and Auditing Organizations	Professional industry organizations convene agencies to exchange ideas and make policy recommendations, then publish findings through trade journals, conferences, newsletters and Internet web sites	PERF; IACP NSA NOBLE PF CALEA Consulting firms and auditing agencies	# of consecutive years of accreditation % of officers with college degrees % of officers with advanced training # of citizen complaints Budget expenditures/budget goals
Performance Measures as a Process of Social Learning	Similarly situated agencies facing an issue often turn to pioneering agencies that are "cosmopolitan" "opinion leaders" for advice and assistance especially when the peer agency has a "good reputation"	CompStat (NYPD) S.W.A.T (LAPD) D.A.R.E (LAPD) G.R.E.A.T (Phoenix PD) Crime Stoppers (Albuquerque PD)	# of DARE graduates # of GREAT graduates % of SWAT crises resolved safely # of drug offender/gang member injunctions issued and enforced # of arrests from "1-800 tip-line"
Performance Measures Stimulated by the Federal Government	Blue ribbon or advisory commissions, investigative commissions and non-profit groups with Congressional mandates often uncover, through investigations and public hearings, chronic problems and new ideas that induce change	President's Crime Commission (1960's) Knapp Commission (NYPD, 1970) Mollen Commission (NYPD, 1994) Christopher Commission (LAPD, 1991) Rampart IRP (LAPD, 2001) NIJ; BJA; NCMEC; NAPA	Total agency inflows (grant dollars) # of community empowerment grants % of officers hired/trained via grants % compliance with agency policy # of missing/runaway juveniles

Modified from The National Research Council (2004:99-103)

The third principle is to prepare legally defensible business plans. A business plan is the agency's written explanation for what it intends to accomplish and performance measures are embodied in it as part of the agency's overall strategy to deliver service. As with any plan that is drafted by the police department, from the outset the position should be that it will be challenged in court or in an administrative hearing. Police executives should ensure business plans do not include performance measures that ostensibly establish quotas, violate any existing labor agreements, or are contrary to existing laws. In most jurisdictions across the United States establishing arrest or traffic summons quotas is prohibited by law or administrative regulation. However, establishing a mandatory minimum number of directed patrols or citizen contacts, for example, is not prohibited. When a business plan is prepared, the best way to ensure it is legally defensible is to base it on empirical data. If research suggests that directed patrols reduce crime, which it does, then defending a plan that uses directed patrols as a performance measure will not be difficult. Empirical data can be derived from documented past experience and historical records from the C.A.D, R.M.S, records division, crime analysis division or wherever data is routinely collected (more about central data collection later).

Remember, imposing performance measures is for administrative purposes and most measures probably will not violate any law, however, the research staff should consult with legal counsel to ensure nothing was inadvertently overlooked (inadvertence is an unwelcome surprise in any organization; reducing unwelcome surprises is the essence of assumption based planning, briefly discussed later). Should the plan become the subject of legal action, then it will be necessary to convince the court (or an arbitrator or a hearing officer) that management has a legitimate interest in establishing standards of employee performance. Employees should not be free to "do what they want" or "do as *they* see fit." They should be given a set of responsibilities that match the type of work they are doing, then be evaluated according to performance indicators for that function. Performance evaluations should be stratified according to work area (geographical location), tour of duty and priority to ensure equal distribution. This will ensure busy work areas or slow tours of duty are not measured against the same standard, since this would not be reasonable. This will help management get out in front of labor leaders and critics and head off grievances or litigation.

The final principle is to involve different layers of staff when developing the performance measures. This can be accomplished through committees that include representatives from the various organizational elements who will be responsible for meeting the standards. This is essential for organizational "buy-in," so those who will eventually be measured cannot claim they were left out of the planning process. The goal here is to renew the commitment to service and give employees a stake in the process that governs their careers. It also means soliciting viewpoints and altering existing measures in the face of new research, new laws and legal decisions, or new empirical data that suggests a better practice. Involving staff in the development process will have more long-term sustainability over setting performance measures that are foisted upon employees without their input.

Types of Performance Measures. There are typically two types of measures, hard and soft. A *hard* measure is usually expressed numerically (quantitative) and usually is easiest to formulate: the number, rate, percent, or ratio of something. A *soft* measure is an intangible attribute or characteristic that is usually expressed in terms of degree of excellence, desirability, attitude or perception (qualitative) and is often output- or outcome-based: citizen satisfaction with police; citizen perception of fear. Soft measures are good for measuring feelings or perceived changes and often complement hard measures by getting at people's emotional state. Since soft measures are typically qualitative they are not usually thought of in numerical terms, but they can be reduced numerically typically through survey questionnaires. Questionnaires that assess satisfaction, attitude or perception, say on a scale of 1 to 10, known as an interval-level scale, can be analyzed like quantitative data. The agency can administer the questionnaire at uniform intervals, such as quarterly, semi-annually or annually to examine qualitative changes. Soft measures should be developed in collaboration with the intended beneficiaries since it is they whom the agency seeks to satisfy. One way to do this is through focus groups, which is discussed in the section under data sources.

Hard and soft performance measures consist of indicators that provide "...evidence that a certain condition exists or certain results have or have not been achieved" (Brizius and Campbell, 1991:A-15) and typically measure input, output, production, process, intermediate objectives and outcomes. "Indicators enable decision-makers to assess progress towards the achievement of intended outputs, outcomes, goals, and objectives. As such, indicators are an integral part of a results-based accountability system" (Horsch, 2006). Input indicators measure the resources necessary to conduct the program, including human, financial and in-kind assets. Output indicators measure either the quantity or the quality of service rendered, based on whether the measure is hard or soft. Production indicators measure economy, efficiency and productivity along the pathway to outcome by describing the monetary value of the program. Process indicators measure the way in which service is delivered and typically includes things that indicate "how long" it takes to achieve a specific result. Indicators that measure intermediate objectives reveal what has been accomplished as of a particular point in the program, such as by a specific date or completion of something important (e.g., closing a case with an arrest). Finally, outcome indicators measure the impact of the initiative and usually reveal whether the initiative achieved its intended result.

Examples of Hard Measures	
Dimension	**Measure**
Inputs	Direct and indirect costs, including personnel, salaries, benefits, equipment, materials and in-kind contributions
Outputs	Number of arrests; total dollars collected in seized assets; percent of guilty pleas
Production	Unit costs; ratio of input:output; ratio of output:input per a defined metric
Intermediate Objectives	Percent of department goals achieved each quarter; semi-annually (interim goals; short-term progress)
Outcomes	Percent reduction in Part I crimes compared to the agency's goal

Examples of Soft Measures	
Dimension	**Measure**
Output	Accuracy and completeness of incident reports; changes in business processes
Outcome	Service adequacy: Percent of citizens who are "very satisfied" with the department; cleanliness of police facilities; appearance of neatly attired, well-groomed professional police officers; professional courteous staff; department reputation; improved citizen quality of life; degree of emergency preparedness
Process	Timeliness; issues measured in terms of adequacy, completeness, perception, preparedness and degree

Performance Indicator Classification System[22]	
Dimension	**Measure**
Indicators showing the required input resources	The total resources including, human, financial and in-kind contributions necessary to ensure program success (number of officers; number of hours; number of patrol cars; number of dollars; dosage level)
Indicators showing the volume of outputs	The number, rate or percentage of activities completed or services provided (throughput)
Indicators showing economy, efficiency and productivity (production)	**Indicators of Economy** measure unit costs to deliver services (cost per unit of service for each type of service delivered; equipment and material costs per unit; salary rate per employee hour). **Indicators of Efficiency** measure the ratio or proportion of budget to output, or of input to output resources (e.g., efficiency = $57,376,481_{\text{patrol budget [input]}}$/ $98,324_{\text{CFS [output]}}$ = $583.55 per CFS handled). **Indicators of Productivity** measure the ratio of output to input resources, usually per a defined metric, and is the inverse of efficiency; efficiency and productivity are equivalent measures, just reversed (e.g., productivity = $98,324_{\text{CFS}}$/ $57,376,481_{\text{patrol budget}}$ = .00171 × $1,000_{\text{metirc}}$ = 1.71 CFS handled per $1,000 of patrol budget expended)
Indicators showing the quality and internal functionality of the organization (process)	Percent of cases that exceed a predetermined service threshold (i.e., timeliness) (e.g., number of days to close a case; number of days to identify a suspect; police response time; cycle time per issue; data entry backlog or other system delays); degree of staff job satisfaction; degree of staff organization and attentiveness; degree of self-discipline and degree of overall agency discipline[23]; degree of emergency preparedness or state of readiness
Indicators showing interim progress toward end outcomes, where tasks are marked by completion within a specified time period (intermediate objectives)	A group of completed tasks or activities that represent progress toward the end outcome of a particular project, program or other goal (milestones). Percent of cases cleared each month; percent of new vehicles ordered and delivered by the end of the first quarter; percent of citizens annually surveyed who respond "satisfied" or "very satisfied;" total overtime expended each week; percent of cases resulting in conviction each month; percent increase in property values each year; total dollars paid semi-annually to settle liability suits; percent of fleet equipped with MDC's each quarter.
Indicators showing effectiveness and service capacity (outcome)	Service adequacy and service allocation by program (e.g., patrol, investigations, traffic, communications etc.) and by victim group (e.g., burglary, robbery, rape, etc.); citizen satisfaction; social impact; degree of courtesy, attentiveness and respect toward customers

Agency executives should select performance measures that are appropriate for the agency or the program and not necessarily rely on measures adopted by other agencies. Simply because one agency measures something, it is not automatically beneficial (or practical) for another agency. This is a common pitfall of the Compstat process; that which gets measured in the New York City Police Department is not necessarily directly transferable nor appropriate to a 5, 15, or 30-member agency. Using the NYPD's measures as an *example* is a good driver to organize ideas. But before any decisions are made to changes in the current data-collection process there should be discussions about feasibility, cost and practicality. This is addressed further under the section on data sources. The Friedman (2005:67-78) four-quadrant model is a good example of how to visualize the interconnectedness of hard and soft measures, how to answer the questions: *"How much did we do? How well did we do it? Is anyone better off?"* and the order of importance for these three questions. Reading this model proceeds from upper left to upper right, then lower left to lower right, where importance goes from least to most.

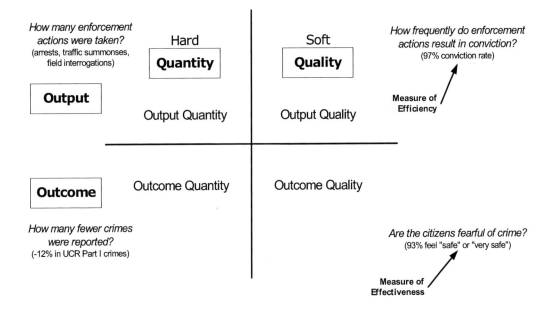

	Quantity	Quality
Effect	How much did we do? **LEAST** Important	How well did we do it? 2nd Most Important
Effect	Is anyone better off? 3rd Most Important	 **MOST** Important

Adopting Suitable Performance Measures for Your Agency. Selecting the most appropriate indicators for a police department can be difficult (Skogan and Hartnett, 1997:74). Developing a successful performance measurement system should be done with input from various members of the command staff, line personnel, those tasked with data collection, and those who will rely on the data. Although table 1 provides numerous examples of performance indicators, not all of them are feasible for every agency to implement. There are two principles that can guide selection:

1. *Principle of Quantity:* The performance measure must make a meaningful and informative contribution to what the agency does as a service organization. It must credible in the eyes of the public and elected officials;
2. *Principle of Quality:* The performance measure must be a valid measure of the activity in question and must support the end outcome.

Horsch (2006) identified a few questions police executives should ask that will help in selecting suitable indicators:

1. *"Does this indicator enable one to know about the expected result or condition?"* Indicators should provide direct evidence that the end outcome is being achieved through this particular activity or service.
2. *"Is the indicator defined in the same way over time? Are data for the indicator collected in the same way over time?"* This is also known as "reliability." If the indicator itself changes or the way in which data on the indicator is captured changes over time, then the results will not be reliable because there are two sets of data for the same thing. Consistency is very important to ensure measurement is accurate-consistency in both the definition and in the capture method.
3. *"Will data be available for an indicator?"* Data should be captured as frequently as possible and presented in a timely manner so decision-makers can act on the information before a new series of data are captured and presented for decision.

4. *"Are data currently being collected? If not, can cost effective instruments for data collection be developed?"* One of the most important features of this question is whether data can be captured and at what cost? If the costs of collection outweigh the decision-making benefits, then it is probably not worth collecting.

5. *"Is this indicator important to most people? Will this indicator provide sufficient information about a condition or result to convince both supporters and skeptics?"* Indicators should be easy to understand and should convey to the end-user a sense that continued reliance on it will help achieve the intended result. The indicator should confirm management's expectations and dispel critics' negative comments or pessimism.

6. *"Is the indicator quantitative?"* Numeric indicators (hard measures) are easiest to understand and are often easiest to capture. Quantitative indicators are often preferred over qualitative ones, however, qualitative indicators do provide valuable and useful information that can lend support and credibility to a program.

In addition to answering these questions, the U.S. General Accounting Office (1996) offers an excellent 3-step guide on how to select performance measures that are meaningful for an organization; the section on performance measurement has been culled and appears below. It reminds executives what they should be mindful of when selecting performance measures.

U.S G.A.O Guide for Selecting Appropriate Performance Measures	
Create performance measures for each organizational element that demonstrate results for that element	Performance measures should tell each organizational element how well it is achieving its goals, in areas such as inputs, outputs, intermediate objectives, production, process and end outcomes
Limit performance measures to a vital few	The number of measures for each goal for a given organizational element should be limited to a vital few. Those vital few measures should cover the key performance dimensions that will enable the organization to assess accomplishments, make decisions, realign processes, and assign accountability
Respond to multiple priorities	Government agencies often face a variety of interests whose competing demands continually force policymakers and managers to balance quality, cost, customer satisfaction, stakeholder concerns, and other factors. Performance measurement systems must take these competing interests into account and create incentives for managers to strike the difficult balance among competing demands. Performance measurement efforts that overemphasize one or two priorities at the expense of the others may skew the agency's performance and keep its managers from seeing the whole picture
Link performance indicators to the organizational function	Performance measures should be linked directly to the offices that have responsibility for making programs work. A clear connection between performance measures and program offices helps to both reinforce accountability and ensure that, in their day-to-day activities, managers keep in mind the outcomes their organization is striving to achieve
Collect sufficiently complete, accurate and consistent data	Performance measures should be accurate, timely, reliable and valid. Police departments should balance the cost of data collection efforts against the need to ensure that the collected data are complete, accurate, and consistent enough to document performance and support decision-making within each organizational element

Modified from U.S. Government Accounting Office (1996:24-27) as depicted in Hatry (1999:221)

When creating performance measures the structure of the measure should include the following elements:[24]

4. **Success Indicator**—"the part of a performance measure that defines the attribute or characteristic to be measured. A particular value or characteristic used to measure outcome or output;"

5. **Performance Indicator**—"the part of a performance measure that describes what is to be measured, typically expressed in quantitative form (i.e., number of...; percentage of...);

6. **Baseline**—"the part of a performance measure that establishes the initial level of measurement (value and date) against which targeted progress, and success is compared. A baseline includes both a starting date and starting level/value; and

7. **Target**—the part of a performance measure that establishes the desired level to be reached in a defined time period, usually stated as an improvement over the baseline."

After these elements are accounted for they should be reduced to a performance measurement statement. For example:

- **Goal: Control Fear and Crime**
  - Reducing crime and criminal victimizations program
    - *Reduce FBI UCR Part I crimes from 2,300 in FY 2007 to 1,955 (- 15%) in FY 2008 by increasing enforcement action.*
      1. **Success Indicator:** FBI UCR Part I crimes
      2. **Performance Indicator:** enforcement action (number of arrests; directed patrols; car stops; traffic summonses; road-safety checkpoints)
      3. **Baseline:** 2,300 FBI Part I crimes
      4. **Target:** 1,955 FBI Part I crimes
    - *Reduce the rate of status offenses from 75 per 1,000 juveniles in FY 2007 to 50 per 1,000 juveniles (-33%) in FY 2008 by increasing juvenile enforcement.*
      1. **Success Indicator:** rate of status offenses
      2. **Performance Indicator:** juvenile enforcement (number of truancy violations; number of curfew violations; number of missing/runaway juveniles)
      3. **Baseline:** 75 per 1,000 juveniles
      4. **Target:** 50 per 1,000 juveniles
  - Holding offenders accountable program
    - *Increase the overall clearance rate for FBI UCR Part I crimes from 25% in FY 2007 to 30% (+20%) in FY 2008 by improving investigative performance.*
      1. **Success Indicator:** overall clearance rate for FBI UCR Part I crimes

      2. **Performance Indicator:** investigative performance (number of days until warrant is issued—arrest or search; number of days until suspect is identified; number of days until case is cleared; number of polygraph examinations conducted; number of voice-stress analyses conducted)
      3. **Baseline:** 25% clearance rate
      4. **Target:** 30% clearance rate

- **Goal: Delivering Public Value through Budgeting Accountability**
  - Using financial resources fairly, efficiently and effectively program
    - *Reducing the cost per citizen to deliver police service from $534 in FY 2007 to $489 (-8%) in FY 2008 through improved service delivery.*
      1. **Success Indicator:** reduced cost per citizen to deliver police service
      2. **Performance Indicator:** improved service delivery (Number of units per year per program delivered; average hours per unit per program delivered; number of personnel required per unit; number of calls diverted to 311 or 7-digit number; percent of police vehicles available for service; total agency inflows; rate of sick-leave days consumed)
      3. **Baseline:** $534 per citizen
      4. **Target:** $489 per citizen

Experience dictates that one of the most effective tools for creating performance measures is through examples. One example is by way of analogy from the restaurant industry. A person's dining experience consists of dimensions beyond food alone. How many times have you heard: *"The food was great but the service was lousy."* This is because the dining experience is more than just the meal; it is a range of qualities that makes the event more enjoyable and typically includes food, décor, service and cost. Restaurant performance, as perceived by the dining public, is evaluated on multiple dimensions, not exclusively food. Although food quality is undoubtedly the first priority for restaurants, it is not the only priority.

Table 1 is a collection of sample multidimensional performance measures, modified from Moore and colleagues (2002:132), which are intended to serve as a model for an agency's annual report or business plan. The table shows an array of disaggregated measures, which can be adopted to help structure the agency's management and performance process: 4 goals, 7 critical dimensions, 30 success indicators, and 235 performance indicators. Notice that most performance indicators have both a hard (quantitative) and soft (qualitative) aspect to them. This is so because a hard measure alone may be insufficient to measure success; for example, the total number of arrests (hard) is meaningless without convictions (soft) (a measure of success may be the ratio of arrests:convictions). Performance measures are only limited by the type of data you are able to collect, the political realities of implementation and the ability to affix accountability.

The performance measures in table 1 are "multidimensional," meaning there is no single best expression of police performance; rather, multiple dimensions better express what police departments do because they include things beyond crime. This means that although controlling crime is nearly universally accepted as a measure of police performance and undoubtedly remains the "first priority of policing" (National Research Council, 2004:85), there are other elements of service delivery that concern constituent groups, such as timely response, courtesy, use of force, transparency and competency (Bratton, 1998; Skolnick, 1999). Such an example comes from Los Angeles, where in December 2006 the police department, through the chief of police, was assessed on seven performance dimensions, with laudable results: 1) crime reduction, 2) compliance with a federal consent decree, 3) deployment strength, 4) diversity in hiring and promotion, 5) homeland security and disaster preparedness, 6) anti-gang policies and 7) fiscal management (McGreevy, 2006). The multiple dimensions used to evaluate the LAPD have equivalent dimensions reflected in table 1:

LAPD Multidimensional Performance Model	
Dimension	**Equivalent from Table 1**
Crime Reduction	Controlling Fear and Crime (reducing victimizations; calling offenders to account)
Compliance With a Federal Consent Decree	Reverence for Law and Authority (practices that promote civil rights integrity; training; audits)
Deployment Strength	Delivering Public Value through Budgeting and Accountability (strength based on proportional need)
Diversity in Hiring and Promotion	Satisfying Customers through Service and Accountability (police personnel profile)
Homeland Security and Disaster Preparedness	Satisfying Customers through Service and Accountability (timeliness to respond; available assets)
Anti-Gang Policies	Reverence for Law and Authority (policies that reflect enforcement and management of gang units)
Fiscal Management	Delivering Public Value through Budgeting and Accountability (reducing/stabilizing costs; overtime)

The LAPD model is a best-practice as it relates to service delivery, which measures the "bottom line" by accounting for things beyond crime control that citizens value as important. There is danger in selecting one-dimensional performance systems; the agency may adopt a measure that they are especially good at achieving at the expense of others. So, while the agency does a good job of controlling crime, perhaps they have alienated the community in the process, thus reducing their legitimacy; ultimately resulting in little or no public support. This is not unrealistic; confidence, support and public perception are often influenced by performance during individual moments rather than by official statistics. This means a single transgression, real or perceived, such as controlling crime through random interdiction along an interstate roadway-the agency's only performance dimension-will define public perception far beyond the overall decline in crime. Some of these soft (qualitative) measures, such as courtesy and competency, may be expressed by ensuring officers provide "practical advice, counseling and referring callers to public and private agencies that are able to assist them further with their problems" (National Research Council, 2004:86).

Several scholars have created multidimensional performance systems. When doing so the idea is to create an exhaustive measurement list that captures all of the service categories for which police are responsible, then, as best as possible, reduce the attributes of each category to mutually exclusive variables to ensure they appear in only one category. Many of these measures can be operationalized and used to conduct intermediate statistical analyses, which is the subject of part two of this text.[25]

Multidimensional Performance Systems				
Michael O'Neil (1980)	Harry Hatry and colleagues (1992)	G. Alpert and M. Moore (1994)	Stephen Mastrofski (1999)	Mark Moore and colleagues (2002)
Crime prevention	Prevention of crime	Doing Justice	Attentiveness	Reduce criminal victimization
Crime control	Apprehension of offenders	Promoting Secure Communities	Reliability	Call offenders to account
Conflict resolution	Responsiveness of police	Restoring Crime Victims	Responsiveness	Reduce fear and enhance personal security
General service	Feeling of security	Promoting Non-criminal Options	Competence	Guarantee safety in public spaces
Police administration	Fairness, courtesy, helpfulness/ cooperativeness, honesty		Manners	Use financial resources fairly, efficiently and effectively
			Fairness	Use force and authority fairly, efficiently and effectively Satisfy customer demands/achieve legitimacy with those policed

A Model for Structuring Police Performance. When thinking about the things the police department should be measured against, think about how the corporate world evaluates its performance. The corporate sector has always been revered for its ability to measure performance and thus has often served as a model for public sectors organizations to emulate. But corporate performance is evaluated on more than just financial profit. Businesses are assessed annually on seven dimensions by *Business Ethics* magazine for their corporate responsibility and how well they serve various stakeholders, not only "bottom line" profits; the stockholders are just one (Maguire, 2003:9). "They are also rated on consumer confidence, responsiveness to customers, and consumer satisfaction using the *American Customer Satisfaction Index* [ACSI]" (Maguire, 2003:9). The ACSI has developed a government model that most police agencies can follow to evaluate performance (diagram 1). "The model used to measure satisfaction with government agencies is identical to the private-sector model, except the component in the private-sector model concerning price and 'repurchase' intentions has been adjusted for the public sector (this occurs in the 'outcomes' component of the model)."[26]

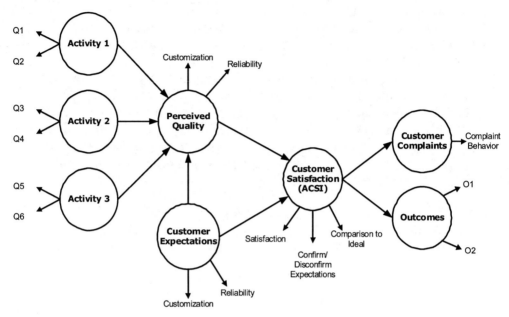

Diagram 1 (http://www.theacsi.org/government/govt-model.html)

The point is that the police must think beyond crime as their only "bottom line" measure of performance, just as corporations think beyond financials (Hoover, 1995). The police department will likely be assessed by various groups for how well they perform on the numerous services they deliver, not just crime. Here is a Police-corporate comparison model using the dimensions from *Business Ethics*:

Primary Corporate Stakeholders	Analogous Police Stakeholders	Police Performance Dimensions
Stockholders	**Taxpayers**: those who have a financial interest in the organization through property taxation	Using financial resources fairly, efficiently and effectively; honoring contractually conferred benefits; reducing employee/ union grievances; reducing occupational injuries and health-related problems
Employees	**Employees**: those who have a human, often long-term, interest in the organization through their employment	
The Community	**Constituent groups**: segments of society that may suffer harm in public or quasi-public places (victims; witnesses; bystanders; informants; complainants; offenders; crowds; peaceful demonstrators)	Reducing crime and criminal victimizations; holding offenders accountable; reducing fear, blight and enhancing personal safety; guaranteeing safety in public and quasi-public places
The Environment	**By-products of police operations**: harmful side effects and sometimes unintended consequences of police action (poor police-community relations; abuse of authority; unlawful or oppressive tactics; excessive force; corruption; differential treatment; involuntary U.S. Department of Justice intervention—consent decree)	Using force and authority efficiently and fairly; increasing early intervention—EWS; developing core competencies and professionalism; reducing citizen complaints

Primary Corporate Stakeholders	Analogous Police Stakeholders	Police Performance Dimensions
Overseas Stakeholders	**Stakeholders**: individuals or groups who have a human or financial interest in the organization and the organization's performance that may be exploited (collaborators, nonprofit groups; community groups; state, county federal government; developers; investors)	Satisfying customer demands and achieving legitimacy with those policed; increasing integrity and fairness; citizen satisfaction; increasing accountability; awards and public recognition; creating a diverse workforce; increasing satisfaction with police services
Minorities and Women	**Minorities, women and other traditionally underserved populations**: segments of society that have historically received inequitable treatment or who have been categorically excluded thus reducing their social status or self-sufficiency (elderly; disabled; juveniles; homeless; mentally ill; domestic violence victims)	
Customers	**Residents and citizens and those who call the police for assistance**: the primary source of work with whom the police must deal	

The performance measures in table 1 parallel those that are widely accepted in the research literature as measures of professionalism. Carter and Wilson (2006) reviewed nineteen studies conducted between 1973 and 2005, which resulted in the list below. Although their research focused on the professionalism of *individual* police officers, particularly the relationship between higher education and professionalism, the performance indicators for department professionalism are the same or very similar (notice the combination of hard (H) and soft (S) measures). The measures they found to be used most frequently were:

Measures of Police Professionalism

Disciplinary actions (H)	Line of duty injuries (H)
Commendations (H)	Verbal or written communications skills (S)
Sick time used (H)	Job knowledge (S)
Police academy test scores (H)	Quality of work (S)
Preventable crashes (H)	Cooperation (S)
Citizens complaints (H)	Probationary evaluations (H)
Volume of arrests or summonses (H)	Response to new training (S)
Use of force incidents (H)	Decision-making ability (S)
Supervisory performance evaluations (H)	Level of commitment (S)
Rank of promotions (H)	Professional attitude (S)

Table 1	Structure for a Performance Measurement Model		
Department Goal	**Critical Dimensions**	**Success Indicators**	**Performance Indicators**
Controlling Fear and Crime	Reducing crime and criminal victimizations	1. Reducing crime and victimization rates (adult and juvenile) 2. Reducing total FBI Part I and Part II crimes 3. Reducing status offenses	1. Number and disposition of arrests for Part I and Part II crimes (by patrol, by detectives, by others) 2. Number and disposition of Part I and Part II crimes 3. Number of Part I and Part II crimes per 1,000 residents 4. Number and disposition of traffic summonses issued (pedestrian, parking and moving) 5. Number and disposition of peddler/vendor-license summonses issued 6. Number of traffic warnings issued 7. Number and disposition of field interrogations 8. Number and disposition of car stops 9. Number and disposition of directed patrols 10. Number and disposition of vertical patrols 11. Number and disposition of street closures[27] 12. Number and disposition of road safety checkpoints. 13. Number and disposition of crackdown operations 14. Number and disposition of decoy operations (narcotics buy/bust; fencing; sting car; street crime) 15. Number and disposition of licensed retail shop inspections (budget motels; pawn; firearms; alcohol) 16. Number of clandestine drug labs disrupted 17. Number and disposition of gangs and organized crime syndicates dismantled 18. Number of gangs and organized crime syndicates dismantled 19. Ratio of recovered stolen vehicles:stolen vehicles (local only) 20. Number and disposition of counterfeiting operations (money; prescriptions; IDs; motor vehicle titles; drivers licenses) 21. Number and disposition of missing/runaway juveniles (NCMEC involvement) 22. Number and disposition of curfew violations 23. Number and disposition of truancy violations 24. Number of juvenile crime victims and perpetrators 25. Number of days to repeat victimization 26. Number and rate of repeat victims[28]

Table 1		Structure for a Performance Measurement Model	
Department Goal	**Critical Dimensions**	**Success Indicators**	**Performance Indicators**
			27. Number of temporary and permanent domestic violence restraining orders served 28. Number of suppressible incidents; ratio suppressible:non-suppressible[29] 29. Value and type of assets seized through civil enforcement (vehicles, property, financial accounts)[30] 30. Number of nuisance locations temporarily and permanently closed via civil enforcement (police padlock) 31. Number of stranger-to-stranger crimes; ratio of stranger:acquantance crimes 32. Number, nature and disposition of successful problem solving/situational crime prevention projects
	Holding offenders accountable	1. Increasing clearance rates 2. Increasing conviction rates 3. Increasing enforcement action (warrants issued and served; evictions; searches; scofflaw) 4. Reducing recidivism (offender compliance with parole and probation; selective incapacitation; "no bail" provisions; preventive detention) 5. Increasing intelligence gathered (prisoner debriefings; confessions) 6. Increasing use of science and technology	1. Number of investigations cleared by arrest 2. Percent of cleared investigations resulting in indictment 3. Percent of successful prosecutions (guilty pleas and trials)[31] 4. Percent of cases turned over to federal government for prosecution 5. Percent and findings from adverse suppression hearings 6. Rate of false witness identifications 7. Rate of false confessions 8. Number and disposition of officers who failed to appear in court after being subpoenaed 9. Percent of investigations with sworn statements and interrogations obtained (victim, witness and suspect) 10. Number and disposition of arrest and search warrants issued and executed 11. Number and disposition of wiretaps conducted 12. Number of warrant checks and percent of "hits" (local and NCIC)[32] 13. Number and findings of polygraph examinations conducted 14. Number and findings of voice-stress examinations conducted 15. Number and disposition of crime bulletin/"wanted" posters issued 16. Number and findings of consent searches undertaken 17. Number and disposition of tenant evictions upon suitable findings

Table 1			Structure for a Performance Measurement Model
Department Goal	Critical Dimensions	Success Indicators	Performance Indicators
			18. Number and findings from K-9 drug-scent detection 19. Number and disposition of drug offender restraining orders/injunctions issued 20. Number and disposition of gang member restraining orders/ injunctions issued 21. Number of hours/days until case is cleared 22. Number of hours/days until warrant is issued (arrests and search) 23. Number of outstanding arrest warrants 24. Number of hours/days until suspect is identified 25. Number of gangs and gang members identified 26. Number and disposition of crime scenes processed 27. Percent of crime scenes processed with usable forensic evidence 28. Percent of forensic samples recovered matched to suspects 29. Number of hours/days to return results from forensic analyses (AFIS; DNA-CODIS, ballistics-NIBIN)[33] 30. Percent of found/recovered property matched to suspect 31. Number and rate of repeat offenders 32. Number of repeat offenders exposed to publicity (billboards; news media; Internet posting) 33. Number of vehicles impounded and persons arrested for scofflaw 34. Rate of local incarceration (county jail) 35. Number of arrestees held without bail (preventive detention) 36. Number of parolees and probationers revoked 37. Number and disposition of 15-minute home visits to parolees and probationers 38. Ratio of arrests:reported crimes[34] 39. Ratio of cases:investigators 40. Number and disposition of investigations initiated from prisoner debriefings and offenders interviews[35]
	Reducing fear, blight and enhancing personal safety	1. Reducing fear (social and physical conditions that contribute to fear and blight; levels of fear; suspicious circumstances)	1. Rate of reported fear and perception of crime through annual community survey 2. Rate of reported security measures through quarterly residential and commercial security surveys

Table 1		Structure for a Performance Measurement Model	
Department Goal	Critical Dimensions	Success Indicators	Performance Indicators
		2. Reporting changes in self-defense measures (levels and types) 3. Empowering communities to help themselves (social capital and social cohesion; partnerships) 4. Reducing harmful student, young adult and underage activities	3. Number of new alarm permits; ratio of permits:structures (commercial and residential) 4. Number of new gun permits by type (handgun, shotgun, rifle; purchase and carry) 5. Number of new community partnerships and neighborhood crime watch groups formed[36] 6. Number and disposition of intergovernmental partnership (FBI, DEA, ATF, state police, victim/witness advocacy) 7. Number and disposition of victim follow-up visits by detectives 8. Number and size of community empowerment grants 9. Number and disposition of police-led community anti-crime/anti-drug marches 10. Attendance during "National Night Out" events (typically held in August) 11. Number of graffiti markings removed within 24 hours of discovery 12. Number and variety of crime prevention seminars (livery services; 24-hour establishments) 13. Number of CFS for suspicious vehicles, persons and shots fired 14. Number and nature of neighborhood conditions corrected within 45 days of notice[37] 15. Number and disposition of abandoned cars impounded. 16. Number and disposition of firearms recovered 17. Number of abandoned structures secured and razed 18. Number and nature of repeat locations identified ("hot spots") 19. Number of students who graduate from DARE and GREAT programs 20. Number and disposition of rave parties disrupted 21. Number and disposition of underage alcohol operations 22. Number and findings of fraternity/sorority inspections 23. Number and disposition of police-led community initiatives (block parties, teen courts, conflict-dispute resolution/mediation, mentoring, forums/discussions, community clean-ups, recreation events

Table 1		Structure for a Performance Measurement Model	
Department Goal	**Critical Dimensions**	**Success Indicators**	**Performance Indicators**
			24. Number and attendance level of community meetings held
	Guaranteeing safety in public and quasi-public places	1. Increasing utilization of parks and other public or quasi-public space (homeless population; EDPs; ridership on public transportation 2. Reducing traffic conditions (fatalities, injuries and property damage; motor vehicle and pedestrian-related problems–DWI, gridlock, cruising, aggressive driving, jaywalking) 3. Increasing property values 4. Increasing safety for vulnerable populations (Internet predation; schools; elderly; juveniles; women)	1. Number of traffic summonses and warnings issued by type (moving, parking, pedestrian) 2. Number and disposition of road-safety checkpoints (street racing, cruising, residential speeding, DWI) 3. Number and disposition of radar operations 4. Number and nature of vehicular and pedestrian accidents 5. Number and findings of bus, taxi, subway and transit portal inspections 6. Number of homeless relocated to shelters; occupancy rate at local shelters 7. Number of citizens using public parks 8. Percent of students using "safe schools" corridors 9. Number of reported crimes on school grounds (bullying, bomb threats, false fire alarms, fights/assaults, vandalism, theft, break-ins) 10. Number and disposition of drunk drivers apprehended 11. Number of intersections cleared of vehicular traffic congestion 12. Number and disposition of car stops for aggressive driving 13. Number of EDPs relocated to hospital/care facility 14. Number and disposition of Internet sting operations 15. Number and disposition of youths detained and arrested for disorderly conduct 16. Number of CCTV cameras installed and results from observations 17. Number and disposition of budget motel disorder operations 18. Number and disposition of registered criminal informants (reliability) 19. Number and disposition of sex-related operations (prostitution, brothel, trafficking) 20. Number of parolees and probationers residing in the community 21. Number of registered sex offenders in community (compliance with the Adam Walsh Child Protection and Safety Act of 2006)

Table 1			Structure for a Performance Measurement Model
Department Goal	Critical Dimensions	Success Indicators	Performance Indicators
Delivering Public Value through Budgeting Accountability	Using financial resources fairly, efficiently and effectively	1. Reducing costs (stabilizing unfunded mandates or priorities; budget compliance; overtime; civilization) 2. Reducing total calls for service (misuse and abuse of 911) 3. Increasing agency inflows (grant funds) 4. Increasing deployment efficiency/ fairness based on proportional need (scheduling efficiency) 5. Reducing occupational injuries and health-related problems	1. Number of police programs delivered (victim/witness assistance) 2. Average cost per citizen 3. Average cost per call for service 4. Average cost per unit per program 5. Total cost to deliver programs 6. Unit cost per prisoner/hospital watch 7. Material cost per unit per program 8. Equipment cost per unit per program 9. Salary rate per employee hour per program 10. Average hours per unit, per program, delivered 11. Number of units per year, per program, delivered 12. Number of personnel required per unit 13. Total employee hours per modality 14. Number of false burglar alarms 15. Total dollars in fines collected for false burglar alarms 16. Number of calls to 311 or 7-digit non-emergency number; ratio emergency:non-emergency calls 17. Number, nature, cost and disposition of employee/union grievances 18. Number, nature, cost and disposition of EEOC companies 19. Total overtime expended by category and division 20. Total cost of parades, festivals, special events and reimbursements 21. Unit cost of property/contraband destroyed 22. Number of property items converted and donated to community groups 23. Deployment level based on semi-annual workload analysis 24. Average number of sworn officers on-duty per tour 25. Relief factor by title 26. Total agency inflows (state, federal and private grant dollars; fines; forfeiture funds; auction; donations) 27. Percent of department goals achieved within budget 28. Percent of police vehicles available for service 29. Number of fleet assets by type 30. Sworn:civilian personnel ratio 31. Sworn officers per square mile 32. Length of staff member service by percent within specific rank 33. Ratio of actual strength:authorized strength

Table 1		Structure for a Performance Measurement Model	
Department Goal	**Critical Dimensions**	**Success Indicators**	**Performance Indicators**
			34. Number and rate of sick-leave days consumed 35. Number of light duty hours consumed; total personnel on light duty 36. Percent of workforce satisfied with employment conditions and relationships at work 37. Number of officers disarmed/restricted-duty status 38. Number of officer-hours consumed by restricted duty status 39. Number and disposition of on-duty injuries 40. Number and findings of police vehicle collisions (at-fault, contributory, not at fault) 41. Number of volunteer hours; total volunteers 42. Number of reservist hours; total reservists 43. Number of auxiliary hours; total auxiliaries 44. Percent of property converted for department use.
Reverence for Law and Authority	Using force and authority fairly, efficiently and effectively	1. Reducing citizen complaints (use of force; police shootings; pursuits; resisting arrest) 2. Reducing settlements in liability suits 3. Increasing early intervention 4. Increasing competencies and professionalization[38] (education level; department accreditation)	1. Number and disposition of citizen complaints by category 2. Average internal affairs investigation time (days) 3. Ratio of citizen complaints sustained:not sustained 4. Percent of personnel in compliance with department policy (drug screening; integrity tests; bureau and division audits) 5. Percent compliance with consent decree during a defined time period 6. Total dollars paid in lawsuit settlements 7. Incidence and prevalence of in-custody deaths and injuries 8. Incidence and prevalence by disposition of police shootings (fatalities and injuries) 9. Incidence and prevalence by disposition of police firearms discharges 10. Percent of SWAT incidents resolved without injury or force 11. Number of bullets fired by police officers 12. Incidence and prevalence by disposition of obstructing/interfering with an officer 13. Incidence and prevalence by disposition of use of force incidents (chemical spray; dogs; mounted; TASER; baton; firearm; ASP) 14. Number and disposition of officer-initiated citizen encounters 15. Incidence and prevalence by disposition of resisting arrest 16. Incidence and prevalence by disposition of aggravated assault on police officer

Table 1		Structure for a Performance Measurement Model	
Department Goal	**Critical Dimensions**	**Success Indicators**	**Performance Indicators**
			17. Number and disposition of officers identified and retrained through early warning system (EWS)
			18. Number and disposition of secondary (spin-off) investigations from ICV review
			19. Number and nature of personnel retrained
			20. Number of hours and variety of training offered (career development seminars)
			21. Percent of personnel who fail firearms qualification
			22. Percent of command rank personnel who satisfactorily complete advanced management training (FBINA, Northwestern Police Staff and Command, PERF SMP)[39]
			23. Percent of officers and detectives who satisfactorily complete discretionary and state mandated in-service training
			24. Percent of supervisors and mid-level managers who satisfactorily complete advanced supervision training
			25. Percent of personnel with baccalaureate and advanced (graduate) degrees
			26. Percent compliance with Freedom of Information Act (FOIA)
			27. Percent of promulgated policies codified in department manual within 30 days
			28. Percent and nature of personnel receiving commendations/award citations
			29. Percent of officers who receive satisfactory and "above average" performance evaluations
			30. Percent of prisoners who escape from police custody
			31. Percent of prisoners who exceed holding-time thresholds
			32. Average time to process a single prisoner from custody to release (cycle time)[40]
			33. Number of consecutive years of department accreditation (CALEA)[41]
			34. Percent of accreditation goals achieved
			35. Number and disposition of police pursuits
Satisfying Customers through Service and Accountability	Satisfying customer demands and achieving legitimacy with those policed	1. Increasing satisfaction with police services (response times; PSAP mandates; service contacts) 2. Increasing citizen perception of integrity, equatability and fairness 3. Meeting or exceeding	1. Percent of citizens satisfied with police service via annual community survey 2. Percent of response time goals achieved 3. Average response time to CFS by type of call (including queue and travel time) 4. Number and disposition of CFS dispatched 5. Percent of dispatched CFS that are "unfounded"[42] 6. Percent of CFS by final disposition type 7. Percent of queue goals achieved

Table 1		Structure for a Performance Measurement Model	
Department Goal	**Critical Dimensions**	**Success Indicators**	**Performance Indicators**
		established total service-time thresholds 4. Increasing information/technology assets	8. Percent of total service-time thresholds achieved 9. Percent of citizens who perceive the police as fair and legitimate via annual community survey 10. Percent of beat/sector boundaries that correspond with identifiable neighborhoods 11. Number of calls expedited by telephone reporting unit (TRU) 12. Ratio of calls dispatched:calls expedited via TRU 13. Number of emergency calls for service answered in under 11 seconds 14. Number of non-emergency calls for service answered in under 21 seconds 15. Number of abandoned 911 calls to the PSAP 16. Number of 911 calls received 17. Number and disposition of telephone calls received via "1-800 tip-line" (internal affairs; narcotics; vice; Crime Stoppers) 18. Number of web-page "hits," forms downloaded and services used 19. Number of email list serv messages sent 20. Number of positive/favorable department issued press releases in print 21. Number of public service announcements (PSAs) 22. Number and disposition of directed citizen contacts (informal social contact) 23. Percent of victims contacted by detectives within 24 hours for follow-up 24. Percent of vehicle owners notified within 48 hours their vehicle is in police custody (recovered or impounded) 25. Number and disposition of personal service contacts handled (senior citizen escorts and check-ins, death notifications, vacant house checks, MV lockouts, check welfare, funeral escorts) 26. Number and variety of victim-witness services provided and the number served (transportation, violent crime compensation, social service referrals) 27. Percent of found/recovered property returned to owner 28. Number of pieces and value of stolen property recovered 29. Percent of found/recovered property linked to a criminal suspect

Table 1		Structure for a Performance Measurement Model	
Department Goal	Critical Dimensions	Success Indicators	Performance Indicators
			30. Percent of the workforce that resembles the community's demographic profile (level of racial, ethnic, and gender diversity)[43]
			31. Percent of the workforce that is bi- or multilingual (read, write or speak; sign language)
			32. Number of desktop computers, MDCs and hand-held devices deployed[44]
			33. Percent of recruiting goals achieved
			34. Number of public recognition awards
			35. Number of Citizens Police Academy classes and graduates
			36. Overall attrition rate
			37. Number and findings from exit interviews of separated employees
			38. Percent of personnel vacancies filled within 90 days of the vacancy
			39. Percent of practical exercises that meet or exceed department performance standards (the capacity to respond as measured by: 1) timeliness and level of deployment-time to muster at staging area; 2) number of required assets activated-equipment; 3) percent of availability-personnel recall and staffing strength; 4) level of redundancy, and 5) number of hours to: a) declare the situation "under control," b) restore general community normalcy, and c) restore normal operating environment)
			40. Number of permits/applications processed within 30 days (firearms, parades, block parties)
Modified from Moore, et al (2002:132)			

Chart 1 is an example of a partial organizational plan that identifies which organizational elements may be responsible for capturing certain performance measures toward the agency's goals. Only the parent command is shown with the exception of the traffic division and the training division. The performance measures under each organizational element *are not* necessarily performance indicators for the specific division in which the measures appear; however some of the indicators may be just that. For example, the number of firearms discharges, the number of police shootings or the number of bullets fired *is not* a performance measure for the internal affairs bureau. These are performance measures the department as a whole should embrace in pursuit of the goal: *Reverence for Law and Authority*. How the department structures its policies and programs should work to achieve that goal, and through training, every member of the agency should work toward that goal. However, the quality of the individual investigations and the amount of time to complete a single investigation (in days or hours) *is* a performance indicator for internal affairs. Similarly, false burglar alarms may be captured and reported by the communications division, but this is not a performance indicator for that division itself; the number of calls expedited via TRU, the number of abandoned 911 calls and the number of 911 calls answered in less than 11 seconds, however, are measures for that division. Ideally performance indicators should be linked to the department's policies and programs, preferably through logic models that are embodied in written business plans, where the strategies for improving service delivery are articulated.

Individual (officer level) performance indicators may be derived from empirical data based on officers serving in those roles and should be aligned with job specifications (civil service title descriptions). Collective (bureau or division level) performance indicators should also be derived from empirical data based on the division's or bureau's operational function and should be aligned with the department's policies and programs that articulate the responsibilities for that organizational element.

Although it is not likely all of the performance measures identified in table 1 would be adopted, indeed it is not necessary, there are several performance measures that may prove valuable to both citizens and elected officials (i.e., input resources, production and end outcomes—*"how much will this cost and what do I get for it"?*) as they evaluate department performance, and to the police executive and his or her subordinate staff as they manage daily police operations (i.e., output, process and intermediate objectives—*"the employees are doing what is expected of them, they are organized, attentive to detail and they are meeting the department's interim goals"*).

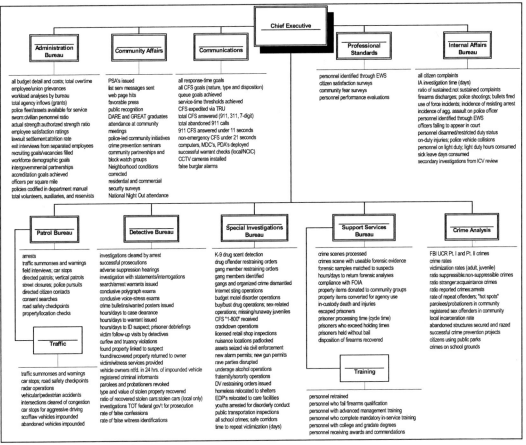

Chart 1 - Partial Organizational Plan

Problem Specification as a Route to Better Performance

When a police department sets out to measure performance it may be predicated upon an existing problem. In this regard the first aspect of measurement is to adequately specify the problem. Much the same way a physician must diagnose a patient's illness, lest they treat only the symptoms, so, too, must the police properly diagnose the problem requiring intervention (both internal and external). Analyzing the problem will not only help commanders develop an appropriate logic model (more about logic modeling ahead), which will guide the intervention, but it will help define the nature and extent of the problem, the necessary dosage and the data elements useful for measurement. According to the Center for Problem Oriented Policing "problems must be described precisely and accurately and broken down into specific aspects of the problem. Problems often aren't what they first appear to be."[45] This suggests that if the problem is not correctly specified, then there is an increased risk of treating only the symptoms, not the causes, and any measurements that are collected and acted upon will be inaccurate. Problem specification should take this form before measurements are taken:[46]

I. **NATURE:** must be specific or risk treating symptoms not the problem
II. **MAGNITUDE:** is this worthy of intervention in terms of size or extent? (# of cases; # of locations; incidence and prevalence)
III. **SERIOUSNESS**
    A. What is the resulting harm?
       1. Property (blight; abandoned or unsafe structures; vacant retail locations)
       2. Physical (death or injury)
       3. Economic (lost sales revenue; lost property tax revenue; reduced property values; reduced tourism; civil liability)
       4. Psychological (residual emotional impact)
       5. Societal (loss of respect and legitimacy in the agency or the community as a whole)
    B. Does this merit/deserve intervention?
IV. **RATE OF CHANGE**
    A. Examine trends over time
    B. Historical trend
    C. Are there any critical incidents?
    D. Baseline measures or composite index (take measurements at the beginning to serve as a baseline for future comparisons and projections)
    E. Gather as much data as possible for a trend analysis
    F. Triangulation
V. **PERSONS AFFECTED**
    A. Victims
    B. Offenders
    C. Police
    D. Families
    E. Potential offenders
VI. **SPATIAL ASPECTS**
    A. "Hot spots;" which neighborhoods?
    B. Without spatial analysis the problem is assumed to be everywhere
VII. **TEMPORAL ASPECTS**
    A. Time of day
    B. Day of week
    C. Week of month
    D. Month of year
    E. Season
    F. Without temporal analysis the problem is assumed to occur all the time
VIII. **SYSTEM RESPONSES**
    A. What has been done in the past?
    B. What was the outcome?
    C. Necessary to prevent duplicating services
IX. **PROJECTIONS**
    A. Forecasting
    B. Provides a good illustration of where you might be without intervention

X. **ORIGINS/CAUSAL ASSUMPTIONS**
   A. What is the cause? (criminological, sociological theory; operational breakdown or perform-
      ance slowdown)
   B. What is the relationship between behavior and consequences?
   C. Policy must deal with causes and origins, otherwise the response is only dealing with
      symptoms

Strategic Management as an Element of Performance

A Japanese proverb is fitting to introduce this section: "Vision without action is a daydream. Action without vision is a nightmare." Said somewhat differently: a vision about what you want to do is an idea; a written document about what you want to do is a plan! Taking action without a written document describing the things that need to done and the procedure for doing them leaves you to founder on the shoals of poor planning with little recourse. Developing strategic plans to fulfill a mission requires detailed analytic information about the problem, proportional need, costs for services, coordination of resources, minimum staffing requirements and appropriate performance indicators.[47] Whether the police department is expanding a crime control program, creating a new overtime initiative, reorganizing, hiring personnel, or evaluating their past success (or failure), measuring performance begins with a written analytic plan.

The Strategic Management Process. Improving performance has two basic parts. First, things must be organized according to a logical process. Second, performance indicators must be identified and collected. This means the agency must have the capacity to capture, analyze, report on, and disseminate findings in a meaningful way to ensure accountability, such as through the Compstat process. Using a modified research process identified by Babbie (2002:102) may make this process more clear. Figure 1 illustrates the process of organizing the approach to performance measurement.

The process follows a series of sequential steps that begins with an interest to address a problem. The interest may be either internally or externally generated and is usually championed by a member of the command staff or the chief executive. The interest is then translated into a concept while concurrently selecting an implementation strategy and identifying input resources. A concept is an abstract principle, whose meaning must be clearly defined to ensure all who come into contact with it have a complete understanding by what is meant. The choice of implementation strategy includes the organizational element, or combination thereof, that will execute the plan and monitor progress.

Next, success indicators must be identified, those things that, if accomplished, suggest the agency is achieving what it stated in the concept. Once you know where success will manifest itself, the next step is to operationalize how that success will be measured. This is generally a quantity or quality of something, such as the number or percent of crimes, or the percent of satisfied citizens. After the measures have been designed the plan must be implemented by the responsible organizational element. This typically follows a detailed implementation order, promulgated by the chief executive, which identifies responsibilities and affixes accountability.

Following implementation, data collection begins on the individual actions taken and services delivered (output). The output data that is collected must be transformed into a form suitable for analysis. This means the raw data must be reviewed for errors and quality, then entered into a database or spreadsheet such as MS Excel©. After the data has been processed it must be analyzed and conclusions should be drawn about the observations; intermediate objectives should be evaluated along the pathway to end outcome to ensure the goals will be achieved. The intermediate objectives serve as markers (milestones) so adjustments to the program can be made. Finally, a report should be prepared about the extent to which the agency achieved its end outcome (goal). The report should be made available to command staff members, elected officials, community members and funding agencies, as appropriate.

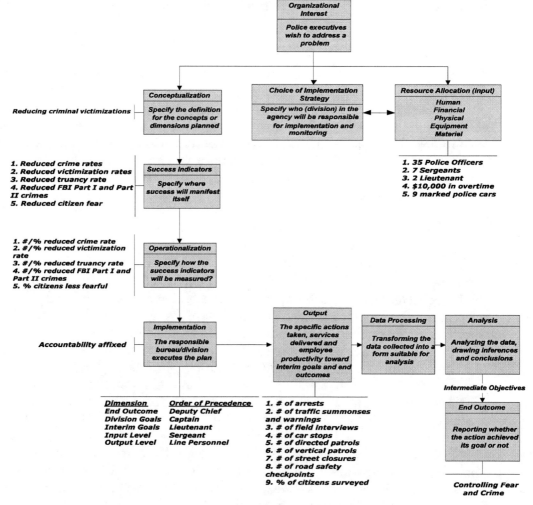

Figure 1 - Performance Measurement Process

One question that often arises in strategic management is: *Which comes first the budget or the plan?* The answer is: *Neither; strategic management is an iterative process meaning it is circular: plans affect budgets and budgets affect plans.* Developing performance standards is accomplished through a strategic management model of successive steps, each building on the preceding steps but not ending simply by returning to the starting point. In fact, it is a revolving process that ensures the agency and the employees are achieving efficiency and performance at optimal levels. Performance measures are determined by the success indicators: *where will success manifest itself?* These measures primarily reflect the direct outputs of the department's core programs, which focus on service delivery. Figure 2 is Jankofsky's rendering of a strategic management model annotated with performance dimensions.

Performance measures make the department's end outcomes and objectives more clear and meaningful.

They also serve to:

1) "promote customer satisfaction,
2) emphasize employee teamwork,
3) focus on measurable results,
4) support 'management by fact',
5) engender top management commitment, and
6) strive for continuous improvement" (Jankofsky:9).

Performance measurement can also help improve:
1) "decision making,
2) performance appraisal,
3) accountability,
4) public service performance,
5) public participation,
6) civic discourse" (National Center for Public Productivity, 2006:8),
7) "workforce productivity, and
8) [cost reduction]" (Plateau/Knowledge Infusion, 2006:3).

Figure 2 Annotated from D.P. Jankofsky (n.d.)

Measuring Outcome vs. Output

There is a distinct difference between measuring output and measuring outcome. To better measure organizational success, police departments must shift from solely measuring units of *output* (e.g., arrests, summonses and field interrogations), to more meaningful measurement of *outcomes* (e.g., end result). Outputs are the direct products of personnel activities. Output questions usually ask *how many* (i.e., the number of something; the percent of...; the ratio of...; the incidence of...). Outcomes are the results from that specific activity and often ask the question *What*. Such as, *What is the result of the output from effecting 126 arrests for drug sales?* Or, did we achieve our end outcome of reducing drug calls for service by 15%?(i.e., did we accomplish what we intended to accomplish?)[48] The basic difference between outcome and output can be stated in terms of goals and objectives, which is a more familiar concept in policing. "Goals [outcomes] describe desired future states, some intended change in the problem. Generally goals are broad statements intended to provide direction for change" (Welsh and Harris, 2004:92). If the goals are vague, then it is likely that the program or policy will not achieve its intended results. When designing goal statement they should be simply stated; one or two sentences that begin with an action verb, that capture the essence of the policy or program and that offer a rationale for its creation and its structure (Welsh and Harris, 2004:92).

On the other hand, "objectives specify explicit and measurable outcomes" (Welsh and Harris, 2004:92). Outputs are the type of measurement that supervisors and middle managers typically ask of their subordinates. Although outputs are easy to measure (e.g., number of arrests; number of DWI checkpoints; number of summonses issued; number of directed patrols[49]; number of citizen contacts), they provide only limited information about the impact or benefit provided to the community. Objectives consist of four major components:

1. "A *time frame*: a date [or time] by which the objective will be completed.
2. A *target population*: who will evidence the intended change?
3. A *result*: the key outcome intended; [or] a specific change in the problem.
4. A *criterion*: a standard for measuring successful achievement of the result" (Welsh and Harris, 2004:97).

For example, the objectives of the widely regarded Minneapolis Domestic Violence Experiment conducted by Sherman and Berk[50] (1984) were:

1. "*Time Frame*: 6 months;
2. *Target Population*: Two precincts with the highest density of domestic violence;
3. *Result*: Fewer repeat incidents of domestic abuse;
4. *Criteria*: Two measures: 1) police arrest records, and 2) victim self-reports (follow-up interviews were conducted every two weeks for 24 weeks)" (Welsh and Harris, 2004:98).

A good way to think of objectives is the individual steps that lead to the goals. One way to conceptualize output measures is to think of the specific performance indicators that will lead to achieving the goal that has been established. DeMaio (no date) uses the acronym S.M.A.R.T to conceptualize performance measures:

1. "Specific
2. Measurable
3. Accountable
4. Results-Oriented
5. Time-Bound" (DeMaio:18).

For example, the goal for a repeat domestic violence (DV) program might be reducing recidivism by 20% and increasing victim satisfaction by 10% in one year. If the goal is to reduce the incidence of repeat domestic violence, then what are the indicators of success? (e.g., number of arrests for DV; percent of cases referred to court and social services; number of temporary restraining orders-TRO-issued; number of follow-up visits by officers and detectives;

number of CFS from the same complainant for DV.) Since objectives must be time-bound and measurable, it is important to identify what actions officers can take to reach the established goal. First, here is an example of a performance measurement statement that might guide the program. Next, table 1-1 is an example of how the performance measures integrate across the dimension areas for a repeat domestic violence program. When selecting outcome measures, it is important to consider input from the command staff, supervisors and line officers to ensure the program evaluation measurements are closely aligned with those the agency finds to be important and worthy of tracking.

- **Goal: Controlling Repeat Domestic Violence**
  - Reducing domestic violence recidivism program
    - *Reduce reported domestic violence crimes from 1,245 in FY 2007 to 996 (-20%) in FY 2008 by increasing protective action.*
      1. **Success Indicator:** reported domestic violence crimes involving the same victim or offender
      2. **Performance Indicator:** protective action (number of temporary restraining orders applied for and granted by the judge; % of domestic violence cases granted a "no-bail" provision; number of 15-minute follow-up home visits by patrol officers)
      3. **Baseline:** 1,245 reported domestic violence crimes
      4. **Target:** 996 reported domestic violence crimes
    - *Reduce total domestic violence CFS from 3,183 FY 2007 to 2,387 (-25%) in FY 2008 by increasing protective action.*
      1. **Success Indicator**: total calls for service for domestic violence
      2. **Performance Indicator:** protective action (number of temporary restraining orders applied for and granted by the judge; % of domestic violence cases granted a "no-bail" provision; number of 15-minute follow-up home visits by patrol officers)
      3. **Baseline:** 3,183 CFS for domestic violence incidents
      4.. **Target:** 2,387 CFS domestic violence incidents
  - Increasing citizen satisfaction program
    - *Increase the citizen satisfaction rating with police domestic violence services from 80% in FY 2007 to 90% (+10%) in FY 2008 by improving service delivery.*
      1. **Success Indicator:** citizen satisfaction ratings
      2. **Performance Indicator:** improving service delivery (number of officers redeployed during peak DV call hours;

number of social service referrals by patrol officers; number of 20-minute follow-up home visits by detectives)
3. **Baseline:** 80% satisfaction rating
4. **Target:** 90% satisfaction rating

Table 1-1		Performance Measures for a Domestic Violence Repeat Offender Program			
Resources and Activity		**Intermediate Objectives**		**End Outcome**	
Input	Output	Strategy	Measures	Goal	Criteria
10 police officers 7 DV detectives 1 civilian aide $10,000 in overtime funds	100% of DV victims apply for TRO	Encourage victims' use of temporary restraining orders (TRO) by explaining the benefits and preparing the documents for the victim's signature	Increase the number of DV cases that have a TRO application attached, from 45% to 100% department-wide within 1 month of implementation	Reduce reported domestic violence crimes involving the same victim or the same offender from 1,245 in FY 2007 to 996 (-20%) in FY 2008 by increasing protective action	Official reports of DV Official DV TRO reports Bail receipts and "no bail" notations CAD system location reports CAD system CFS reports
	100% of DV cases are granted a "no-bail" provision	Meet/confer with the Assignment Judge to encourage "no-bail" provision for all DV cases involving a UCR Part I crime	Increase the number of "no bail" provisions for DV cases involving Part I crimes from 22% to 100% department-wide within 1 month of implementation	Reduce total domestic violence CFS involving from 3,183 in FY 2007 to 2,387 (-25%) in FY 2008 by increasing protective action	
	100% of DV offenders receive follow-up home visits by patrol officers	Enhance protective services for DV victim	Increase the number of DV offenders who receive two 15 minute follow-up visits at their home within 2 weeks of the incident to prevent repeat behavior from 0% to 100% within 1 month of implementation		
	25% fewer DV CFS	Enhance protective services for DV victim	Decrease the number of total DV CFS received at the communications center to reduce patrol workload 25% within 1 year of implementation		

Table 1-1	Performance Measures for a Domestic Violence Repeat Offender Program				
Resources and Activity		**Intermediate Objectives**		**End Outcome**	
Input	**Output**	**Strategy**	**Measures**	**Goal**	**Criteria**
	15 police officers redeployed during peak DV call hours	Decrease average response time to each DV call	Decrease average patrol response time to all "in-progress" DV calls from 7 minutes to an average of 5 minutes department-wide within 3 weeks of implementation	Increase the citizen satisfaction rating with police domestic violence services from 80% in FY 2007 to 90% (+10%) in FY 2008 by improving service delivery	CAD system response time reports
	409 referrals by patrol officers and detectives	Enhance police-victim relationship through long-term aftercare	Increase the number of social service agency and victim/witness referrals by 25% through the patrol division and the detective division within 3 months of implementation		DV victim referral reports
					CAD system location reports
					2008 victim satisfaction survey
					90% of victims feel safe and do not fear reprisal
	100% of DV victims receive a follow-up home visit by DV detectives	Increase access to police investigative services and information about the criminal justice process	Increase the number of DV victims who receive one 20 minute home visit within 24 hours of the incident to explain the subsequent CJ process from 0% to 100% within 3 weeks of implementation		90% of victims are satisfied with initial police action and follow-up services
					90% services delivered within allotted budget

Lastly, another format for creating what are known as "business objectives" was developed by SEARCH, The National Consortium for Justice Information and Statistics (2003:10-13). SEARCH uses a six-step process for developing business objectives that can be used to measure the success of any project or program, when properly defined. The six steps are: 1) identify the *basic measure*, 2) indicate the *direction* of the measure, 3) identify the *object* of the measure, 4) identify the expected *value* of the measure, 5) identify *where* the measurement will occur, and 6) identify *when* the measure will be obtained. Business objectives are ideal for projects such as I/T implementation or changes to business logic that may increase performance or efficiency. If measures exist before and after business logic is modified, then statistical comparisons can be made accurately. In many instances business objectives are required by grant funding organizations as part of the application to ensure success can be measured, especially during a process or impact evaluation.

The SEARCH Six-Step Method of Measuring Business Objectives			
Example: *Reducing Total Time in Custody for Felony Arrests*			
Component	**Measure**	**Actual Measure**	**Description**
Basic measure	Total hours in custody	Total hours in custody	**Step 1** identifies the basic measure—what is to be measured? Total hours in custody can be measured empirically and relates directly to how long it takes to process a single prisoner, from arrest to release.
Direction	Reduce	Reduce the total hours in custody	**Step 2** indicates the expected direction of the basic measure—increase or decrease.
Object	Felony arrests	Reduce the total hours in custody for felony arrests	**Step 3** identifies the object of the measure—what are you measuring against: felony arrests, misdemeanor arrests, traffic arrests, warrant arrests? This must be as specific as possible to ensure something different is not inadvertently measured, such as *all* arrests instead of felony arrests only.
Value	36 hours	Reduce the total hours in custody for felony arrests to an average of 36 hours	**Step 4** identifies the expected value of the measure to be achieved. This will be compared to the actual value that is achieved.
Where	Central prisoner processing division	Reduce the total hours in custody for felony arrests to an average of 36 hours at central prisoner processing division	**Step 5** identifies where the measurement will take place, such as at the precinct, at headquarters, at the detective squad or at central prisoner processing division.
When	3 months	Reduce the total hours in custody for felony arrests to an average of 36 hours at central prisoner processing within 3 months of implementation	**Step 6** identifies when the measure will be achieved. When is a return on your investment expected to manifest itself? Allow sufficient time for the project to mature and diffuse throughout the system; don't be overly ambitious insofar as you over promise and under deliver.

Modified from SEARCH, The National Consortium for Justice Information and Statistics (2003:10-13)

The Importance of Logic Modeling

One of the best ways to ensure tangible results is to develop a logic model. Rossi, Lipsey and Freeman (2004:94) define a logic model as "...the expected sequence of steps going from program services to client outcomes." Simply stated "a logic model summarizes the key elements of your program, reveals the rationale behind your approach, articulates your intended outcomes and how they can be measured, and shows the cause-and-effect relationships between your program and its intended outcomes" (Watson, 2000). A logic model can also be thought of as a "logical chain of events providing a blueprint for mission achievement, [and have at its core]:

1. A graphic representation that illustrates the rationale behind a program;
2. Causal relationships between activities, strategies, and end results
3. Goals and performance measures for each phase of a program's life cycle
4. Various program activities into a cohesive whole
5. A vehicle for dialogue, planning, program management and evaluation" (DeMaio:22).

As you begin to conceptualize the logic model, consider these component parts: "1) the program, 2) the purpose, 3) the program inputs, outputs, intermediate objectives and end outcome, 4) performance reporting, and 5) analysis and action" (National Center for Public Productivity, 2006:8).

1. **The Program:** Typically there is a clear division of labor in police departments. The major components of the organization, usually bureaus and divisions, comprise the programs that make up the organization. For example, uniformed patrol officers, anti-crime, and community service officers may constitute the *field operations program*; homicide, sexual assault, robbery and burglary squads may constitute the *criminal investigations program*.

2. **The Purpose:** Articulating a succinct statement about why the program exists and what it is expected to accomplish is an important step toward measuring efficiency and effectiveness. Ideally, a purpose statement should reflect the program's social utility. For example:

   a. *Field Operations Program:* As the department's primary service delivery element, the field operation bureau exists to provide law enforcement and other community services through swift, reliable response to calls for service or through direct contact with community members.

   b. *Traffic Enforcement Program:* The traffic enforcement program exists to provide specialized traffic enforcement across the city through high visibility patrol while focusing on reducing traffic injuries and fatalities, school zone safety during the school year, accident-prone locations, and selective enforcement operations with a social utilitarian purpose.

3. **The Program Input, Output, Intermediate Objectives and End Outcome:**

   a. *Input* is expressed as the financial, human and workforce capital necessary to achieve end outcomes.

   b. *Output* is expressed as the specific actions taken, services delivered and employee productivity toward interim goals and end outcomes.

   c. *Intermediate Objectives* express the defined strategies, which are monitored and adjusted as needed and serve as an interim measure of progress toward end outcomes. Intermediate objectives are reference markers, (e.g., weekly, monthly, quarterly, semi annually), which are used as indicators to orient the agency generally which are used as a point of reference between the point of departure (implementation) and the end outcome.

   d. *End Outcome* is expressed as tangible results, which are linked to the agency's mission and derived from objectives that define success.

4. **Performance Reporting:** A concise summary of the performance indicators and their comparison periods (year-to-date, current year's month to last year's month, etc.) as they compare to end outcomes and objectives of the program as originally conceived. The Compstat process is ideal for monitoring and reporting performance. Performance reporting is usually part of a larger accountability process such as Compstat or weekly staff meetings. Reporting schemes will vary but typically include elements such as:
   a. Efficiency Indicators
      i. Level of Effort
         1. Units per year
         2. Average hours per unit
         3. Total employee hours per modality
      ii. Budgeting
         1. Average cost per unit
         2. Material cost per unit
         3. Equipment cost per unit
         4. Rate per employee hour
         5. Overtime analysis
      iii. Employee Performance
         1. Directed citizen contacts, directed patrols, arrests, traffic summonses and warnings, field interrogations, traffic stops
         2. Citizen complaints (external)
         3. Supervisory complaints (internal)
      iv. Command Performance
         1. Response time
         2. Sick leave ratio
         3. Sector/beat analysis
         4. Crime clearance rate
   b. Baseline
      i. Crime rate
         1. Violence index (murder, rape, robbery, aggravated assault)
         2. Property index (motor vehicle theft, larceny, burglar, arson)
      ii. Victimization rate
         1. Adult
         2. Juvenile
         3. Male
         4. Female
         5. Racial group

5. **Analysis and Action:** This is an outgrowth of performance management that enables police executives to capitalize on organizational strengths, to benchmark weaknesses, to seize opportunities and to forestall threats. Analysis and action may result in a S.W.O.T analysis or a P.E.S.T analysis (See Bryson, 1995 for S.W.O.T and P.E.S.T analysis).

The reason logic models are so important to program success is that they show definitively what it takes to accomplish the end outcomes, what assumptions the plan rests upon and why those assumptions make sense. This helps to establish validity, which "refers to the extent to which an empirical measure adequately reflects the real meaning of the concept under consideration" (Babbie, 2002:139). The success of any plan rests upon whether the indicators appear to be measuring something sensible. The measures should be logically valid; it makes no sense to state that effecting arrests for jaywalking will reduce street robberies. That logic is a *non sequitur*. However, effecting arrests for disorderly conduct and enforcing motor vehicle laws has been shown to reduce the incidence of street robberies (Sampson and Cohen, 1988; Wilson and Boland, 1978) so performance indicators that reflect that type of enforcement make sense. Logic modeling is heavily relied upon by both researchers and practitioners, so much so that the federal government often requires it as part of their grant solicitations and program evaluations.[51]

How to Create a Logic Model. Logic models take on many different forms; there is no singular "right" method, so if you are already familiar with them, then this is one more approach. Start at the end of the model by identifying the end outcomes. Decide what the desired state should be—the final impact. By starting at the end it will easier to identify the component parts that make up the logic model. This method allows you to see which specific parts do not contribute to the end outcome; anything that does not help achieve the desired state should be amended or removed. The logic model development process can be thought this way:

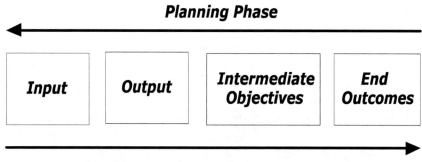

Logic models should be thought of as a series of "If...then..." statements that read from left to right. The "If...then..." decision structure is a series of conditional statements that, when evaluated as true, support the process and permit movement to the next step. When they are evaluated as false the decision is rejected and must be amended before moving to the next step. The logic proceeds like this:

IF given the resources (input), **THEN** I will be able to deliver the planned level of service (output). **IF** I am able to deliver the planned level of service, **THEN** I will be able to meet specific interim goals (intermediate objectives). **IF** I meet the interim goals (intermediate objectives) and I am able to sustain a certain level of service delivery, **THEN** I can expect to meet the goal (end outcomes).

Steps in the development process:
1. Identify and describe the end outcome: what do you ultimately want to achieve?
2. Identify and describe the intermediate objectives: when do you anticipate the first signs of change to manifest themselves? What changes must occur in strategy, knowledge, behavior or conditions to manifest change and when?
3. Identify and describe the intended output: what activities and services support intermediate objectives and the end outcome?
4. Identify the necessary input to support the program: what resources will be required to initiate and sustain the program? If they are not sufficient, then must the entire program be scaled down or only the objectives? Are there alternative resources available for input? How will those resources be secured?

Logic models can be used for specific service programs, such as domestic violence, robbery and burglary suppression and victim/witness advocacy. They can also be used for day-to-day police operations insofar as each organizational element of the department can be considered a discreet "program" (see glossary for definition). In this manner a "program" is defined by the organizational characteristics, such as the services or activities to be delivered (e.g., patrol, criminal investigations, traffic enforcement, communications, prisoner detention, etc.). This is the theory and structure of program budgeting, where the purpose and emphasis is on outcomes rather than the individual components of the program. Using some of the data from table 1, here is logic model for a police department's operations based on desired outcomes:

Table 1-2	Police Performance Logic Model			
	Input	**←Output**	**Intermediate ←Objective**	**←End Outcome**
Description	Financial, human and workforce capital necessary to achieve end outcomes	The specific actions taken, services delivered and employee productivity toward interim goals and end outcomes	Define and monitor strategies, changes, and interim progress toward end outcomes	Tangible results, which are linked to the agency's mission and derived from objectives that define success
	$$$ FTE	# of arrests # of traffic summonses	**Strategy 1** - Reduce criminal victimizations	**Controlling Fear and Crime**

Table 1-2		Police Performance Logic Model		
	Input	**←Output**	**Intermediate ←Objective**	**←End Outcome**
Description	*Financial, human and workforce capital necessary to achieve end outcomes*	*The specific actions taken, services delivered and employee productivity toward interim goals and end outcomes*	*Define and monitor strategies, changes, and interim progress toward end outcomes*	*Tangible results, which are linked to the agency's mission and derived from objectives that define success*
	Equipment Material Supplies	and warnings issued # of field interviews # of car stops # of directed patrols # of vertical patrols # of street closures # of road safety checkpoints $$ value of property recovered # of crackdown operations	Reduce crime rate by 15% Reduce victimization by 25% Reduce truancy rate by 15% Reduce Part I & II crime by 15% Reduce CFS for suspicious vehicles and persons 15%	
	$$$ FTE Equipment Material Supplies	# of investigations cleared by arrest # of successful prosecutions; guilty pleas # of arrest and search warrants issued # of consent searches # of days to case clearance # of days to warrant issued # of forensic samples matched to suspects # of vehicles impounded and persons arrested for scofflaw # of repeat offenders identified Rate of local incarceration # of arrestees held without bail # of parolees and probationers revoked Ratio of reported crimes to arrests # of new investigations initiated from prisoner debriefings	**Strategy 2** - Call offenders to account Increase clearance rates 15% Increase conviction rates 20% Increase arrest and search warrants served 25% Increase consent searches 15% Increase confessions obtained 20% Increase scofflaw enforcement 10% Increase selective incapacitation 10% Increase no-bail provisions 10% Increase parole and probation revocation 5% Reduce recidivism by 15% Increase investigations initiated from prisoner debriefings 15%	
	$$$ FTE Equipment Material Supplies	Rate of reported fear through annual fear survey Rate of reported security measures through quarterly residential and commercial security surveys # of new alarm permits	**Strategy 3** - Reduce fear, reduce blight and enhance personal safety Reduce reported level of fear 25% Reduce reported level of self-defense measures (levels and types) 25% Empower 24 new	

Table 1-2	Police Performance Logic Model			
	Input	**←Output**	**Intermediate ←Objective**	**←End Outcome**
Description	*Financial, human and workforce capital necessary to achieve end outcomes*	*The specific actions taken, services delivered and employee productivity toward interim goals and end outcomes*	*Define and monitor strategies, changes, and interim progress toward end outcomes*	*Tangible results, which are linked to the agency's mission and derived from objectives that define success*
		# of new community partnerships formed # and size of community empowerment grants # of neighborhood conditions corrected # of abandoned vehicles impounded # of blighted structures razed	neighborhoods to help themselves Increase community partnerships by 20% Reduce conditions that contribute to fear and blight 15%	
	$$$ FTE Equipment Material Supplies	# of road-safety checkpoints # of summonses and warnings issued # of radar operations # of vehicular and pedestrian accidents # of homeless relocated to shelter # of citizens using public parks % of students using safe schools corridors # of car stops for aggressive driving	**Strategy 4** - Guarantee safety in public places Reducing traffic fatalities, injuries and damage 20% Increasing utilization of parks and other public spaces 30% Increasing property values 25% Reduce homeless population occupying public space 25% Increase pedestrian students using safe schools corridors 35% Reduce aggressive driving 10%	
	$$$ FTE Equipment Material Supplies	# of programs delivered Avg. hours per unit, per program, delivered # of units per year, per program, delivered # of personnel required per unit Total employee hours per modality Total cost to deliver programs Avg. cost per unit per program Material cost per unit per program Equipment cost per unit per program Salary rate per employee hour per program Total overtime expended	**Strategy 1** - Use financial resources fairly, efficiently and effectively Reduce cost per citizen 5% Reduce cost per call for service 5% Increase grant funds secured 10% Reduce unfunded mandates or priorities 10% Conduct workload/deployment analysis every 6 months Meet 90% of operating budget expenditures Reduce overtime expenditures 20%	**Delivering Public Value through Budgeting Accountability**

Table 1-2		Police Performance Logic Model		
	Input	**←Output**	**Intermediate ←Objective**	**←End Outcome**
Description	*Financial, human and workforce capital necessary to achieve end outcomes*	*The specific actions taken, services delivered and employee productivity toward interim goals and end outcomes*	*Define and monitor strategies, changes, and interim progress toward end outcomes*	*Tangible results, which are linked to the agency's mission and derived from objectives that define success*
		by category Total grant dollars secured % of budget goals achieved Sworn:civilian ratio # and rate of sick leave days consumed # of light duty hours consumed Total personnel on light duty # of volunteer hours; total volunteers # of police vehicle collisions	Increase civilianization 10% Reduce police vehicle collisions 25%	
	$$$ FTE Equipment Material Supplies	# of citizen complaints by category Avg. IA investigative time (days) # of dollars paid in settlements # of police shootings # of use of force incidents # of resisting arrest charges # of police officers assaulted # of personnel retrained # of prisoners who exceeded holding time thresholds # of pursuits initiated	**Strategy 1** - Use force and authority fairly, efficiently and effectively Reduce citizen complaints 25% Reduce settlements in liability suits 30% Reduce police shootings 30% Reduce use of force incidents 30% Reduce pursuits 25%	**Reverence for Law and Authority**
	$$$ FTE Equipment Material Supplies	# of citizen surveys conducted # of dispatched calls serviced within 10 minutes % of citizens who perceive the police as fair and legitimate # of calls processed by telephone reporting unit (TRU) # of calls for service answered in under 10 seconds # of directed citizen contacts	**Strategy 1** - Satisfy customer demands/achieve legitimacy with those policed Increase satisfaction with police services 25% Reduce police response time 20% Increase citizen perception of fairness 25% Meet or exceed established total	**Satisfying Customers through Service and Accountability**

Table 1-2	Police Performance Logic Model			
	Input	**←Output**	**Intermediate ←Objective**	**←End Outcome**
Description	*Financial, human and workforce capital necessary to achieve end outcomes*	*The specific actions taken, services delivered and employee productivity toward interim goals and end outcomes*	*Define and monitor strategies, changes, and interim progress toward end outcomes*	*Tangible results, which are linked to the agency's mission and derived from objectives that define success*
			service-time thresholds by 90% Meet or PSAP mandates by 90%	
	Input→	**Output→**	**Intermediate Objective→**	**End Outcome**

Logic models help police executives, commanding officers and tactical planners explicate program theory to see the relationships between the component parts of the plan and how the theory drives the plan, when applied properly. For example, deterrence theory suggests that if someone is arrested, then there is a strong likelihood that that specific individual will forego re-offending and others will forego offending in general[52] (Paternoster and Piquero, 1995; Stafford and War, 1993); the theory of police omnipresence suggests that the very presence of the police will forestall a criminal behavior (Sampson and Cohen, 1988; Wilson and Boland, 1978). This is why the goal of controlling fear and crime is predicated on output measures such as the number of arrests, car stops, directed patrols, vertical patrols, high visibility patrols, police crackdowns, police raids on drug locations, and field interviews. Logic models help users understand the interrelation or sequence of facts or events that lead to an inevitable outcome. Logic models usually include diagrams or pictures that illustrate the interrelation among important program components by showing a sequence of "if-then" statements that reveal alternate outcome paths, both negative and positive. Figure 3, from Roth and Ryan (2000:5), is their logic model of how the U.S. Department of Justice COPS Office implemented the COPS program.

Exhibit 1. **Logic Model**

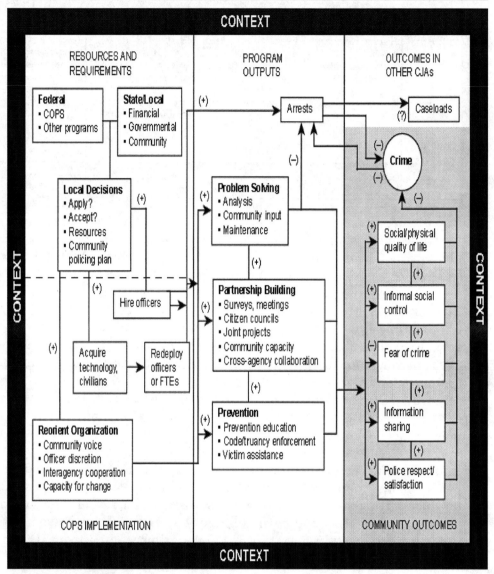

Abbreviations and Symbols:
FTEs: Full Time Equivalents
CJAs: Criminal Justice Agencies
(+): Items listed in preceding box result in positive impact on, or increase in, items listed in the following box.
(−): Items listed in preceding box result in negative impact on, or decrease in, items listed in the following box.

Figure 3 Roth and Ryan, 2000:5

Logic models also help establish the order of precedence. The order of precedence for evaluating performance and affixing accountability should be thought of in terms of the department's hierarchical structure with a clear division of labor demarcated by rank. In a police department the rank structure, including sworn and civilian positions, dictates who will be responsible for achieving established measures. When evaluating performance and affixing accountability think of this question: *what is this rank responsible for?*[53] Given the varying layers of rank in larger police departments, the order of precedence will probably differ according to job title and official responsibilities. Performance measures can be "used to measure results and ensure accountability by: 1) evaluating performance, 2) tracking progress against the plan, 3) establishing success or failure, 4) identifying improvement opportunities, and 5) ensuring management by fact" (Jankofsky:13). This is the order of precedence for the data in table 1:

Dimensions	Performance Measures	Order of Precedence
1. End Outcome →	Reduce Crime; Improve Citizen Satisfaction; Budget Policy Compliance →	Chief / Deputy Chief
2. Division Goals →	Increase Clearance Rate; Reduce Citizen Complaints →	Captain
3. Intermediate Objectives →	Monitor Interim Progress toward Division Goals →	Lieutenant
4. Input Level →	Train, Inspect and Guide Personnel; Apportion Allotted Resources →	Sergeant
5. Output Level →	# of Directed Patrols; # of Cases Cleared; # of Arrests →	Police Officer/Detective/Civilian

Creating a Business Plan

Creating performance measures, analyzing them and reporting on them is good business. Documenting and disseminating where the agency wants to be, how it plans to get there, and the internal and external influences that determine success is best done through a business plan. A business plan is a detailed overview of where the police department is today, where it wants to go (goals) and how it is going to achieve its goals (performance objectives). A solid business plan is critical to a police department's success and is an indispensable management tool that can be used in a variety of situations. A business plan should be thought of as the police executive's blueprint for the agency; just as a developer would not (or could not) begin construction without an architect's blueprint, neither could the police executive before organizing or reorganizing the agency. Before drafting the initial plan, consider these five core questions:

1. What services does the agency provide?
2. Are there any gaps in service delivery that must be satisfied?
3. What are the demographics of your customers?
4. How will the department reach its customers?

5. Other than tax revenue, where will the department acquire the financial resources to:
   a. Reach existing customers?
   b. Start new programs and initiatives?
   c. Implement unfunded mandates?

Answering these questions will help lay the foundation for the department's direction. It will serve as a roadmap as the agency begins efficiency improvements.

The business plan has three basic purposes: communication, management, and planning. As a *communication tool*, it is used to attract investment capital to the city, develop community partnerships and attract strategic government partners (FBI, DEA, ATF, colleges and universities, etc.). It is also the primary means for communicating management's expectations to the workforce, those who are tasked with carrying out the business strategy.[54] Developing a comprehensive business plan demonstrates whether or not a police department has the potential to make a difference in the economic viability of the city and quality of life for the residents. It requires a realistic look at almost every phase of operations and allows the chief executive to show that he or she has worked out all the assumptions and decided on potential alternatives before actually launching the strategy. This is a basic tenet of assumption-based planning (ABP). "Unwelcome surprises in the life of any organization can often be traced to the failure of an assumption that the organization's leadership didn't anticipate or had 'forgotten' it was making. [ABP] is a tool for identifying as many of the assumptions underlying the plans of an organization as possible and bringing those assumptions explicitly into the planning process" (Dewar, 2002:i). ABP is used as a post-planning tool; *after* the initial plan has been developed it should be subjected to ABP to "decrease the risks that assumptions represent" (Dewar, 2002:1).

As a *management tool*, the business plan helps the department monitor and evaluate progress. Because planning is an iterative process, the business plan will be modified as the department gains knowledge and experience. By using the business plan to establish time lines and milestones, the chief executive can gauge progress and compare projections to actual accomplishments. As a *planning tool*, the business plan guides the department through various phases of its business. A thoughtful plan will help identify roadblocks and obstacles so that command staff members can avoid them and establish alternatives. In the ABP process identifying the roadblocks and obstacles is known as identifying "load-bearing vulnerable assumptions;" in the ABP process establishing alternatives are known as "shaping actions and hedging actions" (Dewar, 2002). After the plan is completed it is always a good management practice to distribute the plan among the employees to foster a broader understanding of where the department is going and to secure individual commitment. Figure 4 is Dewar's (2002) assumption-based planning model.

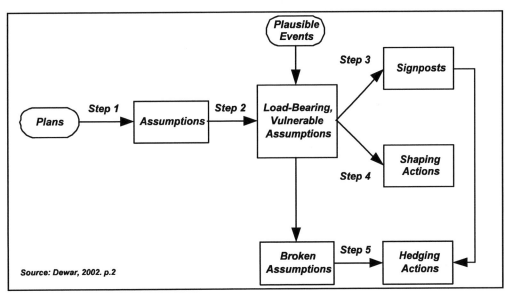

Figure 4

A business plan differs slightly from a strategic plan or a plan of action. The business plan is a larger and broader document that encompasses more operational and management doctrine and charts a course for the entire agency with a long-term purpose. A strategic plan or a plan of action is typically designed for a specific, short-term or intermediate-term purpose, such as addressing a consent decree, or addressing a specific problem. Although the term business plan and strategic plan are used interchangeably, a guiding principle for development should be the length of time it will take to achieve the goals: if the goals are open-ended, with no definitive milestone, then you usually have a business plan.[55] The performance dimensions outlined in table 1 can be incorporated as part of the business plan. Appendix 1 shows an outline for a comprehensive business plan and department annual report along with Internet sources for sample plans.

3

▶ Data Sources

Central Data Collection

Collecting data in a central location is paramount to organizational success; indeed it is the driving principle behind the successful management process known as Compstat and the crime analysis function. Some common problems with data collection are: records are scattered about the department resulting in an incomplete record of the data; the data may be stored and archived in separate divisions and not accessible to managers or analysts; the data may have missing records making analysis unreliable; the data may be replete with clerical errors that compromise analysis; the data may be miscategorized; collection procedures may have changed resulting in two different data sets; the data may have been manipulated to reflect a more favorable position (Jacob, 1984). Without complete and accurate data subsequent analysis may suffer. There are three reasons for collecting data in a central location: 1) to ensure unanimity of purpose across the entire organization, 2) a single organizational element is more likely to bring about improvements in methods for gathering, compiling, organizing and interpreting data and 3) a single collection point is more efficient and economical (President's Commission of Law Enforcement and Administration of Justice, Task Force Report on Assessment, 1967:124). The idea behind central data collection is to assign an individual or an organizational element that will get the data and ensure it is properly archived for future retrieval. The ideal place for this is the records division, which is generally responsible for warehousing data and reports. If you are contemplating modifications to the current data collection process, then asking the right questions beforehand will save time and will help in collecting the right data for the purpose at hand:

1. "What information is currently being gathered?
2. Does the current information meet our needs?
3. What new information needs to be collected?
4. Do any problems exist with data collection?
5. What new or modified forms will be needed to collect data?
6. How cost-effective is it to collect the data?
7. What resources will be needed to manage or collect data? Hardware, software? Storage?
8. Are there any constraints to collecting data? Money, technology, etc.?
9. How often can or should data be collected?
10. Who should collect data?" (Jankofsky:28-29).

The data that is captured today and used tomorrow for analysis is retrieved easiest from automated computer systems such as computer-aided dispatch (CAD) systems and records management systems (RMS). These systems also promote data integrity; that is, all of the data is preserved in its original specified format and is not subject to tampering or loss. If, however, all that is available is hard-copy paper forms, then it is necessary to centralize collection and have a single point serve as the clearinghouse to ensure the records are accurate and the information is made available to managers in a collated format and in a timely manner.

Internal Data Sources

Data that is captured and stored in a Computer-aided dispatch system (CAD) and a records management system (RMS) has great value. Data conversion, changing digital data from one format to another so it can be used in a different software application, is a common problem in CAD and RMS development projects. If the agency is planning a technology project, then data conversion is something that needs to be considered. A CAD and RMS become populated very quickly. Deciding whether to discard the old data, maintain two systems for a period of time or convert the data for the new system is a matter of necessity. If the agency opts for data conversion, then there will be a more complete data set from which to work. However, this is an expensive, time-consuming and highly technical process that could add both cost and time to a technology project.[56]

The CAD System. Most police departments today have CAD systems, no matter how rudimentary. Just as the patrol division is the core of a police department's field operations program, the CAD system is the core of a police department's decision support process. The CAD system is the point of entry for calls for service data that enables management to retrieve timely information regarding calls for service, dispatching records, self-initiated assignments and other relevant data that are usually complete with full incident records for downstream use. The efficiencies of capturing information from a single point of entry are reducing effort, eliminating redundancy, conserving resources (human and materiel) and easily retrievable information that is timely and secure. Some CAD systems utilize an Oracle-based© database, others use Microsoft© products such SQL (pronounced "sequel"). It is important to know in what format the data will be captured and stored because this will affect downstream retrieval and analysis. The CAD system should have the ability to export data into various commercial spreadsheet or statistical software formats such as Microsoft Access©, Microsoft Excel©, SPSS©and MapInfo.© Commercially available software products are the foundation for the analysis described in this text; there is no need for proprietary software to conduct the analysis presented here.

The RMS System. An emerging technology in police departments is RMS. RMS systems are designed for creating, querying, and managing written records, such as incidents reports, field interrogations, impounded vehicles reports, accident reports, and arrests, among the many. The newest RMS packages also have the ability to capture, archive and format data that is easily retrievable for the National Incident-Based Reporting System (NIBRS) and the FBI Uniform Crime Reporting (UCR). What makes RMS particularly attractive to managers is the ease of retrieval and the ability to collate massive amounts of data without sifting through hard-copy paper reports; hard-copy reports have a tendency to get lost or destroyed and are easily misplaced. In a secure RMS the written record is always available and is not subject to the problems associated with hard-copy paper.

The same parameters that apply to the CAD system also apply to the RMS, which is to ensure the data format is exportable to a commercially available software package for analysis. If the CAD and RMS vendors is one and the same, then it usually is not a problem. However, database applications across vendors (i.e., one vendor for CAD and a different vendor for RMS) tend to suffer from integration problems and the data elements are not necessarily readable by each piece of technology. Every effort should be made to avoid multiple vendors for CAD/RMS projects, if possible.[57]

Agency Records and Documents. It is inevitable: some police departments do not have automation capabilities and are relegated to using hardcopy documents to conduct analysis. This is the least efficient way to do so; however, it is better than sitting idle. In fact, hardcopy reports serve as the basis for all analyses that a police department undergoes inasmuch as the reports are the official record of something having taken place (e.g., a crime incident; an arrest, a field interview; an impounded vehicle; a summons issued, etc.). What is most important is that the reports are channeled through a central location that is responsible for processing them and parsing them to the respective analyst. For example, when incident reports are generated in five different locations (e.g., five different police precincts), it is incumbent upon someone to ensure all of the particular reports arrive at their destination, this is usually a commanding officer: all of the robberies from across the city arrive at the robbery squad and so forth. The commanding officer is then responsible for ensuring the analyst receives a complete roster of all the reports in a timely manner.

The various bureaus and divisions of a police organization are unique. Each organizational element captures different information that is germane to that command. Absent an RMS that processes investigative reports the bureau or division commander must capture information in a comprehensible format that lends itself to analysis. One way to do this is to design a desk-top relational database application, such as Microsoft Access,© that enables easy data storage and retrieval. Although stand-alone database applications are not necessarily efficient, they are better than hundreds or thousands of unreadable, wrinkled paper reports that may be out of order sequentially. Moreover, the paper reports do not lend themselves to analysis; the data must be entered into a software program so analysis can be performed. The chief executive of the department must first identify what it is they want to analyze (the output measure) and what they expect to get out of the analysis. Once they determine this, then they must specify what data elements are necessary and how they must be reported in order to satisfy their goal. The individual bureau and division commanders must be made to report the data in a periodic manner, such as each week, to ensure the data is being captured properly.

External Data Sources

Surveys. One of the best ways to assess performance is through citizen surveys. The U.S. Department of Justice published a guide entitled *Conducting Citizen Surveys: A practical Guide for Law Enforcement Agencies*. The document is accessible at the National Criminal Justice Reference Service (NCJRS), www.ncjrs.org (NCJ# 178246). Another excellent resource for designing surveys is *Survey Research Methods* 3rd edition, by Floyd J. Fowler. This short text explains how to design, collect, and analyze survey data to conduct evaluations. The idea behind community surveys is for law enforcement executives to assess how they are performing in the eyes of their customers—the citizens. Citizen surveys are very useful for uncovering latent organizational problems; uncovering responsible and irresponsible behavior; and assessing program effectiveness among the many. Another benefit to surveys is that they can be tailored to each agency for a specific purpose and they can be administered over the telephone, which minimizes organizational disruption and the impact to service delivery. An administrative element of the agency, such as the Research and Planning Division or the Administrative Services Division, is usually tasked with developing, administering and archiving surveys.

Focus Groups. The focus group has grown in popularity over the years because, as Krueger (1988:47) noted:

1. "The technique is a socially oriented research method capturing real-life data in a social environment,
2. It has flexibility,
3. It has high face validity,
4. It has speedy results and
5. It is low in cost."

A focus group is a form of qualitative research in which a small group of stakeholders, typically between 8 and 15 people, assemble and participate in a guided open-ended discussion of a particular topic. Generally, the participants should represent the larger community, unless the intent is to gather data from a specific group such as business leaders, the elderly, parents/guardians or high school students. Questions are asked by moderators, such as police department representatives, in an interactive group setting where the participants are encouraged to offer their opinions, personal experiences, perceptions, and recommendations for resolving an issue or deciding on a course of action for a program or policy. The idea is for police planners to get a cross-section of feedback to ensure the issue is resolved, or a program or policy is delivered to as many people as possible in as many different ways as possible. Focus groups can be used both before and after agency decisions are made. For example, police planners may assemble a focus group *before* the police department applies for a federal or state grant opportunity to see what people want from their local government or how they can help shape the idea. Or, they may assemble a focus group *after* a program is implemented to solicit feedback and opinion about the relevance and impact of the program. Another unique way to employ focus groups is to use them as a device for generating survey questions for subsequent use (Morgan, 1993). The data that is captured can easily be reduced to numerical form and analyzed quite thoroughly to measure performance. Focus groups have been widely adopted by marketing researchers with great success.

U.S. Census Bureau. The United States Census Bureau (www.census.gov) collates a massive amount of demographic information that is particularly useful to police departments. For example, the FBI Uniform Crime Report (UCR) identifies a number of factors that influence the volume and type of crime that occurs from place to place. When analyzing the nature and predictors of crime it is absolutely essential to include data elements such as:

1. "Population density and degree of urbanization;
2. Variations in composition of the population, particularly youth concentration;
3. Stability of population with respect to residents' mobility, commuting patterns, and transient factors;
4. Modes of transportation and highway system;
5. Economic conditions, including median income, poverty level, and job availability;
6. Cultural factors and educational, recreational, and religious characteristics.
7. Family conditions with respect to divorce and family cohesiveness;
8. Climate;
9. Effective strength of law enforcement agencies;
10. Administrative and investigative emphases of law enforcement;
11. Policies of other components of the criminal justice system (i.e., prosecutorial, judicial, correctional, and probational);
12. Citizens' attitudes toward crime;
13. Crime reporting practices of the citizenry" (Federal Bureau of Investigation, 2004:v-vi).

Many of these data elements (e.g., population composition; residential mobility; unemployment; income level; poverty level; educational level, etc.) are captured by and available from the U.S. Census Bureau. The data is available by census tract, which is particularly useful for assessing police performance in specific neighborhoods. Data that is analyzed at the census tract level can be paired with police performance indicators such as response time to evaluate if performance differs significantly with respect to race, or income, or employment status within the tract. This way the department can identify problems such as differential treatment based on extra-legal factors. This level of analysis will help executives uncover inequitable deployment and distribution of services. One of the best sources for commercially-formatted census data is GeoLytics©️ (www.geolytics.com). GeoLytics©️ is an industry leader that provides demographic data for researchers, demographers, government agencies and others who need reliable datasets in a compatible easy-to-use format.

Bureau of Justice Statistics (BJS). The Bureau of Justice Statistics is "a unit of the U.S. Department of Justice whose principal function is the compilation and analysis of data and the dissemination of information for statistical purposes." The BJS (www.ojp.usdoj.gov/bjs) is the central data collection center of the Office of Justice Programs, which archives a nearly limitless variety of useful data. The data can be downloaded into MS Excel©️ or SPSS©️ for further analysis. What makes the BJS data especially attractive is the data archives can be utilized for comparison purposes without having to collect it from an original source—the leg-work has already been done. The archived data sets include:

1. **On-Line Data**
    a. "Criminal offenses from the Uniform Crime Reports for all 50 States and local agencies with coverage of 10,000 population or greater;
    b. Homicide trends and characteristics for all 50 States and localities of more than 250,000 population;
    c. Law enforcement management and administrative statistics for State and local agencies with more than 100 sworn officers;
    d. Local prosecutors' offices in the United States."
2. **Spreadsheet Data**
    a. A compilation of spreadsheets from the *Crime and Justice Electronic Data Abstract* that are aggregated from a wide variety of published sources.
    b. The data is intended for analytic use, the files include crime, justice and sociodemographic variables. Many of the files contain data over time and by:
        i. State
        ii. Locality
        iii. Federal district
3. **Datasets and Codebooks** On-line tabulations of microdata for some datasets.[58]

One of the most comprehensive data sources on law enforcement compiled by the BJS is the *Law Enforcement Management and Administrative Statistics (LEMAS) survey*. The most recent data file is from 2000, which has data for individual state and local agencies that employ 100 or more officers. The 2000 LEMAS survey covers subject areas such as personnel, expenditures, wages, operations, community policing, policies and programs, and computers and information systems for 755 local agencies and 49 State agencies. The complete file can be downloaded in .pdf or ASCII format directly from the B.J.S web site. The document can also be retrieved for the National Criminal Justice Reference Service (N.C.J.R.S); www.ncjrs.org under NCJ# 203350.

In addition to law enforcement data, the BJS also has archived data on:

1. Crime and Victims
2. Prosecutors' Offices
3. The Federal Justice System
4. Courts and Sentencing
5. Criminal Offenders
6. Special Topics
   a. Drugs and crime
   b. Homicide trends
   c. Firearms and crime
   d. Reentry trends
   e. International statistics
7. Corrections
8. Expenditure and Employment
9. Criminal Record Systems[59]

Lastly, the B.J.S is noted for producing one of the most comprehensive documents for criminal justice statistics known as the *Sourcebook of Criminal Justice Statistics*. The publication includes statistics from over 100 sources about all aspects of the criminal justice system. The full document can be downloaded from www.albany.edu/sourcebook. The document is also available in print version for a premium and earlier versions are available for a premium on CD. In addition to the BJS web site you can locate the documents at the N.C.J.R.S, NCJ# 208756 or 203302.[60]

Internet Resources. Two leading Internet-based resources for data are the *National Consortium on Violence Research (NCOVR)* and the *Inter-University Consortium for Political and Social Research (ICPSR)*. Since 1995 NCOVR has been collecting data for research and training purposes by specializing in violence research.

Some of NCOVR's data sets are:

1. FBI UCR offenses and arrests reported to police
2. National Incident-Based Reporting System (NIBRS) incident-based police reports of offenses and arrests
3. National Crime Victimization Survey (NCVS) national victimization survey data
4. FBI UCR supplemental homicide reports (SHR) from police
5. Decennial census data
6. Firearm injury surveillance system (FISS) data from emergency rooms

Users only need Internet access and a standard web browser to access NCOVR data,[61] which can be accessed at http://www.ncovr.heinz.cmu.edu//// home.htm. Since 1962 the ICPSR has maintained and provided access to a vast archive of social science data for research. Users simply need to create an on-line account to access the data. The ICPSR is maintained by the University of Michigan, Ann Arbor, MI.; the data can be accessed at http://www.icpsr.umich. edu/access/index.html. Both NCOVR and ICPSR data sets support MS Excel© or SPSS.©

PART TWO
Statistics and Data Analysis

4

▶ Statistics and the Value of Numerical Data

Value in Expressing Solutions Numerically

"Statistics refers to the branch of mathematics that deals with the collection, analysis, interpretation and presentation of masses of numerical data."[62] The idea behind statistics is to create value in your presentation by translating data into meaningful information upon which program or policy decisions can be made. The nineteenth-century physicist, Lord Kelvin, for whom the Kelvin temperature scale is named, often remarked about measurement:

- *"To measure is to know"*
- *"If you cannot measure it, you cannot improve it"*
- *"...I often say that when you can measure what you are speaking about, and express it in numbers, you know something about it; but when you cannot measure it, when you cannot express it in numbers, your knowledge is...meagre and unsatisfactory...."*[63]

There is something intuitive about numbers and what they represent. It may be that numbers represent a natural science that works so well because they are consistent. For example, there is nothing inherently correct about 5,280 feet being the standard measure of a mile; it is a social artifact, which means someone just created it! In the metric system the equivalent measure of a mile is 1.6 kilometers, or 3,280.8 feet. These are two different measurement systems that arrive at the same answer. The right thing, whether you are measuring distance in feet or in kilometers, is that whichever measurement system you use it be consistent. Because of this consistency, different measurement systems measuring the same thing can derive reliable results time after time by employing the same calculations. This gives numbers a sort of infallible reputation—you may have heard the expression "the proof is in the numbers!" The fact is that most people have a certain comfort level in their own knowledge when they can express something numerically or when they can equate something numerically with their own frame of reference. When a plan is supported by statistics it is usually more persuasive than an undocumented, uncorroborated plan. Expressing your plan numerically is a way to quantify your ideas in a manner that lends both credibility and precision to your claim.

This section identifies a few common techniques for describing statistics and presenting findings from your analysis. The techniques listed here are in use in most agencies employing a Compstat model.[64]

Techniques for Describing Statistics

Descriptive Statistics. When you have a plan that conveys a message, the first step is to describe the data. Describing the data means visually inspecting a summary of the data to see what preliminary conclusions may be drawn. It is also a time to more closely examine the data set for any problems—outliers, for example, that might be the result of data entry error or another administrative or clerical error. Analyzing incorrect data inevitably wastes time and will surely make your conclusions suspect. "Descriptive statistics is a branch of statistics that denotes any of the many techniques used to summarize a set of data. In a sense, we are using the data on members of a set to describe the set. The techniques are commonly classified as:

1. Graphical description in which we use graphs to summarize data.
2. Tabular description in which we use tables to summarize data.
3. Summary statistics in which we calculate certain values to summarize data."[65]

Descriptive statistics are useful for any report or plan that conveys a message numerically, such as a budget, a tactical plan, or a Compstat book. As used in these examples, descriptive statistics set the stage for the details that follow and await an interpretation by a staff member. The summary data is presented at the beginning of the report and the full data set is appended to the end of the report or plan so the executive does not have to review superfluous detail before rendering a decision, asking a question or approving a document. In essence, this is a form of completed staff work (Iannone, 1987:29).

The descriptive data in Table 1a is an example of the level of effort required for a hypothetical traffic division of a police department. It is useful for an executive to know what the level of effort looks like for a given organizational element of the police department in a single summary table. A police executive need only glance at a few rows of information to get a snapshot of the effort required for the traffic division, instead of having to peruse the entire dataset. Summarizing the data in a single table gives the reader better visual insight into the division's performance. The MS Excel© output in Table 1-1 is the traffic division's workload. The data in Table 1-2 summarizes the data in Table 1-3 for a more comprehensive picture of how the division is performing.

Table 1-3	Level of Effort for a Traffic Division					
			Acuity			
	Service Demands	Hours Per Unit	Units Per Year	Officers Required	Total Employee Hours Per Modality	Percentage Allocation
	Arrest	1.5	400	2	1,200	2.72%
	Radar Operations	2	950	2	3,800	8.60%
	Selective Enforcement Operations	2	998	4	7,984	18.08%
	Assist Officer (back up)	0.25	300	2	150	0.34%
	Funeral Escorts	6	90	2	1,080	2.45%
	Court Appearances	1	660	4	2,640	5.98%
	Road Safety Checkpoints	4	104	6	2,496	5.65%
	DWI Checkpoint	4	52	6	1,248	2.83%
	Motor Vehicle Accident (with or without injuries)	1.5	1,244	1	1,866	4.22%
	Parking Violation Enforcement	2	2,233	1	4,466	10.11%
	School Crossing	2	180	5	1,800	4.08%
	Traffic Control	2	1,544	5	15,440	34.96%
	Total		8,755		44,170	100%

Table 1-4	Descriptive Statistics for Traffic Division Workload						
Hours per Unit		Units per Year		Officers Required		Total Employee Hours per Modality	
Mean	2.354	Mean	729.583	Mean	3.333	Mean	3680.833
Standard Error	0.453	Standard Error	197.875	Standard Error	0.541	Standard Error	1224.895
Median	2.000	Median	530.000	Median	3.000	Median	2181.000
Mode	2.000	Mode	#N/A	Mode	2.000	Mode	#N/A
Standard Deviation	1.568	Standard Deviation	685.458	Standard Deviation	1.875	Standard Deviation	4243.161
Sample Variance	2.460	Sample Variance	469852.992	Sample Variance	3.515	Sample Variance	18004416.333
Kurtosis	1.578	Kurtosis	0.460	Kurtosis	-1.624	Kurtosis	5.574
Skewness	1.247	Skewness	1.018	Skewness	0.213	Skewness	2,284
Range	5.750	Range	2181.000	Range	5.000	Range	15290.000
Minimum	0.250	Minimum	52.000	Minimum	1.000	Minimum	150.000
Maximum	6.000	Maximum	2233.000	Maximum	6.000	Maximum	15440.000
Sum	28.250	Sum	8755.000	Sum	40.000	Sum	44170.000
Count	12.000	Count	12.000	Count	12.000	Count	12.000

Interpreting the MS Excel© output for table 1-2 reads as follows:

1. **Mean:** This is the arithmetic average.

2. **Standard Error:** In statistics, the average amount by which an individual observation in a sample differs from the value predicted when using a particular statistical measure. In regression analysis the standard error is typically reported with the coefficient estimate. By social science convention, it is possible to say with 95% confidence that the true coefficient is within +/- 2 standard errors of the estimate.

3. **Median:** This is the point that splits an ordered dataset in half; exactly half the cases are above this value and half the cases are below this value. The dataset must be ordered from low to high: 0 1 2 3 4 5 6 7 8 9 10 11 12. If there is an even number of cases, then you must take the mean of the middle two cases. There are 13 cases 0-12. The middle two cases are 6 and 7. The mean is 6.5 (6+7=13/2=6.5). If there are an odd number of cases, then the median is the middle case. If the number-line ranged from 1 to 12, then 6 would be the median value.

4. **Mode:** The mode is the value that appears with the highest frequency in the distribution of data. In other words, the modal value is the value of the number that occurs most frequently. For example, the number 15 occurred 25 times, and no other number appears as frequently as 15, therefore 15 is the mode. If a distribution has more than one mode, then it is known as a bi-modal distribution.

5. **Standard Deviation:** The standard deviation measures how far apart (how spread out) the values in a dataset are. More specifically, standard deviation is a measure of the *average difference* between the values of the data in the set. If the data points are all relatively similar (e.g., 5, 6, 7, 8, 7.5, 6.2, 5.5), then the standard deviation will be low (closer to zero). A low standard deviation means the data points are more alike (more consistent). If the data points differ greatly (e.g., 2.8.5, 15.9, 3, .25, 36), then the standard variation will be high (further from zero). A higher standard deviation means the data points are not similar and do not reflect consistency. The standard deviation is useful for examining consistency, such as satisfaction with police service, response time or crime rate.

6. **Sample Variance:** A measure of a random variable's statistical dispersion indicating how far from the expected value its values typically are.

7. **Kurtosis:** A measure of the peakedness of a frequency distribution. A normal distribution has a kurtosis value of 3. A negative value characterizes a relatively flat distribution, whereas a positive value characterizes a relatively peaked distribution. The most desirable kurtosis value is that which is closest to 0. Acceptable skew values range from +1.00 to –1.00.

8. **Skewness:** Skewness is a numerical index that represents the degree of asymmetry of a distribution around its mean. Positive skewness indicates a distribution with an asymmetrically longer tail extending in the direction of more positive values. Negative skewness indicates a distribution with an asymmetric tail extending in the direction of more negative values. The most desirable skew is that which is closest to 0. Acceptable skew values range from + 1.00 to –1.00.

9. **Range:** The range is the difference between the largest and smallest value.

10. **Minimum:** The minimum is the smallest value in the data set.

11. **Maximum:** The maximum is the highest value in the data set.

12. **Sum:** The sum is the total of the values in the data set.

13. **Count:** The count is the number of observations in the data set.

Percentages. "A percentage is a method of expressing a proportion, a ratio or a fraction as a whole number, by using 100 as the denominator."[66] Another way to think of percentages is a fraction over (divided by) 100. Expressing numbers in percentages gives the reader an idea of what portion of the whole is accounted for by a particular category. If the question is: *How many people are released from custody within 2 hours of their arrest?* and the answer is 60%, then you know 6 out of 10, 60 out of 100 and 12 out of 20 people are being released (provided you know the raw numbers). Percentages give the executive a snapshot of how well (or how poorly) a division is performing with just a few words. If 60% of the people who are arrested are released within 2 hours of being processed, and if 2 hours is goal, then 40% of the people remain in custody. This is important to know and might necessitate an investigation. It also helps to identify gaps in processes that might be improved; process improvements usually strengthen efficiency, reduce costs, reduce liability and ensure compliance. In the traffic division data (Table 1-3) we see that nearly 35% of the division's time is spent conducting traffic control, followed by selective enforcement operations (18%). At a glance, a police executive should question why more than one-third of the traffic division's time is spent handling traffic control? Is it possible that someone else, other than sworn officers can conduct traffic control operations, such as school crossing guards or civilian traffic enforcement personnel? If so, then perhaps economies of scale can be capitalized on. Creating efficiency can be achieved through a process known as benchmarking.[67]

Ratio. A ratio is an expression of the relationship between two quantities. Ratios are useful when, for example, you want to examine the relative amount of individual output to the whole division. The convention for expressing a ratio is the colon (:), which means "to" as in the ratio 2:1 (2 *to*1). To calculate a ratio you simply divide the frequency of one category by the frequency of another category. So, if you want to know the ratio of traffic summonses issued per officer, for the whole division, sum the total number of summonses in the division (e.g., 124,878), then, divide by the number of officers (e.g., 167) (e.g., $124,878 \div 167 = 747$ or 747:1). This means the ratio of summonses to officers is 747 to 1; for every officer there were 747 summonses issued. Using ratios helps identify individual performance and whether personnel are meeting goals and expectations. If you wanted to express the relationship of arrests across precincts, you might set up a table like this:

Table 1-5			Expression of Ratios	
Precinct	Arrests	Ratio	Interpretation	Expression
East	120	0.96	For every arrest effected in the west there are .96 arrests effected in the east	.96:1
West	125	1.59	For every arrest effected in the west there are 1.6 arrests effected in the central	1.6:1
North	124			
South	148			
Central	199			
Total	**716**			

Another way to visually represent ratios is in a single matrix that expresses each of the parts to each other for comparison purposes, as in table 1-4. The ratios read from left to right:

1. The south:east arrest ratio 1.2:1; the south effects 1.2 arrests for every arrest effected in the east.
2. The east:south arrests ratio .81:1: the east effects .81 arrests for every arrest effected in the south.
3. The central:north ratio is 1.6:1; the central effects 1.6 arrests for every arrest effected in the north.
4. The west:south ratio is .84:1; the west effects .84 arrests for every arrest effected in the south.

Table 1-6		Ratio of Arrests by Precinct				
Precinct	Arrests	Precinct				
		East	West	North	South	Central
East	120		0.960	0.968	0.811	0.603
West	125	1.042		1.008	0.845	0.628
North	124	1.033	0.992		0.838	0.623
South	148	1.233	1.184	1.194		0.744
Central	199	1.658	1.592	1.605	1.345	

When calculating ratios it is important to factor only those frequency categories for personnel who are eligible in that category. For example, of the 160 police officers in this example, perhaps only 150 officers are eligible to actually issue summonses. This is because 10 officers are assigned to administrative duty and do not issue summonses. You cannot use 160 as your denominator since 100% of the group is not eligible for inclusion. The same rationale applies to all ratio calculations; groups of officers, for example, should be stratified to keep from having skewed results.

Another common example is calculating sick leave ratio by rank. If the entire division has a sick leave ratio of 8:1, this may be skewed for superior officers, *as a group*, who may have a lower ratio than police officers. This is because ratios are sensitive to the quantities under observation (in this example, sick leave days). To obtain a more accurate picture you must stratify, divide or arrange into classes, by rank before conducting the analysis. For example, Table 1e reflects the division's sick leave ratio is nearly 9:1; however, the ratio for sergeants is much lower (4:1). To suggest the sick leave ratio *for everyone* is 9:1 is an unqualified statement. You should specify the ratio for each rank.

Table 1-7														Sick Leave Ratio by Division by Rank
Complement	Rank	Jan	Feb	Mar	Apr	May	Jun	Jul	Aug	Sep	Oct	Nov	Dec	Total	Ratio
172	Police Officer	102	135	102	148	115	162	168	189	174	133	119	122	**1669**	9.70
34	Sergeant	12	13	11	14	12	10	9	7	11	16	9	17	**141**	4.15
11	Lieutenant	7	6	8	9	4	7	11	8	9	4	2	1	76	6.91
1	Captain	0	0	0	0	0	1	0	1	0	0	1	0	3	3.00
1	Deputy Chief	0	1	0	0	0	1	0	0	1	0	0	1	4	4.00
219														1893	8.64:1

Rates. A rate is a ratio that expresses a relationship between two measurements with different units and is a "fundamental descriptive statistic" (Maxfield and Babbie, 2001:387). Rates are useful for standardizing a metric for comparison purposes. For example, suppose there are 15,239 Part I index crimes for a population of 275,221. The rate 15,239 ÷ 275,221 compares the number of Part I index crimes per the number of people in the population. The word "per" in the equation means "divided by." Crime rates are often expressed in terms of rate *per* 100,000 or rate *per* 10,000 and so forth. This designation merely uses base-10 (a decimal notation) to figure the denominator. If you want to express the crime rate, the victimization rate, or the robbery rate, you first divide the denominator by the metric you wish to express (i.e., 100,000; 10,000; 1,000, etc.). In this example, the crime rate is calculated like this: $15{,}239_{\text{Part I crimes}} \div 2.75221_{\text{denominator}} = 5{,}537$. With denominators that are smaller than the desired metric it is more meaningful to change the rate to a smaller notation. For example, if the population was 27,522 instead of 275,221, then a more comprehensible way to calculate the crime rate would be per 10,000 people, since 27,522 is of the 10,000 metric not the 100,000 metric. Table 1-8 compares crime rates per 100,000 people for seven U.S. cities. The table shows Newark, New Jersey had the fewest number of Part I crimes in 2004; however, they also have the smallest population base. After the crime rate is standardized using the 100,000 metric, at 5,804 Newark's crime *rate* is comparable to other major U.S. cities that have much higher population bases. The city of Los Angeles has a population base that is 13.8 times higher than Newark, yet Newark's crime *rate* is 32% higher than the nation's second largest city.

Table 1-8	2004 Crime Rate per 100,000 People			
City	Part I Crimes	Population	Population per 100,000	Crime Rate per 100,000
New York	55,688	8,101,321	81.01321	687.394
Los Angeles	169,912	3,864,018	38.64018	4,397.288
Phoenix	104,249	1,428,937	14.28937	7,295.563
Detroit	75,062	914,355	9.14355	8,209.284
Houston	148,107	2,043,446	20.43446	7,247.904
Newark	16,243	279,857	2.79857	5,804.036
Honolulu	75,536	906,589	9.06589	8,331.890
Source: 2004 FBI UCR (www.fbi.gov)				

Measures of Central Tendency

Simply stated, central tendency is the degree to which values cluster in a statistical distribution. The three most common forms of measuring central tendency are the arithmetic mean (the average), the median (the middle point) and the mode (the most frequent value that occurs in a data set). Using measures of central tendency helps clarify summary data and gives the reader some idea of what is typical for a given distribution of data. There are nuances with each measure and it is important to know when using one measure is better than another. We will use a single data set to describe the mean, median and mode and explain the nuances (Table 1-9).

Mean. The mean value (arithmetic average) is by far the most common way to express a given data set. To compute the mean score simply sum the values and divide by the individual number of scores. For example, the mean score in the data set of Table 1-9 is 275 (e.g., $275_{\text{(mean)}} = 3020_{\text{(sum)}} \div 11_{\text{(cases)}}$). The mean is very useful for most expressions of central tendency, but it is subject to disproportionate or extreme values, either high or low. In Table 1-9 we see the scores are relatively stable except case #11 has a value of 899. This is known as an outlier: a single score that is a great distance from the other scores. A great distance is relative but as you can see in this example the distance between the second highest score (320) and the highest score (899) is 579 points away. Therefore, 899 skews the mean score. Without 899 in the data set the mean drops to 212 from 275; the median becomes 187; and the mode remains the same (145). Whenever you have a data set it is imperative to examine the data for outliers. If removing the outlier will not jeopardize accuracy or comprise integrity, then it is permissible to do so. Otherwise, the outlier should remain with an explanation of why the score is anomalous (i.e., very high or very low).

Median. The median value is the center score that splits the data set into two groups, the upper half has higher values and the lower half has lower values. When you have a data set that has an odd number of cases (e.g., 11), then you find the middle case that bisects the data. In this example case number 6 with a value of 215, is the median; exactly five scores are situated above position number 6 and 5 are exactly below position number 6. Note that position 6 is not the median, the value that occupies position 6 is the median, in this case 215.

When you have a data set in which an even number of cases (e.g., 10), divide the number of cases (10) by 2 and add 1. Then, average the two scores that occupy the middle two positions (e.g., $159 + 215/2 = 187$). If this data set had 10 cases, then the median value would be 187 (the average of the two middle scores). The median value is not sensitive to outliers as is the mean.

Mode. The mode, also known as the modal distribution or the modal score, is the value that occurs most frequently. This is a simple statistic that allows the reader a quick and easy indicator of central tendency in a data set. The modal score in our example is 145 since 145 occurs three times in the data set. This is useful when you want to portray the most popular or most frequently recurring value in a data set.

Table 1-9		Three Measures of Central Tendency										
Data Set		145	145	145	156	159	215	222	302	312	320	899
Mean	275											
Median	215											
Mode	145											
Cases	11	1	2	3	4	5	6	7	8	9	10	11

You can combine measures of central tendency in narrative form to help the reader visualize what is happening. For example, if you are describing a robbery pattern you might say: *"Over the last six months we have experienced 2,544 robberies at a rate of 21.2 per 100 people. This is a victimization rate of 1.18. The average number of robberies per day was 14. The most frequent age of the victim was 23."*

Measures of Dispersion

A measure of dispersion is a real number that is equal to zero if all the data in a given set are identical and which increases as the data becomes more diverse. Said differently, a measure of dispersion is a measure of the variability in a data set; the greater the spread in the data, the greater the dispersion. One common measure of dispersion is the range—the difference between the maximum and minimum values in a data set (e.g., $10 - 2 = 8$ point range). The most common measure of dispersion is the standard deviation. "Simply put, standard deviation measures how spread out the values in a data set are. More precisely, it is a measure of the average difference between the values of the data in the set. If the data points are all similar, then the standard deviation will be low (closer to zero). If the data points are highly variable, then the standard variation will be high (further from zero). A large standard deviation indicates that the data points are far from the mean and a small standard deviation indicates that they are clustered closely around the mean."[68] The reason standard deviation is an important concept in efficiency is because, in terms of performance, a low standard deviation reveals consistency and reliability; by contrast, a high standard deviation means inconsistent or uncertain performance.

Consider this example: you are contemplating purchasing service from a police department from a neighboring community; this is known as inter-local contracting for municipal law enforcement services.[69] You want to award a contract to the police department that has the most consistent response time. You request the average response time from two neighboring towns for the last twelve months. The mean for police department 1 is 7.2 minutes; the mean for police department 2 is 7.6 minutes, not a major difference. So, which department has a more consistent response time? You cannot make that determination from the mean response time value only. You need to know how the data is spread out across each month. When you calculate the standard deviation the results regarding their level of service differ in a major way. The standard deviation for department 1 is .265 with a range of .87. The standard deviation for service 2 is .785 with a range of 2.9. The response time for police department 1 is more consistent; the standard deviation is lower (closer to zero) while police department 2 is closer to 1 (more variability). Although both departments have similar average response times, department 1 is clearly more consistent. Measures of dispersion can be used for analyzing a variety of management issues, such as response time; time to case clearance; time to warrant issuance; and time to warrant service.

Table 1-10	Mean Police Response Times for 12 Months	
	Police Department 1	**Police Department 2**
Jan	7	8
Feb	7.1	7.9
Mar	7.3	8
Apr	7.2	7
May	7.09	9.2
Jun	7.77	6.3
Jul	7.2	7.5
Aug	7.45	7.22
Sep	7.6	6.8
Oct	6.9	7.99
Nov	6.98	7.4
Dec	7.06	8.5
Mean	7.22	7.65
Standard Deviation	0.265	0.785
Range	0.87	2.9

Software Tools for Data Analysis and Presentation

Basic Data Analysis. Creating efficiency generally only requires modest data analysis with basic software. Data analysis is the act of transforming data with the aim of extracting useful information and facilitating decisions or drawing conclusions. Depending on the type of data and the question, this might include application of statistical methods.[70] One of the best and simplest data analysis tools is probably on everyone's desktop computer: the Microsoft Office© suite of products. MS Office© contains three valuable tools for conducting basic analysis and reporting the results: MC Excel©, MS Access© and MS Word©. MS Excel© is a very robust spreadsheet application that can perform all of the basic analyses necessary for creating efficiency. It is not necessary to invest in expensive proprietary software products since most of the calculations involve only basic formulae, and, since MS Excel© has advanced statistical features built-in, it may not be necessary to invest in anything more than MS Office©. The statistics shown in this text were developed with MS Excel© and many police departments employing the Compstat process use Excel©.

Also, MS Access© is a user-defined desktop relational database application that can harness large amounts of information and perform the same analysis functions as Excel©. One especially attractive feature of MS Access© is that it is easily customizable to your individual needs; it is as robust as Excel© utilizing the same analysis tools and it has customizable printable reports. The single most important aspect of data analysis is capturing the data. MS Access© does a good job of capturing and analyzing most of the data elements you will need to create a more efficient workplace.

MS Word© is simply a word processing program, but, more importantly, Word© has the ability to handle imported objects and other sources of data rather well. For example, it is possible to conduct statistical analysis in SPSS© (a statistical software application), or create charts in Visio©, then copy the objects into MS Word© for presentation. Whatever word processing package you settle on, make sure it has the ability to handle imported objects from other software applications since conveying your findings is a critical aspect of improving performance. For an excellent source for preparing presentations see RAND, Guidelines for Preparing Briefings, accessible at http://www.rand.org/pubs/corporate_pubs/CP269/CP269.pdf.

Intermediate Analysis. There are other software packages that are more robust and do a better job at performing complex statistical calculations than MS Office© products. The industry leader in statistical reporting software is SPSS© (Statistical Package for the Social Sciences; www.spss.com). SPSS© is a very robust statistical analysis software application that can easily handle imported data from MS Excel©, MS Access©, or from other similar spreadsheet and database applications. SPSS© has analysis capabilities that far exceed MS Excel© and its calculations are accurate to several decimal places. SPSS© can easily handle predictive analytics. Predictive analytics is similar to a science known as predictive modeling, which can enable police executives and command staff officers to making real-time judgments about the likelihood that a particular location is going to experience a crime or whether a suspect is lying during an investigation (e.g., detecting insurance fraud). Both the Richmond, Va. and Atlanta, Ga. police departments have had success using predictive analytics in management areas such as officer deployment; identifying the correlation between minor crimes and violent crimes; and accelerating the investigative process.[71] SPSS© also offers a variety of add-on products that can make data-mining easier and more efficient than ever before.

Presenting Data. After the data analysis is complete, presenting the findings is next. Also known as data visualization, this aspect of efficiency is an important part of conveying the results from the analysis, especially when a police executive is attempting to inform or persuade listeners or readers. It is a good idea to consult a text that specifically deals with writing about and reporting on numbers and quantitative data; one of the most widely regarded original texts on this topic is by Miller (2004). Whether you are presenting your findings to the department's command staff, a community group, or the jurisdiction's elected officials, if the primary purpose is to inform them, then there are three criteria against which your presentation will be evaluated:

1. Whether the information was conveyed *accurately?*
2. Whether the information was conveyed *clearly?*
3. Whether the information was *meaningful* and *interesting* to the reader? (Lucas, 1992:280).

If the primary purpose is to persuade the listeners or readers, then your goal is to convince people to do something they may have been reluctant to do, such as vote in favor of something or change their position on a topic. Presenting the results of a management study must be persuasive since oftentimes processes or policies are at issue. When processes are at issue this may mean that people who have been comfortable in their position may lose that position through improved efficiency (e.g., civilianization; information/technology enhancements; consolidation). When policy is at issue the key topic is often funding; how much will this cost and what is the predicted return on the investment? Advocating for policy initiatives nearly always have money at their core since whether the policy is a new crime control initiative (road safety checkpoint), social program (Weed and Seed), or meeting budget specifications (filling vacant police officer positions) the police executive must accurately, clearly and meaningfully convey their message to convince lawmakers that they need what they are requesting. There are two ways to augment the narrative portion of a report that can help inform or persuade people, charts, graphs and tables.

Charts and Graphs. "A chart or graph is a type of information graphic that represents tabular numeric data. Charts are often used to make it easier to understand large quantities of data and the relationship between different parts of the data."[72] Charts complement narrative text and serve as a visual snapshot of the raw data from which they were derived. There are different charts for presenting a given data set. For example, data that represents a portion of the total, such as budget categories, or workload categories, are best depicted by a pie chart, which permits readers to compare the relative size of each category by segment. Pie charts often display data as a percentage or proportion of the total and sum to 100 (or sum to 1 for proportions). When it is necessary to illustrate numeric data that changes over time, such as a residential burglary trend, then a bar chart or line chart is appropriate. According to Miller (2004:102), creating effective charts and tables have these elements in mind:

1. "Readers should be able to identify the purpose of chart or table and interpret the data simply by reading the titles and labels;
2. Tables and charts should be self-contained, including units, context, source of the data and definitions of abbreviations;
3. The design of tables and charts should contribute to the understanding of patterns in the table and coordinate with the written description."

Line Chart. Line charts are used to show change in some variable (e.g., poverty rate; robbery rate; auto thefts) over time. By convention the predictor (independent) variable appears along the X (horizontal) axis and the outcome (dependent) variable appears along the Y (vertical) axis. Figure 5 shows an 11-hour residential burglary trend; there is an obvious spike around 12:00 with a leveling effect around 17:00.

Pie Chart. A pie chart summarizes data through visual representation of the relationships among individual categories as a part of the whole. Figure 6 depicts the patrol workload distribution for each of three duty tours. It is readily apparent that the 1600 x 2400 tour has slightly more of the workload (37%) than the day tour (36%). *Column/Bar Charts*. Column/bar charts are similar except that the orientation may be vertical or horizontal. A column chart is vertical and has rectangular bars of different heights that are usually proportional to the magnitude or frequency of what they represent. A column chart may not be proportional if the chart did not start at zero. A bar chart is a horizontal version where the rectangular bars are of different lengths. Both types of charts display the same data, only in a different orientation. Figure 7 is column chart and figure 8 is bar chart.

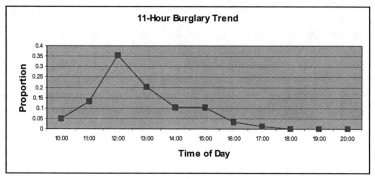

Figure 5

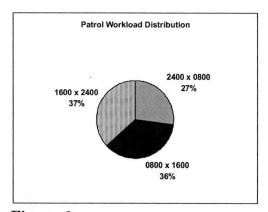

Figure 6

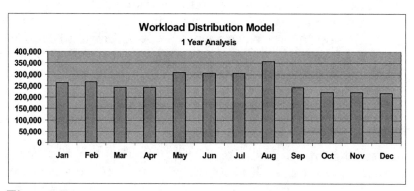

Figure 7

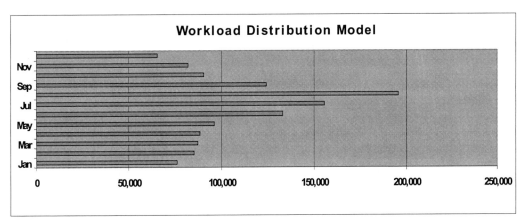

Figure 8

Scattergram (or scatterplot). "A scattergram or scatterplot is a graph used in statistics to visually display and compare two or more sets of related quantitative, or numerical, data by displaying only finite points, each having a coordinate on a horizontal (X) and a vertical (Y) axis."[73] Scatterplots are used to visualize the relationship between the data elements and to conduct an initial screening of the data for outliers. Scatterplots are commonly used before performing an intermediate statistical technique such as linear regression analysis. Figure 9 is a scatterplot with a trend line showing the relationship between personnel and the crime rate. This scatterplot reveals a *negative* relationship. A negative relationship means that as the predictor variable (horizontal X axis) increases there is a corresponding decrease in the dependent (vertical Y axis) variable. Here we see as the number of personnel increases there is a corresponding decrease in the crime rate. The opposite of a negative relationship is a positive relationship. In a *positive* relationship as the predictor variable increases there is a corresponding increase in the dependent variable. An example of a positive relationship might be as the unemployment rate increases (horizontal X predictor variable) there is a corresponding increase in the crime rate (vertical Y dependent variable). For further reading on designing graphs see Kosslyn (1994).

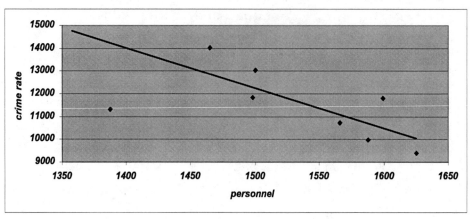

Figure 9

Tables. A table is constructed of a series of rows and columns that help convey raw or summarized data in a comprehensible format. Similar to charts, tables help the reader make sense of the information and help with interpretation. The data need not be numeric; categorical data (i.e., nominal level data) can be displayed to show the relationship between different dimensions, such as a matrix format. The same principles of construction apply to tables as they do for charts and graphs:

1. "Readers should be able to identify the purpose of chart or table and interpret the data simply by reading the titles and labels;
2. Tables and charts should be self-contained, including units, context, source of the data and definitions of abbreviations;
3. The design of tables and charts should contribute to the understanding of patterns in the table and coordinate with the written description" (Miller, 2004:102).

Table 1-11 is a basic table consisting of 5 rows of data, 1 row of column headings and 1 label row. There are 3 categories displayed in the columns.

Table 1-11	FTE Requirements for 24/7 Coverage Based upon RF	
Relief Factor	**Tours/Shifts**	**FTE Requirement**
1.3	3	3.9
1.4	3	4.2
1.5	3	4.5
1.6	3	4.8
1.7	3	5.1

Cross tabulation table. "A cross tabulation (often abbreviated cross tab) table displays the joint distribution of two or more variables.[74] Whereas a frequency distribution provides the distribution of a single data element, a cross tab table describes the distribution of two or more data elements simultaneously. Each cell in a cross tab table shows the specific combination of responses, that is, each cell contains a single cross tabulation for the columns and rows. Cross tabs are frequently used because:

1. They are easy to understand. They appeal to people that do not understand more sophisticated measures;
2. They can be used with any level of data: nominal, ordinal, interval, or ratio – cross tabs treat all data as if it is nominal;
3. A table can provide greater insight than single statistics;
4. It solves the problem of empty or sparse cells.[75]

Table 1-10 is an example of a 2 × 3 cross tab table of gender and assignment (clerical, patrol, detective bureau). The variable "assignment" has three categories; the other variable "gender" has two categories. Each cell shows the number of personnel in a given assignment, sorted by gender. The column and row totals are also displayed for quick visual reference.

Table 1-12	Gender-Assignment Category Cross Tabulation			
Gender	**Assignment**			
	Clerical	Patrol	Detective	Total
Female	206	0	10	216
Male	157	27	74	258
Total	**363**	**27**	**84**	**474**

5

▶ Solutions to Common Police Management Issues

There are many different management issues that lend themselves to analysis. Whether the issue is related to a program, a policy or daily operations there is an analysis technique to help solve the problem. This section deals with important issues that are fundamental to daily operations. For example, when the agency is accused of differential treatment based on community demographics and management cannot wait for answers from a consultant or an outside group for answers. The crime phenomenon changes rapidly and is ever evolving as criminals and technology coalesce. Fortunately, by incorporating statistical analysis into a broader management process, such as Compstat, department executives can gain the upper hand on crime problems by evaluating which tactics are working and which ones are not and by evaluating the prospective costs associated with delivering those services.

Proportional Staffing

In its mission to improve service delivery among law enforcement agencies through a body of national standards, the Commission on Accreditation for Law Enforcement Agencies (CALEA) has determined that allocating and distributing personnel according to a detailed workload analysis is essential for proper management. CALEA standard 16.1.2 states: "The agency allocates personnel to, and distributes them within all organizational components in accordance with documented periodic workload assessments" (CALEA, 2001:16-2). The purpose of this standard is "...to encourage the appropriate deployment of personnel by determining service demands through the use of 1) workload assessments and 2) computer-based or manual methods of personnel allocation and distribution" (CALEA, 2001:16-1). Allocating and distributing personnel is reflected in the department's operating posture, which, in financial terms, is set forth in the department's budget.[76]

Two common management issues faced by law enforcement executives are staffing and budgeting. Staffing and budgeting are executive functions; staffing may be influenced by the volume of work or by a steady-post requirement, regardless of volume. Indeed, steady-post requirements may be a contractually conferred agency obligation; regardless of workload they must be staffed. Budgeting is a continuous process that is directly affected by both steady-post requirements and volume of work. The basic premise for conducting a workload assessment is to ensure equalization of work among and within organizational units. Thorough workload analyses contribute to efficiency by minimizing over-

or under-staffing based on historical patterns of work that account for seasonal fluctuations, anomalies, temporal and geographic diffusion, time and effort to complete certain tasks.

Staffing Problems

A common problem in police departments is calculating how many personnel are needed for staffing. Many police departments operate with a clear division of labor among the different elements, so factoring a workload analysis is the first step. Quite often personnel are assigned by steady position and not on volume of work. The steady-post position formula is not necessarily the best or most efficient method of assignment since this method does not account for the level of effort required to accomplish the task. This is often the case when calculating how many personnel are required to staff a radio-car, with one or two officers, 24-hours per day, 365 days per year. What tends to happen is that a commander is given a predetermined number of people based upon the required positions without any thought to the amount of work they will encounter. Said another way: make do with what you have! This does not translate into good service delivery, nor does it consider efficiency or safety.

One example of how a staffing problem may arise in the police department's communications division is when the Chief makes the following statement: *"Captain, I am receiving complaints from the community that the non-emergency telephone lines at the communications center are not being answered in a timely manner. I am also receiving complaints from the patrol commander that the dispatchers are not answering the units in the field in a timely manner; officers in the field must call over the radio two and three times, sometimes four times before a dispatcher answers the radio. The officers might need help out there! What's going on? Are there enough people to handle the workload? If not, how many do you need?* This is a relatively easy question to answer provided the commander knows exactly how to prepare a staffing plan that accounts for level-of-effort and the relief factor (more about relief factoring later). A comprehensive workload/staffing analysis will provide an accurate answer.

The same is true of other divisions of the police department such as patrol, investigations, traffic enforcement, and the municipal jail facility. The patrol force is the largest and, perhaps, the most important element of the police department. The members of the patrol force are first to respond to a call for help and their safety is paramount! Yet, too often police officers, particularly in major cities, are disrupted from one assignment to handle another assignment. This diminishes service quality and can jeopardize safety. In some departments a two-officer patrol unit is split apart to handle two different assignments at two different locations simply to suppress the pending queue assignments: one officer is dropped off at one location to take a report while the other officer responds to take a report in another part of the city. Essentially there are too many assignments and not enough police officers. Or are there?

The question that must be resolved is whether the patrol force is adequately staffed and if so, are the personnel distributed proportionally according to the work. This section presents formulas for developing three different staffing plans: the patrol force, the communications center, and the investigations division to ensure the workforce is proportionately distributed.

Developing a Staffing Model and the "Relief Factor"

Staffing is an executive function that involves allocating personnel based upon demonstrated need, specialty or individual skills. In its simplest form, staffing involves utilizing human resources by distributing them when and where they are needed most. The only logical and defensible means of assigning personnel is to analyze the tasks associated with the function and arrive at a conclusion based upon the volume of work.

Developing an accurate staffing model has multiple applications. It can be used to determine the department's staffing requirements and assist with preparing the department's annual budget. It can also be used to estimate historical leave patterns by employees, since one accurate indicator of future workforce behavior is historical trends. "Many staffing issues and their attendant problems, such as excessive overtime costs, the inability to cover required positions, or the inability to free staff from their position for training, can be attributed to inaccurate calculations of the *actual* number of hours personnel are available to work in their assignment" (Leibert and Miller, 2003:2). A critical step in determining how many personnel are required for each position is to collect and analyze information that provides an accurate picture of the *actual* number of staff hours that are available to be scheduled for each full-time position (Leibert and Miller, 2003:8). This is commonly known as the "relief factor;" other terms are "non-productive FTE (full-time-equivalent)," "availability factor" and "staff adjustment factor (SAF)."

The term "relief factor" (RF) describes the number of full-time-equivalent (FTE) staff required to fill a single position that requires relief (i.e., a post or position that must be continuously covered 24 hours per day, 365 days per year). The RF accounts for predictable absences such as weekends, vacation or sick leave. For example, a police department might have a relief factor between 1.3 and 1.7 depending on the allotted time off. With a relief factor of 1.3, to cover a single post, 24-hours per day, 7-days per week, 3.9 staff members are needed. Expressed another way the post requires 3.9, rounded to 4, full-time personnel to staff the post continuously. The FTE requirement is derived by multiplying the RF by the number of tours the post must be covered (1.3 x 3 = 3.9). This is what different FTE requirements might look like depending on the department's RF:

Table 2 FTE Requirements for 24/7 Coverage Based upon RF		
Relief Factor	Tours/Shifts	FTE Requirement
1.3	3	3.9
1.4	3	4.2
1.5	3	4.5
1.6	3	4.8
1.7	3	5.1

The RF is calculated by dividing the number of days (or hours) the post needs to be covered by the number of days that a particular job title of staff is available for work during a typical year. For example, if the post must be continuously filled 365 days a year and a staff member is available to work 230 days, the RF is 1.58 (365 ÷ 230 = 1.58). For actual staffing purposes with a RF of 1.58, management must make some decisions regarding the .58 personnel required to staff the post: 1) pay overtime, 2) reassign personnel from another area for the period of time required, 3) hire two employees instead of one or 4) leave the post vacant.

When developing the relief factor, consistency is important. The methodology used by the department should be mathematically precise and conform to the best practices for calculating relief factors. One element of consistency is updating the RF calculations annually to ensure personnel distribution conforms to the most recent workforce behavior patterns. "The benefits of precision and conformity are:

1. A longer, organizationally relevant data time line smoothes out trends and protects the department from anomalous spikes in either direction;
2. The model results are more defensible when clear, simple and comprehensive;
3. The model can be applied with confidence, others can be easily trained in its use; and
4. Future applications and analyses are based on consistently defined and updated data" (San Francisco Board of Supervisors, 2002).

The RF calculation usually considers basic authorized leave categories such as vacation, holiday, funeral leave, compensatory time, personal time, training, and sick leave when estimating a staff member's availability. When calculating the RF, each agency should account for all of the allotted time off that personnel are entitled to, due to contractual stipulations or other employer benefits. A relief factor that exceeds 1.7 should be examined more closely as this may be an indicator of poor personnel management. However, 1.7 is only a guide, not a rule, because many labor agreements include lucrative benefits for employees that may raise the RF. The labor contract is generally beyond management's control, with the exception of excessive sick leave, which may be directly attributed to poor management controls.

Regardless of how necessary relief factoring may be to produce accurate personnel schedules, the inescapable reality is that some overtime will always be encountered. This is because it is not prudent to forecast or budget for *every* eventuality that *might* occur, indeed some categories of time off might never occur for some employees (e.g., maternity leave, military leave, light duty, or jury duty). If the agency were to account for every conceivable event that might take an employee away from their job, then the agency would be stuck paying for too many FTE's, and this is inefficient. Some other categories of time off that may not necessarily affect every employee are:

1. Long-term medical disability,
2. Provisions of the Family and Medical Leave Act of 1993,
3. Light-duty assignments required for injured staff members,
4. Leave of absence without pay,
5. Time away from the job while on special assignment,
6. Time it takes to fill a vacancy,
7. Jury duty,
8. Worker's compensation time off,
9. Unexcused absences (away without leave–AWOL) (Leibert and Miller, 2003:8).

When calculating the relief factor, using "hours" as the unit of analysis instead of "days" is the preferred method because hours are a more discreet and flexible work unit. This method generates what is known as the Net Annual Work Hours (NAWH), a convention that facilitates calculating FTE's. An excellent source-document for such calculations is the *"Staffing Analysis Workbook for Jails,"* which is published by the National Institute of Corrections and is widely available (Leibert and Miller, 2003). Although this document focuses on jail and custody operations, the model is directly transferable to any operation that requires continuous coverage. NAWH represents the number of hours staff members are actually available to work, based on the contracted number of hours per year (e.g., 40 hours per workweek × 52.14 weeks per year = 2,086 hours) minus the number of hours off per staff member per year. Calculating an accurate NAWH will help control costs such as overtime, because actual figures will be used to calculate the number of FTE's required to provide coverage. An accurate NAWH for each job title requires information on all possible time-off categories. Different classifications of employees will have different NAWH because of the amount time off allotted for the particular job title. Experience has demonstrated that leave patterns vary for different groups of workers. Therefore, for purposes of calculating FTEs and relief factors, tracking and reporting leave activity should be done by job title rather than aggregated for the entire workforce.

To begin calculating the relief factor first, determine how many people are needed to fill each post; it is necessary to calculate how many hours an employee in each job title is *not* available for regular work, then it is easy to calculate how many hours the employee is actually available. The total number of hours of coverage needed annually for each job title is then divided by the NAWH per employee for that classification. This yields the number of staff required in the particular job title. For example, if a post must be covered 24 hours per day, 7 days per week, or 8,760 hours per year and a person assigned to the post is available 1,619 hours per year, 5.41 FTE staff positions will be needed for coverage (8,760 ÷ 1,619 = 5.41). Using MS Excel©, here is how to calculate the relief factor for each job title:

Table 3		Steps for Calculating the Relief Factor
	Task	**Description**
1	**Identify each Job Title**	In matrix form list the various job titles across the top in columns.
2	**Establish the Work Year**	Identify the hours in the work year for each job title. This will probably be dictated by contract.
3	**Identify the Time-Off Categories**	Itemize the various categories of time off the department offers (e.g., vacation, sick, holiday, training, etc.). Only those categories that can be *reliably* projected to should be used. It is not wise to include obscure or infrequently used categories because it is not likely that the personnel will experience this type of time off. It may be more prudent to pay overtime if the need arises.
4	**Calculate the Hours Off by Category**	Beneath each job title place the corresponding number of hours off in the appropriate category. For example 224 hours of vacation for the Deputy Chief equals 28, 8-hour days.
5	**Sum the Allotted Hours Off**	The first line beneath the last category is the sum of hours allotted for time off.
6	**Calculate the Net Annual Work Hours (NAWH)**	Subtract the allotted time off from the total hours identified by contract. In the case of the Deputy Chief: NAWH = (2,086 – 528 = 1,558)
7	**Calculate the Relief Factor**	Finally, divide the NAWH by the total hours in the work year and round to two (2) decimal places. In the case of the Deputy Chief: RF = (2,086 ÷ 1,558 = 1.34).

Table 4 presents the completed relief factor chart. Calculating the relief factor is essential for all staffing plans, therefore it should be the first step in any meaningful management analysis involving personnel distribution and assignments. After the relief factor is calculated the next step is to analyze the workload for the organizational element under examination.

Table 4		Relief Factor Chart by Job Title					
		Job Title					
	Category	Deputy Chief	Captain	Lieutenant	Sergeant	Police Officer	Civilian Aide
1	Total hours identified by contract (based on a standard 40-hour work week (40 x 52.14 = 2,086)	2,086	2,086	2,086	2,086	2,086	2,086
2	Vacation	224	216	208	200	192	120
3	Compensatory Time	40	32	24	24	24	24
4	Sick Leave	160	160	160	160	160	96
5	Training	24	24	24	32	32	16
6	Personal Time	40	40	32	32	32	16
7	Funeral Leave	40	40	40	40	40	40
8	Break Time (may vary based on contract)	0	0	0	0	0	0
9	Other (specify)	0	0	0	0	0	0
10	Other (specify)	0	0	0	0	0	0
11	Total Hours Off/year (sum lines 2 through 10)	528	512	488	488	480	312
12	Net Annual Works Hours (subtract line 11 from line 1)	1,558	1,574	1,598	1,598	1,606	1,774
13	Relief Factor (divide line 1 by line 12 and round to 2 decimal places)	1.34	1.33	1.31	1.31	1.30	1.18

Now, with an understanding of how to determine relief for continuous positions, we will proceed with workload staffing plans for three elements of a police department: the patrol force, the communications center and the investigations division.

Patrol Force Workload Analysis

Interest in analyzing police workloads, especially calls for service, emerged in the mid 1960s. This coincided with studies by criminal justice researchers who sought to examine more closely what the police are actually responsible for (Wilson, 1970; Reiss, 1971.) A theme emerged from this body of knowledge that "police work" was much more than crime control and law enforcement, as conceptualized during the "professional era" (Walker, 1977). Today's forward-thinking police executives recognize that a comprehensive patrol workload analysis can help them understand the nature of police work, which means better service delivery, better crime control strategies and better order maintenance. Routinely conducting workload analyses can also help reduce the "overload hypothesis," which dictates that "as crime rates increase, capacity is strained, so less energy is devoted to each case, which reduces the certainty of [apprehension and] punishment" (Klinger, 1997:279). Overload is a contributing factor to what Klinger (1997) identifies as the amount of *vigor* and *leniency* that are afforded various neighborhoods serviced by a police department. What may develop from patrol overload is less vigor and more leniency; police officers become less vigorous in their duties such as "making arrests, taking reports and conducting investigations" in favor of short cuts that increase personal efficiency by being more lenient in their response to calls for service. Consequently, those neighborhoods that are most in need of vigorous police service, ones that may be suffering from a high rate of crime and disorder, may not receive it because of the workload imbalance. This means that equalizing the workload as best as possible is an important aspect of management that should be tended to regularly and accurately. Finally, a workload analysis also helps ensure an officer's precious time is spent wisely and that individual performance includes more than responding to calls for service.

A patrol workload analysis is "the process of collecting and analyzing data on patrol activities for the purpose of more efficient scheduling and deployment of manpower" (Hale, 1981:163). The patrol force has long been considered the "backbone" or the "heart" of the police department. If the "backbone" serves to keep the rest of the agency upright, then management must overcome the problems associated with inadequate staffing and deployment. Unfortunately, the manner in which police administrators develop staffing plans does not receive the scrutiny they deserve. One oft cited comment by police administrators and elected officials is how many police officers per capita the city employs. This method does not account for the most fundamental aspect of police work: workload. Population or square mileage does not necessarily dictate patrol force staffing, in fact population alone does not reveal anything about how much work the patrol force will encounter nor the complexity of the work.[77] Workload, or the level of effort facing the patrol force, based on historical data, is the only logical and defensible means for calculating how many officers will be required. "The practical implications of utilizing the appropriate data include:

1. Decision-makers could know the impact of fielding a given number of patrol officers (e.g., effects on response time);
2. Department managers would be able to effectively monitor patrol performance;
3. The closer that allocation levels and schedules match the reactive patrol force to demand for its service, the more efficient the delivery of that service becomes;
4. Improved matching of resources to workload also results in a more effective patrol force in terms of performance standards, such as response and delay time;
5. Workload among officers becomes more equitable; the department can better justify its budget for patrol operations because of better performance information generated by the computer" (Thomas, 1984:64-67).

Once the workload analysis is completed, the data is valuable for developing an activity-base budget (ABB); ABB is a topic that is covered later in this text, and as you will see ABB is very useful for creating a nexus between workload and costs.

In developing an accurate workload analysis, the first step is to gather existing data on patrol force activities. The best method is to extract dispatched calls-for-service (CFS) data from the computer-aided dispatch system (CAD) and download the data into a spreadsheet application such as MS Excel©. The date range should be three to five years worth of data but not less than one year. This will give you a smoother picture of the workload fluctuations, anomalies and natural expansion and contraction of work based on season, time of day, day of week, special events (parades and festivals) and personnel attrition. This is known as a "bottom up process" or "bottom up methodology," which enables the administrator to look at the required staffing level based on the total amount of work, the amount of work each employee and organizational element is expected to do and the performance standard associated with the work (Sullivan, Bellmio, Hubler, Somers, and Adkins, 2001:27-28).

The CFS are also known as "principal modalities," which are the major activities of the patrol force. The spreadsheet is divided into six columns: CFS, Hours per unit, Units per Year, total Employee Hours per Modality, Officers Required and Percentage allocation.

Table 5		Principal Data Categories for Workload Analysis
Column	Task	Description
1	Calls for Service (CFS)	Itemize each type of call the patrol force must answer. To account for seasonal fluctuations or anomalies in the data, at least one full year's worth of data should be analyzed. CFS are also known as "units" or "units of work."
2	Hours per Unit	The amount of time it takes to handle a single CFS of that particular type. When calculating hours per unit it is best to calculate the *average* amount of hours. Any portion of an hour must be captured as such, for example 20 minutes is depicted as .33; 42 minutes is depicted as .70; 25 minutes is depicted as .42; one and a half hours is depicted as 1.5 hours. Actual time will vary based upon the circumstances of each call, so calculating the average will give police executives some administrative flexibility when assessing workload.
3	Units per Year	The number of CFS of that particular type for the year. Once the units per year is calculated for each type of call, sum the units per year (see table 6: UPY = 60,115). This figure will be used again later for other calculations.
4	Officers Required	The number of officers required to handle the assignment. Stated differently, this is how many officers will be dispatched to handle the call safely. There is no standard, this figure will differ based upon policy or managerial prerogative.
5	Total Employee Hours per Modality	The amount of time it takes to handle all of the CFS of that type. The sum is derived by multiplying the hours per unit (3) by units per year (41) by officers required (2) (e.g., Murder = 3 × 41 × 2 = 246). Once the total employee hours per modality is calculated for each type of call, sum the hours (see table 6: 122,927). This figure will be used again later for other calculations.
6	Percentage Allocation	The sixth column is optional but recommended because knowing how much time each type of call consumes lends itself to greater efficiency. The percentage allocation is derived by dividing the total employee hours per modality by the grand total of employee hours and multiplying by 100 (e.g., Murder = 246 ÷ 122,927 = .002 × 100 = .20%).

Table 6 depicts the first part of the workload analysis.

Table 6	Principal Modalities (Major Activities) for the Patrol Workload Analysis				
			Acuity		
Calls for Service (CFS)	Hours Per Unit	Units Per Year	Officers Required	Total Employee Hours Per Modality	Percentage Allocation
Arrest (average for all types of arrests)	1.5	15,264	2	45,792	37.25%
Arson	1	51	2	102	0.08%
Assault (shooting, stabbing, blunt force)	0.75	1,000	2	1,500	1.22%
Assist Officer (back up)	0.25	152	2	76	0.06%
Bomb Threat	1	12	2	24	0.02%
Burglar Alarm (residential, commercial)	0.33	2,555	2	1,686	1.37%
Burglary	1	1,877	2	3,754	3.05%
Carjacking	1	77	2	154	0.13%
Code Enforcement Violations	0.33	315	1	104	0.08%
Court Appearances	1.5	1,234	5	9,255	7.53%
Directed Patrol Activities	0.33	5,475	2	3,614	2.94%
Disorderly Conduct (fight, loud music, noisy crowds)	0.3	2,555	2	1,533	1.25%
Domestic Violence	1.25	3,255	2	8,138	6.62%
Drug Sales	0.3	5,041	2	3,025	2.46%
DWI	1	44	2	88	0.07%
Emotionally Disturbed Person	1	120	2	240	0.20%
Fire (car, house, building)	1.5	123	2	369	0.30%
Fraud	0.75	211	1	158	0.13%
Gambling Offense	0.42	468	1	197	0.16%
Juvenile Condition (curfew, truancy and all others)	0.75	457	1	343	0.28%
Kidnapping	3	11	2	66	0.05%
Man with a Gun	0.42	401	4	674	0.55%
Motor Vehicle Accident (with or without injuries)	1	1,825	2	3,650	2.97%
Murder	3	41	2	246	0.20%
MV Pursuit	0.75	81	4	243	0.20%
Prostitution	0.33	1,003	2	662	0.54%
Rape	1.5	88	2	264	0.21%
Robbery	1.5	2,110	2	6,330	5.15%
School Crossing	2	1,080	3	6,480	5.27%
Shots Fired	0.33	730	2	482	0.39%
Sick/Injured Person	0.75	720	1	540	0.44%
Stolen Vehicle Report	0.75	2,645	1	1,984	1.61%
Street Collapse	1	14	2	28	0.02%
Suicide	1.5	22	2	66	0.05%
Theft (shoplifting and all others)	0.58	6,522	2	7,566	6.15%
Traffic Control	2	2,190	3	13,140	10.69%
Train Accident	8	1	6	48	0.04%
Vicious Animal	0.33	214	2	141	0.11%
Warrant Service	0.75	73	2	110	0.09%
Wires Down	1	58	1	58	0.05%
Total		60,115		122,927	100.00%

One workload element that is not captured for this analysis is self-initiated assignments. Self-initiated assignments do not reflect the reactive workload; they are a product of other factors, including officers' initiative and self-motivation, the number of officers available to undertake self-initiated assignments, the time of day, and the reactive workload itself. There is usually an inverse relationship between CFS and self-initiated work: when CFS are high, self-initiated assignments are low and vice versa (Thomas, 1984:65). In research by Webster (1970:99) a police sergeant characterized the police as "order takers" because of the amount of time officers spent handling calls for service. This is an accurate statement and depending on how much time is apportioned among the three categories will directly impact proactive (self-initiated) assignments. Although it may be useful to calculate self-initiated assignments as a barometer of individual performance, self-initiated assignments do not necessarily affect deployment staffing, which is why sufficient time must be allotted for proactive activities. This will ensure that officers have enough time throughout their day to handle proactive assignments such as directed patrol activities, traffic stops, pedestrian stops, and community policing activities. As Sweeney (1982:1) stated, "Traditionally, prevention and interception activities have been relegated to a secondary status, to be accomplished in that unpredictable amount of time between calls for service." Managers should work diligently to reverse this trend.

The next step in the workload analysis is to distribute the officer's time across management categories, which is known as weighting or prioritizing. This is critical to the process because what happens with the distribution of time directly affects how many officers will be needed. The three primary management categories are service demands (i.e., CFS), administrative activities and proactive activities. The first category, service demands, is crucial since the other categories receive their allotted time based on what is allotted in this category. The sum of employee hours per modality (122,927) represents 100% of the workload. Obviously, there are other things police officers must do besides respond to calls for service, such as administrative activities (i.e., submitting reports, attending meetings) and proactive activities (i.e., community policing, directed or self-initiated activities). It is not realistic to formulate a workload analysis around 100% of the total employee hours per modality without factoring a police officer's other responsibilities. This is where prudent management decisions must be made regarding how much of the officers' time the department is willing to distribute across these three categories. Stated another way, the lower the percentage of time that is allocated for service demands, the more police officers the department will need. The reality is that police officers will often find a way to stretch out each assignment unless service-time thresholds are set; a service-time threshold is the upper limit of the total time a request for service is allotted. A frequent discussion among police executives is that if a police officer works 6 out of 8 hours, then that is considered a "good" work day. The remaining two hours is consumed with travel time between assignments, stretching each assignment for a few more minutes than is necessary, meal breaks and personal breaks among the many. These conditions will affect the distribution of time.

For illustration purposes the allocation is 60 percent for service demands, 10 percent for administrative activities, and 30 percent for proactive activities. Research has shown that most citizens desire a swift response to crimes in progress. However, the faster the response time, say, for example, within one minute, the police department would need to employ a huge number of officers to meet the standard. Most, if not all, jurisdictions could not afford it. Therefore, the most sensible course of action is to undertake a cost-benefit approach, which involves selecting the number of field units the jurisdiction can afford that also meets a reasonable performance standard as safely as possible.

Based on our distribution of time in this example it will take 134 police officers to handle 204,878 hours of CFS for the year. Once the total hours are calculated, the next step is to calculate the "effective strength" of the patrol force;[78] the effective strength differs from the actual strength, which will be explained later. Based on a work-year of 2,086 hours, the effective strength is 98.23 full-time equivalent (FTE's) patrol officers. This is derived by dividing the total number of hours of work (204,878) by the availability (2,086). Since police officers do not actually work 2,086 hours per year, one additional calculation is necessary, the relief factor. Table 7 depicts the distribution of time across the three primary management categories, the effective strength, the relief factor and the actual patrol force strength.

Table 7			Distribution of Time	
Activity	%	Time	Daily/Minutes	Daily/Hours
Service Demands	60%	122,927	288	4.8
Administrative	10%	20,488	48	0.8
Proactive	30%	61,463	144	2.4
Total	**100%**	**204,878**	**480**	**8**
Availability		2,086	(40 hours per week, 52.14 weeks per year)	
Effective Strength		98.23	FTE Patrol Officers	
Relief Factor		1.360	FTE Patrol Officers	
Actual Strength		134	FTE Patrol Officers	

Actual Patrol Force Strength and the Relief Factor

Actual patrol force strength is the number of officers required for patrol assignment in order to handle the workload. This example begins with a work year 2,086 hours for police officers. Next, subtract 552 hours of allotted time off (Table 8, Nonproductive FTE). The difference is "personnel availability." The work year (2,086) is then divided by "personnel availability" (1,534) to produce the relief factor. The quotient is 1.36. This means it takes 1.36 police officers for every officer position to provide an acceptable level of service 365 days per year, 24 hours per day. Table 8 presents the relief factor calculations for this example; time off in days is depicted for illustration purposes only, the preferred unit of analysis is hours.

Table 8	Nonproductive FTE (Relief Factor)	
Time Off	**Days**	**Hours**
Vacation	28	224
Compensatory	5	40
Sick Leave	15	120
Personal	3	24
Training	8	64
Bereavement	10	80
Total Time Off	**69**	**552**
Work Year	260.70	2,086
Personnel Availability	191.70	1,534
Relief Factor	**1.360**	**1.360**

The final step is to determine "actual" patrol strength. Actual patrol strength is determined by multiplying the "effective strength" by the relief factor. The effective strength is 98.23; the actual strength is 134 ($134 = 98.23 \times 1.36$). Thus, according to the distribution of time as depicted in table 7, 134 officers are required to carry out 204,878 hours of patrol operations over a period of one year. Now that the level of effort has been quantified the personnel must be apportioned according to need. There are three steps:

Table 9	Steps for Distributing Personnel	
Step	**Task**	**Description**
1	**Create the Distribution Model**	Collecting data from a representative period of time, preferably one year to smooth cyclical fluctuations or anomalous conditions.
2	**Identify the Proportional Workload**	Determining the percentage of work by tour. The best method is to analyze data according to the pre-approved tours of duty.
3	**Allocate the Personnel**	Assigning staff according to the relative need as described in the proportional workload. For example, if the 1600 x 2400 tour of duty accounts for 36% of the work, then that tour should receive 36% of the resources.

Step 1: Creating the Distribution Model

To create the distribution model using MS Excel©, format a matrix of sixteen columns and twenty-seven rows:

1. 12 columns, one for each month

2. 1 column to identify the tour of duty
3. 1 column to identify the hour of the day
4. 1 column that sums the total calls per tour
5. 1 column that shows the percentage of work by tour
6. 24 rows, one for each hour of the day
7. 1 row to serve as column headings
8. 1 row to subtotal the calls per month
9. 1 row to sum up for the grand total of calls

In each cell under the appropriate hour of day, enter the number of calls for that hour for the month. Continue this for each month. Next, sum the calls by month and by tour. The completed matrix should look like table 10:

Table 10					Workload Distribution by Month Sorted by Tour										
Tour	Hour	Jan	Feb	Mar	Apr	May	Jun	Jul	Aug	Sep	Oct	Nov	Dec	Total Calls per Tour	% by Tour
2400 x 0800	0	125	102	201	32	125	125	149	102	235	125	123	125		
	1	201	235	120	32	100	144	954	120	215	12	122	120		
	2	125	94	111	162	200	456	95	126	149	149	111	120		
	3	124	2	120	120	124	124	889	125	64	136	145	124		
	4	111	111	112	215	111	111	978	148	188	125	98	88		
	5	235	125	258	215	235	125	788	144	201	123	198	78		
	6	215	12	158	120	215	100	100	126	321	145	124	78		
	7	149	149	142	126	148	149	258	159	126	158	125	98	16,561	27%
0800 x 1600	8	64	136	145	125	164	954	658	200	201	166	147	191		
	9	188	125	98	148	588	95	587	149	129	135	189	100		
	10	144	235	101	144	645	889	744	201	145	112	100	89		
	11	154	211	98	126	101	545	369	95	147	111	125	489		
	12	142	102	144	159	131	84	741	231	114	120	99	147		
	13	125	103	100	200	138	256	188	125	135	189	75	125		
	14	12	198	122	201	897	478	156	974	112	199	80	12		
	15	100	124	78	321	578	562	78	523	111	188	97	99	22,075	36%

Table 10						Workload Distribution by Month Sorted by Tour									
Tour	Hour	Jan	Feb	Mar	Apr	May	Jun	Jul	Aug	Sep	Oct	Nov	Dec	Total Calls per Tour	% by Tour
1600 x 2400	16	32	125	98	126	158	465	116	744	120	156	100	32		
	17	14	147	191	201	489	698	145	569	123	198	78	14		
	18	16	102	100	129	135	598	800	699	145	124	78	16		
	19	129	100	211	145	112	125	545	849	158	125	98	129		
	20	201	99	103	147	111	977	875	598	166	147	191	133		
	21	147	132	147	114	120	589	689	895	135	189	100	147		
	22	115	123	122	126	144	899	122	188	112	199	116	100		
	23	38	102	133	122	147	878	133	160	111	188	104	38	22,479	37%
Sub Total		2906	2994	3213	3556	5916	10426	11157	8250	3663	3519	2823	2692		
Grand Total		61,115													

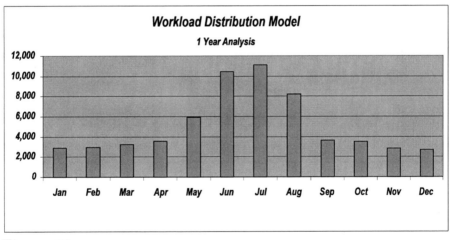

Figure 10

For clarity, you can express the matrix graphically to get a visual sense of how the workload patterns appear for the year.

Step 2: Identifying the Proportional Workload

Using the established tours, determine the proportional workload by tour: 2400 x 0800 = 16,561, 27%; 0800 x 1600 = 22,075, 36%; 1600 x 2400 = 22,479, 37%. For clarity, you can express this graphically with a pie chart to show the relative distribution.

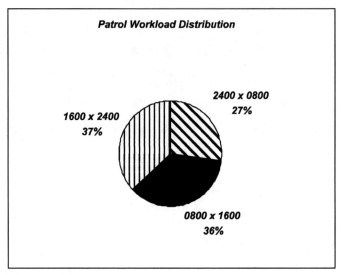

Figure 11

Step 3: Allocating Personnel

The final step is allocating personnel according the proportional need. Here, simply multiply the total staff by the proportional workload to determine how many personnel are required (e.g., 134 ×.27 = 36).

Table 11	Proportional Distribution of Personnel		
Tour	**Workload**	**Calculation**	**Staff**
2400 x 0800	27%	134 x .27	36
0800 x 1600	36%	134 x .36	48
1600 x 2400	37%	134 x .37	50

Communications Center Workload Analysis

"If the patrol force is the heart of the police organization, the communications center is the central nervous system. It is through the communications center that vital information is received and transmitted to patrol units" (Hale, 1981). The communications center is the first line of defense against problems encountered by the community. Therefore, it is imperative a sufficient number of personnel are allocated to handle the volume of work. Assigning the right number of personnel will achieve maximum efficiency.[79]

There are two approaches to solving this staffing problem. One is through steady-post positions and the other is through volume-based positions. Steady-post positions demand staffing regardless of the volume of work imposed, such as dispatch floor supervisors. Volume-based positions include transaction positions that are evaluated based upon the amount of work that flows through them, such as call taker stations. Most staffing plans for communications centers include a combination of steady-post and volume-based formulas because neither method is mutually exclusive. That means every communications center has supervisors, which are generally calculated by steady-post formula and the call-taker positions that are calculated by volume-based formulas.

Steady-post Positions

Restated, these positions are staffed regardless of the amount of work encountered. Examples include police departments where a single person performs both dispatching and call reception functions (i.e., incoming calls are received and dispatched by the same person); most supervisory positions; radio dispatch positions in communications centers where there are separate personnel processing calls for service and conducting dispatching (i.e., call takers only process incoming telephone calls and radio dispatchers only control field units) (Shane, 2004). The formula for steady-post positions has three elements: 1) the number of positions, 2) the number of tours and 3) relief factor.

Table 12	Elements for Calculating Steady-Post Positions
Variable	**Description**
R = Required Personnel	The total personnel required to staff the position
P = Positions	The number of positions that must be continuously staffed.
T = Number of Tours	The number of tours the position must be staffed.
RF = Relief factor	Calculated using the formulas previously s described.

The staffing equation can be expressed as: $R = (P \times T \times RF)$

Sample Steady-Post Staffing Plan

The new commanding officer of the communications center must staff seven (7) positions, twenty-six (26) personnel each tour (0800 x 1600; 1600 x 2400; 0000 x 0800). The seven positions are: 1) tour commander, 2) dispatch supervisor, 3) radio dispatchers, 4) relief dispatchers, 5) call taker supervisor, 6) call takers and 7) relief call takers. The functions are as follows:

1. **Tour Commander:** Responsible overall management and supervision of the communications center for the tour.
2. **Dispatch Supervisor:** Responsible for supervising all radio dispatchers, queue suppression and communications' transmissions.

3. **Radio Dispatchers:** Responsible for managing all police field assets, dispatching pending assignments, and all related work.
4. **Relief Dispatchers:** Responsible for providing meal and personal break relief to all dispatchers.
5. **Call Taker Supervisor:** Responsible for supervising all call takers and incoming/outgoing telecommunications.
6. **Call Takers:** Responsible for processing all incoming/outgoing communications' requests for police, fire or emergency medical service and general service related assistance.
7. **Relief Call Takers:** Responsible for providing meal and personal break relief to all call takers.

Using a matrix format in MS Excel© with the following:

Table 13		Steps for Developing Steady-Post Staffing Model
Column	Task	Description
1	Identify each Job Title	List the various job titles in the first column
2	Identify the Number of Required Positions	List the number of required positions for each title
3	Identify the Number of Tours	List the number of tours the position must be continuously staffed
4	Calculate the Relief Factor	List the RF for each job title
5	Required Personnel	The results of multiplying the positions, the tours and the RF. The formula is: (# of required positions × # of tours × RF) (e.g., Tour Commander Position: 5 = 1 × 3 × 1.56).
6	Total	Finally, sum the number of required positions and the number of required personnel

The resulting staffing plan looks like table 14:

Table 14	Communications Center Steady-Post Staffing Model			
Job Title	# of Required Positions	# of Tours	Relief Factor	# of Personnel Required
Tour Commander	1	3	1.56	5
Dispatch Supervisor	2	3	1.56	9
Radio Dispatchers	7	3	1.42	30
Relief Dispatchers	2	3	1.42	9
Call Taker Supervisor	2	3	1.42	9
Call Takers	10	3	1.33	40
Relief Call Takers	2	3	1.33	8
Total	26			110

To staff 7 positions, 24-hours per day, 365 days per year, with 26 personnel per tour, it will take 110 total personnel. Once the format is designed in MS Excel© it is versatile and can be easily adjusted as the need arises, including creating quick budgets.

Volume-based Positions

Volume-based positions are those that are staffed according to an antici-pated or existing workload, typically based upon historical experience (e.g., volume of 9-1-1 emergency and non-emergency telephone calls processed each year). Calculating the staffing needs for volume-based positions requires a workload analysis similar to the patrol force. Most sophisticated public safety telephone systems can capture the amount of time a call taker spends pro-cessing an incoming call. The telephone trunk lines are usually designated emergency and non-emergency so analyzing the calls by type is not difficult. If the telephone system is not equipped for this, then hardcopy call taker log sheets will suffice.

The methodology begins with an itemized workload analysis just like the patrol force. Again, for administrative flexibility you take the average time it takes to handle each call. This format gives management the most precise and accurate picture of their call reception program. The formula for this calculation has six variables: 1) Calls per Hour, 2) Hours per Year, 3) Calls per Year, 4) Performance Standard, 5) Effective Strength, and 6) Relief Factor.

Table 15	Elements of Volume-based Positions
Variable	Description
CPH = Calls per hour	The average number of calls per hour a call taker is expected to process while still considered efficient. This includes accounting for all of the ancillary functions including CAD database entry, preparing a log sheet, or NCIC entries. A lower CPH value requires more personnel; a higher CPH value means fewer personnel.
HY = Hours worked per year	The number of hours scheduled to work per year, *not counting prearranged absences,* such as days off, vacation and other permissible absences.
CPY = Calls per year	This includes all 9-1-1, 3-1-1, non-emergency, administrative, and seven-digit calls.
ES = Effective strength	The number of required personnel
P = Total positions required	The number of positions required in a 24-hour period to process the number of calls per year using the CPH standard.
RF = The relief factor	As previously discussed on page 42
PS = Performance standard	The average number of calls per year a call taker would be expected to process while still considered efficient (expression: CPH × HY). The PF is agency specific and is based on reasonable expectations of employee ability and actual operations.

The staffing equation is expressed in two steps:

Step 1 $PS = (CPH \times HY)$
Step 2 $(CPY \div PF) = ES \times RF$

Sample Volume-Based Staffing Plan

The new commander of communications is conducting an operations audit. The analysis begins by reviewing the communications center's historical workload. For illustration purposes the communications center is expected to process 3.19 million calls per year. The commander must determine how many personnel it will take to handle this many calls. The first step is to gather the information on the types of calls being handled, just as the patrol force. Table 18 is a replication of Table 6 except one additional column was added: average minutes. The average minutes will help determine the performance standard (PS); if management knows the average telephone call takes 6 minutes to process, then an efficient call taker should be expected to handle 10 calls per hour. In this model the call takers only work 6.5 hours per day, so, theoretically, the maximum number of calls a single call taker could handle per tour is 65. The next step is to calculate the relief factor. Calculating the relief factor is well established by now, so Table 19 is simply a completed RF table. For illustration purposes we are using the RF for the "call taker" job title. The last step is to distribute time across three categories, emergency calls, non-emergency calls, and administrative calls, and to determine the actual strength.

Table 16		Principal Data Categories for Volume-based Staffing Model
Column	Task	Description
1	Calls for Service (CFS)	Itemize each type of call the call takers will process. To account for seasonal fluctuations or anomalies in the data, at least one full year's worth of data should be analyzed. CFS are also known as "units" or "units of work."
2	Hours per Unit	The amount of time it takes to handle a single CFS of that particular type. When calculating hours per unit it is best to calculate the *average* amount of hours. Any portion of an hour must be captured as such, for example 20 minutes is depicted as .33; 42 minutes is depicted as .70; 25 minutes is depicted as .42; one and a half hours is depicted as 1.5 hours. Actual time will vary based upon the circumstances of each call, so calculating the average will give police executives some administrative flexibility when assessing workload.
3	Average Minutes	The average number of minutes for all CFS.
4	Units per Year	The number of CFS of that particular type for the year. Once the units per year is calculated for each type of call, sum the units per year (see table 18: 3,196,305). This figure will be used again later for other calculations.
5	Call Takers Required	The number of call takers required to handle the call. Aside from the novice or call taker in training, the number is probably 1.
6	Total Employee Hours per Modality	The amount of time it takes to handle all of the calls of that type. The sum is derived by simply multiplying the hours per unit (3) by units per year (41) by officers required (2) (e.g., 3 × 41 × 2 = 246). Once the total employee hours per modality is calculated for each type of call, sum the hours (see table 6, 122,927). This figure will be used again later for other calculations.
7	Percentage Allocation	The sixth column is optional but recommended because knowing how much time each type of call consumes lends itself to greater efficiency. The percentage allocation is derived by dividing the total employee hours per modality by the grand total of employee hours and multiplying by 100 (e.g., 2,048 ÷ 319,358 = .0064 ×100 = .64%).

Table 17		Steps for Calculating Volume-based Staffing Model	
Step	Task	Description	Calculation
1	Establish Calls per Hour (CPH)	Based on the "average minutes," the amount of calls per hour an efficient call taker is expected to handle. For illustration purposes one call taker is expected to process ten (10) calls per hour (1 call every 6 minutes, on average).	$10\ CPH = 60_{minutes} \div 6_{minutes}$
2	Establish the Performance Standard (PS)	Based on the "average minutes," the amount of calls per year an efficient call taker is expected to handle. The formula is (PS = CPH × HY).	$18{,}250_{PS} = 10_{CPH} \times 1{,}825_{HY}$
3	Calculate the Effective Strength (ES)	The total number of required positions. The CPY (3,196,305) is divided by the PS (18,250); the quotient is the "effective strength:"	$175_{ES} = 3{,}196{,}305_{CPY} \div 18{,}250_{PS}$
4	Calculate the Actual Strength (AS)	The total number of required personnel. Finally, multiply the effective strength by the relief factor to determine how many actual personnel are required for staffing: (AS= ES × RF);	$227_{AS} = 175_{EF} \times 1.30_{RF}$

If it is not possible to capture the individual calls for service and the hours per unit, then begin by reasonably estimating the length of the average incoming call. You can also separate the calls into emergency and non-emergency categories. This is less efficient but it will still produce a reasonably accurate volume-based analysis. For example, if you estimated that the average incoming call is 6 minutes, then you could begin the CPH calculations. Table 18 is the completed first step to creating the volume-based staffing model.

Table 18	Communications Center Volume-based Staffing Model					
Principal Modalities (Major Activities)						
				Acuity		
Calls for Service	Hours Per Unit	Average Minutes	Units Per Year	Call Takers Required	Total Employee Hours Per Modality	Percentage Allocation
Administrative Calls	0.083	5.0	24,581	1	2,048	0.64%
Arson	0.100	6.0	365	1	37	0.01%
Assault (shooting, stabbing, blunt force)	0.083	5.0	4,877	1	406	0.13%
Bomb Threat	0.117	7.0	55	1	6	0.00%
Burglar Alarm (residential, commercial)	0.067	4.0	8,541	1	569	0.18%
Burglary	0.100	6.0	13,255	1	1,326	0.42%
Carjacking	0.133	8.0	421	1	56	0.02%
Code Enforcement Violations	0.100	6.0	412	1	41	0.01%
Disorderly Conduct (fight, loud music, noisy crowds)	0.100	6.0	32,655	1	3,266	1.02%

Table 18		Communications Center Volume-based Staffing Model				
Principal Modalities (Major Activities)						
			Acuity			
Calls for Service	Hours Per Unit	Average Minutes	Units Per Year	Call Takers Required	Total Employee Hours Per Modality	Percentage Allocation
Domestic Violence	0.083	5.0	14,741	1	1,228	0.38%
Drug Sales	0.117	7.0	102,569	1	11,966	3.75%
Emotionally Disturbed Person	0.100	6.0	199	1	20	0.01%
Fire (car, house, building)	0.050	3.0	210	1	11	0.00%
Fraud	0.083	5.0	7,411	1	618	0.19%
Gambling Offense	0.083	5.0	647	1	54	0.02%
Juvenile Condition (curfew, truancy and all others)	0.100	6.0	1,233	1	123	0.04%
Kidnapping	0.183	11.0	44	1	8	0.00%
Motor Vehicle Accident (with or without injuries)	0.083	5.0	10,236	1	853	0.27%
Murder	0.167	10.0	125	1	21	0.01%
Non Emergency Calls	0.100	6.0	2,866,387	1	286,639	89.75%
Person with a Weapon	0.083	5.0	5,487	1	457	0.14%
Prostitution	0.100	6.0	14,000	1	1,400	0.44%
Rape	0.117	7.0	254	1	30	0.01%
Robbery	0.117	7.0	8,975	1	1,047	0.33%
Shots Fired	0.083	5.0	26,987	1	2,249	0.70%
Sick/Injured Person	0.100	6.0	9,855	1	986	0.31%
Stolen Vehicle Report	0.083	5.0	15,689	1	1,307	0.41%
Street Collapse	0.100	6.0	122	1	12	0.00%
Suicide	0.100	6.0	55	1	6	0.00%
Theft (shoplifting and all others)	0.100	6.0	25,102	1	2,510	0.79%
Train Accident	0.117	7.0	4	1	0	0.00%
Vicious Animal	0.067	4.0	712	1	47	0.01%
Wires Down	0.100	6.0	99	1	10	0.00%
Total		6.00	3,196,305		319,358	100%

Table 19	Relief Factor Calculations					
Non-productive FTE (Relief Factor)	Time Off in Hours					
Time Off	Captain	Lieutenant	Sergeant	Police Officer	Detective	Call Taker
Vacation	224	216	208	200	200	112
Compensatory	40	40	40	40	40	32
Sick Leave	120	120	120	120	120	128
Personal	24	24	24	24	24	32
Training	64	64	64	64	64	32
Funeral	80	80	80	80	80	80
Total Time Off	552	544	536	528	528	416
Work Year	1,825	1,825	1,825	1,825	1,825	1,825
Personnel Availability	1,273	1,281	1,289	1,297	1,297	1,409
Relief Factor	1.43	1.42	1.42	1.41	1.41	1.30

Table 20	Distribution of Time Across Management Categories				
Activity	%	Hours/year	Daily/Minutes		Daily/Hours
Emergency Calls	4%	12,774	15.6		0.26
Non Emergency Calls	90%	287,422	351		5.85
Administrative Calls	6%	19,161	23.4		0.39
Total	100%	319,257	390		6.5
Hours per Year		1,825	(35 hours per week, 52.14 weeks per year)		
Effective Strength		175	Effective FTE's		
Actual Strength		227	Actual FTE's		
Relief Factor		1.30			

The last step is allocating personnel. Using the same method as previously discussed, there are three steps: 1) creating the distribution model, 2) identifying the proportional workload and allocating personnel.

Creating the Workload Distribution Model

To create the workload distribution model using MS Excel©, format a matrix of sixteen columns and twenty-seven rows:

1. 12 columns, one for each month
2. 1 column to identify the tour of duty
3. 1 column to identify the hour of the day
4. 1 column that sums the calls per tour
5. 1 column that shows the percentage of work by tour
6. 24 rows, one for each hour of the day
7. 1 row to serve as column headings
8. 1 row to subtotal the calls per month
9. 1 row to sum up the grand total of calls

The completed matrix should look like table 21:

Table 21						Workload Distribution by Month Sorted by Tour								
Tour Hour	Jan	Feb	Mar	Apr	May	Jun	Jul	Aug	Sep	Oct	Nov	Dec	Tour Total	% by Tour
2400 x 0800 0	12,592	1,258	1,254	2,101	4,896	9,988	8,589	8,756	3,654	2,544	2,011	1,233		
1	1,203	3,256	8,569	7,125	1,222	2,111	2,325	3,666	9,852	1,020	1,022	1,033		
2	1,203	1,247	1,200	2,011	2,012	1,233	1,488	1,200	1,369	1,950	1,233	1,000		
3	1,029	1,456	1,022	1,366	1,000	1,222	1,478	1,598	1,000	1,010	1,011	1,000		
4	1,236	4,589	1,244	1,325	3,266	1,999	1,588	1,477	1,544	1,222	2,311	1,211		
5	15,161	15,161	15,161	15,161	15,161	15,161	15,161	15,161	15,161	15,161	15,161	15,161		
6	13,131	13,131	13,131	13,131	13,131	13,131	13,131	13,131	13,131	13,131	13,131	13,131		
7	21,354	21,354	21,354	21,354	21,354	21,354	21,354	21,354	21,354	21,354	21,354	21,354	**751,382**	**23.51%**
0800 x 1600 8	1,656	1,656	1,656	1,656	1,656	1,656	1,656	1,656	1,656	1,656	1,656	1,656		
9	94,115	94,115	12,479	12,479	94,115	12,479	12,479	94,115	12,479	12,479	12,479	12,479		
10	25,984	25,984	22,944	22,944	25,984	22,944	22,944	25,984	22,944	22,944	22,944	22,944		
11	1,249	1,249	25,189	25,189	1,249	25,189	25,189	1,249	25,189	25,189	25,189	25,189		
12	1,203	3,256	8,569	7,125	1,222	4,562	6,458	1,022	1,544	1,020	1,022	1,033		
13	1,203	1,247	1,200	2,011	2,012	1,223	1,225	1,233	1,369	1,950	1,233	1,000		
14	1,029	1,456	1,022	1,366	1,000	1,222	1,478	1,598	1,000	1,010	1,011	1,000		
15	1,236	4,589	1,244	1,325	3,266	1,999	1,588	1,477	1,544	1,222	2,311	1,211	**1,082,306**	**33.86%**
1600 x 2400 16	25,694	25,694	55,858	55,858	25,694	55,858	55,858	25,694	55,858	55,858	55,858	55,858		
17	1,203	3,256	8,569	7,125	1,222	23,145	23,142	23,255	9,852	1,020	1,022	1,033		
18	1,203	1,247	1,200	2,011	35,485	23,145	12,458	12,452	1,369	1,950	1,233	1,000		
19	1,029	1,456	1,022	1,366	12,458	14,589	25,648	47,856	1,361	1,010	1,011	1,000		
20	1,236	4,589	1,244	1,325	3,266	14,576	12,489	15,489	1,544	1,222	2,311	1,211		
21	12,000	12,000	12,000	12,000	12,000	12,000	12,000	12,000	12,000	12,000	12,000	12,000		
22	12,548	12,548	12,548	12,548	12,548	12,548	12,548	12,548	12,548	12,548	12,548	12,548		
23	12,458	12,458	12,458	12,458	12,458	12,458	12,458	12,458	12,458	12,458	12,458	12,458	**1,362,617**	**42.63%**
SubTotal	261,955	268,252	242,137	242,360	307,677	305,792	304,732	356,429	241,780	222,928	223,520	218,743		
Grand Total	3,196,305													

For clarity, you can express this table graphically to get a visual sense of how the workload patterns appear for the year.

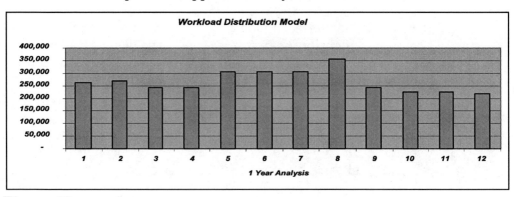

Figure 12

Identifying the Proportional Workload

Using the established tours, determine the proportional workload by tour: 2400 x 0800 = 751,382, 23.5%; 0800 x 1600 = 1,082,306, 33.8%; 1600 x 2400 = 1,362,617, 42.6%. Again, for clarity, you can express this graphically with a pie chart to show the relative proportions.

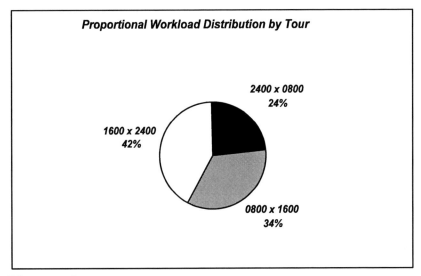

Figure 13

Allocating Personnel

The final step is allocating personnel according the proportional need. Simply multiply the total staff by the proportional workload to determine how many personnel are required (e.g., 227 × .2351 = 53).

Table 22	Proportional Distribution of Personnel		
Tour	Workload	Calculation	Staff
2400 x 0800	23.51%	227 x .2351	53
0800 x 1600	33.86%	227 x .3386	77
1600 x 2400	42.63%	227 x .4263	97

As with any staffing plan you may find that the current tour configuration is not necessarily the most efficient for personnel assignments. You may also find that the distribution model warrants creating an "overlap" tour, sometimes referred to as an "umbrella tour" to address peak workload demands. Overlapping tours can be thought of as a "tour within a tour" where the overlap begins a few hours after the primary tour and ends a few hours after the primary tour ends (e.g., 1000 × 1800; 1100 × 1900; 1900 × 0300; 1700 × 0100; 1800 × 0200;

2000 × 0400). Overlapping tours augment the primary tours and also ensure additional coverage during primary tour shift change.

Investigative Division Workload Analysis

Being assigned to the investigations division can be a rewarding assignment in the police department, except when the volume of work is so overwhelming that you cannot conduct a proper or thorough investigation, or when a large percentage of cases remain open because there is not enough time to conduct an adequate follow-up, or cases are lost at prosecution because mistakes were made during initial crime scene processing and evidence collection. The amount of evidence collected at the scene of a crime or whether a suspect is identified in the initial report, among other factors, contributes to case clearance. These shortcomings are generally manifestations of an excessive case load where sacrifices are made in the interest of time or when competing demands leave the investigative function short-handed. Policy decisions regarding staffing exist in all government bodies, not just police departments, and often reflect the will and priority of the individual agency. Although the research is mixed on whether the amount of time a detective spends on a case directly influences case closure, such as burglary or robbery, there is more evidence in support of this notion than opposed (Brandl and Frank, 1994).

One method to help reduce the volume of work is to use a decision model. A decision model is an objective way for personnel to decide if a follow-up investigation will proceed or if it will be suspended (Swanson, Chamelin and Territo, 1996:185-190). An example of a decision model is the investigative case screening process recommended by the Commission on Accreditation for Law Enforcement Agencies (CALEA, 2001:42.1.2). The CALEA standard recommends using "solvability factors" (Swanson, Chamelin and Territo, 1996:185) that yield the greatest chance of case clearance. Decision models can be used in conjunction with a workload analysis to "...improve management control over the productivity of investigations" (CALEA, 2001:42.1.2).

There is no direct comparison between the amount of work the patrol force will handle and the amount of work the detectives will handle. Patrol staffing levels can be evaluated in terms of response time or assignment thresholds for different types of calls, distribution of time for proactive police work, and other performance factors set by police administrators. Methods for evaluating investigative staffing needs are somewhat less sophisticated. Detectives only handle a portion of what patrol actually responds to, but the distinction is the complexity or degree of specialization, the rigor necessary to successfully prosecute, and the amount of time devoted to handling a single investigation.[80] The investigative workload is generally an outgrowth of what the patrol force generates and what the community directly makes the police department aware of, such as vice and narcotics complaints, self-initiated investigations notwithstanding. Some of the variables that affect investigative performance are:

1. "Role of patrol officers in conducting preliminary and follow-up investigations;
2. Skill level and knowledge of investigative techniques on the part of both patrol and investigative personnel;
3. Quality of preliminary investigation reports completed by patrol officers;
4. Effectiveness of quality control procedures for preliminary investigations;
5. Level of support from crime analysis and other information systems;
6. Level of community willingness to participate in the justice system;
7. Degree to which investigators spend time on administrative or support functions;
8. Effectiveness of efforts to collect, analyze, and present physical evidence in court" (Sullivan, et. al., 1994:43).

Equally frustrating for many detective commanders is the department's stance on creating new detectives positions. What most often happens is that an arbitrary number of detectives positions are created with no thought given to the amount of work they will encounter. Detectives usually number between 10% and 30% of the total sworn force; a traditional number is about 10% or 12% of the patrol force, but this is arbitrary, and is not linked to empirical data. Granted, there is a budgetary impact in promoting detectives but the costs to the city could be far greater if crimes are not solved, offenders are not held accountable and the citizens are not satisfied. Using the figures described in the patrol force workload analysis, Table 6, we will examine how many detectives are required to investigate the crimes documented by patrol.

The detective division does not investigate every call the patrol force responds to answer. They only investigate a percentage of the calls for various reasons, among them: 1) patrol officers determine that no crime has been committed, 2) the crime reported differs from the actual crime, 3) the crime is exceptionally cleared and does not require an investigation, or 4) the crime occurred in another jurisdiction. The procedure for establishing the investigative workload derives from the method for the patrol force workload. In fact, when designing the patrol workload spreadsheet in MS Excel© it is wise to create the investigative workload worksheet at the same time using figures derived from the patrol workload. This will save development time, but also will link the worksheets so as changes are made in one, they are simultaneously made in the other. Table 23 reveals that based upon patrol's workload, the investigation division will handle 34,622 investigations totaling 96,040 hours.

Table 23			Investigative Workload Analysis			
			Investigative Acuity			
Investigative Demands	Hours Per Unit	Units Per Year	Detectives Required	Total Employee Hours Per Modality	Detectives Assigned	% of Patrol Workload
Arrest (average for all types of arrests)	1.5	17,458	1	26,187	21	---
Arson	6	51	1	306	0	100
Assault (shooting, stabbing, blunt force)	4	900	1	3,600	3	90
Back up for Other detectives' assignments	1.5	365	2	1,095	1	---
Bomb Threat	5	12	1	60	0	100
Burglary	6	1,126	1	6,757	5	60
Carjacking	4	62	1	246	0	80
Court	1.5	246	3	1,107	1	---
Domestic Violence	5	3,092	1	15,461	12	95
Drug Sales	3	1,512	2	9,074	7	30
Fire (car, house, building)	5	123	1	615	0	100
Fraud	4	42	1	169	0	20
Juvenile Condition (curfew, truancy and all others)	3.5	229	1	800	1	50
Kidnapping	20	11	3	660	1	100
Murder	30	41	2	2,460	2	100
Rape	11	79	1	871	1	90
Robbery	8	1,477	1	11,816	9	70
Stolen Vehicle Report	0.75	2,513	1	1,885	2	95
Suicide	4	22	1	88	0	100
Theft (shoplifting and all others)	3	3,261	1	9,783	8	50
Warrant Service	0.75	2,000	2	3,000	2	---
Total		34,622		96,040	77	

A few points need clarification in the "detectives assigned" column. First, it will take 21 FTE detectives to handle arrests, not that 21 additional detectives will need to be assigned; rather, the amount of work, in hours, is equivalent to losing 21 detectives. Said differently, it means that the work entailed in processing 17,458 1½ hour arrests is equivalent to 21 full-time detectives. Next, notice there are zeros entered beside a few categories of investigations, such as suicide, fraud and carjacking. This does not mean that a detective is not needed to investigate the matter, quite obviously the crime must be investigated. Rather, it means that an FTE detective is not required because so few assignments over the course of one year do not necessitate a full-time detective. Those assignments that have zeros entered for the "detective assigned" category can be investigated by other detectives without any impact to the detectives' other work demands.

After establishing the principal modalities, the next step is to distribute the detectives' time across three management categories: investigative, administrative and proactive activities. Similar to patrol officers, detectives do not only handle investigations but have other responsibilities such as attending meetings, preparing and organizing case files, preparing for trial and proactive field work. Table 24 shows the distribution of time. In this example detectives will spend 80% of their time conducting investigations, 10% handling administrative details and 10% conducting proactive field work. This distribution of time necessitates assigning seventy-seven (77) detectives to handle 120,050 hours of investigations.[81] For simplicity and illustration purposes only, this staffing model does not include the relief factor. If detectives were required to work two or three tours, then the appropriate relief factor would be calculated. This example is based on a 5-day, 40-hour schedule, Monday through Friday.

Table 24		Distribution of Detectives' Time		
Activity	%	Hours/year	Minutes/daily	Hours/daily
Investigative	80%	96,040	384	6.4
Administrative	10%	12,005	48	0.8
Proactive	10%	12,005	48	0.8
Total	100%	120,050	480	8.0
Availability		1,558	Hours/yr	
Actual Strength		77	Detectives	

Activity-base Budgeting[82]

Creating a Nexus Between Workload and Costs

At some point in an executive's career they will be required to develop a budget for something. Indeed it is a prime responsibility. A budget is merely a plan described in financial terms. Knowing which budget plan to choose is a matter of what message needs to be conveyed. There are many different budget styles, each with a different purpose. For example, the most common government budget is the *line-item* style, which answers the question: what is to be bought? This budget plan is oriented toward control and economy. A *program budget* answers the question: what is to be achieved? This budget plan is oriented toward planning and effectiveness. And a *performance budget* answers the question: what is to be done? This plan is oriented toward management and efficiency (Riley, and Colby, 191). Each has its place depending upon the goal. However, one budget style, which has gained popularity over the last few years, has the ability to link activities to costs, giving executives a better understanding of the full costs of service and resource allocation. This plan is an activity-base budget (ABB). ABB has been used successfully by small police departments, such as Van Buren, Arkansas, and large police departments, such as Newark, New Jersey, to validate deployment efficiency and service delivery costs.

Activity-base budgeting is an economic model that grew out of Activity-base costing (ABC), which is similar to zero-based budgeting (Maddux, 1999). This budget type accounts for how staff members allocate their effort among activities. Once the full cost of each activity has been calculated, drivers can be established that link support activities to the primary activities of the organization—in a law enforcement environment the primary activities are the direct costs of program delivery (Maddux, 1999) (e.g., patrol services, investigations, tactical operations, communications, traffic control, jail operations, etc.). By developing a comprehensive activity-base budget executives are able to create a clear nexus between workload and costs. Once developed, executives and managers can exercise control in several ways:

1. Assign personnel based upon a demonstrated need,
2. Expand or contract personnel proportionately as the need changes,
3. Uncover waste and hidden costs,
4. View which activities are most and least expensive, thus subjecting them to review,
5. Assess the full efficiency of the organization,
6. Identify places to cut spending,
7. Establish a cost baseline that may be influenced through process or technology changes that reduce effort requirements for the activity, (Maddux, 1999:228) and, perhaps most importantly,
8. Argue from an informed, objective position in favor of the organization's budget.

There are 13 steps to creating an activity-base budget:

1. Identify the principal modalities (the major activities) and factor the acuity
2. Distribute time across management categories
3. Calculate the relief factor
4. Identify the supervisory staff
5. Identify the management staff
6. Identify the support staff
7. Identify the total FTE complement
8. Perform salary calculations
9. Identify material costs
10. Identify equipment costs
11. Create the present level of service (i.e., the ABB)
12. Create a budget summary
13. Create a budget allocation graph

Since workload, staffing and relief factoring have already been discussed, this section will analyze the activities of a hypothetical patrol force to determine: 1) how many personnel are required to handle the workload, 2) the salary, material and equipment costs, and 3) the distribution of time across primary management categories. This example presumes an existing department budget from which to begin; ABB is not a zero-base budget.[83] This section begins with a discussion of some basic budgeting principles and strategies for successful budget preparation followed by a sample activity-base budget for the patrol force.

Accountability and the Politics of Budgeting

Accountability

Being entrusted with public monies requires the utmost integrity and responsibility. In recent years there have been efforts afoot to make budgets more readable and understandable and public policy advocates have created laymen's guides to navigating budgets.[84] An ABB is transparent and eliminates hidden costs. Not only does it afford a reader the ability to see where the funds are being spent, it gives a manager who has oversight the ability to see at a glance the most expensive activities and where to exercise control.

One of the keys to accountability is to ensure the manager assigned to the budget has real control over the resources that take the form of decision-making authority, information and skills. "A manager cannot be responsible for a budget in which they have no authority to approve expenditures" (Maddux, 1999:20).

The Politics of Budgeting

Appropriations battles are common. In fact, as an executive charged with budget implementation and control, appropriations battles are expected from subordinate personnel who look to the executive to exercise leadership and argue on their behalf, for what they need to carry out their functions. Police Chief Gil Kerlikowske, Seattle Police Department, echoed these sentiments at the 2006 ASC meeting in Los Angeles. In his presentation Chief Kerlikowske mentioned that policing is an expensive, labor-intensive endeavor that has enormous budget implications; the cost of policing urban America is a leadership challenge police executives must assume within a defined budget.[85] In preparing for battle it is useful to know a few things about the budget process: 1) "budgets reflect choices about what government will and will not do, 2) budgets reflect priorities—between police and flood control, day care and road repair, 3) budgets reflect the relative proportion of decisions made for local and constituency purpose, and for efficiency and effectiveness, and broader public goals. Public budgets are not merely technical managerial documents; they are also intrinsically and irreducibly political" (Rubin, 2000). Since budgets are politically driven it is also useful to know the elected leaders' platform, which is often mutually beneficial when seeking funds. The police department will compete with the other departments of city government for limited funds, so it is of paramount importance for the executive to prepare a sound budget justification.

To that end one of the best things a police executive can do to maximize his or her chances of being successful during budget appropriations hearings is to develop and adhere to performance standards, such as those suggested earlier. A study by McManus (1984) revealed that 8 out of 10 "...Houston-area local governments did not report measures of effectiveness or efficiency (Grizzle, 1987; in Miller, Hildreth and Rabin, 2001:203). She concluded that without creating a nexus between inputs and outputs "any justification of spending cuts or reordering of priorities is extremely difficult and likely to subject those doing the cutting and reordering to charges of political favoritism" (in Miller, Hildreth and Rabin, 2001:203).

Successful Budget Strategies and Justification

Strategies

Strategies differ from justifications. A strategy is an approach; a careful plan or method; the art of devising or employing plans toward a goal. A justification means to prove or show to be just, right, or reasonable; to show to have had a sufficient legal reason.[86] The chief executive's goal is to retain the agency's base budget, and, if possible, to increase it above the current year's appropriations. Developing a logical strategy is the means to that end.

In November 2002, the Police Executive Research Forum (PERF) posted the final draft of roundtable discussions with several police chiefs from around the country. Among the different budget strategies that were considered, using crime and workload data was first on the list (PERF, 2002). Other research by Greene, Bynum and Cordner (1986) revealed that "increased workload was the second greatest factor contributing to an increase in positions" (Greene, Bynum and Cordner, 1986). While not infallible, workload data is reasonable and objective. The other strategies discussed by PERF were to: 1) "capitalize on sensational crime incidents (ideally not occurring locally), 2) carefully mobilize interest groups, 3) plan strategically, 4) participate fully in the federal grant process, 5) maintain a close working relationship with the local chief executive and governing board members, and 6) involve all levels of the police department" (PERF, 2002:2).[87]

Other data that can support a budget proposal includes: 1) aggregate population and population density, 2) racial and ethnic composition of the city, 3) age composition, 4) gender composition, 5) education levels, 6) median household income, and 7) per capita and household income.

Justification

Budget strategies and their attendant analysis are important, but justification is the main ingredient to the success for the agency's budget. A solid justification includes all of the relevant information for the legislative body, the budget office and the city's chief executive. Performance measures are a very important part of justifying one's budget. Grizzle's research (1985:357) helped to "...develop a tool that agencies can use to screen potential performance measures systematically in order to choose measures worth including in their budget request justifications." When deciding on performance measures a series of questions "...should be answered in order to evaluate each potential measure against a specific criterion" (Grizzle, 1985:357).

The resulting framework was this:

I. **"TECHNICAL ADEQUACY**
    A. Valid. Does the measure logically represent the concept or construct to be measured?
        1. Complete. *Does the measure cover the entire concept or construct?*
        2. Unique. *Does the measure represent some concept or construct not covered by any other measure in this set?*
    B. Reliable. *If a measurement is repeated, will the results be identical? Are there fluctuations in the characteristics to be measured, changes in transient personal or situational factors, or inconsistencies in the measurement procedure that cause variation in the measurement obtained?*
    C. Accurate. *Is the measurement free of systematic error?*
II. **PRACTICALITY**
    A. Cost. *How much will data collection or analysis cost?*
    B. Ease of data collection. *What is the anticipated ease or difficulty of obtaining data needed to make the measurement?*
III. **UTILITY-USER INDEPENDENT**
    A. Comparable. *Can this measure be used to compare different programs with each other?*
    B. Sensitive. *Is the discriminating power of the measurement procedure sufficient to capture the variation that occurs in the object, event or situation being measured?*
    C. Clear. *Can the meaning of the measure be understood?*
IV. **UTILITY-USER DEPENDENT**
    A. Relevant to decision. *Does the measure provide information needed to make a decision about the performance of a program or agency?*
    B. Timely. *Are changes in the objects, events, or situations being measured reflected quickly enough in the measurements to be available before the decision must be made?*
    C. Controllable. *To what extent can the user of the measure affect the measurements, providing resources are made available?"* (Grizzle, 1985:359).

Budgets should be justified in three separate spending categories: mandatory, base and discretionary.

Budget justification categories

Mandatory expenditures are those governed by federal, state or local law (e.g., social security, pension, unemployment contributions, and contractually negotiated benefits). Salaries may also fall into this category, except for those that may be considered discretionary. It is best to justify mandatory budget expenditures by citing the applicable laws (i.e., federal, state, local).

Base expenditures are defined as those that are essential for the agency's continued operation. These include utilities, equipment, supplies and materials, printing and other consumables (i.e., operating expenses). Justification in this category comes from analyzing previous budgets and projections for service delivery. The executive must be prepared to explain increases in operating expenditures, such as developing a special task force to address a spike in drug crime. Workload data and performance-improvement data are always welcomed by budget review members.

Discretionary expenditures are those that enhance an existing level of service. These expenditures do not affect the agency's operations, but they do contribute to improved service delivery or a particular program's efficiency. A good example is hiring; by hiring more officers the agency expects to improve response time, and reduce fear of crime, but not having the extra officers does not adversely impact the agency's ability to provide basic service. In defending discretionary spending it is imperative for the executive to convince the budget review members of necessity or worthiness of the proposal. Once again workload and performance data are at the top of the list for developing the rationale.

The Workload Analysis

A recurring theme in budget development is objectivity. An objective budget, based on empirical data, is the most reasonable and the easiest to justify. A question that is often raised in law enforcement circles is: how many officers do we need? Or, how many officers should we have? Typical responses sound like this: as many as we can afford; as many as the Mayor and Council want; as many as the people of the city are willing to pay for. While there is merit to these statements, "the only logical and defensible means of determining how many persons should be assigned to patrol duty is through a careful and systematic analysis of the duties performed by patrol officers" (Hale, 1981). This is true of any position within the police department, and the first step toward a logical budget justification is a workload analysis.

Collecting the Data

The workload analysis that supports ABB is identical to the workload analysis examples presented earlier in this text. We will proceed through another workload example to illustrate all of the steps in ABB. The ABB process begins by collecting data on activity, in the case of the patrol force this is calls for service (CFS). Again, it is important to have at least one full year's worth of data in order to account for seasonal fluctuations or other anomalies that might occur. A better data set is two full years worth of CFS data to account for the same fluctuations and also to account for personnel trends. For example, if officers are hired or officers are separated from employment throughout the year this may adversely impact how CFS are handled including the amount of time required to do so. The data set must include the same items as previously discussed when developing a workload analysis:

1. Type of call (principal modalities)
2. Average number of hours spent handling a single call[88]
3. Number of calls of that type (for the year or the period being examined)
4. Number of officers required to handle a single call, and
5. Total employee hours per modality, and[89]
6. Percentage allocated

The first step involves two parts:

1. capturing the principal modalities and
2. factoring the acuity

There are some basic calculations that must be performed here since the remainder of the analysis is predicated upon the level of effort that is required.

The first step is to identify the principal modalities. In the case of the patrol force the principal modalities are the service demands (i.e., the calls for service), which must be itemized in the first column. The second column is the *hours per unit*. The individual calls for service are also referred to as "units," a single call for service is 1 unit. This is the average amount of time it takes to handle a single call for service of the type (e.g., handling a single stolen vehicle report will take an average of 1 hour to complete). Again, any portion of an hour must be calculated as such (e.g., .5 = 30 minutes; .75 = 45 minutes). To find the portion of an hour simply divide the number of minutes by 60 (e.g., 25 minutes = 25 ÷ 60 = .416 hours; 1 hour and 25 minutes = 1.416 minutes). If you already know the portion of an hour and want to know how many minutes the portion represents, simply multiply the portion by .6, then multiply the product by 100 (e.g., (.416 × .6) × 100 = 25 minutes).

The third column is *units per year*. The units per year is the total number of CFS for that type (e.g., there were 58 CFS for wires down for the year). Here you must identify how many units there are for each modality. After you have itemized each call for service, sum the column, this figure will be used again later. The sum of the units per year is 115,044. The fourth column is *officers required*. This is the number of officers that are typically needed to handle the call safely and efficiently. There is no standard and the numbers will vary based upon labor agreement or managerial prerogative. The fifth column is the *total employee hours per modality*. This represents the total number of hours required to handle all of the units.

The total employee hours per modality is derived by simple multiplication:

total employee hours per modality = hours per unit × units per year × officers required

For example, a call for an animal complaint takes 1 officer one half hour to complete. Over the course of one year 1,825 animal complaints were received for a total of 913 employee hours (e.g., 913 = .5 × 1825 × 1). Repeat these calculations for each modality and then sum the total employee hours per modality. The sum of units per year and total employee hour per modality serve as the foundation for future calculations and for ABB development. The sum of hours per employee modality is 318,216. The last column is *percentage allocated*. This is optional but recommended since it will give the reader an excellent visual representation of which activities consume the most and least of the budget. The percentage allocated is derived by dividing the total employee hours per modality by the sum of the employee hours per modality, then multiplying the product by 100 (e.g., 15.4 = (49000 ÷ 318216) × 100).

Table 25 shows that arrests consume 30.75 percent of the time and court appearances consume 15.4 percent of the time. The percentages can be ordered from highest to lowest, or vice versa, and contrasted against each other for comparison purposes. This is where efficiency begins to reveal itself. Restated, this method allows the executive to see where time is spent, thus influencing processes or technology changes that reduce effort requirements for the activity. This completes the first part of the ABB. The next step is to distribute the officers' time across management categories.

Table 25		Patrol Workload Analysis					
Principal Modalities (Major Activities)							
				Acuity			
Service Demands	Hours Per Unit	Units Per Year	% of Total	Officers Required	Total Employee Hours Per Modality	Percentage Allocation	
Aggravated Assault	1.5	1,365	1.19%	2	4,095	1.29%	
Animal Complaint	0.5	1,825	1.59%	1	913	0.29%	
Arrest (average for all types of arrests)	1.5	32,612	28.35%	2	97,836	30.75%	
Arson	2	242	0.21%	2	968	0.30%	
Assist Officer (back up)	0.25	152	0.13%	2	76	0.02%	
Assist Other Agency (EMS, Fire, Public Works)	0.75	2,269	1.97%	1	1,702	0.53%	
Bomb Threat	1	12	0.01%	2	24	0.01%	
Burglar Alarm (residential, commercial)	0.5	3,285	2.86%	2	3,285	1.03%	
Burglary	1	2,292	1.99%	2	4,584	1.44%	
Carjacking	1	77	0.07%	2	154	0.05%	
Code Enforcement Violations	0.33	414	0.36%	1	137	0.04%	
Court Appearances	2	2,450	2.13%	10	49,000	15.40%	
Criminal Mischief/Vandalism	0.5	3,002	2.61%	1	1,501	0.47%	
Disorderly Conduct (fights, crowds)	0.75	6,210	5.40%	2	9,315	2.93%	

Table 25				Patrol Workload Analysis		
Principal Modalities (Major Activities)						
				Acuity		
Service Demands	Hours Per Unit	Units Per Year	% of Total	Officers Required	Total Employee Hours Per Modality	Percentage Allocation
Domestic Violence	1.5	3,255	2.83%	2	9,765	3.07%
Drug Sales	0.75	5,041	4.38%	2	7,562	2.38%
DWI	2	52	0.05%	2	208	0.07%
Emotionally Disturbed Person	1	120	0.10%	4	480	0.15%
Fire (car, house, building)	1.5	123	0.11%	2	369	0.12%
Fraud/Forgery	1	313	0.27%	1	313	0.10%
Gambling Offense	0.75	468	0.41%	1	351	0.11%
HazMat Condition/Dangerous Circumstances	1	2,366	2.06%	2	4,732	1.49%
Juvenile Condition (curfew, truancy and all others)	0.75	1,211	1.05%	2	1,817	0.57%
Kidnapping	3	11	0.01%	2	66	0.02%
Liquor/Tavern Violation	1.5	3,548	3.08%	2	10,644	3.34%
Motor Vehicle Accident (with or without injuries)	1.5	1,825	1.59%	2	5,475	1.72%
Murder	4	81	0.07%	2	648	0.20%
MV Pursuit	0.75	177	0.15%	4	531	0.17%
Noise Complaint	0.33	1,987	1.73%	2	1,311	0.41%
Open Door Condition	0.75	1,547	1.34%	2	2,321	0.73%
Parking Complaint	0.33	3,698	3.21%	1	1,220	0.38%
Person with a Weapon	0.42	401	0.35%	4	674	0.21%
Prostitution	0.33	2,113	1.84%	2	1,395	0.44%
Public Intoxication/Public Consumption	1	3,321	2.89%	2	6,642	2.09%
Rape	2.5	85	0.07%	2	425	0.13%
Receiving Stolen Property	1	2,221	1.93%	2	4,442	1.40%
Robbery	1.5	1,304	1.13%	2	3,912	1.23%
School Crossing	2	900	0.78%	5	9,000	2.83%
Shots Fired	0.33	1,460	1.27%	2	964	0.30%
Sick/Injured Person	0.75	720	0.63%	1	540	0.17%
Simple Assault	1.1	2,478	2.15%	1	2,726	0.86%
Stolen Vehicle Report	1	6,018	5.23%	1	6,018	1.89%
Street Collapse	1	14	0.01%	2	28	0.01%
Suicide	1.5	22	0.02%	2	66	0.02%
Suspicious Person/Vehicle	0.5	2,899	2.52%	2	2,899	0.91%
Theft (shoplifting and all others)	0.75	6,522	5.67%	2	9,783	3.07%
Traffic Control	4	2,190	1.90%	5	43,800	13.76%
Train Accident	8	1	0.00%	4	32	0.01%
Vicious Animal	0.4	214	0.19%	2	171	0.05%
Warrant Service	4	73	0.06%	11	3,212	1.01%
Wires Down	0.75	58	0.05%	2	87	0.03%
Total		**115,044**	**100%**		**318,216**	**100%**

Distributing Officers' Time Across Management Categories

The next step is one of the most important in the budget development process, because what happens with the distribution of time directly affects the budget. After the baseline calculations are performed it is necessary to distribute the time across three primary categories: service demands (i.e., CFS), administrative, and proactive activities.[90] These are industry-accepted categories and may differ based upon local priority. The categories can also be more specific to give managers a better understanding of how an officer's time is delegated. For example, instead of capturing the broad category of "proactive activities," a manager could be more specific by listing directed patrols, community policing activities and street surveillance.

The first category, service demands, is critical since handling calls for service is usually the police department's first priority. Gay, Schell and Schack (1977) characterize calls for service as the "the single most important element for structuring and directing police patrol operations."

When you begin with service demands the other categories receive their allotted time based on what is allotted in this category. The sum of employee hours per modality (318,216) represents 100% of the workload. Obviously, there are other things police officers must do besides respond to calls for service, such as administrative activities (i.e., submitting reports, attending meetings) and proactive activities (i.e., community policing, directed or self-initiated activities). It is not realistic to formulate a budget around 100% of calls for service without accounting for a police officer's other responsibilities. This is where prudent management decisions must be made regarding how much of the officers' time the department is willing to distribute across these management categories. Stated differently, the lower the percentage of time that is allocated for service demands, the more police officers the department will need.

To create the distribution matrix, begin with five columns and six rows. The column headings are: 1) activity, 2) percent, 3) hours per year, 4) daily minutes and 5) daily hours. The row headings are: 1) service demands, 2) administrative activities, 3) proactive activities, 4) total, 5) scheduled hours and 6) effective strength. For illustration purposes the distribution is 55 percent for service demands, 10 percent for administrative activities, and 35 percent for proactive activities. Ironically, the first calculation to be performed is the total hours per year; this will tell you how many hours per year are required to conduct patrol operations. This is derived by dividing the total employee hours per modality by the percentage of time allocated for service demands; in this case 55% of the time is allotted for service demands (578,575 = 318,216 ÷ .55). The next step is to apportion the remaining 45% of hours to the other activity categories, in this case administrative and proactive activities. This is accomplished by multiplying the percentage allotted by the total hours per year (578,573 administrative activities = 578,575 × .1; 202,501 proactive activities = 578,575 × .35).

The next two steps are to calculate how many daily minutes and how many daily hours each category represents. The "daily minutes" are derived by multiplying the percentage of time allocated to the category by the number of minutes in the work day; a standard 8-hour work day equals 480 minutes. The amount of time spent handling service demands is 264 minutes (264 = .55 × 480). The "daily hours" are derived by dividing the daily minutes by 60. In this example service demands account for 4.4 hours per day (4.4 = 264 × 60). The last step is to calculate the effective patrol strength. This is derived by dividing the total hours per year by the number of hours an officer is *scheduled* to work, not by how many hours the officer is *available* to work. The number of scheduled hours is simply the hours per week multiplied by the number of weeks in the year. In this example the officers are scheduled to work 2,086 hours per year (2,086 = 40 × 52.14). The effective patrol strength is 277 officers for 578,575 hours of work per year (277 = 578,575 ÷ 2,086). Once again, since officers do not work 2,086 hours per year the relief factor must be calculated. The relief factor in this example is 1.34 making the actual patrol strength 371 officers. Table 26 is the completed time distribution matrix.

Table 26		Distribution of Time Across Management Categories		
Activity	%	Hours/year	Daily/Minutes	Daily/Hours
Service Demands	55%	318,216	264	4.4
Administrative	10%	57,857	48	0.8
Proactive	35%	202,501	168	2.8
Total	**100%**	**578,575**	**480**	**8**
Scheduled Hours		**2,086**	(40 hours per week, 52.14 weeks per year)	
Effective Strength		**277.41**	FTE Patrol Officers	

Relief Factor

We have already discussed how to develop a relief factor model, so table 27 is simply the completed RF model for the ABB presented here.

Table 27 (Relief Factor)	Time Off in Hours					
Time Off	Captain	Lieutenant	Sergeant	Police Officer	Detective	Civilian Aide
Vacation	224	216	208	200	200	112
Compensatory	40	40	40	40	40	16
Sick Leave	120	120	120	120	120	96
Personal	24	24	24	24	24	16
Training	64	64	64	64	64	16
Bereavement	80	80	80	80	80	40
Total Time Off	**552**	**544**	**536**	**528**	**528**	**296**
Work Year	2,086	2,086	2,086	2,086	2,086	2,086
Personnel Availability	1,534	1,542	1,550	1,558	1,558	1,790
Relief Factor	**1.36**	**1.35**	**1.35**	**1.34**	**1.34**	**1.17**

Management, Supervisory and Support Staff Positions

All police departments operate with command rank personnel, supervisors and support staff. These positions are usually determined by fixed-post formula or by accepted industry ratios, in some cases they are established by labor agreement. The first subsection is management. This is the command staff personnel for the division. In this example there is one captain who is assigned as the commanding officer (CO) and one lieutenant who is assigned as the executive officer (XO). Both the CO and XO are assigned by fixed-post position not by formula. Also, neither the CO nor the XO require relief so the relief factor does not apply. Table 28 is the management plan.

Table 28	Management Staff		
Not by ratio (fixed post): 1 Captain per command	**Captain**	**1**	effective strength
Not by ratio (fixed post): 1 Executive Officer	**Executive Lieutenant**	**1**	effective strength
	Total	**2**	FTE Command Staff (managers)

The supervisory staff in this example is devised by formula. The sergeants' position is calculated at 1 sergeant per 7 officers and the lieutenants' position is calculated at 1 lieutenant per 5 sergeants. To calculate the number of sergeants required simply divide the number of police officers by the predetermined number of sergeants, in this case seven ($53.06 = 371 \div 7$). The same formula applies to the lieutenants' position ($10.61 = 53.06 \div 5$). Table 29 shows that based on 1:7 ratio for sergeants and 1:5 ratio for lieutenants a total of 64 supervisors will be required to supervise the workload.

Table 29	Supervisory Staff		
By ratio: 1 Sergeant per 7 officers	**Sergeants**	**53.06**	effective strength
1 Lieutenant per 5 Sergeants	**Lieutenants**	**10.61**	effective strength
	Total	**63.67**	FTE Supervisory Staff

The supervisory staff in this example is also derived by formula. The job title "civilian aide" is apportioned at 2 per manager. Since we have identified two managers, the captain and the executive officer, then 4 support staff members are required. This is simple multiplication of managers by the ratio of support staff ($4 = 2 \times 2$). Table 30 is the completed support staff model.

Table 30	Support Staff for Management		
By ratio: 2 support staff members per manager (Civilian aides)		**4**	effective strength
	Total	**4**	FTE Support Staff

Identify the Total FTE Complement

The total FTE complement is a matrix that displays all of the division's personnel after the relief factor is calculated for each position. This is simply a subtotal of personnel and the actual strength for each job title based upon both the workload requirements and the staffing needs. Table 31 is the completed FTE subtotal.

Table 31	FTE Complement (includes relief factor)			
	Complement	Work Hours	Relief?	
Captain	1	9-5 MF	No	Actual Strength
Executive Lieutenant	1	9-5 MF	No	Actual Strength
Lieutenant	14	24/7	Yes	Actual Strength
Sergeant	71	24/7	Yes	Actual Strength
Patrol Officer	371	24/7	Yes	Actual Strength
Civilian Aides	4	9-5 MF	No	Actual Strength
Total FTE's	**462**			Actual Strength

The total personnel required to staff the patrol division is 462. Now that workload and staffing has been projected, the results will be used to develop the activity-base budget.

Budget Development

In this section we begin to attribute costs to operations based upon salaries and the costs for materials and equipment. There are eight components of the budget:

1. Salaries
2. Salary rate per employee hour
3. Cost for materials
4. Unit cost for materials
5. Cost for equipment
6. Unit cost for equipment
7. ABB present level of service
8. Budget summary

Salary Calculations and the Rate per Employee Hour

The first element of ABB is calculating salaries. The largest expenditure of virtually every budget is personnel; in many instances personnel account for more than 90 percent of total budget expenses. The goal in this section is to establish the rate per employee hour. The purpose of establishing this figure is to create a baseline from which to work. This figure is also necessary for monitoring purposes: if cuts must be made, it may not be possible to do so from salaries since salaries are usually governed by the labor agreement. Knowing how much it costs to perform the required work is beneficial to managers and supervisors as they monitor individual and collective performance. Begin by creating a table with five columns: 1) FTEs, 2) salaries, 3) benefits cost, 4) salary cost and 5) job title.

Next, transcribe the FTE requirements from the FTE complement table (figure 18). Then, insert the salary for each job title and the cost for benefits. Benefits are usually calculated as a percentage of the salary costs. Next, calculate the salary costs for each job title. This is accomplished by adding salary and benefits and multiplying by the FTE's (patrol officers = $30,869,938

= ($69,255 + $13,851) × 371.45). Perform this calculation for each job title and sum the salaries. Once you have the total salary costs, divide the total salary costs by the total employee hours per modality. This will give you the rate per employee hour ($123.92 = $39,433,294 ÷ 318,216).To calculate the rate per employee hour use this equation:

**rate per employee hour = (salary × "X"% benefits) × FTE
÷ total employee hours per modality**

Table 32 is the completed salary calculations and the rate per employee hour.

Table 32				Salary Calculations (includes relief factor)
FTE	Salary	Benefits at 20%	Salary Cost	Job Title
371.45	$69,255	$13,851	$30,869,938	Patrol Officers
1.00	$96,104	$19,221	$115,325	Captain
1.00	$87,573	$17,515	$105,088	Executive Lieutenant
14.36	$86,573	$17,315	$1,491,621	Lieutenant
71.42	$78,310	$15,662	$6,711,432	Sergeant
4.00	$29,144	$5,829	$139,891	Civilian Aides
463.23			$39,433,294	Total Salary Cost
		divided by	318,216	total employee hours per modality
		Rate per employee hour	$123.92	

Calculating Materials and Equipment Costs

The next two categories to be accounted for are materials and equipment. In lean fiscal times training and equipment budgets are the first to be reduced. Materials usually consist of consumable supplies such as pens, paper, flares, crime scene tape and other office supplies. Finding the unit cost for materials is a simple calculation based on a fixed amount per employee. In this example materials are appropriated at $2,500 per employee, or $1,158,075 total. The unit cost is derived by dividing the total cost ($1,158,075) by the number of units per year (115,014). The unit cost for materials is $10.07.

Table 33	Materials	
Training, Fuel, Paper, Pencils, Reports, Forms, Crime Scene Tape, Flares and all other Consumable Supplies (@ 2,500 per employee)	$1,158,075	
	$1,158,075	
divided by	115,044	units per year
Unit Cost	$10.07	

Equipment is a larger category that consists of all the items necessary to carry out the patrol function properly and safely. The equipment category consists of tangible assets acquired through donation, purchase, loan, or capital lease with a useful life of more than one year and a cost of $2,000 or more; however, this is not a rule, just a guidepost. Equipment costs are calculated by spreading the cost of individual items across the useful life of the equipment. Since having to incur the full cost of the equipment will not come until it must be fully replaced, the cost is predicated upon its useful life. The equation is:

cost = (quantity × unit cost) ÷ useful life in years

The total cost for equipment is $1,647,211. The unit cost is derived the same way as the unit cost for materials; the unit cost for equipment is $14.324. Table 34 depicts the total and unit cost for materials and equipment.

Table 34	Equipment			
	Quantity	Unit Cost	Useful Life/yrs	Cost
Computers	100	$1,500	5	$30,000
Shotguns	80	$700	15	$3,733
Typewriters	100	$300	3	$10,000
Marked Police Cars	110	$35,000	3	$1,283,333
Prisoner Vans	4	$40,000	5	$32,000
First Aid Kit and Replacements	75	$140	2	$5,250
Non Traditional Vehicles	7	$19,000	6	$22,167
Night Vision Equipment	3	$7,500	7	$3,214
Portable Police Radios	500	$1,200	7	$85,714
Walk-through Metal Detector	4	$5,500	10	$2,200
Gas Masks	500	$320	7	$22,857
Siren and Police Radio	80	$3,000.00	5	$48,000
Mesh Traffic Vests	200	$30	2	$3,000
Tripod Scene Lighting	3	$1,000	6	$500
Megaphones	6	$90	7	$77
Prisoner Leg irons	5	$43	10	$22
Snow Blower	2	$2,600	7	$743
Laser Printers	30	$1,400	4	$10,500
Unmarked Police Cars	10	$28,000	5	$56,000
Traffic Cones	200	$35	5	$1,400
Suites of Furniture	20	$4,000	8	$10,000
Photocopier	3	$25,000	5	$15,000
Fax	10	$300	2	$1,500
				$1,647,211
			divided by	115,044 units per year
			=	$14.32 equip. per unit

Present Level of Service

The final step is to calculate the costs for the present level of service. This is where all of the previous calculations are reconciled to form the ABB. The first step is to replicate the table that holds the principal modalities. Again, the principal modalities serves as the foundation upon which the remainder of the budget will rest. A few additional calculations are necessary to arrive at the total cost. These include salary per hour, salary per unit, material per unit, equipment per unit, and unit cost.

Salary per Hour

The salary per hour per modality cost is calculated by multiplying the rate per employee hour ($123.92, table 32) by the total number of officers required. For example, the total number of officers required to handle a murder is 2; multiply this by the rate per employee hour and the salary per hour is $247.84.

salary per hour = rate per employee hour × total officers required

Per Unit Costs

"Unit costs compare the volume of work anticipated to the items needed to complete the work and the funds required to purchase the items. This method [is] used to justify the need for personnel or equipment..." (Riley and Colby, 1991:54). This is the most salient feature of activity-base budgeting since identifying the individual costs is what this budget plan seeks to accomplish.

Salary per Unit

The salary per unit cost is calculated by multiplying the hours per unit (3) by the salary per hour (murder = $247.84). The salary per unit cost for the modality "murder" is $991.36.

salary per unit = hours per unit × salary per hour

Unit Cost

The unit cost is the sum of salary per unit ($991.36), materials per unit ($10.07), and equipment per unit ($14.32) costs. The unit cost for "murder" is $1,015.74.

unit cost = salary per unit + material per unit + equipment per unit

Total Costs

The total cost is the final calculation in the budget. Total costs are derived by multiplying the units per year for each modality (murder = 81) by the unit cost ($1,015.74). The total cost for the modality "murder" is $82,275.24.

total costs = units per year × unit cost

Table 35 is the completed ABB plan outlining the entire cost for salaries, materials and equipment. It is readily apparent that the percentage of the budget allocated per modality in table 34 very closely approximates the percentage of time allocated per modality in table 25.

Table 35					Activity Based Budget: Present Level of Service						
	Hours per unit	Units Per Year	Officers Required	Total Hours	Salary per hour	Salary per unit	Material per unit	Equipment per unit	Unit Cost	Total Cost	Percentage Allocated
Animal Complaint	0.5	1825	1	913	$123.92	$61.96	$10.07	$14.32	$86.34	$157,578.55	0.37%
Arrest (average for all types of arrests)	1.5	32,612	2	97,836	$247.84	$371.76	$10.07	$14.32	$396.14	$12,919,053.41	30.59%
Arson	2	242	2	968	$247.84	$495.68	$10.07	$14.32	$520.06	$125,855.50	0.30%
Aggravated Assault (shooting, stabbing, blunt force)	1.5	1365	2	4,095	$247.84	$371.76	$10.07	$14.32	$396.14	$540,736.78	1.28%
Assist Officer (back up)	0.25	152	2	76	$247.84	$61.96	$10.07	$14.32	$86.34	$13,124.35	0.03%
Assist Other Agency (EMS, Fire, Public Works)	0.75	2,269	1	1,702	$123.92	$92.94	$10.07	$14.32	$117.32	$266,209.03	0.63%
Bomb Threat	1	12	2	24	$247.84	$247.84	$10.07	$14.32	$272.22	$3,266.69	0.01%
Burglar Alarm (residential, commercial)	0.5	3,285	2	3,285	$247.84	$123.92	$10.07	$14.32	$148.30	$487,179.82	1.15%
Burglary	1	2,292	2	4,584	$247.84	$247.84	$10.07	$14.32	$272.22	$623,938.01	1.48%
Carjacking	1	77	2	154	$247.84	$247.84	$10.07	$14.32	$272.22	$20,961.27	0.05%
Code Enforcement Violations	0.33	414	1	137	$123.92	$40.89	$10.07	$14.32	$65.28	$27,025.10	0.06%
Court Appearances	2	2,450	10	49,000	$1,239.20	$2,478.40	$10.07	$14.32	$2,502.78	$6,131,817.06	14.52%
Criminal Mischief/Vandalism	0.5	3,002	1	1,501	$123.92	$61.96	$10.07	$14.32	$86.34	$259,205.92	0.61%
Disorderly Conduct (fights, crowds)	0.75	6,210	2	9,315	$247.84	$185.88	$10.07	$14.32	$210.26	$1,305,741.37	3.09%
Domestic Violence	1.5	3,255	2	9,765	$247.84	$371.76	$10.07	$14.32	$396.14	$1,289,449.25	3.05%
Drug Sales	0.75	5,041	2	7,562	$247.84	$185.88	$10.07	$14.32	$210.26	$1,059,942.39	2.51%
DWI	2	52	2	208	$247.84	$495.68	$10.07	$14.32	$520.06	$27,043.33	0.06%
Emotionally Disturbed Person	1	120	4	480	$495.68	$495.68	$10.07	$14.32	$520.06	$62,407.69	0.15%
Fire (car, house, building)	1.5	123	2	369	$247.84	$371.76	$10.07	$14.32	$396.14	$48,725.73	0.12%
Fraud/Forgery	1	313	1	313	$123.92	$123.92	$10.07	$14.32	$148.30	$46,419.26	0.11%
Gambling Offense	0.75	468	1	351	$123.92	$92.94	$10.07	$14.32	$117.32	$54,907.81	0.13%
HazMat Condition/Dangerous Circumstances	1	2,366	2	4,732	$247.84	$247.84	$10.07	$14.32	$272.22	$644,082.60	1.52%
Juvenile Condition (curfew, truancy and all others)	0.75	1,211	2	1,817	$247.84	$185.88	$10.07	$14.32	$210.26	$254,630.08	0.60%
Kidnapping	3	11	2	66	$247.84	$743.52	$10.07	$14.32	$767.90	$8,446.94	0.02%
Liquor/Tavern Violation	1.5	3,548	2	10,644	$247.84	$371.76	$10.07	$14.32	$396.14	$1,405,519.49	3.33%
Motor Vehicle Accident (with or without injuries)	1.5	1,825	2	5,475	$247.84	$371.76	$10.07	$14.32	$396.14	$722,963.10	1.71%
Murder	4	81	2	648	$247.84	$991.36	$10.07	$14.32	$1,015.74	$82,275.24	0.19%
MV Pursuit	0.75	177	4	531	$495.68	$371.76	$10.07	$14.32	$396.14	$70,117.52	0.17%
Noise Complaint	0.33	1,987	2	1,311	$247.84	$81.79	$10.07	$14.32	$106.17	$210,962.96	0.50%
Open Door Condition	0.75	1,547	2	2,321	$247.84	$185.88	$10.07	$14.32	$210.26	$325,278.89	0.77%
Parking Complaint	0.33	3,698	1	1,220	$123.92	$40.89	$10.07	$14.32	$65.28	$241,398.14	0.57%
Person with a Weapon	0.42	401	4	674	$495.68	$208.19	$10.07	$14.32	$232.57	$93,260.53	0.22%
Prostitution	0.33	2,113	2	1,395	$247.84	$81.79	$10.07	$14.32	$106.17	$224,340.58	0.53%
Public Intoxication/Public Consumption	1	3,321	2	6,642	$247.84	$247.84	$10.07	$14.32	$272.22	$904,056.77	2.14%
Rape	2.5	85	2	425	$247.84	$619.60	$10.07	$14.32	$643.98	$54,738.64	0.13%

Table 35					Activity Based Budget: Present Level of Service						
	Hours per unit	Units Per Year	Officers Required	Total Hours	Salary per hour	Salary per unit	Material per unit	Equipment per unit	Unit Cost	Total Cost	Percentage Allocated
Receiving Stolen Property	1	2,221	2	4,442	$247.84	$247.84	$10.07	$14.32	$272.22	$604,610.08	1.43%
Robbery	1.5	1,304		23,912	$247.84	$371.76	$10.07	$14.32	$396.14	$516,571.99	1.22%
School Crossing	2	900	5	9,000	$619.60	$1,239.20	$10.07	$14.32	$1,263.58	$1,137,225.12	2.69%
Shots Fired	0.33	1,460	2	964	$247.84	$81.79	$10.07	$14.32	$106.17	$155,010.53	0.37%
Sick/Injured Person	0.75	720	1	540	$123.92	$92.94	$10.07	$14.32	$117.32	$84,473.56	0.20%
Simple Assault	1.1	2,478	1	2,726	$123.92	$136.31	$10.07	$14.32	$160.70	$398,205.56	0.94%
Stolen Vehicle Report	1	6,018	1	6,018	$123.92	$123.92	$10.07	$14.32	$148.30	$892,495.64	2.11%
Street Collapse	1	14	2	28	$247.84	$247.84	$10.07	$14.32	$272.22	$3,811.14	0.01%
Suicide	1.5	22	2	66	$247.84	$371.76	$10.07	$14.32	$396.14	$8,715.17	0.02%
Suspicious Person/Vehicle	0.5	2,899	2	2,899	$247.84	$123.92	$10.07	$14.32	$148.30	$429,934.34	1.02%
Theft (shoplifting and all others)	0.75	6,522	2	9,783	$247.84	$185.88	$10.07	$14.32	$210.26	$1,371,343.83	3.25%
Traffic Control	4	2,190	5	43,800	$619.60	$2,478.40	$10.07	$14.32	$2,502.78	$5,481,093.62	12.98%
Train Accident	8	1	4	32	$495.68	$3,965.44	$10.07	$14.32	$3,989.82	$3,989.82	0.01%
Vicious Animal	0.4	214	2	171	$247.84	$99.14	$10.07	$14.32	$123.52	$26,433.36	0.06%
Warrant Service	4	73	11	3,212	$1,363.12	$5,452.48	$10.07	$14.32	$5,476.86	$399,810.79	0.95%
Wires Down	0.75	58	2	87	$247.84	$185.88	$10.07	$14.32	$210.26	$12,195.33	0.03%
Total		115,044		318,216	15,242					$42,238,580	100.00%

Budget Summary

Once the ABB is prepared, it is useful to create a small budget summary by category. The categories for this budget are salaries, materials and equipment. The budget summary will help you reconcile the individual pieces of the budget. The total cost presented in table 35-1 is $42,238,580. When summing the categories (salaries, materials, equipment) in the budget summary, the total must equal the ABB Present Level of Service total; otherwise an error was made somewhere in the calculations. A simple pie chart of the finished budget gives the reader a quick visual perspective of how the funds are distributed.

Table 35-1	Budget Summary	
Total from Salary Calculations	**Salaries**	$39,433,294
Total from Materials Calculations	**Materials**	$1,158,075
Total from Equipment Calculations	**Equipment**	$1,647,211
	Total	**$42,238,580**

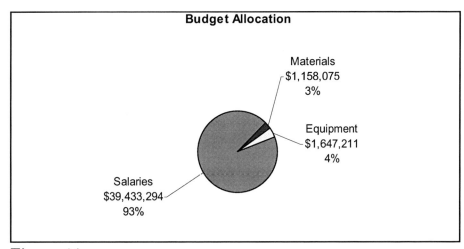

Figure 14

The ABB is an objective way to link workload to costs. It is also easy to design. Each division of the police department can create an ABB to see how efficiently they are operating; link all the individual budgets and the department now has a comprehensive picture of its operating posture. The ABB contained on the Resource CD shows five separate division budgets: patrol, investigations, communications, traffic and prisoner processing, linked together to form a total department budget. Click on the worksheet named "Org. Recap," which is the recapitulation of the individual budgets for an overview of the entire budget. Table 35-2 shows the budget recap for those divisions.

Supervisors can use ABB to make adjustments in processes or shift personnel. Administrators can use ABB to create partnership programs with the police department. In this sense it is useful to see the proportion of the ABB that is allocated to each partner (i.e., public, private or non-profit). Another internal use for ABB is to justify hiring and promoting personnel. By using accepted industry standards of span of control, an executive can argue in favor of hiring and promoting based upon the volume of work. Table 35-2 shows the budget recap, which summarizes the financial aspects, as well the personnel complement and the performance.

Table 35-2			Anytown Police Department			
			Budget Recap			

Budget Allocation

Category	Patrol	Criminal Investigations	Communications	Traffic	Prisoner Processing	Total
Salaries	$54,140,663.77	$13,522,442.06	$4,824,412.05	$3,163,995.50	$12,615,840.62	$88,267,353.99
Materials	$1,588,607.16	$398,154.02	$196,208.45	$39,280.59	$453,793.78	$2,676,044.00
Equipment	$1,647,210.55	$123,705.74	$85,818.78	$151,181.44	$41,705.40	$2,049,621.92
Subtotal	$57,376,481	$14,044,302	$5,106,439	$3,354,458	$13,111,340	$92,993,020
Percent	61.70%	15.10%	5.49%	3.61%	14.10%	100%

Personnel Complement

Job Title	Patrol	Criminal Investigations	Communications	Traffic	Prisoner Processing	Total
Captain	1	1	1	1	1	5
Exec. Lieutenant	1	1	1	1	1	5
Lieutenant	19	4	4	1	3	31
Sergeant	98	17	4	3	14	136
Detective	0	133	0	0	0	133
Police Officer	512	0	27	30	127	696
Call Takers	0	0	30	0	0	30
Civilian Aide	4	4	11	4	5	28
Subtotal	635	159	78	39	151	1,064
Percent	59.74%	14.97%	7.38%	3.69%	14.22%	100%

Performance Indicators

	Level of Effort			Level of Production (Economy, Efficiency and Productivity)				
Division	Units per Year	Avg. Hours per Unit	Total Employee Hours per Modality	Overall Cost per Unit (Efficiency)	# of Units Serviced per $1,000 Expended (Productivity)	Material Cost per Unit (Economy)	Equipment Cost per Unit (Economy)	Rate per Employee Hour (Economy)
Patrol	98,324	1.54	526,102	$583.55	1.71	$16.16	$16.75	$257.27
Investigations	61,492	4.65	206,514	$228.39	4.38	$6.47	$2.01	$88.49
Communications	337,925	0.136	53,774	$15.11	66.18	$0.58	$0.25	$89.72
Traffic	8,755	2.35	63,100	$383.15	2.61	$4.49	$17.27	$71.63
Prisoner Processing	152,871	0.712	168,721	$85.77	11.66	$2.97	$0.27	$74.77
Bail/ROR				$29.49	33.91			
In-Custody				$85.93	11.64			

Beyond its internal uses, ABB has other merits. Many grant programs require an ABB for the grantor to see where their money is being spent and how efficiently the grantee can administer the program. ABB can easily be turned in to a performance-based budget by attaching performance standards. ABB can also be used together with benchmarking to identify best practices (Ammons, 1999).[91]

The basic steps in corporate benchmarking are:

1. Decide what process to benchmark,
2. Study the process in your own organization,
3. Identify benchmarking partners,
4. Analyze the processes of benchmarking partners to identify differences that account for superior performance,
5. Adapt and implement "best practices," and
6. Monitor and revise (Ammons, 1999:43).

In this example, effecting patrol-related arrests consume nearly 21 percent of the activity. The arrest process could be benchmarked to determine if there is a more efficient way to process them, including new technology that reduces the effort or changes in the required documents. Activity-base budgeting holds some promise as a solution to the faults and frustrations of traditional budgeting methods:

1. "Traditional budgets don't identify waste. ABB exposes non-value costs.
2. Traditional budgets focus on workers. ABB focuses on workload.
3. Traditional budgets focus on division cost. ABB also focuses on process cost.
4. Traditional budgets focus on fixed versus variable costs. ABB also focuses on used versus unused capacity.
5. Traditional budgets measure "effect." ABB measures root "cause" (Pryor, 2004).

ABB is an alternative to traditional government budgets. The line item may be required by law, but there is nothing preventing an organization from adopting ABB to solve internal problems.

6

▶ **Intermediate Statistical Analyses**

This book is about using data to solve problems and how to make the agency data driven. The performance measures listed in Table 1 are meaningless unless they are analyzed and compared to other meaningful measures. Beyond the introductory concepts of basic mathematics, such as percentage increase or decrease, numerical average and descriptive statistics, police executives can use a variety of intermediate statistical procedures to draw inferences and make predictions. Intermediate statistical analyses enable law enforcement agencies to "go granular" into the data and understand "why things are happening," help "reduce uncertainty in decision making," "react faster to public service needs," empower command staff officers, uncover hidden relationships that would otherwise go unnoticed, and "forecast future resources."[92] The idea is to examine relationships between discrete pieces of data to uncover patterns of association and whether the data can predict things such as crime control, case clearance or response time. These techniques have been widely used by marketing researchers, Wall Street and other business analysts, sales managers, medical and pharmaceutical researchers, sociologists, demographers, criminologists, and public administrators, to name a few. One intermediate technique that will be explored measures the strength and direction of the relationship between two variables. Another technique helps build a mathematical model that can predict one value from the value of other "predictive" data elements (Norusis, 2000).

The value in using these techniques comes when a police executive must answer difficult questions such as, *"If we allocate 1,000 hours of overtime, then what will be the predicted crime rate?"* Or, *"Given our current level of output, which performance measures have the greatest influence on the crime rate?"* Or, *"Given our current rate of absenteeism, what is the predicted response time?"* Answering the second question helps establish economies of scale, where administrators are able to reduce resource input levels while producing greater output levels toward end outcomes. When you know which output measures have the greatest influence on the crime rate, then you can direct specific resources toward specific tasks while modifying or discontinuing other tasks. This is known as adjusting the dosage level. By applying a medical model to controlling crime and quality of life conditions, if the dose (input) is too low, it will be ineffective against the prevailing conditions, while excessive doses will be inefficient and may be intolerable to the community. By monitoring output and end outcomes it is possible formulate detailed "dosing schemes," which can guide supervisors and command staff officers on the correct level of police intervention and make adjustments in case of over or under staffing. Simply put, using certain intermediate statistical techniques is as close to a crystal ball as you will get.

Statistical Analysis in Law Enforcement

Criminal behavior, like most other human behavior, is predictable. Criminal behavioral patterns have been explained quite well through a variety of "opportunity" theories such as routine activities (Clarke and Felson, 1998; Felson, 1987), crime pattern theory (Brantingham and Brantingham, 1984, 1991), and the rational choice perspective (Cornish and Clarke, 1986).[93] Criminal propensities and offending patterns usually come in the form of comfort zones, which may appear as hot spots, or specific time periods throughout the day (temporal distribution). One of the best ways to identify patterns and predict risk is through data mining—an analytic technique that helps to establish relationships and identify patterns that accurately predict behavior. Data mining tools can be used to analyze huge archived files of CAD and RMS data to structure tactical plans and risk-based deployment strategies, to model violent crime, to detect fraud, and to conduct risk and threat assessment in the post 9/11 environment (Bonasia, 2005; McCue, 2003).

Two law enforcement agencies that have had success using data mining and intermediate statistical techniques are the Atlanta, Ga. and Richmond, Va. police departments. Both agencies have used statistics to help accelerate the investigative process, make better deployment decisions, identify potential violent crimes from relatively minor crimes, analyze offenders' criminal histories to produce a "most dangerous criminals" list and enhance officer safety.[94] All of this good analysis begins by collecting the data in a central repository and transforming it into a useable format. Although a full discussion of data mining and the software applications used in the data mining process are beyond the scope of this text, there are some intermediate statistical procedures that are readily available through MS Excel© that accomplish a similar end.

Linear Regression Analysis and Correlation

The intermediate statistical procedures we will discuss in this section are best when an executive wants a snapshot of the agency's performance at a given point in time. For example, taking measurements of the same variables (e.g., crime rate, response time, poverty level, unemployment level) at the same point in time, perhaps monthly, quarterly, semi-annually or annually, the executive can see how the agency is meeting established end outcomes. The method is known as linear regression analysis and the snapshot that results is known as cross-sectional analysis. Another method related to linear regression is known as correlation. When two things are correlated they are related, particularly when one implies the other. Correlation is used to examine the relationship between two variables. Correlation does not explain causation but, as a measure of association, it does explain the strength and direction (positive or negative) of the relationship between variables.

The statistic that results from a correlation analysis is known as the correlation coefficient or Pearson's *r,* and takes a value from -1.00 to +1.00, with 0 indicating no relationship, +1 indicating a perfect positive relationship and -1 indicating a perfect negative relationship. The stronger the relationship, the closer the correlation coefficient will be to +1.00; the weaker the relationship, the closer the correlation coefficient will be to -1.00. A significant shortcoming of MS Excel's© correlation feature is that it does not identify statistically significant relationships between the variables, which is essential for analysis. Nevertheless, the feature is still robust enough to produce accurate strength and direction analyses from which to draw inferences.

Linear regression is a technique for estimating the expected value of one variable (typically known as the "y" or dependent variable) given the value of another variable or variables (typically known as the "x" or independent variables). The concept of regression might seem odd since the term regression is usually associated with backward movement (i.e., to regress). However, in the world of statistics, regression analysis is used to predict a future value. Linear regression requires an interval-ratio dependent variable. This means that continuous numeric data are necessary; a dependent variable that has only limited values, such as "yes" or "no" or 0 or 1 are not suitable.

Linear regression is a statistical technique that uses data collected after observing many units (e.g., people, time, condition, income) *at the same point in time*, or without regard to differences in time. Because this is only a snapshot in time the agency executive can compare how well (or how poorly) the agency is performing to different time periods, say compared to the last six months, last year or the last five years. This analysis technique differs from something known as time-series data analysis, which follows change in a single unit over the course of time.[95] Cross sectional analysis also differs from a technique known as longitudinal data analysis, which is where repeated measures of the same variables are taken over a period of time. Neither time series analysis nor longitudinal analysis will be illustrated in this text.

The procedures for cross-sectional analysis are not necessarily more difficult to execute, they simply require more patience to interpret. Admittedly, most police executives do not have experience using these techniques, so it is a matter of knowing the data set, working with the software and following the instructions here for interpretation. A full recitation about intermediate statistical models is beyond the scope of this text. However, a good textbook on statistics will ensure you fully understand the logic behind the procedures and which procedures are permissible with the specific type of data that has been collected. Five very good textbooks on introductory and intermediate statistics are:

1. Healey, J.F. (2002). <u>Statistics: A Tool for Social Research</u>. 6th ed. Belmont, Ca: Wadsworth.

2. Bachman, R. and Paternoster, R. (2004). <u>Statistics for Criminology and Criminal Justice</u>. 2nd ed. New York: McGraw-Hill.
3. Knoke, D., Bohrnstedt, G.W. and Mee, A.P. (2002). <u>Statistics for Social Data Analysis</u>.   4th ed. Belmont, Ca: Wadsworth.
4. Walker, J.T. and Madden, S. (2005). <u>Statistics in Criminology and Criminal Justice: Analysis and Interpretation</u>. Boston, Ma: Jones and Bartlett.
5. Wholey, J. S., Newcomer, K. E., and Hatry, H. (ed.). (2004). <u>Handbook of Practical Program Evaluation</u>. San Francisco: Jossey-Bass. See sections *"Using Statistics Appropriately"* and *"Using Regression Models to Estimate Program Effects."*

Once again we will use Microsoft Excel[©] in these examples to conduct the analysis. There are better and more sophisticated software programs that advanced statistics users may wish to consider such as SPSS.[© 96] A good resource for learning how to execute statistical procedures, including building regression models in MS Excel,[©] is a workbook by Dretzke (2001). If you purchase SPSS,[©] then two good reference books are by George and Mallery (2006) and Norusis (2000).

Formulating Hypotheses

Before you begin any data collection or conduct any analysis it is important to think through what you are trying to explain or the message you are trying to convey. As a police planner or chief executive you undoubtedly have some idea about the cause of a particular phenomenon or, if not the cause, at least the contributing factors. The idea about the relationship between things, or how one thing causes another thing is known as a hypothesis. A hypothesis is an educated guess that seems valid in the face of the available information. More specifically, a hypothesis is a specific statement about the relationship between two variables that is testable. As a chief executive your responsibility is to develop hypotheses; the police planners and crime analysts are responsible for proving or disproving the hypotheses by collecting and analyzing the appropriate data. Hypotheses are often symbolized H_1, H_2, H_3 and so forth, to denote the number of hypotheses being stated.

A hypothesis or set of hypotheses will direct the data collection effort and the analysis procedures. If, for example, you are interested in the relationship between crime and police officer activity (output), your hypothesis might be: *as the rate of arrest, field interrogations and hours of overtime increase, the rate of crime will decrease.* This is a specific statement about the nature and direction of the hypothesis: the nature of the hypothesis is police officer activity (output measures); the direction is a decrease (in the crime rate). This statement is testable and can be confirmed or dispelled by collecting the appropriate data.

Restated, hypotheses are important because they guide data collection, analysis and beliefs about certain things. Creating hypotheses during staff meetings such as CompStat, table-top exercise or "scenario" planning sessions helps shape intervention strategies and determine if those strategies are worthwhile or need to be revised. The following examples each have stated hypotheses to show these statements relate to the actual data collection and analysis.

Limitations of Statistical Procedures

Using intermediate statistics in policing has distinct advantages, however, it is not a free-for-all; there are limitations. First, the data and the associated statistical procedures are not infallible. They are very good but when certain procedural assumptions are violated, linear regression will not be the best method for assessing the relationship or making predictions. The reason linear regression was selected as the procedure to demonstrate is because much of the data police departments collect is known as continuous data, or interval-ratio data. Data elements such as response time, number of arrests, number of traffic summonses and incarceration rate are examples of interval-ratio data. The dependent (Y) variable must be continuous when using linear regression. Statistical procedures for analyzing limited dependent variables, such as yes (1) or no (0) require a different, more complex statistical analysis, one that is beyond the scope of this book. However, limited dependent variables are very useful for analyzing things such as citizen satisfaction surveys. There are five data assumptions that must be met before you can opt to use linear regression for analysis:

Table 36	Data Assumptions for Using Linear Regression	
Assumption	**Description**	**Example**
The observations are independent	The result in which the independent variables used in regression analysis are not related to each other instead they are related to the dependent variable; if the independent variables are correlated with each other, this is known as colinearity	In a multivariate analysis the poverty rate should be related to the crime rate, not the other predictor variables such as education level. If the poverty rate is related to education, then the variables are not independent.
The relationship between the two variables is linear	A relationship between two variables that is illustrated by a straight line (contrast against a nonlinear relationship)	This can be assessed by examining a scatterplot to see how closely the data clusters around the trend line
For each value of the independent variable, there is a normal distribution of the values of the dependent variable	The data values are concentrated near the mean, they decrease in frequency as the distance from the mean increases and they are represented by a bell-shaped curve	This can be assessed by examining a histogram or column chart for outliers and to see how closely the data clusters around the mean value
The distributions have the same variance	The values of the dependent variable and the independent variables are approximately the same	The spread of crime rate (dependent variable) at all values of poverty rate (independent variable) can be assessed by examining a scatterplot
The dependent variable is continuous (interval/ratio level)	A quantitative variable with an infinite number of attributes that can be subdivided into an unlimited number of sub-units for measurement	Response time; numeric crime data; numeric census data; age; things measured in days, weeks, months or years

Intermediate Statistical Analyses

The next limitation is the law of parsimony. The law of parsimony states that it is always advisable to make as few assumptions as possible, eliminating those that make no difference in the prediction. For example, it would be nice to say that 100% of the crime problem is related to poverty. Then, all we need to do is eliminate poverty and the crime would disappear. But we know this is not the case. Crime is related to many other social circumstances such as education level, unemployment, residential stability, the proportion of the population under 25 years, as well as poverty. Tactical planners and crime analysts can observe the law of parsimony by selecting the fewest variables that capture the greatest amount of explanatory power. The law is violated when more and more variables are added to a regression equation until a statistically significant result is achieved. Each time a new variable is added to the equation a certain element of uncertainty is also introduced. It is inevitable that a statistically significant result will occur if enough variables are added to the equation. This is not the point of data analysis; it is not "achieve a statistically significant result at any cost." It is a matter of analyzing the situation, appealing to the criminological and sociological literature to see which variables are indeed necessary and which ones can be discarded. One way for tactical planners and crime analysts to do this is simply run different regression models, observe the results, then exclude the variables that do not contribute to the explanatory power of the model.

Statistical Procedures and Types of Data

If you are thoroughly familiar with some of the more intermediate or advanced statistical procedures and wish to use them, then here is a table of the data types and statistical procedures required:

Table 36-1 | **Statistical Procedures for Bivariate Analyses** | | |

...and the independent variable is...	If the *dependent variable is...*		
	Categorical	Continuous	Dichotomous
Categorical *(nominal)*	Joint Contingency	ANOVA	Joint contingency
Continuous *(interval or ratio)*	--	Correlation	Correlation
Dichotomous (e.g., *yes or no*)	Joint Contingency	Difference of Means or Correlation	Joint Contingency or Correlation

	Statistical Procedures for Multivariate Analyses
If the *dependent variable is...*	...then use this statistical procedure
Categorical *(nominal)*	Loglinear and Multinomial Logistic Regression
Continuous *(interval or ratio)*	Ordinary Least Squares (OLS)/Linear Regression and Poisson (count)
Dichotomous (e.g., *yes or no; true or false)*	Logistic Regression
Time Dependent	Cox Proportional Hazards and Kaplan Meier
Source: Spring 2006, Dr. Bonita Veysey, Rutgers School of Criminal Justice	

Statistics are useful but they can be very complex. There are a variety of web sites and books to help crime analysts, police planners, consultants and students use statistics properly. One way to ensure your work product is complete and accurate is to seek help from a consultant, a local university or other organizations that use statistics on a regularly basis (Clarke and Eck, 2005:54). Before you begin using statistics to you must know what questions to ask, then what type of data will answer the questions. Use this guide as a frame of reference to ensure you capture the right type of data for your statistical analysis:

Table 36-1.1		Types of Data Useful for Law Enforcement Statistics		
Category	Description	Measurement	Question?	Data Type
Nominal	Categorical data; data that is described by the qualities of a category and is not ranked or ordered according to the values. The values are usually not numerical.	Counts; counting the number of cases in a particular category; cannot make judgments about "greater than" or "less than;" categories must be mutually exclusive and exhaustive	Who? What? What? When? Where? Where? How? Why? Weapon? Weapon Type? Occupation? Gang member?	Sex (male, female); Race (white, black, Hispanic, Asian) Crime (robbery, burglary, arson, theft, assault, rape) Victim/Offender Relationship (stranger, friend, family member) Day of week (Sunday—Saturday) Location (street, house, retail store, alley, motel) Division (patrol, detectives, traffic, PSAP, precinct) Point of attack(front, back, side, roof, door, window) Motive (revenge, jealousy, financial, domestic) Displayed or possessed (yes, no) Handgun, shotgun, knife, rifle, club, car, stick, bat Status (unemployed, student, professional, nurse) Status (current, former; gang name)
Ordinal	Ordered data; data that quantifies differences by order such as "larger," "smaller," "higher," "lower," "more" or "less," not magnitude; the size of the interval is not specified	All of the above, plus judgments about "greater than" and "less than"	What? What? Who? Why?	Fear of crime and citizen satisfaction with police service—survey responses, attitude/opinion scales and other "Likert-type" scales (very satisfied, somewhat satisfied, satisfied, neutral, dissatisfied, somewhat dissatisfied, very dissatisfied; agree, neutral, disagree) Social class (upper, middle, working and lower class) Victim or offender build (tall, average, short) Increase or decrease in performance (high morale, low morale)
Interval	Continuous data; data that is divided into ranges that represent quantities in terms of equal intervals but whose zero point is arbitrarily fixed (the zero point means that, although a value of zero is possible, zero does not mean the absence of the phenomenon under analysis). This is data that is represented in numbers.	Includes all the measures used in nominal and ordinal data and also includes other mathematical operations (addition, subtraction, division, square root, multiplication, exponents)	Who? How many?	Victim or offender's age Performance—things calculated in number of days or hours (days to case clearance; hours off sick or injured; days to serve a warrant; hours to process a single prisoner—cycle time); number, percentage, rate or proportion of something (victimization rate; number of traffic accidents; number of citizen complaints; clearance rate; percent unemployed; number of personnel; arrest rate); monetary value (overtime; per-unit cost; salary rate; assets seized)

Table 36-1.1	Types of Data Useful for Law Enforcement Statistics			
Category	Description	Measurement	Question?	Data Type
Ratio	Continuous data; data that is represented in terms of equal distance between points and an absolute zero point (the absolute zero point typically means the absence of zero). This is data that is represented in numbers.		How many? When? What? Why?	Crime and quality of life conditions (crime rate; composite index of quality of life indicators) Time (response time; time of day; week or day of year—chronological) Percent of incidents deemed suppressible Increase or decrease in performance (number of officers on sick, injured or vacation leave; number of officers on restricted duty; deployment strength)

Drawing Inferences and Making Predictions

Predicting the Crime Rate Based upon Overtime Allocation

Overtime funds are a scarce resource. Mayors, business administrators and finance directors do not like to part with the city's money for overtime. That is, unless the police department can demonstrate what the return on their investment (ROI) will be. As a matter of course it is imperative to have a written plan in hand before asking for additional overtime funds for a crime control program. Part of that plan is to have empirical data that demonstrates what the predicted ROI will be, given the historical data and how the police department arrived at its ROI determination. In this example, the police department can use regression analysis to predict the future crime rate based on the overtime history; the predicted crime rate is the ROI for 1,000 hours of overtime. Let's begin with this question: *"How much is the crime rate predicted to decline if the city allocates 1,000 hours of overtime?"* This can also be stated slightly differently, which answers a second important question: *"For every 1,000 hours of overtime the city allocates, what is the predicted crime rate?"* These are two different questions but they use the same data set and the same analysis techniques. The hypothesis is: H_1: *as the number of overtime hours increases, the crime will decrease.*

The first step is to collect the data; in this example we will use 10 years worth of data, but you could use 1 or 2 years or 6 months. The two variables we need are crime-rate data and overtime data; for illustration purposes the crime rate is calculated per 100,000 people. The data should be arranged in two columns (Table 36-2). Anytime you are using only two variables (e.g., crime rate and overtime hours) you have what is known as a bivariate analysis.

Table 36-2	10-year History of Overtime Hours and Crime Rate	
Year	Overtime Hours	Crime Rate per 100,000 People
1993	1125	15709
1994	1258	15301
1995	1599	14025
1996	1478	13043
1997	2589	11796
1998	2269	9402
1999	2988	9976
2000	3899	10743
2001	3989	11825
2003	4268	11304

Just by looking at the data presented in table 36-2 it is impossible to infer what the predicted crime rate will be or what the relationship is between overtime and the crime rate, likewise it is impossible to determine if there is a positive or negative relationship A positive relationship means as the independent variable (overtime hours) increases, there is a corresponding increase in the dependent variable (crime rate). A negative relationship means as the independent variable (overtime hours) increases, there is a corresponding decrease in the dependent variable (crime rate). Therefore, the next step is to create a correlation matrix. A correlation matrix will analyze the strength and direction of the relationship, which will give you better insight into what type of relationship exists between these two variables.

With the data arranged in two columns, as shown in Table 36-3, select **Tools > Data Analysis** from the Excel© toolbar. Next, select **Correlation** from the **Data Analysis** dialog box. The input range is the column of data, including the row with labels if you labeled the data. Select whether the data is grouped by columns or rows and whether the first row or column includes labels. Next, select **Output Range**, which is simply the available cell in the worksheet where you want the correlation matrix to appear. Then, select **OK**. The resulting output summary should look like Table 36-3:

Table 36-3	Bivariate Correlation of Overtime Hours and Crime Rate	
	Overtime Hours	*Crime Rate per 100,000 People*
Overtime Hours	1	
Crime Rate per 100,000 People	-0.685	1

First, notice that the relationship when correlated with itself is always 1. This is because the relationship is a perfect fit. By convention, in a correlation matrix the association of the variables with themselves is left blank; for illustration purposes the value 1 is shown but would not be shown in a report promulgated for readers. Next, notice the relationship between the crime rate per 100,000 people and overtime hours has a moderately strong negative relationship (-0.685). This means there is an inverse relationship: as overtime hours increase, the crime rate decreases. This is a good finding, except we do not know if the relationship exists by chance or if it exists because there truly is a relationship between overtime hours and crime rate. Therefore, the next step is to create a scattergram of the data to collect a little more information.

A scattergram is also known as a scatterplot or an XY scatter chart. A scattergram is a graph of data plotted along a horizontal (X) axis and a vertical (Y) to represent bivariate data. By convention the "X" axis plots the independent variable and the "Y" variable plots the dependent variable. Each bivariate element being plotted has both a horizontal and vertical position and is often accompanied by a line of "goodness-of-fit" for the data; the more tightly the data points cluster around the line, the better the fit, which means the stronger the relationship. A scattergram is useful when you are trying to show whether there is a positive or negative relationship between two variables (such as the crime rate and overtime hours). In this example our hope is to find a negative relationship: as more overtime hours are appropriated, there is a decrease in the crime rate.

To obtain a scattergram in MS Excel© select: **Insert > Chart > XY Scatter**. Select the default in the chart sub-type. Then, select **next** and choose the **Series** tab. For the **X** values select the entire column labeled **overtime hours** and press enter. Then, for the **Y** values select the entire column labeled **crime rate** and press enter. Select **next** and fill the **chart options** with your choices. The resulting chart should look like this:

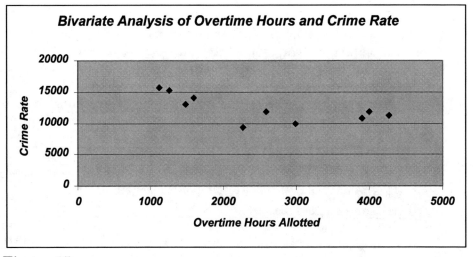

Figure 15

You can visually see there is a slight downward slope from the upper left corner toward the lower right corner. This indicates a possible negative relationship. To confirm this and see just how much the crime rate declines with each hour increase in overtime, we want to add a few things to the chart: 1) a trend line, 2) an equation and 3) the R-squared value on chart. The trend line will confirm the direction, positive or negative; the equation is the statistical equation that is used to answer the question: *"What is the predicted crime rate based upon overtime hours?"* and the R-squared value explains the amount of variance in the dependent variable (crime rate) by the independent variable (overtime hours) (more about R-squared ahead). To insert these three chart options, highlight the chart and select **chart** from the tool bar. Then, select **add trend line**; select **linear**. Next, select the **options** tab and check the boxes named **display equation on chart** and **display R-squared value on chart**.

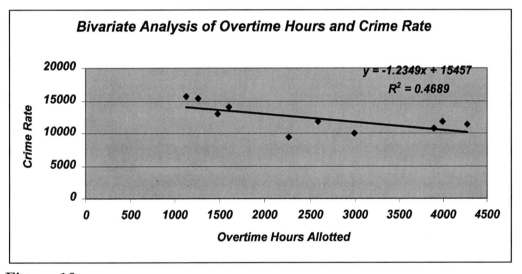

Figure 16

Depending on your data, you will show a positive or negative trend. If there is no trend at all, then you will have a nearly horizontal trend line. Figure 16 is the completed chart from the data in Table 36-2. Notice the pronounced downward trend line. This confirms a negative relationship: as overtime hours increase, the crime rate decreases. Next, notice the equation. The formula for linear regression is: $y = a + bx + e$, where:

1. $y =$ the predicted value (in this example it is the crime rate we are trying to predict);
2. $a =$ the intercept (this is the value if all independent variables are equal to zero; in this example this is the predicted crime rate if we did not have any overtime hours allocated);

3. b = the slope (this is the amount of change in the dependent variable for every one-unit change in the independent variable; for every metric increase in overtime hours the slope will change the value of the dependent variable by that much—in this example the metric for the independent variable is every one hour);

4. e = the error term ("The error term represents the unpredicted or unexplained variation in the response variable; it is conventionally called the 'error' whether it is really a measurement error or not. The error term is conventionally assumed to have expected value equal to zero" and therefore is not computed).[97]

Something that you must understand is that MS Excel$^©$ places the slope before the intercept in the formula; this is a nuance in the software and does not follow statistical convention. So, in this example, using the linear regression formula y = a + bx+ e the equation from figure 15 is expressed like this:

$$y_{\text{(predicted crime rate)}} = \textbf{-15456}_{\text{ (intercept)}} + \textbf{(-1.2349}_{\text{ (slope)}} \times \textbf{1000}_{\text{ (overtime hours)}})$$

Remember, we are asking what the predicted crime rate will be if there is 1,000 hours of overtime allocated for crime control. You can set-up this equation in Excel using the intercept and slope functions located on the toolbar: **insert > function**. Once the formula is entered, all you have to do to answer different overtime predictions is enter a new amount of hours and the formula will recalculate the predicted value for you.[98] What is vitally important here is to recognize the direction of the slope. Notice there is a negative sign before the numerals (-1.2349). This indicates that there is a reduction in the dependent variable (crime rate) by that amount as the independent variable (overtime hours) increases. Since we are interested in the predicted crime rate based upon 1,000 hours of overtime, we simply move the decimal point three places to the right which leaves us with the number -234.9. Said differently, we multiply the intercept by the metric we are using, in this example 1,000 (-234.9 = -1.2349 × 1000). If we interested in predicting the crime rate for 100 hours of overtime, then we would multiply by 100, since 100 would be our metric (-123.49 = 1.2349 × 100). All that is left is to compute the formula (y = a + bx + e):

Table 36-4	Computed Bivariate Regression Formula		
Name		**Value**	**Symbol**
Intercept		15456.6169	*a*
Slope		-1.2349	*b*
Coefficient of Multiple Determination		0.4689	*r sq*
Pearson Correlation Coefficient		-0.6847	*r*
Overtime hours		1000.00	*x*
Dependent Variable (predicted crime rate)		14221.75	*y*

$$14222 \text{ (predicted crime rate)} = 15456 \text{ (intercept)} -1234.9 \text{ (slope)}$$

Notice the predicted crime rate (14222) is reduced by a value of 1,234 (14222 = 15456 −1234). In translation you can say that for every 1,000 hours of overtime that is allocated, the crime rate is predicted to decrease by 1,234 crimes per 100,000 people. If the city allocated 2,000 hours of overtime, then the predicted crime rate would be 12988 (12986 = 15456 − 2470; the slope 2468 is derived by multiplying 1234 by 2). If the city only allocated 500 hours of overtime, then the predicted crime rate would be 14839 (14839 = 15456 − 617).[99]

The R-squared value is .4689, which means .4689 or 46.89% of the variance in the dependent variable is explained by the independent variable. The R-squared value can be transformed into a percent by simply multiplying by 100. In the bivariate model (crime rate and overtime hours) we computed the R-squared, which means nearly 47% of the variance in the crime rate is explained by overtime hours. In social science this is a strong finding, which means that overtime hours accounts for nearly half of the variance in the predicted crime rate. Although slightly more than 50% of the variance remains unexplained, in the next example we will discover how to increase the explanatory power of a linear regression model by including multiple factors that may account for the unexplained 50% variation in the crime rate. The bivariate regression summary output appears in table 37 but requires interpretation.

Interpreting the Data. Table 37 may look confusing at first with language and numbers that do not seem to mean anything. Indeed, most of the language is seldom used by police executives. In fact, there is a wealth of decision/policy information contained in this table. A few moments of explanation will clear up the dismay. The summary output that is created includes three sections:

1. Regression Statistics
2. Analysis of Variance (ANOVA) Summary Table
3. Coefficient Summary Information Table

Table 37		Bivariate Regression of Overtime Hours and Crime Rate					
SUMMARY OUTPUT							

Regression Statistics	
Multiple R	0.6847
R Square	0.4689
Adjusted R Square	0.4025
Standard Error	1666.8387
Observations	10

ANOVA

	df	S.S.	MS	F	Significance F
Regression	1	19621895.2727	19621895.2727	7.0624	0.0289
Residual	8	22226809.1273	2778351.1409		
Total	9	41848704.4000			

	Coefficients	Standard Error	t Stat	P-value	Lower 95%	Upper 95%
Intercept	15456.6169	1295.2420	11.9334	0.0000	12469.7835	18443.4503
Overtime Hours	-1.2349	0.4647	-2.6575	0.0289	-2.3064	-0.1633

The first section is *Regression Statistics*:

1. **Multiple R.** Also known as the correlation coefficient, the multiple correlation R-value measures the strength of the relationship between the dependent variable (crime rate) and the independent variables (overtime hours) and takes a value from 0 to 1. The closer to 1 the greater the strength of the relationship; the closer to 0 the weaker the relationship. The R value in this model is .6847 a moderately strong relationship not often observed in social science. A rule of thumb for interpreting the strength of the R-value is:

    a. 0 to .3 = weak relationship
    b. 4 to .6 = moderate relationship
    c. 7 or greater = strong relationship

2. **R-Square.** The R-Square value explains the amount of variation in the dependent variable (crime rate) by its linear relationship with the one predictor variable. The R-Square takes a value from 0 to 1 with the same rule of thumb for interpretation as described for Multiple R. In this model the R-Square is .4689. This means that 46.89% of the variation in crime rate can be explained by the one predictor variable, overtime hours. This is a moderate finding.

3. **Adjusted R-Square.** The adjusted R-Square value more closely reflects the degree of fit than does R-square. The adjusted R-square is often preferred over the R-squared value. If you use a statistics package that only reports the R-squared value, then settle on R-squared as good measure of variance. In this model the Adjusted R-Square is .4025. This means that 40.25% of the variation in crime rate can be explained by the one predictor variable, again a moderate finding.

4. **Standard Error.** The Standard Error is the average amount by which we err if we use the regression equation to predict crime rate. In this model the Standard Error is 1666.83 a relatively low standard error.

5. **Observations.** Observations is number of observations in the model. In this example there are 10 years of data (10 observations).

Analysis of Variance (ANOVA). The ANOVA output is the next section. ANOVA is a test of no linearity between the predictor variable and the dependent variable. What is most important in this section is the Significance F. Recall when you first set up the regression equation in the Regression dialog box, you selected the 95% confidence level. This means that you are willing to tolerate being wrong about your observations 5 chances out 100 (5%). The statement *"willing to tolerate being wrong"* means that what you observe is occurring by chance alone and not because of the activity expressed in your equation. Said differently, if your Significance F level is at .05 or lower (e.g., .04; .03; .01), then you can interpret that as being right about your prediction 95 times out of 100; your prediction will only have occurred by chance 5 times in 100. We are seeking to rule out chance alone in a regression model. We do not want the crime rate to decrease by chance, we want it to decrease based on the output level, in this case overtime hours. In this model the Significance F is 0.0289, which means that there are less than 2 chances in 100 that you will obtain an F value of 7.0624. Stated differently you will be right about your prediction about 98 times out of 100 (i.e., that the predicted crime rate is correlated with overtime hours). The regression model also includes degrees of freedom (df), the sum of squares (S.S.) and the mean sum of squares (MS). These statistics are not particularly important for our purposes.

The Significance F is also known as significance level, the alpha level, or the "p" value, and is vitally important to statistical interpretation. Social science convention dictates that the absolute minimum significance level is 95% (or .05). The .05 significance level was originally adopted by the pharmaceutical industry as a criterion for evaluating drugs. The psychology discipline followed seeking equally rigorous research standards. They adopted the same level and many police researchers today insist that any compromising on the .05 level weakens the integrity of research. If you create a bivariate regression or multivariate regression model that does not display a significance level at least at the .05 level, then you cannot say that the independent variable(s) caused the change in the dependent variable. For example, if you set the significance level at .05 and the Significance F in the regression output reads .15, then you must reject the model as not statistically significant. The same holds true if the Significance F output shows .06, since both .15 and .06 are higher than the industry-standard of .05. To create more certainty in your model you can increase the significance level to .01 or to .001. At the .01 level you are willing to tolerate being wrong only once in 100 chances (meaning you will be right about your prediction 99 times out of 100); at the .001 level you are willing to tolerate being wrong only once in 1,000 chances (meaning you will be right about your prediction 999 times out of 1,000). As you increase the significance level you decrease the amount of times that what you are observing is due to chance alone, and eliminating chance is very important.

Coefficient Summary. The last section is the Coefficient Summary, which includes some of the most valuable data in the model.

1. **Intercept.** The Intercept is the value of "Y" when "X" equals 0. The intercept is the value of the dependent variable if all independent variables equal zero. The *t-Stat* is a test that the slope is significantly different from zero. Notice the p-value is 0.0000, which means that there is a significant difference from zero (remember, the p-value 0.0000 is less than .05). This means that if all the predictors in the model were equal to zero, then the crime rate would be 15456.62. The intercept of the regression equation is 15456.6169.

2. **Coefficients.** MS Excel$^{©}$ displays the unstandardized coefficient for the predictor variables. In statistical parlance the unstandardized coefficient is also known as the beta coefficient or the regression coefficient and is symbolized by a capital "B." The beta coefficient measures the amount of change in the dependent variable (crime rate) for every unit increase in the independent (X) variable and the sign indicates the direction of the change. The beta coefficient -1.2349 indicates that for every 1-unit increase in the independent variable (overtime hours) there is a corresponding *decrease* in the dependent variable (crime rate) by the stated amount (-1.2349). The negative sign indicates a decrease; if this was a positive number 1.2349, then there would be a corresponding *increase* in the dependent variable. Said differently, for every 1-hour increase in overtime hours, the crime rate is predicted to decrease by 1.2349 crimes per 100,000 people.

3. **Standard Error.** The standard error is the average amount of error that results from predicting the dependent variable (crime rate) using the regression equation. The standard error is 1295.2420.

4. **t-stat.** The t-statistic refers to a test that the intercept is significantly different from zero. The t-value is 11.9334 and is statistically significant from zero as shown by the p-value.

5. **P-Value.** The p-value is the exact probability that any change is due to randomness or chance alone. The p-value is derived by setting the significance level at the beginning of the equation. The significance level is also known as the alpha level. Significance does not mean importance or meaningfulness. In statistics, a result is statistically significant if it is unlikely to have occurred by chance. Meaningfulness is exercising good judgment. Here we are seeking to reduce the opportunity for chance in favor of a statistically significant finding that what we are observing occurred because of our efforts, not by chance alone. With the significance level set to 95% (significance level of .05), a p-value of .05 or lower is statistically significant. This means we can affirmatively say that we have reduced the opportunity of chance alone having an effect, and we can say that only 5 times in 100 will we see such a result occur by chance alone. Said differently, in 100 decisions about accepting or rejecting whether what you are observing is true, you will be wrong 5 times and right 95 times. The p-value is critical to our interpretation since we do not consider any variables that do not meet the accepted level of statistical significance (the social science standard is .05).[100] For example, in our equation, overtime hours have a p-value of 0.0289. This is statistically significant, which means that we can rule out that chance alone may be operating. Said differently, the crime rate is decreasing *because of* the amount of overtime hours allocated, not simply by chance alone. We will accept this decision and in doing so we will be wrong twice (2) and right ninety-eight (98) times out of 100.

6. **Lower and Upper 95%.** Remember what we are doing in a regression model: we are making predictions! Neither humans nor the data are infallible and no one can predict the future with absolute certainty. What we can do is reduce the opportunity for chance alone to be operating against us, which is why we set the significance level to .05. But we are never absolutely certain that the prediction is 100% correct. The lower and upper 95% confidence interval helps us say, with a certain level of confidence (95% confidence actually) that the true value of the coefficient falls between the lower and upper limit. For example, the predicted crime rate is 14222. We can say with 95% confidence that the true crime rate falls between 12469 (lower) and 18443 (upper). The same interpretation holds for each coefficient interpretation under the lower and upper 95% limit.

Armed with this information a police executive can make an intelligent and informed presentation to the appropriations committee when asking for additional overtime funds. But, simply because more overtime hours are allocated does not mean that officers are creating more output units (e.g., arrests, traffic summonses, directed patrols, field interviews etc.). In fact, rarely is there ever a situation in real life when a bivariate relationship is all that exists. In many law enforcement applications the results from bivariate analyses often do not hold when you control for other factors, such as the aforementioned output units. It is better to try and answer the following statement with more statistical data: *"Given the department's **current level of output,** if we allocate 1,000 hours of overtime what is the predicted crime rate?"* The statement *"current level of output"* is important because the amount of overtime hours allocated is only one indicator of controlling crime. Yes, appropriating overtime is important, indeed it is the first step to getting officers deployed into the field since no one works for free. Other output measures that help control crime include the arrest rate, the summons rate, the directed patrol rate, the incarceration rate and the number of personnel in the department. There are obviously other crime control indicators, but for illustration purposes we will use these performance indicators to conduct another variety of linear regression known as multiple regression. Once these indicators are controlled statistically, the resulting measure will show how much overtime contributes to the variability in the crime rate.

Predicting the Crime Rate Based Upon Existing Output Measures

One especially important management task is to know how effective a specific police activity is at controlling crime. If an executive knows how effective, say arrests, are at reducing the crime rate, then the executive can direct policy initiatives toward making arrests. What often happens in the real world is that more than one enforcement activity is underway at any given time (e.g., arrests, traffic summonses, field interrogations, directed patrols).[101] In this case you no longer have a bivariate model; you now have a multivariate model. The challenge becomes how to separate the individual data to see which activity has the greatest causal influence on controlling the crime rate. Then, management can direct resources toward those activities and forego other less effective activities. The technique for analyzing multiple possible causes at one time and their effect on something, such as crime rate, is known as multivariate regression analysis (also known as multiple regression analysis).

Multiple regression analysis examines more than one variable at a time, and this tends to produce a more realistic prediction. The general purpose of multiple regression analysis is to learn more about the relationship between several predictor variables (those things that are thought to cause something else to change) and a criterion or dependent variable (those things thought to change or result in a particular outcome). Staying with our previous example the predicted crime rate (dependent variable) may depend on the following factors:

1. How many police officers are employed (predictor variable);
2. The arrest rate (predictor variable);
3. The traffic summons rate (predictor variable);
4. The directed patrol rate (predictor variable);
5. The incarceration rate (predictor variable), *as well as*
6. The number of overtime hours allocated (predictor variable).

Multiple regression analysis will help identify which of these predictor variables have the greatest (and least) causal influence over the crime rate.

A typical line of inquiry into performance that may arise during a management meeting is this: *the chief of police wants to know how well the crime rate can be predicted given the current level of performance, specifically the arrest rate, the traffic summons rate, the directed patrol rate, the incarceration rate, the number of existing personnel and the number of overtime hours allocated.* If the prediction equation works well for the current level of output, then the equation could presumably be used to direct personnel into specific activities. This line of inquiry may be put to the police chief from an elected official sitting on the public safety committee. Or, better yet, the inquiry may be put to a command staff officer *from* the chief of police *before* the chief appears before the appropriations committee. The hypothesis is: H_1: *as police officers increase their level of output, there will be a decrease in the crime rate.*

Because multiple regression permits simultaneous analysis of many predictor variables on a single dependent variable, the technique enables a police executive to ask (and hopefully resolve) the question: *"What is the best predictor of..."* The ...that needs to be completed in this particular management question is: *"What is the best predictor of the **crime rate**?"* The police executive is able to insert different predictor variables and examine which ones have the greatest causal influence.

In our crime control example we added five additional predictor variables: 1) the arrest rate, 2) the summons rate, 3) directed patrol rate, 4) the incarceration rate, 5) the current number of police officers, and 6) the current number of hours of overtime. We want to know what the predicted crime rate will be, given our current performance levels. Again, our first step is to collect some historical data. You should gather at least a few years worth of data; this example uses 10 years (Table 37-1).

Table 37-1		Police Performance Variables for Determining Crime Rate					
Year	Arrest Rate	Summons Rate	Directed Patrol Rate	Incarceration Rate	Personnel	Overtime Hours	Crime Rate
1993	14897	30100	1254	458	1358	1125	15709
1994	15989	31210	1256	489	1385	1258	15301
1995	17896	36589	2478	458	1465	1599	14025
1996	14589	35697	1452	587	1500	1478	13043
1997	18989	30217	1569	569	1599	2589	11796
1998	15896	36988	1698	743	1625	2269	9402
1999	18789	40259	1789	707	1588	1369	9976
2000	19878	39520	1889	816	1566	1589	10743
2001	14789	27896	1987	578	1498	2255	11825
2003	19899	39899	1879	789	1388	3255	11304

Let's first create a correlation matrix to see what relationships exist between the predictor variables and the crime rate. To create a correlation matrix with multiple variables, use the same procedure described earlier for a bivariate model. The resulting output summary should look like table 37-2:

Table 37-2	Bivariate Correlations among Predictor Variables					
	Arrest Rate	Summons Rate	Directed Patrol Rate	Incarceration Rate	Personnel	Overtime Hours	Crime Rate
Arrest Rate	1						
Summons Rate	-0.473	1					
Directed Patrol Rate	0.460	-0.062	1				
Incarceration Rate	-0.080	0.571	0.148	1			
Personnel	-0.187	0.538	-0.026	0.015	1		
Overtime Hours	0.389	0.405	0.274	0.589	0.148	1	
Crime Rate	-0.346	-0.441	-0.349	-0.105	-0.795	-0.497	1

The interpretation is the same as described earlier. Those correlations that show a negative relationship indicate that as one variable increases the other decreases, while a positive relationship indicates that as one variable increases the other variables also increase. The interpretation begins with the columnar data, starting with *arrest rate*. Notice that all of the relationships have moderate to weak strength. Next, we will create a multiple regression model to determine whether there is a statistically significant relationship between the dependent variable (crime rate) and the independent variables (arrest rate, summons rate, directed patrol rate, incarceration rate, personnel and overtime hours). The equation for multiple regression equation is similar to the linear regression equation: $y = a + bx_1 + bx_2 + bx_3 ... + e$, where:

1. y = the predicted value (in this example it is the crime rate we are trying to predict)
2. a = the intercept (this is the value if all independent variables are equal to zero, which means this is the predicted crime rate if we did not have any output measures)
3. b_1x_1 = the partial slope (this is the amount of change in the dependent variable for every one-unit change in the independent variable, which means for every metric change in each of the independent variables, there is a corresponding change in the dependent variable by a specified amount);
4. e = the error term (same as described earlier).

The reason the slope ("b" value) is known as a *partial* slope in a multivariate model is because there is more than one independent (predictor) variable. In a multivariate model each independent variable *partially* contributes to the predicted crime rate. In the previous example, only overtime hours contributed to the crime rate. Thus, the multiple regression equation is:

$$y_{\text{(predicted crime rate)}} = a_{\text{(intercept)}} + b_1 x_1{}_{\text{(arrest rate)}} + b_2 x_2{}_{\text{(summons rate)}}$$
$$+ b_3 x_3{}_{\text{(directed patrol rate)}} + b_4 x_4{}_{\text{(incarceration rate)}} + b_5 x_5{}_{\text{(personnel)}} + b_6 x_6{}_{\text{(overtime rate)}}$$

The next step is to execute the multiple regression equation. In MS Excel© begin by selecting **Tools > Data Analysis.** In the **Data Analysis** dialog box select **Regression,** then click **OK.** The Regression dialog box will appear. Next, select **Input Y Range.** The "y" range is the dependent or criterion variable. In our example crime rate is the dependent variable; this means that the crime rate *depends* on what happens in the other variables. Select the entire crime rate column including the heading "crime rate" and select enter. Next, select **Input X** Range. The "x" range is the independent variables. In our example arrest rate, summons rate, incarceration rate, number of personnel, and number of overtime hours are the independent variables. These are the activities thought to cause a change in the crime rate. Select the entire range of the five variables including their headings. Next, check the boxes labeled **Confidence Level** (set the confidence level at 95%, if it is not already selected) and **Labels.** Next, under **Output Options,** select **New Worksheet Ply.** You can leave the remaining boxes unselected. Next, click **OK.** MS Excel© will execute the multiple regression equation and create a model in a separate worksheet. The Summary Output is the same as that created for a bivariate model and the interpretation is the same. Table 37-3 is the regression model output.

1. **Multiple R.** The multiple correlation, R-value, is .9906, an extremely high finding, a near-perfect relationship.
2. **R-Square.** The R-Square value is .9812. This means that 98.12% of the variation in the crime rate can be explained by the six predictor variables. This is exceptionally high, not often seen in social science.
3. **Adjusted R-Square.** The adjusted R-Square value is .9437. This means that 94.37% of the variation in crime rate can be explained by the six predictor variables. Again, this is exceptionally high.
4. **Standard Error.** The Standard Error is the average amount by which we err if we use the regression equation to predict crime rate. In this model the Standard Error is 511.528, a very low standard error.
5. **Observations.** Observations is number of observations in the model. In this example there are 10 years of data (10 observations) with six predictor variables for each year.

Analysis of Variance (ANOVA). The ANOVA output is the next section and ANOVA is a test of no linearity between the predictor variables and the dependent variables. What is most important in this section is the Significance F. Remember, we are seeking to rule out that chance alone is causing the crime rate to decline; we hope that the crime rate is declining because of the work the police officers are doing. In this model the Significance F is 0.011, which means that there is less than 1 chance in 100 that you will obtain an F value of 26.156. Stated differently you will be right about your prediction about 99 times out of 100. This is a highly statistically significant finding.

Coefficient Summary. The last section is the Coefficient Summary, which includes some of the most valuable data in the model.

1. **Intercept.** The Intercept is the value of "Y" when "X" equals 0. The intercept is the value of the dependent variable if all independent variables equal zero. This means that if all the predictors in the model were equal to zero, then the crime rate would be 44350.[102] The intercept of the regression equation is 44350.208.

2. **Coefficients.** MS Excel© displays the unstandardized coefficient for the predictor variables. The independent variable with the greatest causal influence on the crime rate is personnel, with a coefficient of -14.862. The negative sign reflects the direction in which the dependent variable (crime rate) will change with a one-unit change in the independent variable. The interpretation can be stated this way: for every increase of 1 police officer, crime is predicted to decline by 14.862 per 100,000 people. Conversely, the incarceration rate does not help predict a lower crime rate. The incarceration rate shows a positive direction, which means that for every 1 percent increase in the incarceration rate, the crime rate is predicted to increase by 1.372 per 100,000 people. This suggests that the incarceration rate does not support the crime control effort, indeed, holding all else constant, crime is predicted to increase as more people are incarcerated. The incarceration rate is also not statistically significant. The summons rate, directed patrol rate and overtime hours also do not contribute to a reduction in crime in this model. Only one other variable contributes to a reduced crime rate, and is statistically significant, the arrest rate (b = .373, p<.028).

Table 37-3	Crime Rate Regressed on Predictor Variables					
SUMMARY OUTPUT						

Regression Statistics

Multiple R	0.9906
R Square	0.9812
Adjusted R Square	0.9437
Standard Error	511.528
Observations	10

ANOVA

	df	S.S.	MS	F	Significance F	
Regression	6	41063721.907	6843953.651	26.156	0.011	
Residual	3	784982.493	261660.831			
Total	9	41848704.400				

COEFFICIENT SUMMARY

	Coefficients	Standard Error	t Stat	P-value	Lower 95%	Upper 95%
Intercept	44350.208	3695.402	12.001	0.001	32589.788	56110.628
Arrest Rate	-0.373	0.093	-4.024	0.028	-0.668	-0.078
Summons Rate	-0.243	0.094	-2.587	0.081	-0.541	0.056
Directed Patrol Rate	-0.395	0.270	-1.460	0.240	-1.256	0.466
Incarceration Rate	1.372	1.076	1.275	0.292	2.053	4.797
Personnel	-14.862	2.368	-6.277	0.008	-22.397	-7.327
Overtime Hours	-0158	0.437	-0.361	0.742	-1.550	1.234

The full multiple regression equation is:

$$12312 \text{ (predicted crime rate)} = 44350 \text{ (intercept)} + (-.373 \times 14207) \text{ (arrest rate)}$$
$$+ (-.243 \times 4734) \text{ (summons rate)}$$
$$+ (-.395 \times 964) \text{ (directed patrol rate)} + (1.372 \times 1600) \text{ (incarceration rate)}$$
$$+ (-14.862 \times 1497) \text{ (personnel)} + (-.158 \times 1879) \text{ (overtime rate)}$$

In this equation, the mean score for each independent variable is shown as the "X" value that is multiplied by the slope. You should use the number that is most suitable for your purposes.

You now know the performance indicators that are best for predicting the crime rate in this model are the arrest rate and the number of personnel. So, for example, if you wanted to know what the predicted crime rate would be if you increased the average arrest rate by 25%, and increased the average personnel strength by 100 officers, here is what you need to do:

1. Increase the arrest rate by 25%: ($17758.75 = 14207 \times 1.25$).
2. Increase the average personnel strength by 100 officers: ($1597 = 1497 + 100$).

4. Insert the new values for each variable and compute the regression equation as usual.

5. The new predicted crime rate would be 9,504 per 100,000 people.[103]

Drawing Inferences about Police Response Time Based Upon Demographic Data

Response time is a traditional indicator of police performance. Although research suggests that swifter response time does not necessarily lead to more apprehensions, it *does* suggest that it is associated with citizen satisfaction. The police are a service-oriented business akin to any other service-oriented business such as livery service, and the hotel and restaurant industry. Customer satisfaction is predicated on the level of service provided by those on the front lines of delivering that service (i.e., the restaurant maitre d'; the waiter; the bartender; the taxi/limousine driver; the police officer). Since service delivery is one of the most important functions of a police department, it is logical to ensure that it is being delivered in a reasonably efficient and expeditious manner.[104] Assessing service-quality through citizen-satisfaction surveys or through administrative performance review is useful to police executives who want to confirm or dispel citizen attitudes and make adjustments to their patrol program (Kelly and Swindell, 2002).

A frequent criticism of the police is that they respond in a differential manner across neighborhoods, typically based on extralegal factors. Response time has been a source of police-community tension, especially in minority communities, for decades; minority neighborhoods frequently cite poor response time as a source of dissatisfaction with the police (Kelly and Swindell, 2002b). Therefore, police executives will do well to redouble their efforts to ensure the police department is providing police service equitably, in proportion to demonstrated need, and that each neighborhood receives the same level of attention as all other neighborhoods. The hypothesis is: H_1: *police response time does not differ significantly between minority and non-minority neighborhoods.* To assess performance in this area we again turn to multiple regression analysis.

The first step is to conceptualize what needs to be analyzed. If you want to assess the department's response time performance against a demographic profile of the community, then you will need:

1. Response time data, and
2. Community demographic data.

The response time data can be collected from the CAD. If not, then dispatch cards that have the starting time and ending time will be required. Next, you will need to gather the demographic data, which can be collected from the U.S. Census Bureau. Census data is very valuable for this type of performance review. The data can be purchased commercially in a user-friendly format from GeoLytics© www.geolytics.com).

Once you have the data elements you must decide on a unit of analysis. "The unit of analysis is the major entity that is being analyzed in the study. It is the 'what' or 'whom' being studied."[105] This is critical since correctly drawing inferences is predicted on specifying what is being studied. For example, you cannot draw an inference about a neighborhood if the unit under study is individual people, and vice versa. If you think about it logically it does not make sense to draw inferences about two different things: it is not possible to attribute poor response time to individual people if you are examining census tracts. The reverse also holds true. If you fail to carefully specify what it is that you are studying, then you risk drawing incorrect inferences from the analysis and you may commit what is known as an ecological fallacy.[106]

In this example the unit of analysis is going to be census tracts. Census tracts are relatively stable units, meaning they do not change over time like precinct boundaries, sector boundaries or political wards. Also, every address in a jurisdiction has a census tract associated with it. A location's address is a unique identifier; no two locations can occupy the same address and no two census tracts have the same location. The data from GeoLytics© is formatted with census tracts, therefore it is easy to match CAD data, that has a valid address, to a corresponding census tract.

The first step is to collect response times from dispatched assignment from the CAD for at least one year. We are not interested in self-initiated assignments, only those assignments where a police officer was dispatched; dispatched assignments demonstrate response time. You will calculate the amount of time it takes to arrive on scene from the time the call was entered in to the CAD. This usually means simply subtracting the time the officer arrived on-scene from the time the call was entered into the CAD to arrive at the number of minutes it took a police officer to arrive after the caller hung up the phone.

1.	Officer arrived	14:10
2.	Call entered into CAD	14:02
3.	Response time	Minutes: 8

After you have calculated the response times for each call for service, you must select demographic variables. Since we are analyzing police performance across diverse neighborhoods in the community, we will select predictor variables that will help us understand how the social differences among neighborhoods affect response time. Selecting these variables should be based on sociological and criminological theory and is best accomplished by appealing to the social science literature. Some of the predictors may be:

1. The non-white population
2. Residential mobility

3. Unemployment
4. Poverty
5. Female-headed households

There are potentially others, such as divorce rate, education levels, and population under 16: however, we will use only the previously mentioned predictors.

Once we have the variables identified we need to aggregate the data to each corresponding census tract and calculate the mean score for each variable for each census tract. For example, if you had 100 CFS in census tract 1, then you would calculate the mean response time for all 100 calls; then you would calculate the mean score for each of the other variables for census tract 1 and insert them into the spreadsheet, as in Table 38. In our example there are 89 census tracts (let's say they are numbered 1-89). For each case we need the mean score for:

1. Response time
2. The non-white population
3. Residential mobility
4. Unemployment
5. Poverty
6. Female-headed households

You will set this up in Excel© like Table 38. Response time is reflected in minutes and the predictor variables are shown in proportions. In the last row create an overall mean score for each variable. This will give the reader an overall picture for the entire model.

Table 38		Response Time and Census Data Aggregated to the Census Tract Level				
Census Tract	Response Time	Non-white	Mobility	Unemployment	Poverty	FM Households
1	8.95	0.213561	0.377046	0.111388	0.178936	0.200354
2	6.6	0.147822	0.25578	0.127095	0.430708	0.375
3	5.25	0.293962	0.360241	0.169707	0.289838	0.341365
4	4.84	0.032645	0.330237	0.135821	0.258761	0.303278
5	8.15	0.088981	0.20142	0.045515	0.2033	0.299638
6	6.37	0.14504	0.301078	0.092923	0.177332	0.185542
7	5.29	0.526623	0.32491	0.118213	0.217431	0.580808
8	9.6	0.230839	0.250803	0.103687	0.202294	0.387791
9	7.42	0.568261	0.306162	0.165913	0.379599	0.587892
10	6.69	0.63852	0.345187	0.334166	0.433973	0.679715
11	9.03	0.597561	0.188192	0.396	0.209815	0.773437
12	5.65	0.958588	0.348889	0.358416	0.508486	0.464646
13	8.49	0.877871	0.263939	0.185455	0.430403	0.715073

Table 38		Response Time and Census Data Aggregated to the Census Tract Level				
Census Tract	Response Time	Non-white	Mobility	Unemployment	Poverty	FM Households
14	10.53	0.896699	0.203779	0.185	0.420955	0.700361
15	8.08	0.858734	0.348912	0.184818	0.320665	0.548736
16	12.13	0.911007	0.401219	0.150127	0.328922	0.688022
17	9.54	0.931526	0.254297	0.266667	0.285451	0.675324
18	7.03	0.90472	0.242095	0.106557	0.370882	0.569892
19	8.11	0.930632	0.411655	0.158858	0.249682	0.330578
20	9.12	0.938642	0.226658	0.171045	0.131211	0.377162
21	9.58	0.509845	0.259354	0.085528	0.150931	0.256428
22	9.84	0.911382	0.282869	0.106756	0.173347	0.457711
23	8.55	0.925325	0.303843	0.092697	0.219555	0.616459
24	8	0.951184	0.306325	0.123878	0.215362	0.519515
25	13.26	0.868893	0.286678	0.223947	0.348718	0.722397
26	9.18	0.886517	0.4689	0.28481	0.502247	0.734848
27	10.09	0.895101	0.346436	0.172932	0.318732	0.655367
28	6.17	0.85931	0.397048	0.320565	0.335821	0.803797
29	6.42	0.926195	0.337064	0.215569	0.669702	0.830449
30	7.49	0.988593	0.468354	0.241877	0.499351	0.827886
31	8.75	0.884644	0.371381	0.248062	0.409796	0.671641
32	6.48	0.923297	0.289053	0.222543	0.531196	0.734348
33	9.35	0.940291	0.271692	0.139082	0.32113	0.75
34	5.91	0.909622	0.485853	0.198228	0.403384	0.793478
35	7.18	0.954864	0.383544	0.331639	0.499219	0.743534
36	7.85	0.901422	0.537726	0.339888	0.421801	0.816239
37	6.85	0.946553	0.368092	0.162824	0.277727	0.662361
38	8.85	0.972254	0.269923	0.224044	0.256886	0.595505
39	7.25	0.951124	0.279635	0.109375	0.214003	0.651162
40	8.17	0.98687	0.280886	0.255639	0.363541	0.743142
41	5.76	0.97382	0.273066	0.104659	0.173875	0.647482
42	8.1	0.951661	0.305209	0.183788	0.204358	0.640416
43	6.95	0.956271	0.260384	0.118675	0.142946	0.557297
44	5.17	0.922948	0.297547	0.144612	0.220576	0.698481
45	9.1	0.717008	0.366605	0.238045	0.434669	0.697624
46	7.25	0.965365	0.301089	0.159718	0.288032	0.517187
47	4.7	0.83972	0.25155	0.262517	0.392739	0.696498
48	2.8	0.991283	0.308614	0.188435	0.154996	0.529411
49	9.6	0.991283	0.308614	0.188435	0.154996	0.529411
50	6.6	0.968191	0.304407	0.145937	0.15772	0.463601
51	7.58	0.97619	0.30936	0.316219	0.29067	0.708144
52	7.08	0.916481	0.326765	0.174153	0.400301	0.758064
53	5.97	0.438568	0.346154	0.158805	0.355327	0.55
54	4.88	0.819304	0.361194	0.238956	0.546479	0.843342
55	8.41	0.834049	0.40931	0.271255	0.56968	0.733059

Table 38		Response Time and Census Data Aggregated to the Census Tract Level				
Census Tract	Response Time	Non-white	Mobility	Unemployment	Poverty	FM Households
56	5.88	0.904966	0.165201	0.127907	0.163327	0.725
57	6.78	0.986105	0.335896	0.290557	0.437256	0.721153
58	6.61	0.57665	0.269403	0.261993	0.526173	0.657718
59	4.77	0.228365	0.250943	0.109948	0.303786	0.407124
60	2.55	0.013656	0.26592	0.094131	0.141974	0.22268
61	3.1	0.019983	0.208038	0.083998	0.145998	0.045346
62	2.81	0.022047	0.268454	0.130764	0.142767	0.09756
63	2.5	0.007569	0.235838	0.113836	0.177728	0.091743
64	6.18	0.011632	0.237913	0.078014	0.138993	0.075875
65	5.6	0.042828	0.270807	0.1139	0.183434	0.192913
66	4.17	0.181364	0.261735	0.166667	0.285305	0.452631
67	5.14	0.211735	0.316429	0.226827	0.285439	0.391752
68	6.67	0.004988	0.278398	0.087478	0.190491	0.135869
69	5.25	0.015729	0.147277	0.142266	0.171844	0.125373
70	7.38	0.016016	0.220984	0.101174	0.159801	0.060846
71	5.27	0.035289	0.259955	0.123782	0.173405	0.111842
72	5.27	0.434069	0.127069	0.244156	0.44686	0.396984
73	3.81	0.843529	0.249352	0.14653	0.360049	0.647761
74	9.23	0.875	0.400943	0.069565	0.338325	0.842639
75	3.89	0.485993	0.260462	0.452406	0.495544	0.431818
76	8.18	0.743223	0.231156	0.090141	0.277861	0.618055
77	6.14	0.127429	0.326233	0.168647	0.219669	0.491428
78	1	0.311681	0.339836	0.272251	0.378589	0.330882
79	7.2	0.311681	0.339836	0.272251	0.378589	0.330882
80	6.13	0.253661	0.284908	0.164557	0.355372	0.512755
81	7.32	0.630252	0.29652	0.128319	0.330492	0.55967
82	7.23	0.070573	0.278867	0.157696	0.257041	0.472275
83	10.12	0.405269	0.276051	0.201444	0.44223	0.577625
84	6.4	0.246299	0.318264	0.144379	0.28491	0.449564
85	5.13	0.267214	0.354833	0.095439	0.199503	0.345854
86	4.73	0.146667	0.29918	0.101588	0.272978	0.416361
87	4.76	0.355259	0.302001	0.109403	0.277434	0.593277
88	3.77	0.170927	0.348722	0.132403	0.29354	0.586368
89	5.56	0.665668	0.190419	0.44186	0.333333	0.444444
mean	6.84	0.603	0.302	0.182	0.306	0.523

Now, we can examine the scores for each predictor variable at a glance:

Response time	6.84 (minutes)
Non-white population	.603 (proportion)
Residential mobility	.302 (proportion)
Unemployment	.182 (proportion)
Poverty	.306 (proportion)
Female-headed households	.523 (proportion)

The next step is to create a correlation matrix to examine the strength and direction of the relationship between variables. Table 38-1 is the bivariate correlations among predictor variables by census tract. Notice that all of the correlations are positive with generally moderate strength.

Table 38-1	Bivariate Correlations among Predictor Variables by Census Tracts					
	Response Time	*Non-white Population*	*Residential Mobility*	*Unemployment*	*Poverty*	*FM Households*
Response Time	1					
Non-white population	0.455	1				
Residential Mobility	0.143	0.309	1			
Unemployment	0.036	0.357	0.223	1		
Poverty	0.103	0.345	0.383	0.597	1	
FM Households	0.379	0.788	0.406	0.428	0.593	1

Next, with all of the mean scores calculated and the data aggregated to the census tract level, we are ready to execute the multivariate regression model. Remember the question we are trying to answer: *do the police respond differently in areas that have a higher proportion of non-white residents?* The first indication there might be a problem is revealed in the correlation matrix. Notice the relationship between the non-white population and the response time. There is a moderately strong positive relationship (0.455). This means that census tracts with higher non-white populations also have higher response times, the hypothesis has been rejected. The regression procedure is the same as our crime rate model; the dependent (Y) variable will be response time and the predictor variables (X) are the five we collected from the census. Run the regression analysis and the output will look like table 38-2.

Table 38-2	Response Time Regressed on Demographic Variables					
SUMMARY OUTPUT						

Regression Statistics	
Multiple R	0.480
R Square	0.231
Adjusted R Square	0.184
Standard Error	1.976
Observations	89

ANOVA

	df	S.S.	MS	F	Significance F
Regression	5	97.1241	19.4248	4.9751	0.0005
Residual	83	324.0649	3.9044		
Total	88	421.1890			

	Coefficients	Standard Error	t Stat	P-value	Lower 95%	Upper 95%
Intercept	5.433	0.960	5.661	0.000	3.524	7.342
Non-white population	2.459	0.988	2.488	**0.015**	0.493	4.425
Residential Mobility	0.198	3.304	0.060	0.952	-6.374	6.770
Unemployment	-3.876	3.140	-1.234	0.221	-10.120	2.369
Poverty	-0.571	2.575	-0.222	0.825	-5.693	4.551
Female-headed Households	1.423	1.949	0.730	0.467	-2.453	5.298

Let's interpret the data. In the first section, *regression statistics*, we see the strength of the relationship between response time and the five predictor variables is moderately strong: .480. The r-square value is low at .231; 23.1% of the variability in response time is explained by the five predictor variables. The adjusted r-square value is .184 with a low standard error of 1.976 for the 89 observations (the observations are the individual census tracts).

The ANOVA section of table 38-2 reveals that the model is statistically significant (F: 4.9751; p<.0005), which means that we can rule out chance alone. A p-value of .0005 is extremely high. We will be right about our prediction 9,995 times out of 10,000; said differently, we risk being wrong about our prediction less than 5 times out of 10,000 chances. Turning to the coefficient summary we see that only the non-white population is statistically significant at the .05 level (p<.015). None of the other predictor variables are statistically significant, which means that we cannot interpret them, and we cannot say that they have a causal influence on the dependent variable (response time). Just to confirm what we are looking at, we will construct a scatterplot of response time (dependent variable) and the non-white population (predictor variable).

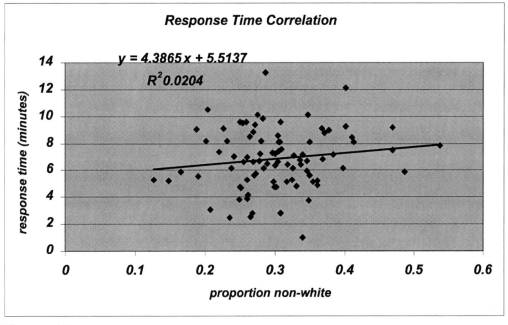

Figure 17

The scatterplot reveals a positive relationship: as the proportion of non-white population increases in each census tract, police response time also increases. The coefficient for non-white population is 2.459 with a positive relationship. This means for every 1 percent increase in the non-white population in the census tracts, response time is predicted to increase by 2.459 minutes. This is clearly a time for introspection. Why are police responding differently in non-white areas? Is the workload greater in these areas? If so, then a workload analysis must be conducted to see if personnel are distributed proportionately. Is there something else about the area that could explain the variability in response time? A thorough management analysis is required to answer what is causing this problem, but the statistics reveal a snapshot of the response time patterns. Also, slightly more than 18% (adj. r-square 18.4) of the variability in response time is explained by the five predictor variables. This leaves about 72% of the variability in response time unexplained. Although one of the variables, residential stability, does approach statistical significance (p<.06), strictly speaking, it is not significant according to convention and should remain treated as such.

Linear regression and correlation are very useful methods for management analysis. Here is another management question that both methods can answer: *what is the relationship between citizen complaints and the volume of calls for service?* As a commanding officer it is your obligation to address all citizen complaints to confirm or dispel their validity. Correlation and regression can help resolve these personnel issues:

1. *Is there a relationship between citizen complaints and volume of calls for service?*
2. *If so, then is the relationship positive or negative?*
3. *What percentage of the variability in citizen complaints can be explained by calls for service? What other factors (predictors) contribute to citizen complaints?*
4. *What citizen complaint rate would you predict for a duty-tour that received 1,000 calls for service? What about 1,500 calls for service?*
5. *Would you expect all duty tours that received 1,000 calls for service to have the same citizen complaint rate?*

Drawing Inferences about Police Response Time Based Upon Absenteeism

A frequent management issue is addressing employee absenteeism, a performance indicators discussed in table 1 that relates to, *"Delivering Public Value through Budgeting Accountability."* A few categories of personnel-leave are particularly critical for management to control, since they are often symptoms of a larger problem. Employees who are chronically sick, injured, placed on light duty, suspended or placed on restricted/modified duty tend to draw management's attention because a police department's number one resource is its people. These symptoms may signify much larger problems, such as alcohol or drug dependency, gambling, personal finances, domestic troubles or misconduct, which often interfere with department performance (see, for example Fyfe and Kane, 2006).

One of the performance areas that may suffer from excessive absenteeism is response time.[107] Response time is directly affected by the number of police officers available to handle dispatched calls for service; fewer officers in the field translates into slower response time and inevitably fewer satisfied citizens. Consequently, management has an obligation to minimize employee absences that are within their control, particularly when department performance is at risk. The hypothesis is: *H_1: as personnel on leave increases, response time increases.* We can use regression analysis to infer what influence these categories of absenteeism have on response time.

First, collect data for a suitable period of time, such as the last 12 months; the data can be collected in monthly or weekly intervals, whichever is preferred. Calculate the average response time in minutes for each period (week, month etc.) for the last 12 months. Then, calculate the average number of days employees consumed, for each period, for sick, injured, light duty and restricted duty. Set up the data in Excel© as shown in Table 38-3.

Table 38-3	Response Time and Predictor Variables				
Month	Response time	Sick	Injured	Light Duty	Restricted Duty
Jan	8.2	25	7	5	5
Feb	7.5	3	9	7	2
Mar	7.66	2	10	7	5
Apr	8.01	20	5	4	2
May	7.95	9	6	6	1
Jun	8.33	25	8	7	5
Jul	7.25	7	9	7	0
Aug	7.8	9	8	5	2
Sep	7.3	2	7	6	3
Oct	7.1	2	4	5	2
Nov	7.6	1	5	5	1
Dec	7.05	4	11	6	7
Mean	**7.646**	**9.083**	**7.417**	**5.833**	**2.917**

Next, perform a bivariate correlation analysis to examine the strength and direction of the relationship, as shown in Table 38-4. What is immediately apparent is that sick leave has a strong positive correlation with response time with a correlation of .8251 (recall that a correlation of 1 is a perfect correlation). In the bivariate model both sick leave and restricted duty have a positive correlation with response time; the other correlations have weak strength at best with a negative relationship, which suggests they do not influence response time in the bivariate model.

Table 38-4	Bivariate Correlations among Predictor Variables				
	Response time	Sick	Injured	Light Duty	Restricted Duty
Response time	1				
Sick	0.8251	1			
Injured	-0.1883	-0.1228	1		
Light Duty	-0.1433	-0.2120	0.6907	1	
Restricted Duty	0.0982	0.2565	0.5293	0.1605	1

The last step is to create the regression model. The dependent variable (Y) is response time; the independent variables (X) are sick leave, injured leave, light duty and restricted duty. These are the categories of leave that are believed to influence response time. The first output measure we want to examine is whether the model is statistically significant. This means that we want to know if response time is really influenced by these performance indicators or whether the results may have occurred by chance alone. We turn first to the *Significance F,* which shows a value of .047. This means the model is statistically significant. A *p-value* of .047 means there is about 5 chances in 100 of obtaining an F value of 4.216, which means the result did not occur by chance. Next, we examine the strength and direction of the model. The *Multiple*

R value is .841, which shows a strong positive relationship. The *R-squared* value is .707 and the *adjusted R-squared* value is .539; using the adjusted R-squared value over the R-squared value is preferred and this model suggests that nearly 54% of the variability in the dependent variable (response time) is explained by the independent variables (sick leave, injured leave, light duty and restricted duty). Next, examine the *p-value* for each independent variable. Notice that only sick leave is statistically significant ($p < .007$), which means we can only interpret sick leave and not the other predictors; the other predictor variables are not statistically significant and they must be treated as such. Sick leave shows a positive relationship, when controlling for the other variables. We can say that for every 1 day increase in sick leave, response time is predicted to increase by .040 minutes or approximately 2.4 seconds ($.040 \times 60 = 2.4$ seconds). So, as sick leave increases so too does response time.

Table 38-5	Response Time Regressed on Predictor Variables					
SUMMARY OUTPUT						
Regression Statistics						
Multiple R	0.841					
R Square	0.707					
Adjusted R Square	0.539					
Standard Error	0.288					
Observations	12					
ANOVA						
	df	*S.S.*	*MS*	*F*	*Significance F*	
Regression	4	1.397	0.349	4.216	0.047	
Residual	7	0.580	0.083			
Total	11	1.977				
	Coefficients	*Standard Error*	*t Stat*	*P-value*	*Lower 95%*	*Upper 95%*
Intercept	7.174	0.540	13.294	0.000	5.898	8.45
Sick	0.040	0.010	3.824	0.007	0.015	0.065
Injured	-0.032	0.070	-0.450	0.666	-0.197	0.134
Light Duty	0.065	0.124	0.526	0.615	-0.228	0.358
Restricted Duty	-0.012	0.055	-0.226	0.827	-0.142	0.117

From this statistical model the executive can set performance outcomes. For example, the executive wants to set a response time goal of no more than 6 minutes. The management question is: *Given the 12 previous months of response time data, on what date can the agency expect to reach the 6-minute response time goal?* An intermediate objective a police executive can set is weekly milestones along the path toward the 6.00 minute response time goal. This can be accomplished through *forecasting*, which is the subject of the next section.

One of the reasons measuring performance indicators such as sick leave, injured leave, light duty and restricted duty is so important is because management may wish to regulate employees through policy by restricting use of these prerogatives. Some of these categories may be contractually conferred benefits, particularly sick leave. Without statistical analysis an executive will have a difficult time demonstrating why management wants to reduce sick leave from, say, 25 days per year to 15 days per year during labor negotiations. Likewise, if a personnel matter goes to arbitration or to court, then management will be well poised to support their case with this type of analysis instead of simply making uncorroborated generalities, such as *"we believe..."* or *"historically ..."* which probably will not hold up in court.

This type of analysis can also be used to justify other personnel decisions such as removing someone from their preferred assignment. Let's argue that instead of predicting response time we want to predict the case clearance rate for the detective division. The same data set could be collected (1 year); the dependent variable would be case clearance rate (it could also be the actual number of cases cleared instead of the rate); the independent variables would remain the same, however, we might also want to control for some other variables such as court time and time spent at meetings. If the results were statistically significant, then we could conclude that case clearance rate is associated with absenteeism. In this case the detective division commander would have to explain the basis for the negative relationship: as sick time increases the division's case clearance rate decreases. Taking this theory one step further, so as not to commit an ecological fallacy, we could examine each individual detective's clearance rates to see if the same patterns were uncovered. Then a commander would be armed with objective information necessary to support his or her request to have someone removed from their assignment for poor performance.

Making Predictions through Forecasting

It is a matter of when, not if, crime will occur that needs a solution. Since we are virtually assured that crime will occur we need a method for forecasting when, where and how much. Predicting when and where is a formidable challenge fraught with all of the inaccuracies, uncertainties and human foibles as any other forecasting technique. Crime mapping, for example, shows where crime is concentrated *after* it occurs, but does not help predict where it will occur beforehand. How often is the local weather forecast inaccurate with all of its sophisticated computer analysis and radar? The Compstat process and all of its associated analyses, particularly spatial and temporal analysis (crime mapping), have significantly advanced crime control management and how law enforcement approaches when and where crime may occur. But predicting *how much* is more than just taking an average of the last several months and drawing an inference.

Predicting crime is best developed through a combination of qualitative and quantitative methods. Qualitative methods explore and answer analysts' questions that "focus on how individuals and groups view and understand their world and construct meaning out of their experiences. It essentially is narrative-oriented and uses content analysis methods on selected levels of communication content."[108] Qualitative research is also laden with minute details and descriptions of social phenomena such as how humans interact with each other and with their environment and manage interpersonal relations. By contrast, quantitative methods explore and answer analysts' questions with numerical data and other data elements that are measurable. The results of quantitative research are generally counts, percentages, positive and negative data relationships, ratios, decimals or a series of numbers that are often presented in tables or charts. Both quantitative and qualitative research is important to predicting crime. According to Schneider (2005) "qualitative methods for forecasting crime include environmental analysis and scenarios. These techniques are useful for identifying the future *nature* of criminal activity. By contrast, quantitative methods are used to predict the future *scope* of crime, more specifically, crime rates. A common quantitative method for developing forecasts is to extrapolate annual crime rate trends developed through time-series models. This approach also involves correlating past crime trends with factors that will influence the future scope of crime, in particular demographic and macro-economic variables" (Schneider, 2005). This is precisely what occurred in the example that dealt with police response time and the socio-demographic predictor variables in the previous example. A full discussion of time-series analysis and its associated analytic techniques (e.g., autoregressive integrated moving average-ARIMA-models) is beyond the scope of this text, however ARIMA is an excellent diagnostic tool (see Shadish, Cook and Campbell, 2002).

Crime forecasting is relatively new to policing but is gaining in popularity thanks to advances in criminological research in areas such as the "criminality of places," the "ecology of crime" and "hot spots" (Gorr and Harries, 2003:551). This section will examine one basic statistical forecasting technique that can help tactical planners make better crime predictions, which will help police administrators develop performance goals and adjust level of deployment.

Forecasting Technique

Crime forecasting helps calculate or predict future values from existing values. This is where baseline measures again are useful; the baseline measure is the existing value, which provides a historical picture of the agency's present state. The forecasted valued is where the agency may wind up if things don't change or unless something is done differently, good or bad (Friedman, 2005:56). O'Shea and Nichols (2002:27), in a report to the U.S. Department of Justices—COPS Office, found that police agencies do consider forecasting a strategic activity that is useful for daily tactical operations. The forecasting technique uses linear regression analysis, a method of estimating a predicted value of one variable (Y) derived from a series of given values of one or more other variables (X). The estimate is derived from values that are known and already exist (both the Y and X are already known). For example, before you can forecast the crime rate for next month, you must have the data from at least the last two previous months; the last two month's data are already known to you since they have already been collected. We also know the time period from which the values are drawn, the last two months. The *forecast period* could be the last 1, 5 or 10 years, or the last week, month or quarter. The forecast period is the length of time that is represented by each observation in the baseline data. The term forecast period is used because the forecast typically represents the same length of time (interval) as each baseline observation. For example, if the baseline data consists of monthly calls for service, then the forecast is usually for the following month. If the baseline consists of quarterly crime data, then the forecast is usually for the following quarter. The new value is predicted through linear regression, which can help forecast a variety of tactical and administrative future perspectives. Some of those perspectives are:

- *How many calls for service can we expect over the next 3 years?*
- *Given the current workload how many arrests can we expect to make next year?*
- *What is our projected workload for the upcoming summer months?*
- *How much can we expect to spend in court overtime for the next fiscal year?*
- *What is our worst and best case for deployment given the anticipated workload for the next 3 years?*
- *What date can we expect to experience "x" number of crimes, given the past trend?*

Analysts that are not familiar with forecasting techniques usually rely on simple averages of the data for the previous time period to estimate the next value. For example, if, in the first quarter of the year the city experienced 102, 320 and 226 Part I crimes, respectively, most analysts would predict that April will experience 216 Part I crimes (102 + 320 + 226)/3 = 216). However, forecasting analysis predicts 340 crimes for April, because forecasting accounts for the covariance between the individual data points and the time periods (Jan, Feb and Mar are known as the intervals), whereas averaging simply factors the numbers.[109] Averages do play an important role in forecasting, particularly for a technique known as *moving average analysis*, which is discussed later.

Forecasting crime is only as accurate as the data and the environment surrounding its creation. This is the point Schneider (2005) was making about the necessity of combining qualitative and qualitative methods to predict when and where crime will occur. If environmental conditions change (e.g., unemployment rate, poverty rate, etc), then it is likely that the prediction will change. This is also the point that was made earlier about taking a snapshot of the agency's performance and accounting for socio-demographic factors that are subject to change, albeit slowly. Forecasting will provide you with reasonable quantitative predictions, *provided* assumptions you make about the qualitative aspects remain constant. So, if you predict a crime rate of 247 per 1,000 residents and a sudden, unexpected shift in population occurs, the crime rate may expand or contract with the population shift.[110] Another very important aspect about forecasting is the further into the future you estimate, the less accurate your prediction will be. Using the linear regression approach, you can make forecasts farther into the future than just one forecast period, but the farther your forecast gets from the most recent actual observation, the weaker the prediction.

MS Excel© has a forecasting function that uses three numeric parameters to create the expression.[111] Forecasting can only be accomplished with numeric data (numbers) not letters. So, for example, if you want to forecast the crime rate or budget expenditures for the next week, you must convert the days of the week (Sunday through Saturday) into numbers (1-7). The same convention applies for monthly parameters (January through December = 1-12). The three parameters for the forecast expression are:

1. X = the data point for which you want to forecast, for example the next month, the next year or the next day.
2. Y = the known dependent variables, for example the number of crimes or the budgeted dollar amount for each interval. The dependent variable is what you are trying to predict.
3. X = the known independent variables, for example the range of years (2000-2005) if you are predicting a yearly crime rate or the range of weeks (1–35) or months (1–10; 1–18; 1–36) if you are predicting weeks or months.

The data for forecasting is located on the Resource CD under the forecasting workbook. The first example is a 1-month forecast. Let's say during a crime control meeting in December the chief wants to know what the projected calls for service will be for the upcoming month (January). This is how to satisfy the requirements of the forecasting function:

1. X = 13 (the first month following 12 months worth of data)
2. Y = the dependent variable (the calls for service)
3. X = the independent variable (previous range of months in your data set, 1 – 12)

To execute the forecast function, find the first empty cell following month #12 on the row of calls for service (cell O3 in the Excel© spreadsheet). Next, select **forecast** from **Insert > function** on the toolbar. When the dialog box appears, enter 13 as the value for the data point which you are predicting (X = the 13th month, which is the successive month from the previous 12-months. We are predicting the calls for service for January 2007, the 13th month, based upon historical data). Next, select the entire range of data that is the subject of the forecast (i.e., the calls for service in the row 2006; this is the (Y) dependent variable). Finally, select the range of data for the time period in question (i.e., the months 1 through 12, these are the (X) independent variables). Excel© executes the forecast function and inserts the projection in the cell you originally selected (O3). Table 39 shows the projected calls for service for January 2007 to be 223,069, given the historical trend.

Table 39	1-Month Projection of Calls for Service												Projection
	Jan	Feb	Mar	Apr	May	Jun	Jul	Aug	Sep	Oct	Nov	Dec	Jan 2007
Month	1	2	3	4	5	6	7	8	9	10	11	12	13
2006	124569	137026	164431	172653	138122	151934	148896	163785	180164	198180	217998	239798	223069

You can repeat the procedure for each successive month for medium and long-range planning exercises. Table 39-1 is the 1st quarter 2007 projection of calls for service, based on the known monthly calls for service from the previous 12 months and the estimated calls for service for January and February 2007.

Table 39-1	1st Quarter 2007 Projection of Calls for Service												Projection		
	Jan	Feb	Mar	Apr	May	Jun	Jul	Aug	Sep	Oct	Nov	Dec	Jan	Feb	Mar
	1	2	3	4	5	6	7	8	9	10	11	12	13	14	15
2006	124,569	137,026	164,431	172,653	138,122	151,934	148,896	163,785	180,164	198,180	217,998	239,798	223069	231265	239461

There are times throughout the year when projections become especially important, namely the summer season (June, July and August) and the Christmas season (November and December). The summer months bring warm weather and increased travel and tourism, which inevitably bring more people together who may be carrying cash or who leave houses and property unattended. Let's say during a crime control meeting in May the chief wants to know what the projected calls for service will be for the upcoming summer months (June, July and August) because he or she is planning a summer initiative. The procedure is the same. Recall, since months are expressed in letters (January–December), we must convert the letters into numbers (months 1–12). First, select the first empty cell beneath June (H25 in the spreadsheet); the data point we are projecting is June (month #6). The dependent variable (Y) is the range of data from January to May. Finally, the independent variable is the months (1 - 5, meaning January to May). Execute the forecast function and you will derive a projection of 166,180 calls for June 2000. Repeat the same procedure for July and August and you get a projection of 172,453 for July and 178,727 for August; the total calls for service for the 3 summer months in 2000 is projected to be 517,360 calls (Table 39-2). Table 39-2 is a similar projection of calls for service for the Christmas shopping months, November and December. This type of analysis is useful for projecting anticipated workload, which affects deploy-ment levels, overtime expenditures and arrest levels, all of which impact the budget. It is a useful tool for tactical planners who may be tasked with design-ing various special initiatives during seasonal times that are subject to fluctuations.

Table 39-2						Summer-Season Projection of Calls for Service						
	Jan	Feb	Mar	Apr	May	Jun	Jul	Aug	Sep	Oct	Nov	Dec
	1	2	3	4	5	6	7	8	9	10	11	12
2000	124569	137026	164431	172653	138122	166180	172453	178727	196599	216259	237885	261674
2001	123548	135903	163083	171238	136990	164818	171040	177262	194988	214487	235935	259529
2002	158799	174679	209615	220095	176076	211844	219841	227838	250622	275685	303253	333578
2003	124599	137059	164471	172694	138155	166220	172495	178770	196647	216311	237942	261737
2004	125495	138045	165653	173936	139149	167415	173735	180055	198061	217867	239653	263619
2005	158786	174665	209598	220077	176062	211827	219823	227820	250602	275662	303228	333551
2006	154895	170385	204461	214684	171748	206636	214437	222237	244461	268907	295798	325377

Table 39-3				Christmas Shopping Season Projection of Calls for Service							Projection	
	Jan	Feb	Mar	Apr	May	Jun	Jul	Aug	Sep	Oct	Nov	Dec
	1	2	3	4	5	6	7	8	9	10	11	12
2000	154856	170342	204410	214630	171704	188875	185097	203607	223968	246364	233836	240645
2001	123548	135903	163083	171238	136990	150689	147675	162443	178687	196556	186560	191993
2002	158799	174679	209615	220095	176076	193684	189810	208791	229670	252637	239790	246772
2003	124599	137059	164471	172694	138155	151971	148931	163825	180207	198228	188147	193626
2004	125495	138045	165653	173936	139149	153064	150002	165003	181503	199653	189500	195018
2005	158786	174665	209598	220077	176062	193668	189795	208774	229652	252617	239770	246752
2006	154895	170385	204461	214684	171748	188922	185144	203658	224024	246427	233895	240706

Another useful application for forecasting is predicting the date on which a given number of something will occur. For example, a commander will want to set end outcomes and expect personnel to meet those outcomes by a specified date. Indeed, meeting milestones is a key indicator of performance. Let's say at the beginning of the year you analyze the preceding 52-weeks of reported crime and find the average number of monthly crimes was 736 (figure 18). Notice the variability in the data, a relatively downward trend with several spikes; the standard deviation is 19, which confirms a moderate spread in the data. Examining the trends, you now want to set an end outcome: to reduce the average number of monthly crimes by 10%. Specifically, the management question you are asking is: *Given the past 12-month crime trend, what is the projected date for a monthly average of 662 crimes?* With the historical spikes in the data and periodic inconsistencies, when can you expect to achieve that end outcome? Using the forecast function the projected date is April 3, 2007.[112] This is how the equation appears:

1. X = 662; 10% reduction from 736;
2. Y = the preceding 52 weeks, measured in 1-week intervals;
3. X = the known number of crimes for each week.

Once the formula is calculated you can make adjustments to your end outcomes by increasing or decreasing the forecasted value (cell BF54 in the "yr month week CFS forecast" worksheet of the forecasting workbook). If your end outcome is a 15% reduction (626 crimes), then, all else being equal, the estimated date is August 16, 2007. By adjusting the forecasted value downward you should notice that it will take longer to achieve that milestone given the historical data.

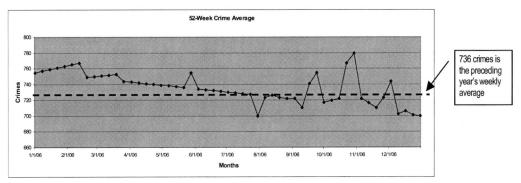

Figure 18

In the previous section we calculated a new agency end outcome: *to reduce average response time to 6.00 minutes.* The projected average response time of 6.00 minutes is a 21.5% reduction from 7.646 minutes. Another useful measurement is to set the projected date when this new response time average will be realized. Using the same forecasting procedure, set up the equation like this:

1. X = 6.00, (the new response time goal) 21.5% reduction from 7.646;
2. Y = the preceding 12 months, measured in 1-month intervals;
3. X = the known average response times for each month.

38717	2/1/2006	3/1/2006	4/1/2006	5/1/2006	6/1/2006	7/1/2006	8/1/2006	9/1/2006	10/1/2006	11/1/2006	12/1/2006	
Jan	Feb	Mar	Apr	May	Jun	Jul	Aug	Sep	Oct	Nov	Dec	**Avg.**
8.2	7.5	7.66	8.01	7.95	8.33	7.25	7.8	7.3	7.1	7.6	7.05	**7.646**

Holding all else constant, the projected date for when the agency will realize the new average response time is March 6, 2007. Knowing this date in January, 2007, the executive will be able to set intermediate objectives along the path to the end outcome, such as 6.3 minutes by January 17, 2007; 6.1 minutes by February 8, 2007; 6.00 minutes by March 6, 2007. The completed forecast equation appears in cell H43 of the "regression workbook" under the "medical services data" worksheet.

Once the predictions are complete, to get the best picture of how to meet the anticipated service demands, tactical planners and administrators can create scenarios. Scenarios are also known as "what-if" analysis; "what-if" analysis is a process of manipulating values (independent variables) to see how the changes affect the outcome (dependent variables). Scenarios are useful for administrative planning to determine the impact on resources. According to van der Heijden (1996:5) scenarios:

1. Provide a test bed for plans and/or policies;
2. Stretch mental models as a means of leading to discoveries;
3. Enhance corporate perceptions about the future;
4. Energize management;
5. Aid top management in providing leadership.

In a somewhat different approach to scenarios Fahey and Randall (1997) described a concept known as *scenario learning*, which is used to:

1. Augment understanding;
2. Produce new decisions;
3. Reframe existing decisions;
4. Identify contingent decisions.

For example, if calls for service are predicted to increase or decrease over the next 2 years, then what level of effort will be required to meet the demand and what is the budget impact? This is useful for long-range planning that must account for personnel attrition and recruiting efforts: If you can project the anticipated workload, and you know the historical attrition rate, then you know when to hire personnel and by what date their training should be complete so they can be assigned accordingly. Using aggregate data in this manner does have limited utility since it does not provide discrete analysis of the *individual* calls for service, which influences the level of effort for *all* of the organizational elements associated with operations (i.e., communications, patrol, investigations, traffic, etc.). For example, simply knowing there is a 3% projected increase in calls for service from June 2007 to June 2008 does not reveal where the work will come from (the principal modalities), only that it will come. Where the work will emanate from is directly relevant to the amount of time it will take to handle a single unit and how many officers will be needed.

Moving Average Analysis

Another method for examining trends in data is moving average analysis. A moving average is another statistical technique used to analyze time-series data. The average is based on the data points over a period of time (days, weeks, months, years etc.) and reveals trends for the latest period. A moving average is a method of smoothing the data by averaging a specified number of terms of the time series; "it is simply the average frequency that an event occurred over some short time period" (Bachman and Paternoster, 2004:90). The average "moves" because for each calculation, the latest "x" number of time periods' data is used. The time period or interval, is the number of data points used to calculate the moving average. The larger the time period, the smoother the moving average line; the smaller the time period, the more the moving average is affected by individual data point fluctuations. For example, to calculate a 12-month moving average, using an interval width of 3, the first data point would be March; March would consist of the average of January, February and March. The next data point, April, would consist of the average of February, March and April, thus the idea behind the interval width of 3. There is absolutely no requirement that the interval width be 3, it could be 4, or 5 or 10 or even larger depending on the data set. By using moving average analysis it is possible to use historical data levels to predict future demand, which enables police executives to better plan financial and human resources.

Let's use the example of court overtime expenditures, you can use moving average analysis for all numerical data (e.g., arrests effected, traffic summonses issued, calls for service). Overtime funds are a scare resource and many labor agreements specify a mandatory minimum payment for an officer's appearance in court, regardless of the length of the appearance. In a short period of time court overtime expenditures can rise quickly and have adverse budget consequences. Budgeting is of paramount importance especially if the city is facing budget deficits. Arresting offenders is the basis for court overtime management and appropriating sufficient funds can be challenging, particularly if there are variable spikes in arrest trends (seasonality). Table 40 shows observed court overtime expenditures for 2006.

Table 40					Court Overtime Expenditures for 2006						
	Jan	Feb	Mar	Apr	May	Jun	Jul	Aug	Sep	Oct	Nov	Dec
Month	1	2	3	4	5	6	7	8	9	10	11	12
2006	$102,456	$245,895	$315,269	$412,456	$102,145	$235,974	$311,455	$201,223	$459,521	$265,487	$145,896	$459,899

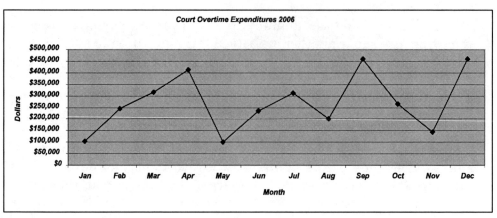

Figure 19

Figure 19 reveals substantial fluctuations in month-to-month court overtime expenditures, suggesting both possible over and under budgeting, neither of which is good for fiscal planning. By creating a moving average, police administrators are able to project expenditures in the forecast period, based on the average value of historical expenditures over a specific number of preceding periods. The moving average will reveal trend information that a simple average of all historical data would conceal, by removing much of the short-term variability. The idea behind using moving average analysis is to reduce static in the baseline data caused by random error in order to provide a more accurate picture of what is actually occurring over time. Table 40-1 shows actual court overtime expenditures and predicted monthly average court overtime expenditures using an interval width of 3 to smooth the data. Figure 20 shows the actual and predicted expenditures; the predicted expenditures give planners a much more even projection for optimal monthly appropriations. Notice the moving average in figure 20 shows much less variability than the actual expenditures.

Table 40-1	Actual and Predicted Court Overtime Expenditures 2006											
	Jan	Feb	Mar	Apr	May	Jun	Jul	Aug	Sep	Oct	Nov	Dec
Actual	$102,456	$245,895	$315,269	$412,456	$102,145	$235,974	$311,455	$201,223	$459,521	$265,487	$145,896	$459,899
Predicted	#N/A	#N/A	$221,207	$324,540	$276,623	$250,192	$216,525	$249,551	$324,066	$308,744	$290,301	$290,427

You may be wondering what the difference is between forecasting and moving average analysis, since both make predictions based on past values. Forecasting uses a linear regression equation, which accounts for the intervals (forecast periods) from which the data was drawn; the number of intervals for when the data was collected and their width (days, weeks, months, years, hours etc.) are part of the linear regression equation. Moving average analysis simply smoothes (averages) the data for given intervals that move forward in time and does not account for the period in which the data was collected. The interval width for which the data was collected does not matter to moving average analysis. The width only matters for how many time periods will be used to calculate the average, not how the data was collected. The interval width in this example is 3, meaning the result is the average of each 3-month period (e.g., March is the average of January, February and March; April is the average on February, March and April, and so on).

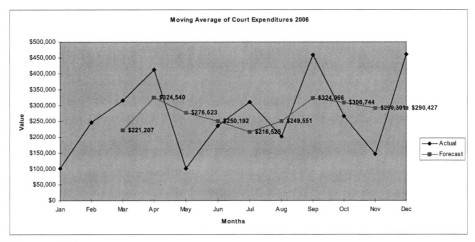

Figure 20

PART THREE
Management and Efficiency

7
▶ **The Compstat Process**[113]

Introduction and Background

Managing, directing and controlling a modern law enforcement organization is a complex and demanding job for the chief executive. It is not sufficient that the executive control the budget and the daily operations of the most visible segment of government, the executive is also *expected* to control the human phenomenon known as crime.

How to control crime and disorder have always been a conundrum. Through the 1970's and 1980's many criminologists posited that "...collective 'root causes' like social injustice, racism, poverty [and economics] caused crime ... [These implications suggested that] crime could only be prevented if *society itself* were radically changed...[therefore] when it came to *preventing* (and thus reducing crime), police did not really matter" (Kelling and Sousa, 2001).[114]

The fact is that the police *do matter* when it comes to preventing crime and keeping cities and towns safe, despite many criminologists' academic explanations that police can do little to prevent crime and restore order. With some reorganization law enforcement executives can put into practice one of the most innovative, deceptively simple, and economical means to controlling crime and disorder—a management process known as Compstat.[115]

The Compstat process was pioneered by former New York City Police Commissioner William Bratton and his management team, after Bratton assumed command of the NYPD in January 1994. "The [Compstat] model is based on the principle that by controlling serious crime, police are better poised to maintain order and solve other community problems in the promotion of public safety" (McDonald, 2002). The Compstat model is a classic example of how re-engineering[116] processes within a bureaucracy can produce significant public safety gains.

The Compstat process can be summarized in one simple statement: "Collect, analyze and map crime data and other essential police performance measures on a regular basis, and hold police managers accountable for their performance as measured by these data."[117] This statement also reflects a larger overall paradigm: accountability and discretion at all levels of the organization. By creating a management structure that keeps everyone focused on the core mission, officers and executives alike will be able to shed the cloak of cynicism that often comes from trying to do a job whose requirements are sometimes in irreconcilable conflict (Kelling, 1995).

This section is a description of how any law enforcement agency, regardless of size, or magnitude of the crime problem, can design and implement Compstat to achieve performance-based outcomes, while holding others to account. The accompanying Resource CD contains the analysis portion of a Compstat book.

The Four Principles of Crime Reduction

The Compstat process is a strategic crime-control technique that has "...diffused widely across the landscape of American policing" (Weisburd, Mastrofski, Greenspan, and Willis, 2004:6). The process is centered on four crime reduction principles: accurate and timely intelligence, effective tactics, rapid deployment of personnel and resources, and relentless follow-up and assessment (New York City Police Department, 1994). These four principles drive the crime-control objectives set by the agency during the reorganization. As the agency re-engineers to support Compstat, the Chief and the executives of the Department must set specific objectives. "This is important because establishing specific objectives sends a powerful message to all [levels of the organization]; the message indicates what the Department determines worthy of focus and attention" (McDonald, 2002).[118] Examples include: reducing gang-related homicides, reducing ATM robberies, and reducing disorderly youth in and around a shopping mall. The New York City Police Department developed ten specific objectives that drove their crime reductions (Henry, 2002:227). Once the objectives are set, the Department uses Compstat to ensure accountability is fixed and the desired goals are achieved.[119] In addition to the core management principles of Compstat, directing and controlling, the process may also serve as the pathway to leadership development by enhancing participants' knowledge, skills and abilities (Delorenzi, Shane and Amendola, 2006).

Accurate and Timely Intelligence

Compstat is an information-driven managerial process. Accurate and timely information is imperative, without these elements the Compstat process would be seriously diluted, and so would any other meaningful managerial process. The basic information necessary for prudent, informed decisions by Department executives can come from a variety of sources: calls for service, field interview reports, prisoner debriefings, incident reports, and UCR reports to name a few. The two most common sources for Compstat data are UCR reports and calls for service.

Information is *accurate* if it reflects what actually occurred at a given time and place. Accuracy can be authenticated through supervisory review and approval. Supervisors usually review and approve all written documents before they become official records. For example, in the case of incident reports that serve as the basis for UCR, a supervisor usually reviews the reports and reclassifies them, when necessary, before they are submitted to the FBI (e.g., a burglary is reclassified to a theft).[120] This quality control mechanism ensures the Department is in receipt of accurate crime reports before they are published or acted on.

In the case of calls for service, the disposition (e.g., no cause) can be compared to the actual call classification (e.g., shots fired). A field supervisor or a communications supervisor may reclassify the call if it is determined that the initial call differs from what was actually discovered (e.g., call for shots fired reclassified to kids with fireworks). Another way to ensure the Department is operating on accurate information is through independent corroboration. Police officers and detectives must always independently corroborate the information they receive. The personal observations of experienced, well-trained police officers will confirm or dispel what is gleaned from police reports and calls for service. Independent corroboration will also confirm or dispel rumors, community rhetoric, and anecdotal information that so often becomes "fact" because of misunderstandings or misinterpretations of events or statements.

Information tends to go stale rather quickly. Information is *timely* if the occurrence of an event and the reporting or recording of it are almost simultaneous. Timely information or "real-time" information is the most current information available, being collected and acted upon as near to the occurrence as possible. Real-time data is generated when officers in the field are able to write police reports and submit them electronically such as via wireless mobile data computer (MDC), where they are immediately stored and can be retrieved instantly. This enables decision makers (i.e., commanding officers, executive staff) to view crime data as near to its happening as possible and respond swiftly and certainly.[121]

Many police departments do not have the capability to submit reports via MDC. They must rely on information that is at least a few days old, in most cases a week old. Responding to week-old crime data is, of course, slightly less advantageous, particularly since the crime phenomenon is dynamic, however, police departments can still successfully deploy around such data. Crime trends and patterns rely on historical data, in fact, the more data the better the analysis. But for purposes of correcting daily conditions, commanders will fare well if they listen to what week-old information is telling them; the same criminals and the same antecedents will inevitably be present when the commander deploys their counter strategy.

Effective Tactics

In the words of Jack Maple, former NYPD Deputy Commissioner for Operations, and one of the founders of Compstat, "Nobody ever got in trouble because crime numbers on their watch went up…trouble arose only if the commanders didn't know why the numbers were up or didn't have a plan to address the problems" (Maple and Mitchell, 1999). Once commanders are in receipt of accurate and timely intelligence, they are required to develop and implement a plan of action. They must devise effective tactics that deal with as much of the problem as possible. It is not enough to simply issue a directed patrol order and leave it at that; the likelihood that a directed patrol order is sufficient to abate a particular problem is small.

For example, in the case of drug-sales emanating from a fast-food restaurant that is open 24-hours, the directed patrol strategy must be augmented by undercover operations (buy-bust operations; street surveillance); inspections from the Code Enforcement, Fire Department, and Health Department. If the problem persists, then the commander can then seek civil enforcement (permanently closing the establishment since it is an identified nuisance) through the city's corporation council. Finally, the police department, through the municipal council, may seek legislation to regulate twenty-four establishments more stringently, such as mandating specific closing times. For tactics to be effective, commanders must direct specific resources toward specific problems. An array of city, county, state, and federal resources exist, some of which include:

Table 41	Various City, County, State and Federal Resources		
Local	County	State	Federal
Housing Authority	County Police	State Police	Coast Guard
Sanitation/DPW Department	Prosecutor's/District Attorney's Office	Attorney General's Office	FBI, DEA, ATF, IRS, INS, EPA
Health and Human Services	County Sheriff's Office	Department of Corrections (DOC)	Marshal's Service
Code Enforcement	Traffic Engineering	National Guard	Customs Service
Parks and Recreation Department	Welfare (Public Assistance)	Probation Department	Social Security Administration
Public Utilities Company	Substance Abuse/ Mental Health/AIDS	Alcoholic Beverage Control (ABC)	Postal Inspectors/ Post Police
Fire Department	Homeless Outreach	Division of Parole	Secret Service
Board of Education	Public Works Department	Department of Community Affairs	U.S. Attorney's Office
Economic Development Corp.	Division of Youth Services	Division of Motor Vehicles (DMV)	Bureau of Prisons
(Modified from McDonald, 2002:17)			

Whatever strategies are eventually devised, Compstat provides the impetus for creative mind-mapping sessions where all the resources are gathered. The Chief of Police and the Deputy Chief of Operations are on hand to ensure responses are created and the resources committed. By having commanders commit their resources there is no delay, and no excuse for not developing effective tactics. Compstat breeds this integrated approach, which is a departure from the traditional model of policing where most elements of the Department operate independently.

Table 42	Traditional Model vs. Performance Model
Traditional Model[122] **(From. . .)**	**Performance Model** **(To. . .)**
Output	Outcome
Incidents	Problems
Summary Results	Feedback
Reaction	Prevention
Control of Serious Crime	Public Safety
Accountability for Rules	Accountability for Problems Solved
Individual Attribute-Based Performance Evaluation	Unit or Agency Performance Management
Intuition	Data
Isolation	Integration
(Source: McDonald, 2002:78-82)	

Devising effective tactics is the point in the Compstat process where accountability attaches; once commanders are in receipt of information about a problem, they are responsible for developing strategies to counter the problem. Failing to act is to risk being derelict in their duties, or worse, insubordinate. If the agency is large enough, commanders may be replaced for failing to act. However, in smaller agencies where there is a restricted number of command-rank personnel, the Chief may use some of these alternatives to compel commanders' participation:

- "Holding one commander to task for a longer period of time during a Compstat meeting by asking an extensive number of probing questions to accelerate the learning curve and underline the criticality of the process.
- Rewarding minimal success, at first, as positive reinforcement until the commander becomes more deeply involved in the process and energized by the satisfaction that comes with success.
- Being stern and finding other ways to communicate displeasure with performance without verbally assaulting or insulting the commander.
- Working with a commander's subordinates to get the job done, in the event that the commander exhibits reluctance initially to get involved (being bypassed tends to send an urgent [and embarrassing] message).
- Seeing that subordinates become invested in the process, with or without the commander, because this will motivate the commander to become involved as a way to reassert command and control.
- Speaking in relatively harsh tones without demeaning the individual, addressing criticism directly to performance or behavior rather than to the personal qualities of the individual (this being the only way, for some personalities, to change the person's level of involvement).
- Demonstrating that the jurisdiction is receiving a lot of praise for its new actions to convince a commander that if he or she does not

participate, promotion or other desirable positions will not be an option" (McDonald, 2002:15).

Once the tactics are developed, it is imperative to deploy them quickly.

Rapid Deployment of Personnel and Resources
Once the appropriate resources are identified, and an appropriate strategy has been developed, the commander must rapidly deploy the personnel and resources. This may include adjusting work schedules, if permitted, to meet the demands. In some instances restrictive labor agreements do not permit changing officers' work schedules as quickly or as frequently as may be needed. The least attractive solution to this problem is paying overtime to counter the crime problem. Overtime is fine for short-term task-force strategies; however funds are usually scarce and limited. Moreover, appropriations probably never reach a level that could be sustained over a long period of time. One effective solution to restrictive labor agreements is the split-force patrol concept. "Under the split-force concept, one part of the patrol force is assigned to respond to calls for service, investigate crimes, and perform other assigned duties. Another part of the patrol force is held in reserve for the express purpose of conducting preventive patrol. [There may be instances when the second portion of the patrol force is required to answer calls for service, however]" . . . the primary intent is for one portion of the patrol force to be devoted exclusively to preventive patrol" (Hale, 1981).[123]

Generally, a good proportion is a two-thirds/one-third split; two-thirds are assigned to answer calls for service and one-third is assigned to proactive patrol. "The primary advantage of split-force patrol is that it allows more attention to be devoted to preventive patrol activities and that officers are assigned this function as a *primary* responsibility" (Hale, 1981:122). The commander now has at his or her disposal a sufficient number of personnel who are unencumbered by the constant demands of the dispatcher; the proactive personnel can focus on the commander's obligations that are derived from Compstat, *and* the commander knows exactly who to hold accountable for the outcomes. The split-force patrol concept has received favorable results, among them:

- Increases calls for service response productivity.
- Increases the arrest-related productivity of the patrol force.
- Results in increased police professionalism and accountability (Tein et. al., 1977).

To gain the upper hand commanders need to set their plan in motion rapidly and decisively, for the next Compstat meeting is only one week away, and the commander will be expected to provide an update on the progress they have made toward alleviating the problem.

Relentless Follow-up and Assessment

The last crime reduction principle is relentless follow-up and assessment. This is considered by many who practice Compstat to be the most onerous and time-consuming principle—also the most important. It is foolish for a commander to design and implement an action plan and trust that it has been carried out without witnessing the results firsthand. A commander cannot **expect** if they do not **inspect!** Periodic follow-up to orders acts as an early warning to detect problems that may arise so that adjustments can be made. The most important question that must be answered in this phase is: did the solution meet the intended end outcomes? If not, why not? A commander should not wait until the day before the next Compstat meeting to follow-up with the supervisors tasked with implementing the action plan. A commander should be able to identify within a few days of executing the plan whether the intended results are being achieved (output and outcome).

If applied properly, the "output" should be linked to the "outcome." That is, if drug sales from a 24-hour restaurant are the problem, then effecting arrests and issuing summonses (output) in and around the restaurant should solve the problem (outcome). This is why relentless follow-up and assessment is essential: it establishes if the treatment (output) achieved the desired result (outcome). Other outcome measures include the ratio of calls handled per officer (e.g., Collective performance might be adversely affected by excessive individual sick time); and response time (e.g., Patrol-car availability, also known as the serviceability factor, might be adversely affected by at-fault and contributory accidents). "Managers need to monitor decision implementation to be sure that things are progressing as planned and that the problem that triggered the decision-making process has been resolved" (Bartol and Martin, 1991:272). A commander will do well to double-back and to make sure the specific end outcomes have been achieved and to ensure the condition is not recurring. To ensure follow-up is being conducted, the Chief designates a Compstat *scribe* who is responsible for taking copious notes during, and reporting back at the next Compstat meeting on what issues required attention. This is known as the recap (recapitulation). The recap notes are distributed to the affected commanders the day after Compstat, and commanders are expected to follow-up on the outstanding issues. During the next Compstat meeting the facilitator will open the session with the recap by asking commanders what has been done to alleviate the problem or correct the condition. The commanders must now answer for what they have done (i.e., the tactics, the deployment, and the investigative follow-up) to abate the problem and expound upon the results. If the commander is successful, the data will usually support them.

The NYPD described some of the methods commanders can use to follow up on their crime control efforts:

- Tour the confines of their precinct; also "management by walking around"
- Review incident reports on a daily basis
- Review the "Unusual Incident Report" each morning
- Talk to uniformed personnel frequently and discuss the issues with them
- Talk to the precinct detective squad supervisor and the detectives frequently about conditions and their investigations
- Review the Compstat reports for individual performance, performance compared to other precincts, trends and patterns (Giuliani and Safir, 1998).

Figure 21 summarizes Compstat's crime reduction principles and how each successive principle flows from the preceding one.

One final word about accountability. The essence of the Compstat process is **results**. Accountability must be affixed in order to achieve results: however, when the "dots on the map" disappear the inevitable result is fewer crimes. In this respect the true measure of success is the absence of crime. The results a commander derives emanate directly from his or her leadership. Strong-willed commitment from the commander to empower personnel with the authority and discretion to carry out a problem-solving effort, and the fortitude to reward creative risk-taking, even when mistakes are made, will yield positive gains. The commander should give personnel working for them the benefit of the doubt. If it turns out that a commander's personnel made a mistake, there will be time to hold them accountable. But if a commander abandons them at the first accusation, and they are later exonerated, the commander will never "wash away the smell of betrayal." The commander will have lost the trust of that employee, *and* of those who have never been accused of making a mistake. Standing behind one's employees is critical to morale, not just for the employee but for the enterprise, too (Giuliani, 2002).

POLICE DEPARTMENT

COMPSTAT Process: Crime Control Strategy

Crime Reduction Principles

If the police are to respond effectively to crime and to criminal events, officers at all levels of the organization must have accurate knowledge of when particular types of crimes are occurring, how and where the crimes are committed, and who the criminals are. The likelihood of an effective police response to crime increases proportionately as the accuracy of criminal intelligence increases.

Effective tactics are prudently designed to bring about the desired result of crime reduction, and they are developed after studying and analyzing the information gleaned from accurate and timely intelligence. In order to avoid displacing crime and quality of life problems, and in order to bring about permanent change, tactics must be comprehensive, flexible, and adaptable to the shifting crime trends that are identified and monitored.

Once a tactical plan has been developed, an array of personnel and other necessary resources must be deployed. Although some tactical plans might only involve patrol personnel, for example, experience has proven that the most effective plans require that personnel from several units and enforcement functions work together as a team to address the problem. A viable and comprehensive response to a crime or quality of life problem generally demands that patrol personnel, investigators and support personnel bring their expertise and resources to bear in a coordinated effort.

As in any problem-solving endeavor, an on-going process of rigorous follow-up and assessment is absolutely essential to ensure that the desired results are actually achieved. This evaluation component permits the Department to assess the viability of a particular response and to incorporate the knowledge acquired in subsequent tactics development efforts. It also permits the redeployment of resources to meet newly identified challenges once the problem has been abated.

Accurate and Timely Intelligence	Effective Tactics	Rapid Deployment of Personnel and Resources	Relentless Follow-up and Assessment

Sources	Intervention Strategies	Resources	Success Measurement
Direct Observation	Gun Buy-Back Program	Decoy Operations	Quality of Life Task Forces	Arrests/Search Warrants Issued
Surveys	Directed Deterrent Patrols	Reverse (Sting) Operations	Robbery Suppression Teams	Suspects Identified/Arrested
Official Reports	Vice Operations	Anti-Gang Program	Street Narcotics Units	Investigations Cleared/Cases Closed
Calls for Service	Search/Arrest Warrant Service	Confidential Surveillance	Gang Enforcement Task Force	Community Perceptions/Fear of Crime
Officer Experience	Narcotics Abatement (Buy-Bust)	Graffiti Abatement	SWAT Team	Reduction in Recidivism
Community Input	Civil Enforcement/Nuisance Abatement	Saturation Patrol	Fugitive Apprehension Teams	Citizen Satisfaction/Declining Crime Rate
Interviews		Vertical Patrols	Burglary Suppression Teams	Elicit Conformity with Local/State Laws
Informants	Educating Others about Vulnerability and How They Unwittingly Contribute to the Problem; Recommending Protective Steps	Plainclothes Street Surveillance	Violence Reduction Task Force	Successful Prosecution/Treatment of Victims and Offenders
Elected Representatives		Community Partnerships	Other Government Resources (Sanitation/Code Enforcement)	Empowering Those Impacted to Solve Own Problems
Prisoner Debriefings	Street-Crime Suppression	Domestic Violence Program	Interagency Coordination (FBI/DEA/ATF/Customs)	Reduction in Calls for Service/Crimes Reported
Information from Other Agencies (Probation, Parole, FBI, DEA, Prosecutor's Office, State Police)	Auto Theft Deterrence Programs	Problem-Solving Partnerships		Reduced Response Time
		Road Checkpoints		Achieving the "Outcome" vs the "Output"
Field Interview Reports	Situational Crime Prevention	Prostitution Operations		Activity Level: Arrests, Summonses, Field Interviews

Figure 21 modified from New York City Police Department, 1994

Additionally, a commander should not consider their mistakes failures per se. It has been said that "a mistake is just another way of doing things. The word failure carries with it finality, the absence of movement characteristic of a dead thing, to which the automatic human reaction is helpless discouragement. But for the successful leader, [mistakes are] the beginning, the springboard to hope" (Bennis and Nanus, 1997).

The Compstat Design

The chief executive of the department is *absolutely critical* to Compstat's design and success. The chief executive must serve as sponsor and must also champion the process with the command staff. "Sponsoring [Compstat] and championing it are different; sponsorship is necessary to provide legitimacy to the process, while championing provides the energy and commitment to follow through. [Compstat] does not just happen—involved, courageous and committed people make it happen. The department's leaders must serve as process champions. These people must believe in the [Compstat] process and be committed to it" (Bryson, 1995:57). Compstat is a performance management model. Without strong leadership the process is likely to fail completely or, at least, degrade into perfunctory weekly meetings that staff members no longer take seriously. Some of the pitfalls that should be considered when designing a Compstat model are: 1) "the cost of data collection in both hard-money and in-kind contribution (human resources), 2) lack of long-term support for the process especially from top management and/or public officials, 3) absence of a 'quarterback' to keep the process running, 4) lack of training, 5) not using data generated by the system in actual operations, and 6) overemphasis on output or workload data as opposed to performance indicators" (National Center for Public Productivity, 2006:8).

When designing the Compstat model for the organization, a few administrative details must be sorted through; they are organizational placement, required attendees, the facilitator, the facility, the equipment, and most importantly data collection, analysis, and the Compstat book.

Organizational Placement

Compstat is a managerial function. Therefore, it should be placed at the top of the organization. Data must flow to the chief executive and the executive staff without delay. There should be as few lines of reporting as possible between the Compstat unit (or the individual responsible for collating the data) and the chief executive. This will ensure that the data is collated, analyzed, and delivered to the chief executive for a preliminary review before the final version is prepared for publication. The Compstat unit should not have to negotiate several organizational layers before the chief executive is handed the completed staff work, particularly because the material is time sensitive.

Required Attendees

Restated, Compstat is a managerial process. It is a process where *managers* assess the operational effectiveness of the Department, and how those entrusted with geographic or organizational command perform in response to a set of given conditions (i.e., the Compstat data). Those that are required to attend Compstat are the Department's executives (Chief, Deputy Chiefs, Captains, Division/Section Commanders) and those decision-makers responsible for developing deployment strategies or committing resources (personnel or matériel). The command-rank personnel are responsible for answering for the state of their command, how well they are performing individually and compared to other commands, and the total crime picture within their command. Commanders of specialty divisions (e.g., narcotics, warrants, robbery, homicide) are responsible for answering what level of support they have committed to an area to reduce a problem, such as arrests effected, canvasses conducted, street surveillances conducted, warrants served, cases cleared, *and* for their command's overall performance.

Each commander is supported by their staff–the executive officer, detective squad supervisor, and crime control officer[124]–during Compstat meetings. The commander must sit at the table, and the support staff sits directly behind him or her. The support staff provides the commander with notes, charts, statistics, and performance data on the strategies undertaken since the last Compstat session. The support staff, particularly the Executive Officer, must be equally attuned to the commander's intentions and presentation.

The Facilitator

The Compstat facilitator **must** be the chief executive or his or her executive-level designee. The chief executive should attend and facilitate Compstat in order to set the tone for the agency: if Compstat is important enough for the chief executive to take time out of his or her schedule, then participants had better respect the process and take it seriously. In the chief executive's absence the facilitator must be a disinterested member of the command staff. Other command staff officers have a biased interest because it is they who are being critiqued. The facilitator moves Compstat along, questioning the commanders, helping devise solutions, ordering information for the recap, and issuing censure when necessary. To be successful the facilitator should have an understanding of patrol and investigative strategies, how to interpret statistics, and analysis skills insofar as linking conditions, performance, and outcome are concerned.

The Compstat Facility

The Compstat facility need not be elaborate. The room must be large enough to comfortably accommodate all of the required personnel and, preferably, guests. The room should also have audio/visual capabilities such as an overhead projector, a projection screen, computers, and an amplification system. All of the visual aids (i.e., charts, graphs, and data) should be supplemented by printed copies for each commander (the Compstat book). This will ensure everyone follows along and remains attentive while discussions are in progress. Figure 22 depicts a typical configuration for the Compstat facility.

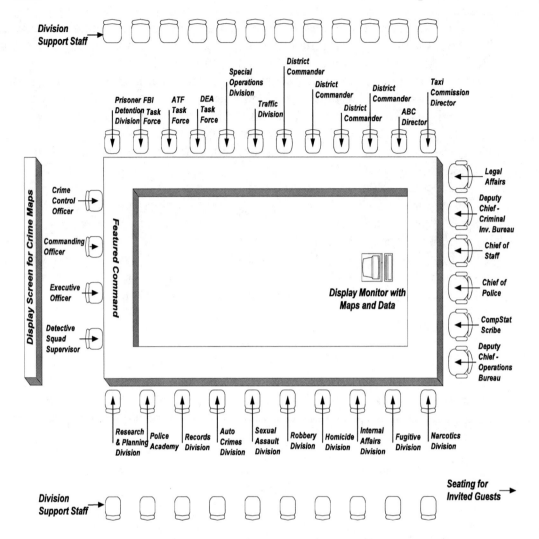

Figure 22

Data Collection, Analysis, and the Compstat Book

Compstat is a process that is grounded in data. The process begins by collecting, analyzing, and mapping crime data. This is the job of the person or unit designated to gather and collate Uniform Crime Report (UCR) data, and performance data. The Compstat book that is eventually prepared becomes the centerpiece of each meeting. Therefore, the book's content and layout are very important.

The Compstat book will vary in size based upon the jurisdiction, and how each Chief wishes to display the data. A large urban agency, for example, may capture recovered guns, panhandling, and prostitution arrests. A smaller suburban agency that is not affected by these conditions may capture DWI, cruising, and shoplifting data. The single best guiding principle for designing the Compstat book is this: *whatever issues are prevalent must be captured and made part of the book.*

The Compstat book is a collated, printed version of the previous Compstat period's activity; the Compstat period usually begins on Monday at 12:01 AM and ends the following Sunday at 11:59 PM. The Compstat period for specialty divisions, such as narcotics and criminal investigations, is every two weeks in order to produce a better trend analysis.[125]

The typical Compstat book is formatted in the following manner and includes the following elements for the Compstat period; the sections are separated by either numbered, lettered or named tab dividers (e.g., precincts and divisions).

Section	Description
Cover Page	Includes the Compstat period dates, the Compstat Conference #, and the name of the featured command
Recap	The previous Compstat period's notes and issues
Numerical Crime Summary	Describes citywide data, which includes the aggregate number of incidents, average number of incidents, percentage change, rate of violent and nonviolent crime and corresponding charts (e.g., pie chart representing crime rates for Pt-I offenses), sorted by offense
Violence Summary	Describes violent crime by offense in detail, sorted by precinct, and includes: gun violence, knife violence, other weapons and physical force
Property Crime Summary	Describes property crime by offense in detail, sorted by precinct
Precinct Profile	Includes commanding officer, executive officer, detective squad supervisor, demographics, personnel strength by rank, aggregate and disaggregate crime data by precinct
Weekly Sector Analysis	Tables comparing crime data and performance across categories, and a citywide analysis. Data is described by current week vs. previous week, the aggregate difference and percentage change
Crime Maps	Includes density comparisons and thematic layers; separate maps for each corresponding crime
Narrative Crime Summary	Brief summary of *every* incident under investigation for the Compstat period, sorted by date, and described by: sector, complaint #, date, time, location, type of premises, and means of attack. Specialty commands may show more data specific to the command or the operation (e.g., recovered guns may have make, model, color, caliber and serial number; narcotics may have packaging description and "brand name")

Section	Description	
Pattern Crimes	Describes confirmed or emerging crime patterns (i.e., commercial robberies, residential burglaries, sexual assaults of college students, auto thefts among church parishioners).	
Performance Indicators	Arrests	Pt-I, Pt-II, and Pt-III Arrests by patrol Arrests by detectives
	Summonses Issued	Moving, parking and by type
	Field Interviews	By sector and precinct
	Warrants and Court Orders Issued and Served	Arrest Search Temporary restraining orders
	Clearance Rates for Detective Squads	Also includes individual detective clearance rates
	Sick Time	By precinct, tour, rank and illness type; includes ratio of sick to officers
	Investigations and Complaints Against Personnel	By division, assignment, rank, sex, and tour; includes ratio of investigations to complaints
	Overtime	By category, sorted by division
	Accidents with City Vehicles	By division, tour and contributing circumstances
	Response Time	By precinct, and tour; includes priority code, # of calls dispatched and # self-initiated, queue goals, avg. queue time, avg. travel time, avg. on-scene time and avg. service time
	Personnel Grievances	By division, rank and category
Optional Data	Supporting data, such as abandoned/unsecured buildings, vacant lots, confirmed gangland areas, "top 10 lists," truancy and curfew violations, found property lists, offenders' residences (burglars, auto thieves), and sex-offender registrants, that helps commanders identify a nexus between non-crime conditions, and crime. This data helps commanders identify the antecedents to existing problems, and whom should be enlisted to control the problem	

Section	Description
Specialty Commands	Commands such as narcotics, traffic enforcement, special investigations, and task force operations should have their own pages depicting their level of performance. These specialty functions will have data that is germane to their command and is pertinent to the Compstat process
Special Programs	Includes programs such as grant-funded initiatives; explains the performance measures specified in the program for monitoring purposes

The best method of capturing calls-for-service and incident-report data is from a CAD system and an RMS. A robust CAD and RMS system can produce most of the Compstat book at the touch of a button. Otherwise, a data-entry clerk or crime analyst must enter the details of *every* incident report, arrest effected, summons issued, case cleared, and any other data the chief executive deems pertinent, into a spreadsheet or database to produce the reports. Essentially every piece of data that is to be presented must be collated in an easy-to-read format, organized in a logical order, and assembled into a coherent book.

Absent CAD or RMS reports: each command must capture the essential data elements each week, and report them to the designated person/unit who arranges the style and format. Collating and analyzing the data is made easy by desktop software applications that have a suite of products such as spreadsheets, databases, and word processing programs all in one. This, coupled with the use of special statistical programs for more complex analysis, is excellent for data reduction.

In displaying the information the first step is to *describe* the data. Descriptive statistics are important because the goal is to arrange the data so that relevant information can be quickly understood and appreciated (Healey, 2002). Descriptive statistics gives a commander a good overview of how their command is faring. Below are the statistics that are appropriate for this summary task:

Table 43	Summary Statistics				
Descriptive Analysis	Maximum	Minimum	Mean	Median	Mode
	Violent and Non-Violent Crime Summary		Aggregate Increase or Decrease		Standard Deviation
Frequency Distribution	Percentage Increase or Decrease	Proportion Across Categories	Ratio and Rates 1. Incidents to Population 2. Performance to Police Officers		
Organization and Presentation of Data	Pie Charts (for percentage of total)		Bar Charts (for aggregate data or rate; e.g., incidents per 100,000 people)		
	Line Charts (frequency polygon). Add trend lines to establish direction		Histograms with a Normal Curve (e.g., response time analysis)		Crosstab Charts

The next step is to *compare* the data. Comparing data enables the chief executive, and command staff to gauge progress, and adjust or compensate for shifts in trends or patterns. The data should be displayed for each precinct and citywide, including the aggregate difference and percentage change in reported incidents:

				Diff.	**% +/-**
1. Day to Day	One chart for each week of the Compstat period				
2. Week to Week	Current Week	vs.	Previous Week	+5	+3%
3. Month to Month	March 2007	vs.	April 2007	-18	-27%
4. Quarter to Quarter	Jan, Feb, Mar	vs.	Apr, May, Jun	+32	+44%
5. Half Year to Half Year	1st six months	vs.	2nd six months	-63	-40%
6. Year to Year	2006	vs.	2007	-27	-2%
7. Year to Date	January 1, 2007	to	present date	Aggregate	
8. Last 12 months	March 15, 2006	to	March 14, 2007	Aggregate	
9. Custom Date	Any time period (days, weeks, months, quarters, years, decades)				
10. Prior Year Period	**Comparisons for each period against the prior period:**				

Week	Current Week 2007	vs.	Same Week 2007
Month	Current Month 2007	vs.	Same Month 2007
Quarter	Jan, Feb, Mar 2007	vs.	Jan, Feb, Mar 2007
Half Year	1st six months 2007	vs.	1st six months 2007
Year	Jan 1, 2007 to present	vs	Jan. 1, 2006 to present
12 Months	Jan 18, 2006 to Jan 17, 2007	vs.	Jan. 18, 2006 to Jan. 17, 2006
Custom	Any custom date period compared with the prior date period		

These charts should be disaggregated for each crime, and a chart depicting the temporal (time) distribution should also be included so commanders can see what time of day crime is occurring.

Next is spatial analysis (crime mapping). Spatial analysis has gained popularity over the last ten years as an inexpensive and valuable resource for police departments to identify and plot the occurrence of crime. Crime analysts can identify "nodes," "paths" and "edges" along which criminals travel;[126] they can create overlays of calls for service vs. arrests effected, or unsolved burglaries with known burglars' residences, or calls for service with abandoned buildings; they can create specialty maps such as sex offenders' residences (Megan's Law registrants), recovered guns, recovered stolen autos, theft of auto headlights; and, what is most important, they can display aggregate data to show relationships among offenses in time space; this is also known as "hot-spot" analysis. Once spatial and temporal analysis is conducted intervention strategies can be developed.[127]

There are a variety of commercial mapping software applications available that integrate very easily with the spreadsheet and database applications that harness the raw data. The data is simply imported to the mapping program, and the reports are run to create the desired maps. One of the best resources for technical assistance and crime mapping implementation is the Police Foundation's (Washington, D.C.) Crime Mapping Laboratory.[128]

Implementation

After the Department has designed their Compstat program, it is now time for implementation. There are a few elements that must be considered; they are training, the Compstat meeting protocols, the interaction (line of questioning), and the roundtable discussion.

Training

Training for Compstat (or the lack thereof) is a frequent complaint of the participants. Training can be accomplished by first preparing a sample Compstat book. The book must be an exact rendition of what will be produced every week. Any subsequent changes to the book must be announced ahead of time so there are no surprises for which someone is held to account.[129] The next step is to conduct a plenary session of all the required attendees, chaired by the Chief and the facilitators, at the facility in which Compstat will be held, using the actual equipment. This will give participants the look and feel of the impending meetings, and ease their transition once the real meetings begin. During the plenary session, the purpose, rationale, techniques, anticipated organizational change, and expectations must be fully described and understood. It is also a good idea to send participants to an actual Compstat session in a practicing city to observe firsthand what they can expect. Some cities practicing Compstat are: [Newark; Philadelphia]; Boston; Indianapolis; Baltimore; New Orleans; Broward County, FL; Washington, D.C.; Austin, TX; Seattle; Mount Vernon, NY: Durham, NC; Lowell, MA; Longmont, CO; Maryland State Police; Los Angeles; Minneapolis; Chicago; San Diego; and of course, New York City (McDonald, 2002:26).

The Compstat Meeting Protocols

Day and Time. The Department must identify the day and time in which to conduct the Compstat meetings. The day and meeting time must be the same each week. This is not only imperative to data collection but to consistency; consistency breeds conformity. Since crime is dynamic and trends emerge and dissipate quickly, particularly due to the commanders' efforts, the Compstat session should be held at least on a weekly basis. For example, if a city has four police precincts, one precinct each week becomes the featured command; therefore the *Compstat period for each precinct* is every four weeks (once per month).[130] Participants should expect to spend two or three hours at each Compstat session in order to cover all of the material.

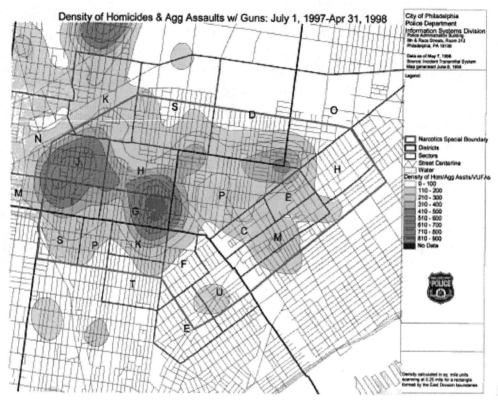

Figure 23 Source: Philadelphia Police Department 1997-1998

Seating Arrangement. The Compstat room should be configured in a square (see figure 22). Seating is assigned; the chief and other executives sit at the head of the table; on either side of the table are the commanders or designated participants; the featured command is seated directly opposite the Chief, facing the executive audience; seated behind the commanders are the division support staff; and guests are seated in the gallery behind the Chief.

Dress Code. All personnel attending Compstat should appear in uniform-of-the-day, preferably the dress uniform. Again, this promotes consistency, and sends a message to both participants and observers: Compstat is a formal process worthy of everyone's undivided attention and professional appearance.

Session Begins. When Compstat begins the Chief will open by welcoming everyone to the Compstat session, and acknowledging the guests by name (if there are just a few, otherwise by their organization). The first order of business is accolades. Insofar as possible, commanders are encouraged to bring personnel to Compstat for an accolade for outstanding performance. The commander calls the officers before the Compstat group, provides a brief overview of the action that led to the accolade and commends the officers. This public display of praise strengthens morale and sends the message that individual efforts produce a synergy that contributes to the whole.

Recap. Restated, the recap is prepared from the scribe's notes of the previous meeting. The facilitator will review the recap items, and the commanders in question are to provide answers for what they did to abate the problem. The answers must be narrowly tailored to the recap question without superfluous detail.

Featured Command. The featured command takes their place at the table, ready to proceed. The session begins by having the featured commander provide an overview of their crime posture, and their crime-control strategies since they last appeared at Compstat. "The [overview] is intended to be a comprehensive and informative recapitulation of criminal activity and police activity within the command, showcasing what the commander is doing to identify and solve problems...The executives may interrupt and direct the [commander] to focus more closely on a particular issue, or they may interrupt to focus on a particular case. The overall process of interaction is fluid and flexible, with few fixed rules.

Overview. The [overview] is the commander's chance to impress executives and other personnel present at the meeting with his or her knowledge, leadership talents, crime-fighting abilities, and overall career potential. This is the commander's [opportunity] to bring problems and issues (especially those concerning the adequacy of resources and crime patterns that cross precinct boundaries) to the attention of the executive staff—in essence to publicly communicate their needs and, in doing so, to place some of the responsibility and some of the accountability on the executives" (Henry, 2002:267). The key to success for any commander is to be **prepared**; being prepared means exhibiting a willingness and commitment to knowing and understanding the data and the underlying conditions within the command, devising effective strategies and tactics, relentlessly following up on initiatives, and the ability to articulate plans and conditions. Author and scholar Jim Collins (2001:88) remarked that great companies "...create a culture wherein people have a tremendous opportunity to be heard, and, ultimately, for the truth to be heard."

Questioning. Once the overview is complete, the facilitator begins the questioning. The facilitator will ask a series of direct, probing questions concerning current investigations, quality-of-life conditions, and crime-control strategies. The questioning may, at times, become adversarial, especially if the commander failed to implement a plan of action. The commanders should maintain their focus and *never* lie as a means to extricate themselves from difficult questioning. Collins (2001:88) identified four dimensions that great companies used to confront the facts of their organization:

1. "Lead with questions, not answers;
2. Engage in dialogue and debate, not coercion;
3. Conduct autopsies, without blame; and
4. Build red flag mechanisms that turn information into information that cannot be ignored."

The Compstat facilitator will do well to adhere to Collins' "four basic practices" as they establish a dialogue during Compstat. The following example is a typical line of questioning that might arise if a robbery pattern was discovered involving two suspects, using a blue vehicle:

Facilitator: I see that six robberies involving the same vehicle occurred between August 3 and August 20 in your precinct. These six robberies account for a 6% increase over last week, a 2% increase from last month at this time, and a 10% increase over this time last year. Explain the increase to me and what you are doing about it?

Commander: Chief, my crime control officer identified the pattern two weeks ago and made the assumption that the drug trade in the area was fueling the problem. Since the robberies occurred between 2200 and 0300 I increased patrols during those times. I issued a directed patrol order for the train station since four of the six robberies occurred in that vicinity. I notified the transit police who patrol the interior and a portion of the perimeter of the train station, and I briefed them on the details. I personally spoke to the Chief of the transit police and advised him to post the crime bulletin where commuters could see them. The transit Chief said he would also increase patrols during those hours and review surveillance tapes from fixed cameras outside the station. I assigned two officers to a task force assembled by the Robbery Division. The M.O. and the vehicle-description are the same on each of the robberies, but I am not certain if one person committed all six robberies or if there are six separate suspects.

Facilitator: Robbery Division commander, what are you doing about it?

Commander: Chief, I deployed a task force of detectives and precinct personnel who are working exclusively on this investigation. Some personnel are in uniform and some are conducting a decoy operation. Another team is conducting street surveillance. So far the results have been negative. I am continuing with these tactics for another week, if the results are still negative, I will reassess the tactics. I issued a crime bulletin to all commands, here is a copy. Tuesday we are going to have the latest victim meet with the police artist to develop a sketch. The earlier victims could not identify the gunman because he wore a mask, but the last victim struggled with the suspect and managed to pull the mask off. The earlier victims said they could identify the voice, a deep male voice. When an apprehension is made I will obtain a voice exemplar and have the victims to listen to it. As for the mask, it was sent to forensics for analysis.

Facilitator: Crime scene commander, what is the disposition of the mask?

Commander: Chief, hair fibers were recovered from inside the mask. It is being tested for DNA right now. Once I have the DNA analysis I will run it through our DNA database to search for a comparison. I should know something by the end of the day. There was no other evidence recovered from any of the other crime scenes.

Facilitator: Place that on the recap: crime scene commander to provide results of DNA testing on the suspect's mask by 5:00 P.M. today.

Obviously robbery is the motive. There was an assertion by the precinct commander that the local drug trade is fueling the problem. This is a high narcotics area. Let me see the map of narcotics complaints. Narcotics Division commander, tell me what you are doing about this? Is there a nexus between the drug trade in the area and the robberies?

Commander: On Monday, Tuesday, and Thursday of last week I conducted twelve different buy-bust operations, two during the A.M. and two during the P.M. hours, which yielded the following: 12 arrests for sale and possession of cocaine or heroin; 15 field interviews, five of which resulted in arrests for outstanding warrants; 6 traffic summonses issued; and we impounded 4 vehicles. Unfortunately, the prisoner debriefings were negative. We are still working to establish a connection to the drug trade and ascertain the suspects' identity.

Facilitator: Gang Division commander, is the vehicle description listed in the gang database? Do any vehicles of known gang members match this vehicle?

Commander: Chief I am not sure. I will check on that and advise the Robbery Division by the end of the day.

Facilitator: Place that on the recap: gang division to review the database of identified gang members to see if any similar vehicles fit the description and notify the Robbery commander by 5:00 P.M. today.

Auto Crimes commander, have any blue vehicles been impounded since August 20th, the date of the last incident?

Commander: Chief, there were three blue vehicles that were impounded. I assigned a single detective to investigate all three vehicles. I also notified crime scene to print each vehicle and advise me of the results. Two of the three vehicles were stolen, the other was towed for street cleaning.

Facilitator: For the recap, the Auto Squad commander is to present the findings of the investigation of the three blue vehicles and the crime scene commander is to present whether latent prints or other forensic evidence was recovered from any of the vehicles by Monday, August 23rd at 1:00 P.M.

Facilitator: Robbery Division commander what is the victimology? Do the victims have a criminal history?

Commander: Chief, all six victims have prior drug arrests. Two are on probation and I notified Agent John Doe of the Essex County Probation Department of that fact on August 16th.

Facilitator: Robbery commander, check with parole and the DOC to determine who is currently on parole and living in the area, and also who was recently released from prison and moved to the area.

Commander: Chief the task force is already working on that. I should have some answers by next Wednesday, August 25th.

Facilitator: For the recap: robbery commander to identify the results of parole and DOC inquiry on parolees' residences by Wednesday, August 25th.

OK. Let's move on. To the commanders I want intense monitoring of this investigation. Advise my office the minute something breaks.

The interaction during Compstat is dynamic, there is not a standard set of questions, with the exception of a few. The things the chief executive will always want to know are:

Motive?   Robbery, jealousy, revenge, thrill, bias, dispute, domestic, debt

Victimology?	A complete history of the victim, including lifestyle, personality traits, employment, and so forth. Examples include: age, occupation, family background, reputation, likes and dislikes, drug/alcohol use, financial troubles/ stability, religious beliefs, the last known person(s) the victim spoke to or was seen with and the circumstances, enemies or any known reason why someone may have wanted to harm the victim, routines/habits such as checking mail or walking the dog, criminal history, connection to area or suspect, DOC history, gang affili- ation, Lexis/Nexis® and AutoTrack/Accurint LE/Accurint LE Plus® summary.
Offender profile?	"Signature," financial troubles/stability, religious beliefs/ fanaticism, reputation/propensity for violence, drug/alcohol use, known hangouts, NCIC inquiry, outstanding war- rants, criminal history, likes/dislikes/obsessions/infatua- tions or perversions, the last known person(s) the offender spoke to or was seen with and the circumstances, enemies, connection to area or victim, DOC history, gang affiliation, Lexis/Nexis® and AutoTrack® summary.
Was the incident suppressible?	Could patrol or a proactive street-crime unit have prevented the incident? Could detectives have been more assertive?
Why is performance up or down?	Patrol or investigative strategies and tactics, road safety checkpoints, supervision, motivated employees, morale, vacation, sick time, personnel strength
Suspects' connection to other crimes?	Multiple victims that can ID, same MO or "signature," other similar unsolved crimes in area, forensic evidence, surveillance tape
What progress has been made to date?	Statements and confessions taken, polygraph adminis- tered, suspects identified, warrants issued or served, com- posite sketch, assets seized
Deployment and Strength Level	Sector cars, overlap/umbrella cars, walking posts, overtime detail, special units, uniformed and plainclothes personnel
Nexus to gangs, drugs or organized crime?	Drug rip-off, drug kingpin, gang leader/member, member of crime family or criminal enterprise, potential for vertical prosecution (RICO) or an enhanced prosecution/sentence

Recovered forensic evidence and its connection to other crimes?	Comparing samples such as DNA, trace evidence, bullets or shell casings, pry or tool marks, latent prints, impressions (tires, shoes), written documents, audio and video tapes, liquids, paint chips, shards of glass, examining computer hard drives, and Internet history
What is the plan of action or what are the next steps?	Develop a task force, serve warrants, raze buildings, tow derelict autos, padlock notorious businesses, issue summonses/MV enforcement, seize assets, conduct inspections: buses, taverns, bodegas, ATMs, convenience stores, gas stations, and taxi cabs, present case to a Grand Jury, seek civil enforcement (nuisance abatement), increase patrol, overtime initiative

One thing the chief executive *does not* want is a recitation of the incident report. On occasion it may be useful to summarize the incident report, and if so, the chief executive will ask for it. Otherwise, reciting the incident report amounts to a superfluous detail, it also appears as though the commander is temporizing because they are unprepared. Commanders must expect a variety of questions that are unique to each investigation.

Once the crime presentation is over, the performance presentation is next. The commander must answer for how their command is performing as compared to other commands. As with any other portion of Compstat, the commander is expected to articulate why performance has increased or decreased, what action plans he or she has, where adjustments to strategies must be made, if necessary.

The last portion of Compstat is the roundtable discussion. During the presentations other commands should not interject issues that are not related to the discussion causing the facilitator to engage in boundering.[131] They should make notes and save their comments for the roundtable. During this portion the chief executive polls all the other commands and asks if they have anything to discuss. Now is the time for administrative elements to discuss training issues, announce other city or department initiatives, review budget issues or procurement problems, and the like. When the roundtable discussion is finished, the chief executive will thank everyone for their attendance and the session will be dismissed.

Adaptability

One of the distinctions about Compstat is its adaptability. The Compstat process is easily adaptable to subdivisions of the organization, or to other segments of government. For example, the Internal Affairs (IA) function is subject to Compstat. When organized properly, IA Compstat can reduce personnel complaints, reduce corruption, and increase integrity. This promotes a much higher degree of overall organizational discipline and "a well-disciplined work force is in voluntary compliance with the rules and regulations of the organization and works efficiently to attain the goals of the organization" (Schroeder, Lombardo and Strollo, 1995:232-233).

Purchasing and procurement is another element subject to Compstat. Scrutinizing the purchasing process will ensure much-needed equipment and matériel is acquired as expeditiously as possible. Compstat can identify unscrupulous vendors and practices, uncover contractual problems, system delays in the purchasing process, and funding obstacles. Because purchasing often involves other elements of local government, participants may include the city manager/business administrator, the budget director, and the purchasing agent.

Compstat's adaptability is evidenced by how the Philadelphia Police Department uses the process to focus on specialty units. Because of its size and decentralized command structure, every fourth week the Philadelphia Police Department holds Compstat meetings that focus exclusively on the Department's specialized units, including SWAT, Canine, Mounted, Aviation, Bomb Disposal, Environmental Response, Marine, and Accident Investigation. At these meetings, performance measures such as the number of cases involving barricaded persons handled by the SWAT Unit; the number of vehicle pursuits in which Aviation Unit officers were engaged; and the number of code enforcement violations issued by the Environmental Response Unit are identified and discussed.[132] The City of Baltimore uses "CitiStat," a variant of Compstat, to monitor all of the city's operations.[133] The City of New York also created a variant known as "HealthStat, a citywide initiative that would draw upon the resources of more than 20 city agencies in a massive community [health care] outreach effort" (O'Connell, 2001:22).

Law enforcement agencies will do well by embracing the Compstat process. "By adopting a flexible, accountability-driven law enforcement structure, cities that have made little progress to date can achieve reductions on par with the most dramatic declines in urban crime during the last decade, while those cities that already experienced success can continue to force crime down to ever lower levels" (Kelling and Borbett, 2003). Crime rates among the cities practicing Compstat reveal the program's true success: in New York City over the last ten years crime is down 64%; in Philadelphia crime fell 23% between 1995 and 2002; in Baltimore crime fell 31% between 1995 and 1999; and in Newark crime fell 51% between 1995 and 2001.[134]

Law enforcement agencies need invest only a negligible amount of money to implement Compstat, and even fewer dollars if they can live without audio/visual equipment. The *key* is for law enforcement agencies to structure for success. "Creating that structure requires extensive central data collection and analysis, and constant feedback and review of the effectiveness of police programs. Perhaps, most importantly of all, a culture of accountability must be instituted within the structure. At every level, from the whole city to a single street, the law enforcement personnel entrusted with preventing crime must take responsibility for [mistakes], and be recognized for success" (Kelling and Corbett, 2003:5). Compstat is a transparent accountability system where performance is objectively measured, and those responsible are open to scrutiny.

The Compstat process is not just more police rhetoric. It has been studied and the results are favorable. "Case studies conducted in six New York City police precincts in 2000 show that precinct commanders use Compstat technology to identify when specific types of crime, such as robbery and burglary, become unusually serious problems. Incidences of such crimes fell after the commanders employed specifically devised tactics to combat the identified problem" (Kelling and Sousa, 2001:1).

Aoristic Crime Analysis

Tactical Planning for Crimes without a Definitive Starting Time
    According to Iannone (1987:14-15) "tactical plans are those which are prepared to meet exigencies encountered by police such as…unusual crime problems…" One of the most vexing issues facing efficient deployment is how to handle crime trends that have no definitive starting time. What makes these incidents an "unusual crime problem" is that they occur out of the presence of someone who is "capable" of reporting them, such as a homeowner, car owner or "place manager" (Felson, 1987). When this happens, the best that tactical planners can do is estimate, within a range of times, when the crime occurred. For example, a homeowner leaves for work 8:00A.M. and returns at 4:00 P.M. to discover their home has been burglarized. Or, a shopper leaves their car parked at the mall from 12:00 PM to 3:30 PM, when she returns she discovers the car has been stolen. Similarly, an apartment building superintendent conducts an inspection of the grounds at 9:00 AM and again at 12:00 PM and discovers spray painted graffiti on an exterior wall. Deploying more officers between 8:00 A.M. and 4:00 P.M. or hiring more apartment security guards is not (necessarily) the answer.

No government entity could ever hope to employ all of the police personnel they will ever need to meet service demands or prevent crime. The better approach is to work smarter. Research suggests that randomized preventive patrol does not have the effect once believed (Kelling et. al., 1974); rather, a growing body of research suggests tactical and directed patrol activities based upon intelligence might be far more effective (Cordner, 1981; Cahn and Tien, 1981; Gay, Schell and Schack, 1977; McGarrell, Chermak, Weiss, and Wilson, 2001; Sherman, Shaw and Roga, 1995). This is the theoretical underpinning of an emerging policing concept known as "intelligence-led policing," (Carter, 2005), and one of the analysis techniques employed in this policing concept is aoristic crime analysis.

What the previously mentioned crime patterns have in common is that they have a range of possible times when the incident may have occurred; we do not know the precise time because no one saw the event occur. Obviously, this is quite different from an assault or robbery that is reported by the victim (or a witness) who knows exactly when the crime occurred. With wide time ranges and high-volume crime it is nearly impossible to deploy personnel efficiently to the coverage area (hot spot). Police executives must narrow the estimated time the crime occurred and deploy personnel when they have the greatest chance of deterring or apprehending an offender. Creating aoristic signatures is one plausible method.

Aoristic analysis is an emerging analytic tool that police departments are increasingly relying on to better estimate the probability of when an unwitnessed crime occurred to improve the likelihood of prevention and apprehension. The technique uses a "...methodology [that] generates a probability estimation that an event or number of events occurred within user-specified temporal parameters based on the overlap between the search time frame and the time span of each incident (Ratcliffe, 2002:26-27). Aoristic analysis...calculates the probability that an event occurred within given temporal parameters, and sums the probabilities for all events that might have occurred to produce a temporal weight in a given area..."(Ratcliffe, 2002:27). What this means is that the time span is weighted according to the number of time intervals between the starting time and the ending time of the reported event. The resulting probability gives police executives a better estimate of when the event likely occurred, which provides better reconciliation between the event and deployment. A separate aoristic model must be developed for each crime under examination; one model for burglary, a separate model for theft and a separate model for auto theft. This will ensure the idiosyncrasies of each crime are captured without undue influence on each other.

Developing an Aoristic Model

An aoristic model relies on user-specified time intervals, for instance, days, weeks or hours. For illustration purposes we use the more discreet time interval hours, as we did with activity-base budgeting and workload analysis. During a twenty-four hour period all of the crime incidents are distributed across one-hour time intervals, beginning at 00:00 and ending at 23:59 (midnight). Incidents that are not witnessed by someone have a range of occurrence times, where the actual incident occurred somewhere in between. It is this 'somewhere in between' that we are trying to narrow. Begin with an Excel© spreadsheet that lists the 24-hour time period across the top row. The starting time will be 1:00 AM, the intervals will be 1 hour and the ending time will be 24:00. In the last column create a "total" that will sum the probability values in each row. The total column is to ensure the calculations are correct and that proper weight is given to each incident.

Next, begin entering the data for the first incident in the cells below the appropriate one-hour bracket. For example, Table 44 represents an aoristic model for burglary for a 10-hour period. There are ten incidents (A-K). Each incident represents a maximum value of 1: one incident is equal to 100%. The first incident occurred between 10:00 and 14:00, a four-hour time frame. If we knew the exact time the incident occurred (e.g., 11:00), then 11:00 would receive a value of 1. Since the incident occurred sometime over a four-hour period, then we must divide the full value (1) by the number of intervals in the period (4): $1 \div 4 = .25$. The quotient (.25) is the proportional value assigned to each 1-hour interval for the first incident. Likewise, continue entering the data and calculating the proportional values for each incident for the entire 24-hour period. The pattern that begins to develop should appear like that in table 44.

Table 44	10-Hour Aoristic Model for Burglary									
Incidents	Hour of the Day									
	10:00	11:00	12:00	13:00	14:00	15:00	16:00	17:00	18:00	19:00	20:00
A	0.25	0.25	0.25	0.25							
B		0.5	0.5								
C	0.25	0.25	0.25	0.25							
D			1								
E			0.2	0.2	0.2	0.2	0.2				
F		0.2	0.2	0.2	0.2	0.2					
G			1								
H				1							
I					0.5	0.5					
J		0.14	0.14	0.14	0.14	0.14	0.14	0.14			
Aoristic Sum	0.5	1.34	3.54	2.04	1.04	1.04	0.34	0.14	0	0	0
Aoristic Probability	0.05	0.134	0.354	0.204	0.104	0.104	0.034	0.014	0	0	0
% of Total	5.00%	13.40%	35.40%	20.40%	10.40%	10.40%	3.40%	1.40%	0.00%	0.00%	0.00%

Modified from Ratcliffe, 2002:27

After the probability values for each time interval have been calculated, the next step is to sum the values for each time interval beneath each column. This is known as the aoristic sum, which is the probability weight for each 1-hour interval (10:00 a.m. = .59; 11:00 a.m. = 1.34; 12:00 p.m. = 3.54, and so on). Next, you create the aoristic probability by dividing the aoristic sum by the total number of cases (10:00 a.m. = .5 ÷ 10 = .05; 11:00 a.m. - 1.34 ÷ 10 = .134). Then, convert the aoristic probability to a percentage to show the relative contribution of each 1-hour interval to the total (10:00 a.m. = .5 ÷ 10 = .05 × 100 = 5%).

This is where efficiency begins to reveal itself. Notice that nearly 56% (55.80 = 35.4 + 20.4) of the probability of a burglary occurring is in the one-hour time period from 12:00 to 13:00. This dramatically narrows the original 10-hour time span. Looking further we see that nearly 80% (79.60) of the probability of a burglary occurring is between 11:00 and 15:00 (79.6 = 13.40 + 35.40 + 20.40 + 10.40); if you extend the time span to 16:00, then you capture 90% of the probability. Coupling the temporal analysis with geographic analysis (i.e., crime mapping) will give police tactical planners a much more reliable chance of deterring or apprehending a burglary than if he or she only knew a burglary pattern developed between 10:00 and 17:00.

Finally, after all the data has been entered and all the calculations have been performed, create a line chart to graphically depict how the aoristic probability values spread across the time period, in this case 11-hours (figure 24). This gives tactical planners a better visual representation of how the probability values spike, then decline.

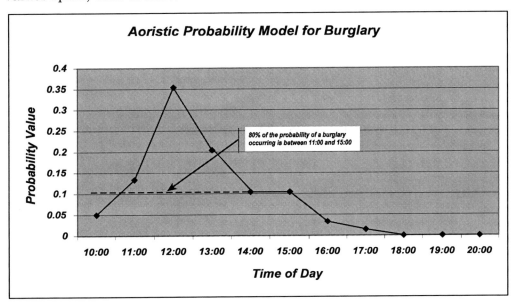

Figure 24

Table 45 is a larger representation of how aoristic analysis can be used to estimate the probability of an event. The complete data-set is too large to portray in the text, so for illustration it was purposely reduced to 140 cases; the full data-set of 1,014 cases appears on the Resource CD. Nearly 50% (48.17) of the probability of an auto theft occurring is between 8:00 AM and 11:00 AM; nearly 60% (59.84) of the probability is between 8:00 AM and 12:00 PM.

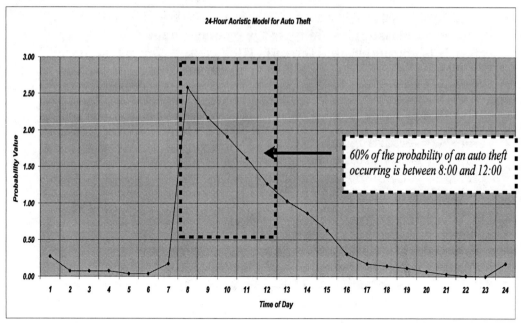

Figure 25

The public value created by aoristic crime analysis is the continued development of the "intelligence-led policing" paradigm (Carter, 2005). By thinking more analytically, using computer technology and working smarter, police agencies will be able to create efficient deployment plans that yield a higher probability of apprehending or deflecting offenders. "Aoristic signatures cannot tell us the hunting patterns of individual offenders. The start and end times of incidents are a better indication of the behavior of victims and their routine activity than a signal of offender movement. But by better understanding the routine activities of victims we can get a clearer view of not just their personal victimization liability, but also a better idea of the criminal opportunities associated with the property they leave unguarded" (Ratcliffe, 2002:42).

Efficiency Analyses

Cost-Benefit Analysis and Cost-Effectiveness Analysis

Measuring program efficiency is one of the most important facets of police management. Whether programs have been successfully implemented as designed (process) and whether they have achieved the intended end outcome (impact) is critical to success and the program's continued existence. In fact, evaluating programs is at the core of management efficiency and effectiveness. Conducting an efficiency assessment of individual programs gives the police executive the opportunity to see just how well the program is performing (outcome) in relation to the cost of doing it (input). It also helps the executive make adjustments as necessary. Although efficiency analyses are excellent ways to examine program performance, they are not without controversy. A large part of that controversy resides in attaching a monetary value to things that cannot be easily quantified—things such as a person's quality of life, fear, and community well-being, are abstract concepts that do not lend themselves to simple quantification. This is so because "it is usually difficult to evaluate the long-term effects of social interventions. There are many different social variables to measure and control for, and this complexity often defies measurement" (Welsh and Harris, 2004:7; see also Thompson, 1980). How much is it worth to improve someone's quality of life by adding a single foot patrol officer to the neighborhood? How much is it worth to reduce fear by 10%? These questions are difficult to answer. In some sense they are purely political and monetizing the benefits may be irrelevant—the police department is going to deliver the program regardless of the cost-benefit relationship. This mandate will usually come from elected officials.

The primary difference between cost-benefit analysis and cost-effectiveness analysis is whether a monetary value can be placed on the end outcome. If it is not possible to place a dollar value on the end outcome, then a cost-effectiveness analysis should be undertaken. Since it is controversial to place a dollar value on human services programs, even if it can be done so accurately, monetizing benefits may be considered outright offensive and inconsistent with the purpose of government.

Nevertheless, efficiency analyses are useful for police executives who must make policy decisions regarding whether to continue, modify or dissolve a program, assess the utility of a program at different points in time (cross-sectional analysis) (Rossi, Lipsey and Freeman, 2004:341) or adjust dosage levels (Yates, 1996). Knowing the costs, benefits and effectiveness of programs also helps when the department is seeking external funding. For example, conducting a retrospective cost-benefit analysis of a police-led after school athletic program, designed to keep children ages 13 to 17 occupied until parents/guardians are home from work, can yield particularly useful information that a grantor may wish to have before they fund the project.

This section examines two types of efficiency analyses: cost-benefit and cost-effectiveness.

Ex ante Efficiency Analysis and _Ex post_ Efficiency Analysis. Whether the efficiency analysis takes place *before* or *after* a program is implemented will produce different results. An *ex ante* analysis is also known as a *prospective* analysis. Here, police management may undertake the analysis based upon anticipated or projected costs and benefits; this is another example of how conducting linear regression analysis, forecasting and moving average analysis can have added value. All of the inputs (costs) and end outcomes (benefits) must be estimated. This may be either very easy, if there is historical data or experience to infer from, or very difficult if the program is novel and has not been implemented before. Naturally, there is always the risk of over- or underestimating the costs and benefits but this is also expected when dealing with the human element of social intervention. One of the advantages of *ex ante* analysis is to compare alternatives: how else can the department achieve the same or similar results and what are the costs? Or, could the funds be put to better use to achieve an entirely different public safety goal? These are political judgments based more on emotion and human sentiment than objective criteria. As Rossi, Lipsey and Freeman (2004:336) stated "Political and moral controversies may result from placing economic values on particular input or outcome measures, controversies that could obscure the relevance and minimize the potential utility of an otherwise useful and rigorous evaluation."

A management question that may arise from the chief executive prompting *ex ante* efficiency analysis is this: *I want to analyze different strategies for addressing robberies. How does our anti-crime program compare to the costs and benefits of two other successful strategies used by other police departments?* The *ex ante* evaluation method is useful if there is sufficient time to wait and conduct the analysis before an intervention program is decided upon.

One of the most difficult considerations in conducting an *ex ante* efficiency analysis is whether it is better to prevent the problem or allow it to occur because treating the result of the problem may be less expensive. Sometimes this is a difficult proposition to sell; after all, how can a police executive publicly declare they have examined the costs and the benefits and it is less expensive to investigate a robbery than to try and prevent it. Therefore, the police department will no longer try to prevent robberies. Regardless of whether this is true, it is highly offensive and perhaps illegal. Even crime control programs that have been evaluated with scientific rigor and found *not to work*, or legislative policies have yielded little or no public value, continue to be implemented all the time because they make the community "feel good" and they symbolize what people want from their government (Marion, 1997; Sherman et al, 1998). The decision to implement these types of programs is immutably political.

Quite frequently police programs are implemented before any prospective cost-benefit analysis has been conducted. When this occurs, it is typical to examine the relative costs and benefits that have been derived and whether the cost of the program can be justified by the magnitude of the end outcome (Lipsey, Rossi and Freeman, 2004:339). This is known as an *ex post* efficiency analysis, or a *retrospective* efficiency analysis. There is some benefit to undertaking an *ex post* efficiency analysis, namely, in real terms, the costs and benefits are now known and do not have to be estimated, which makes the analysis and subsequent decisions more sound.

Cost-Benefit Analysis (CBA). A cost-benefit analysis "compares present values of all benefits less those of related costs when benefits can be valued in dollars the same way as costs."[135] The key here is to express benefits in monetary terms. If that can be accomplished, then cost-benefit analysis may be preferred over cost-effectiveness analysis because there is a direct common metric against which to measure the outcome: money. In fact, developing a common measure is absolutely essential before any meaningful comparison can be undertaken, whether that measure is money (U.S. dollars) or level of effort (time in hours), it must be standardized. Again, the most challenging part is to quantify things that are difficult and controversial to place dollar figures on, such as human life and injury. For illustration purposes we conduct a retrospective cost-benefit analysis that makes the following assumptions: 1) the benefits can be monetized, 2) we know where the benefits will be derived and 3) all else being equal, the reduction in crime is attributed to the program.

Let's say the police department is interested evaluating the success of an anti-crime program that was implemented last year. Using the principles outlined previously in the sections on logic models, activity-base budgeting (ABB) and workload analysis, we will construct an anti-crime program and evaluate that program's costs and benefits for efficiency. There are ten steps to creating the CBA:

1. Define the intervention strategy and identify resources
2. Create conceptual definitions
3. Identify success indicators
4. Operationalize how success is to be measured
5. Identify outputs
6. Identify outcomes
7. Value inputs (costs)
8. Value outcomes (benefits)
9. Analyze intermediate objectives, and
10. Compare costs with benefits (see similarities by Dhiri and Brand, 1999:15).

These ten steps are essentially defined in the performance measurement approach outlined in Figure 1. Conducting a CBA is an executive decision based upon input from the command staff. The ten steps to the CBA model can be thought of this way:

Dimension	Example
Define the intervention strategy and identify resources	Create an anti-crime program as a separate section of the patrol division to proactively address crime and violence
Create conceptual definitions	1. **Crime:** Any FBI UCR Part I Offense 2. **Victimization:** Any FBI UCR Part I crime that affects a single individual person or a single household 3. **Household:** All individuals who live in the same housing unit 4. **Victimization Rate:** For *individual persons*, the number of victimizations among people within city limits per 1,000 residents; for *household crimes*, the number of victimizations per 1,000 households
Identify success indicators	1. Reduce the crime rate 2. Reduce Part I crimes 3. Reduce the victimization rate

Dimension		Example
Operationalize how success is to be measured	1.	Number of Part I crimes
	2.	Number of victims
	3.	Crime rate per 1,000 people
	4.	Victimization rate per 1,000 residents
Identify the outputs	1.	Number of arrests effected
	2.	Number of summonses issued
	3.	Number of directed patrols conducted
	4.	Number of road safety checkpoints
Identify the end outcomes	1.	Reduce Part I crimes by 10%
	2.	Reduce Victimization Rate by 15%
Value the inputs (costs)	1.	Personnel $2,659,393
	2.	Materials $81,927
	3.	Equipment $59,797
Value the outcomes (benefits)	1.	Average robbery $1,760
	2.	Average burglary $1,657
	3.	Average sexual assault $42,534
	4.	Average aggravated assault $83,000
	5.	Average arson $17,044
Analyze intermediate objectives	1.	Sum quarterly and semi-annual data on costs, benefits and progress toward end outcome
Compare costs with benefits	1.	Total Costs: $2,801,117
	2.	Total Benefits/1 yr: $11,939,558
	3.	Total Net Benefits: $9,138,441
	4.	Monthly Net Benefit: $761,537
	5.	Part I Crimes averted: 226
	6.	Break Even Point: .235 of a year
	7.	Months to ROI: 2.82 or 2 months 25 days
	8.	Cost-Benefit Ratio: $4.26:$1

We will use the ABB and workload method to derive inputs and values. The following tables represent the ABB after one year of operation for the anti-crime program.

Table 45-1		Anti-Crime Program Acuity			
Service Demands	Hours Per Unit	Units Per Year	Detectives Required	Total Employee Hours Per Modality	Personnel Needed
Arrest (anti-crime only)	1	960	2	1920	2
Court Appearance	2.5	1200	3	9000	7
Proactive Investigations	12	720	2	17280	14
Prisoner Debriefings	0.416	897	1	373	0
Warrant Service	0.75	190	2	285	0
Total		3,967		28,858	23

Table 45-2		Distribution of Time		
Activity	**%**	**Hours/year**	**Minutes/daily**	**Hours/daily**
Investigative	80%	28,858	384	6.4
Administrative	20%	7,215	96	1.6
Proactive	0%	-	0	0
Total	**100%**	**36073**	**480**	**8**
Availability		**1558**	Hours/yr	
Actual Strength		**23**	Police Officers	

Table 45-3	Supervisory and Support Staff		
Supervisory Staff			
By ratio: 1 Sergeant per 8 detectives	**Sgt's**	**2.89**	effective strength
1 Lieutenant per 4 Sergeants	**Lt's**	**0.72**	effective strength
Total		**3.61**	FTE Support Staff
Management Staff			
Not by ratio (fixed post): 1 Captain	**Capt.**	**1.000**	effective strength
Not by ratio (fixed post): 1 Executive Officer	**Exec. Lt.**	**1.000**	effective strength
			FTE Command Staff
Total		**2.000**	(managers)
Support Staff for Management			
By ratio: 2 support staff members per manager		**4.000**	effective strength
Total		**4.000**	FTE Civilian Aides

Table 45-4		Nonproductive FTE (Relief Factor)				
		Time Off in Hours				
Time Off	**Captain**	**Lieutenant**	**Sergeant**	**Police Officer**	**Detective**	**Civilian Aide**
Vacation	224	216	208	200	200	112
Compensatory	40	40	40	40	40	16
Sick Leave	120	120	120	120	120	96
Personal	24	24	24	24	24	16
Training	64	64	64	64	64	16
Bereavement	80	80	80	80	80	40
Total Time Off	**552**	**544**	**536**	**528**	**528**	**296**
Work Year	2086	2086	2086	2086	2086	2086
Personnel Availability	1534	1542	1550	1558	1558	1790
Relief Factor	1.36	1.35	1.35	1.34	1.34	1.17

Table 45-5	FTE Subtotal (includes relief factor)			
	Complement	Work Hours	Relief?	
Captain	1	9-5 MF	No	Actual Strength
Exec. Lt.	1	9-5 MF	No	Actual Strength
Lt.	1	24/7	No	Actual Strength
Sgt.	3	24/7	No	Actual Strength
Detectives	23	24/7	No	Actual Strength
Civilian Aides	4	9-5 MF	No	Actual Strength
Total FTE's	33			Actual Strength

Table 45-6	Salary Calculations (includes relief factor)			
FTE	Salary	Benefits at 20%	Salary Cost	Title
23	$70,255	$14,051	$1,951,954	Detectives
1	$96,104	$19,221	$115,325	Captain
1	$87,573	$17,515	$105,088	Executive Lt.
1	$86,573	$17,315	$75,167	Lt.
3	$78,310	$15,662	$271,969	Sgt.
4	$29,144	$5,829	$139,891	Civilian Aides
33			$2,659,393	Total Salary Cost
		divided by	28858	total employee hours per modality
	Rate per employee hour		$92.15	

Table 45-7	Materials, Supplies, Equipment and Other Expenses				
Materials, Supplies and Consumable Supplies		Equipment			
			Useful		
		Qty	Unit Cost	Life/yrs	Cost
Training, Fuel, Paper, Pencils, Reports, Forms, Crime Scene Tape, Flares and all other Consumable Supplies (@ $2,500 per employee) $81,927		Computers	20	$1,500	5	$6,000
$81,927		Shotguns	5	$700	15	$233
divided by 3967 units per yr.		Typewriters	22	$300	3	$2,200
		Non Traditional Vehicles	5	$19,000	6	$15,833
Unit Cost $20.65		Night Vision Equipment	1	$7,500	7	$1,071

Table 45-7	Materials, Supplies, Equipment and Other Expenses				
Materials, Supplies and Consumable Supplies	Equipment				
		Qty	Unit Cost	Useful Life/yrs	Cost
	Prisoner Leg irons	2	$43	10	$9
	Laser Printers	10	$1,400	4	$3,500
	Unmarked Police Cars	4	$28,000	5	$22,400
	Suites of Furniture	5	$4,000	8	$2,500
	Photocopier	1	$25,000	5	$5,000
	Fax	7	$300	2	$1,050
					$59,797
			divided by		3,967 units per yr
			equip. per unit	=	$15.07

Table 45-8	The Activity Base Budget: Present Level of Service										
	Hours per unit	Units Per Year	Officers Required	Total Hrs.	Salary per hour	Salary per unit	Material per unit	Equipment per unit	Unit Cost	Total Cost	Percentage Allocated
Arrest (average)	1	960	2	1920	$184.31	$184.31	$20.65	$15.07	$220.03	$211,232.31	7.54%
Court	2.5	1200	3	9000	$276.46	$691.15	$20.65	$15.07	$726.88	$872,256.57	31.14%
Investigations	12	720	2	17280	$184.31	$2,211.70	$20.65	$15.07	$2,247.42	$1,618,143.07	57.77%
Prisoner Debriefings	0.416	897	1	373	$92.15	$38.34	$20.65	$15.07	$74.06	$66,433.41	2.37%
Warrant Service	0.75	190	2	285	$184.31	$138.23	$20.65	$15.07	$173.96	$33,051.77	1.18%
Total		3,967		28,858						$2,801,117	100%

Table 45-9	Budget Summary
Salaries	$2,659,393
Materials	$81,927
Equipment	$59,797
Total	$2,801,117

We see the cost of establishing the anti-crime unit is $2.8 million, (input). But what is the return on the investment (ROI)?

As its name suggests the anti-crime program was designed to prevent crime and criminal victimization; this aligns with the logic model. The first step toward defining the ROI is to examine the reduction in crime (end outcome), attach dollar-values to each crime, and attach dollar-values to the estimated savings from the reduced workload.[136] The "savings per victim" dollar value is the FBI's estimate of dollars lost due to the crime itself, based on supplemental reports submitted by law enforcement agencies (FBI UCR, 2004:34.). The crimes of robbery, burglary and arson do not include other tangible costs such as hospital/emergency medical care, emergency medical transport to the hospital, psychological/mental health care, wages; nor do they include intangible costs such as diminished quality of life, personal or community fear and anxiety. The crimes of sexual assault and aggravated assault include some medical and mental health costs but none of the other tangible costs mentioned above and none of the intangible costs. The "savings per victim" then is the inverse of the cost to the victim; since the crime was averted it is shown as a benefit. The reduction in crime is attributed to the anti-crime program and therefore results in accrued savings, which is captured as a program benefit. Table 45-10 shows the following estimates:

Dimension	Benefits
Benefit per Victim	Savings per victim per type of crime
Total benefits per victim	Accrued savings per victim per number of crimes
Arrests	Accrued savings from averted arrest processing
Court Appearances	Accrued savings from averted police court appearances
Patrol Response	Accrued savings from averted police patrol response
Communications	Accrued savings from averted processing incoming 911 calls for service
Prisoner Debriefing	Accrued savings from averted prisoner debriefings
Prisoner Processing	Accrued savings from averted prisoner processing

Table 45-10   *Ex ante* (Retrospective) Cost Benefit Analysis of an Anti-Crime Program

Costs

Personnel	$2,659,393
Materials	$81,927
Equipment	$59,797
Total	**$2,801,117**

Crimes Averted and Benefits Derived from 226 Fewer Crimes

Benefits	# Fewer Crimes	Benefit per Victim	Total Benefits per Victim	Arrests	Court Appear-ances	Patrol Response	Communica-tions	Investigation	Prisoner Debriefing	Prisoner Processing	Total Social Benefit
Robbery											
Bank	1	$4,221.00	$4,221	$220.03	$726.88	$803.63	$14.29	$2,247.42	$74.06	$772.90	**$9,080.22**
Supermarket	2	$1,529.00	$3,058	$440.07	$1,453.76	$1,607.26	$28.58	$4,494.84	$148.12	$1,545.81	**$12,776.44**
Gas/Service Station	10	$1,749.00	$17,490	$2,200.34	$7,268.80	$8,036.28	$142.92	$22,474.21	$740.62	$7,729.05	**$66,082.22**
Push-in/ Residential	6	$1,488.00	$8,928	$1,320.20	$4,361.28	$4,821.77	$85.75	$13,484.53	$444.37	$4,637.43	**$38,083.33**
Convenience Store	7	$653.00	$4,571	$1,540.24	$5,088.16	$5,625.40	$100.05	$15,731.95	$518.43	$5,410.33	**$38,585.55**
Person/Street	57	$923.00	$52,611	$12,541.92	$41,432.19	$45,806.80	$814.65	$128,102.99	$4,221.52	$44,055.56	**$329,586.63**
Sub Total	83		$90,879	$18,262.79	$60,331.08	$66,701.13	$1,186.25	$186,535.94	$6,147.13	$64,151.08	**$494,194.39**
Average Benefit		$1,760.50									
Burglary											
Residential	18	$1,607.00	$28,926	$3,960.61	$13,083.85	$9,829.35	$311.09	$40,453.58	$1,333.11	$13,912.28	**$111,809.86**
Non-residential	12	$1,708.00	$20,496	$2,640.40	$8,722.57	$6,552.90	$207.39	$26,969.05	$888.74	$9,274.85	**$75,751.91**
Sub Total	30		$49,422	$6,601.01	$21,806.41	$16,382.25	$518.48	$67,422.63	$2,221.85	$23,187.14	**$187,561.77**

Table 45-10			Ex ante (Retrospective) Cost Benefit Analysis of an Anti-Crime Program								
Average Benefit		$1,657.50									
Sexual Assault	6	$42,534.00	$255,204	$1,320.20	$4,361.28	$6,367.09	$94.72	$13,484.53	$444.37	$4,637.43	$285,913.62
Sub Total	6		$255,204	$1,320.20	$4,361.28	$6,367.09	$94.72	$13,484.53	$444.37	$4,637.43	$285,913.62
Average Benefit		$42,534.00									
Aggravated Assault											
Gun Shot	65	$154,000.00	$10,010,000	$14,302.19	$47,247.23	$68,976.77	$860.96	$47,247.23	$4,814.01	$50,238.80	$10,243,687.19
Stab/Cut Wound	39	$12,000.00	$468,000	$8,581.31	$28,348.34	$41,386.06	$516.57	$87,649.42	$2,888.41	$30,143.28	$667,513.39
Sub Total	104		$10,478,000	$22,883.50	$75,595.57	$110,362.84	$1,377.53	$134,896.65	$7,702.42	$80,382.07	$10,911,200.58
Average Benefit		$83,000.00									
Arson											
Structure	1	$22,071.00	$22,071	$220.03	$726.88	$803.63	$16.09	$2,247.42	$74.06	$772.90	$26,932.02
All Other	2	$12,017.00	$24,034	$440.07	$1,453.76	$1,607.26	$32.17	$4,494.84	$148.12	$1,545.81	$33,756.03
Sub Total	3		$46,105	$660.10	$2,180.64	$2,410.88	$48.26	$6,742.26	$222.19	$2,318.71	$60,688.05
Average Benefit		$17,044.00									
TotalSavings			$10,919,610	$49,727.61	$164,274.99	$202,224.18	$3,225.25	$409,082.00	$16,737.96	$174,676.43	$11,939,558.41
% of Total			91.46%	0.42%	1.38%	1.69%	0.03%	3.43%	0.14%	1.46%	100.00%

The estimated accrued social benefits are nearly $12 million. The estimated costs are $2.8 million. This immediately reveals the program's efficiency since the benefits exceed the costs. The next step is to provide a small summary of the analysis, which will give the executive a concise look at the cost-benefit comparison (table 45-11).

Table 45-11	Cost-Benefit Summary	
Total Pt I Crimes Averted	**226**	
Total Costs	**$2,801,117**	
Total Gross Social Benefits in 1 year	**$11,939,558.41**	
Net Social Benefit (total social benefits in 1 year - total costs)	**$9,138,441.29**	
Monthly Net Social Benefit from 226 Fewer Crimes (net social benefit ÷ 12)	**$761,536.77**	
Break Even Point (total cost ÷ total social benefits)	**0.235**	of a year
Months to ROI	**2.82**	2 months and 25 days
Cost-Benefit Ratio	**$4.26**	to $1

The total net social benefit of 226 fewer crimes, over the course of 1 year, is approximately $9.1 million; the "profit" is the difference between the costs incurred and the benefits accrued, which is the most obvious direct comparison of costs and benefits. The estimated monthly benefit amounts to $761,537. The break even point is .235 of a year, which is approximately 2.82 months, or 2 months and 25 days. This means the anti-crime programs pay for themselves in about 3 months. The cost-benefit ratio is $4.26 to $1 meaning that for every $1 spent on the anti-crime program there is a direct benefit of $4.26 to the victim, the police department and to society in general. As you can see from table 45-10, over 91% of the direct and indirect benefit is "paid" to the victim and society in terms of safety, security, quality of life and dollars from *not* having been a crime victim. The other 9% is "profit" for the police department by *not* having to answer and investigate an additional 226 crimes.

Some of the intangible benefits may not be readily apparent and may be difficult to "see," such as feelings of safety and security or communal well-being. But these things can translate into tangible benefits that manifest themselves through increased housing prices, new home construction, increased use of public space, increased retail commerce, increased pedestrian traffic and fewer signs of social and physical disorder.

Cost-Effectiveness Analysis (CEA). A cost-effectiveness analysis is "a criterion for comparing alternatives when benefits or outputs cannot be valued in dollars. This relates costs of programs to performance by measuring outcomes in non-monetary form. It is useful in comparing methods of attaining an explicit objective on the basis of least cost or greatest effectiveness for a given level of cost."[137] For example, a patrol-based anti-crime program where officers are assigned proactive duties may be more cost-effective than creating a separate anti-crime program if it produces fewer FBI UCR Part I crimes for the same or lower costs, or the same rate of Part I crimes for a lower cost. Because of the controversy surrounding monetizing human service programs, such as treatment or police services, cost effectiveness analysis is often regarding as more appropriate than cost-benefit analysis: "cost-effectiveness analysis requires monetizing only the program's costs, its benefits are expressed in outcome units...Efficiency, then, is expressed in terms of the costs of achieving a given result. That is, the efficiency of a program in attaining its goals is assessed in relation to the monetary value of the inputs required for a designated unit of outcome" (Rossi, Lipsey and Freeman, 2004:340-341).

Restated, the primary difference between cost-benefit analysis and cost-effectiveness analysis is monetizing the value of the benefit. When this can not be achieved, a cost-effectiveness analysis is preferred since the same methodology and procedures for measuring costs is applied. The relationship between input (costs) and end outcome (effectiveness) is expressed as the monetary value of reaching a substantive goal (Rossi, Lipsey and Freeman, 2004:363). Since only costs are compared, efficiency reveals itself by examining various degrees of program input to anticipated levels of outcome.

For example, let's say the police department has decided to create a truancy program. Prior research and model programs suggest that police-led truancy interventions may produce statistically significant results for school attendance, which may reduce the incidence of juvenile crime (Bazemore, Stinchcomb, Leip, 2004). The program will consist of individual educational needs assessment, return to school field enforcement, police case management, social service follow-up and extra-curricular activity. The chief executive tasks a commander with exploring the most cost-effective method for delivering this initiative. The commander identifies four program options ranging from about $760,000 (program D) to over $960,000 (program C); the results of the analysis appear in table 45-12:

1. **Program A:** Situate the truancy program in the existing Youth Aid Bureau where the truancy responsibilities will be assumed by the existing detectives;
2. **Program B:** Situate the truancy program in the existing Youth Aid Bureau and appropriate overtime for Youth Aid Bureau detectives and police officers department-wide to carry out the program;
3. **Program C:** Create a school-based partnership with the Youth Aid Bureau, or
4. **Program D:** Create a police-nonprofit partnership with the Youth Aid Bureau.

Table 45-12	Cost-Effectiveness Analysis of a Police-Led Truancy Intervention Program			
	Youth Aid Bureau **Program A**	**Police Overtime** **Program B**	**School Partnership** **Program C**	**Police-Non-profit** **Partnership** **Program D**
Personnel	$6,879,596.00	$6,521,458.00	$6,525,896.00	$7,102,230.00
Materials	$2,564,785.00	$2,548,565.00	$1,200,142.00	$129,889.00
Equipment	$1,201,225.00	$1,023,000.00	$1,201,458.00	$2,556,699.00
Subtotal	**$10,645,606.00**	**$10,093,023.00**	**$8,927,496.00**	**$9,788,818.00**
Juveniles Serviced	5896	5989	6984	8896
Cost per Case	$1,805.56	$1,685.26	$1,278.28	$1,100.36
Truancy Component Costs	$878,589.00	$896,985.00	$965,269.00	$758,954.00
Truants Serviced	1589	2697	2754	2987
Cost per Truant	$552.92	$332.59	$350.50	$254.09
Total Truancy Costs/ Total Program Costs	8.25%	8.89%	10.81%	7.75%
Cost per truant/cost per case	30.62%	19.74%	27.42%	23.09%
Total Cost with Truancy Component	**$11,524,195.00**	**$10,990,008.00**	**$9,892,765.00**	**$10,547,772.00**

There is a wealth of policy information contained in this table and some decisions will have to be made. The most expensive program with the fewest clients serviced is program A: the program costs $11.5 million, services 1,589 truants at $553 per truant. The least expensive program is program C: the program costs $9.8 million, services 2,754 truants at a cost of $350.50 per truant. The policy decision that must be made is not between the most and least expensive program since it is clear the least expensive program is more cost-effective. The decision is whether to spend more money to reach more clients, which can be achieved in programs B and D, or use the money for a competing police priority?

Competing priorities are inevitable in policing. This is why cost-benefit and cost-effectiveness analysis are essential to fiscal responsibility, which is subsumed in competent management. As Rossi, Lipsey and Freeman (2004:366) point out, many people do not necessarily agree with efficiency analyses because they "…deal chiefly with 'dollars' not 'people'." While there is merit to that argument, nonetheless it is not possible for government to satisfy every single person all the time, which is why a utilitarian approach is often best: the greatest good for the greatest number. Government resources are finite and, as previously stated in the section on activity-base budgeting, the police department will compete with other elements of government for those resources. This means demonstrating efficiency by comparing alternatives is perhaps the best way to deliver police services and meet public demands.

Virtually every police program is linked to its economic potential, although admittedly there will be times when a program creates a deficit but is still carried out because of its "feel" rather than its efficiency or effectiveness (see, for example Sherman et. al., 1998). The social utility of a program that runs a deficit may look like this: the program may leave people "feeling safer," → feelings of safety and security bring more people out into public places → more people in public places produces social vibrancy with a concurrent upturn in retail commerce → a strong economic base promotes community growth and social interaction, which is an element of "collective efficacy," which may reduce crime (Bellair, 1997; Morenoff, Sampson and Raudenbush, 2001).

Insofar as possible, police executives should subject the department's policies and programs to efficiency analysis on a regular basis to see where adjustments can be made. It is also good management to conduct *ex ante* efficiency analyses before deciding on a course of action to compare projected costs and benefits. Conducting efficiency analyses ensures accountability and raises the standard of "…substantive and managerial competence in the performance of public responsibilities" (Lynn, Jr., 1980).

▶ Conclusion

Scholars from the John F. Kennedy School of Government at Harvard University recently documented why Americans have lost trust in their government. They chronicled public policy initiatives that have, over the last three decades, eroded Americans' confidence in government. One of these policy areas was criminal justice. Overall, comparing the 1990's with the 1960's, Americans believed fear of crime, the incidence of crime (per 100,000 people), success in solving completed crimes (clearance rate) and personal safety, all grew worse. After comparing two 15-year periods, 1960-1975 and 1975-1990, only modest progress was reported (Nye, Zelikow and King, 1997:66-71). There may be more to this than just perception: According to the FBI Uniform Crime Report, between 1985 and 2004 violent crime in the United States reached its apex in 1991; during this 20-year period violent crime peaked at a rate of 758 per 100,000 people. During the same period property crime also reached its apex at a rate of 5,140 per 100,000.[138] And in 2006 the surge in violent crime was widely documented; preliminary estimates from the FBI indicate reported violent crime rose 3.7% from January through June (FBI UCR, 2006; Police Executive Research Forum, 2006). Surely, law enforcement leaders can do much more to restore public confidence in their agencies.

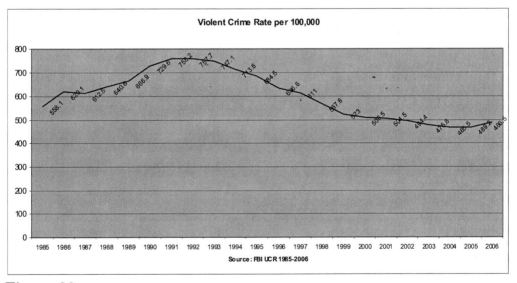

Figure 26

Technology has improved, research and scholarship has diffused through the criminal justice system and is reaching more practitioners, and training and education are more prevalent in policing today then ever before. These combined aspects have all contributed to more professional police departments (Glenn et. al., 2003). The trend toward individual (officer) and collective (department) performance standards is an essential element of police professionalism. Measuring these standards, redefining them in the face of new information or research, and disseminating results is all part of transparent government.

Measuring police performance is a complex endeavor. It is made easier by simply taking the time to think through the specific problem, identifying where success will manifest itself, identifying the activities correlated with success, collecting the data in a central location, subjecting the data to analysis and making necessary adjustments toward end outcomes. The basic premise is to ensure the police department's policies and programs have clearly defined goals and performance objectives built on the foundation of logic. It is bad policy to "throw cops" at a problem without first explicating the problem in detail. Throwing cops at a problem and ordering arrests may not be the answer; if America could incarcerate its way out of the crime problem, then America would be the safest place on earth since no other industrialized democracy incarcerates more people than the U.S.[139]

Police departments who measure their performance can compare their organization against nationally-recognized standards, or, if none exists, against a jurisdiction of similar qualities (size, population, demographics). This is a necessarily crude method but nonetheless serves as a benchmark for inherently arbitrary, political and intangible phenomena known as "satisfaction" and "success."

Bok (1997:55-56) stated, "Some observers might say that the best index of [a] government's performance *is* the verdict of public opinion. In a democracy, after all, the ultimate aim of the government is to satisfy its citizens... a democratic regime that has so completely lost the confidence and trust of the people must, ipso facto, be doing a bad job." Because the police are the largest, most visible and authoritative segment of government, it is only natural they are tasked with leading social interventions that can improve quality of life and improve citizen-government relations.

The theme throughout this text has been to give police executives, crime analysts, police planners, elected or appointed officials, consultants and students the tools necessary to improve individual and collective performance. The causes of crime are multifaceted and interwoven with social and environmental stimuli that meet law enforcement executives at their doorstep. Being able to wade through the morass of phenomena that the police can control and call upon other agencies for those things they can not, is part of the police executive's responsibility. This can be accomplished through an iterative process of strategic and assumption-based planning, data collection, analysis and implementation. The "profit" will come in the form of cost-effective service delivery and renewed public confidence.

Finally, an excerpt from Clarke and Eck (2005:61) summarizes the premise of this book rather neatly:

> *"The 21st century is becoming the century of analysis in policing, and you can make a large contribution. A hundred years from now, analysis will be firmly established in policing, and much will have changed. The technology will certainly be different. But more importantly, our successors will know a great deal more about crime than we do. And they will know this because you and people like you asked important questions, collected and analyzed data, and reported results with honesty and clarity."*

24-Hour Rule   As part of practicing Compstat, a rule that states commanders are not expected to answer intimate details of a crime or condition occurring in the 24-hour period immediately preceding the Compstat session. The rule exists so commanders are not surprised by questions that arise from a spontaneous event they have not had sufficient time to explore.

Abandoned Call   A call placed to a 9-1-1 communications center in which the caller disconnects before the call can be answered by the PSAP. May be used a performance indicator for a PSAP.

Accountability   An obligation or willingness to accept responsibility and to proffer a statement or explanation of reasons, causes, or motives to account for one's actions. Accountability requires the agency to: 1) clarify what is expected, 2) examine activities and performance measures and compare actual performance with what is expected, 3) act on findings to improve activities and performance measures, and 4) communicate findings in accordance with agency and regulatory policy. See *NOAA Strategic Planning Office*, Definitions for Performance Measurement, p.1.

Accreditation (also national accreditation)   To recognize (as in a law enforcement agency) as adopting and maintaining standards that qualify the agency as conforming to accepted industry practices. National accreditation is such a status conferred by the Commission on Accreditation for Law Enforcement Agencies-C.A.L.E.A) (see www.calea.org).

Accurate and Timely Intelligence   Principle #1 in the Compstat process. **Accurate** information reflects what actually occurred at a given time and place. **Timely** information reflects whether the occurrence of an event and the reporting or recording of the event are almost simultaneous. Accurate and timely information or Areal-time© information is the most current information available, being collected and acted upon as near to the time of occurrence as possible.

Activity-base Budget (A.B.B)   A budgeting system in which funds are allocated on the basis of the costs required to achieve expected output levels. See *economic model*.

Actual Strength   The number of personnel assigned to a particular function, such as patrol, investigations, communications or traffic.

Acuity In an activity-base budget, the individual data elements that comprise the workload analysis. The component pieces of acuity include hours per unit, units per year, percent of the total, personnel required, total employees per modality and percentage allocation.

Adam Walsh Child Protection and Safety Act of 2006 A law to protect children from sexual exploitation and violent crime, to prevent child abuse and child pornography, to promote Internet safety, and to honor the memory of Adam Walsh and other child crime victims (H.R. 4472; 109th U.S. Congress (2005-2006)). Became Public Law No: 109-248 on July 27, 2006. A full-text copy of the law is available from http://www.govtrack.us/data/us/bills.text/109/h/h4472.pdf as of November 4, 2006.

Adjusted R-square (symbolized adj. R^2) In a multivariate linear regression model, adjusted R-square measures the proportion of the variance in the dependent variable (Y) accounted for by the predictor variables (X). Adjusted R-square is typically considered a more accurate reflection of goodness-of-fit than R-square.

Aggressive Driving An informal term applied to drivers who operate motor vehicles and typically commit a combination of moving traffic offenses so as to endanger other persons or property; also, to operate a motor vehicle and commit more than one moving violation as part of a single continuous sequence of driving acts, which is likely to endanger any person or property. The National Highway Traffic Safety Administration (NHTSA) identified a variety of motor vehicle violations that are typically associated with aggressive driving. They are presented here with a few additions: 1) exceeding the posted speed limit, 2) following too closely, 3) erratic or unsafe lane changes, 4) improperly signaling lane changes, 5) reckless driving, 6) careless driving, 7) improper passing and 8) failure to obey traffic control devices (stop signs, yield signs, traffic signals, railroad grade cross signals, pedestrian crosswalks).[140]

Alignment In an organization, assessing the extent to which programs, projects and activities contribute to meeting the mission and desired outcomes.

Analysis of Variance (ANOVA) In statistics, analysis of variance (ANOVA) is a collection of statistical models and their associated procedures that compare means by splitting the overall observed variance into different parts. A quantitative dependent variable is required. ANOVA procedures include one-way ANOVA and two-way ANOVA techniques.

Annual Report	A formal public document released by the police department each year that accounts for the activities and financial performance of the agency. An annual report may be voluntary or legally mandated. See *The Police Annual Report as a Performance Accountability System, Final Report*, by Stanley Vanagunas, National Institute of Justice for a critique of police annual reports. Incorporating the principles outlined in this text into a business plan and ultimately into an annual report will improve accountability and public image between the police and constituent groups.
Aoristic Crime Analysis	A crime analysis technique that considers all incidents, which might have occurred within a specified period of time, when the actual time of occurrence is not known and which produces a probability estimate of when the crime may have occurred. See *Ratcliffe*, 2002.
Assumption-based Planning	A judgment or evaluation about some characteristic of the future that underlies the plans of an organization. See *Dewar*, p.229.
Assumptions	In assumption-based planning, the facts, beliefs or propositions that underlie a plan. See *Dewar* p.2.
Authorized Strength	The total sworn strength of the department as authorized by the governing body as depicted in the adopted budget.
Autoregressive Integrated Moving Average Model (A.R.I.M.A)	In statistics, an autoregressive integrated moving average (A.R.I.M.A) model is fitted to time-series data either to better understand the data or to predict future points in the series.
AutoTrack®	A premium service that enables subscribers to access information databases that search and cross-reference enormous amounts of data from various sources, such as addresses, drivers' licenses, property deed transfers, telephone listings, and corporate information, and unifies it into a single report. AutoTrack® is useful for conducting criminal and civil investigations, identifying fraud, locating witnesses, finding missing children or locating and verifying assets. (See www.autotrack.com).
Baseline (also baseline data)	A data set arranged in chronological order that establishes the status of the data as of a specific date. Baseline data is used to provide a starting point for subsequent measurements and comparisons. For example, the baseline for case clearance rates may be the national clearance rate for the crime being measured, for cities of comparable size; or it may be the police department's clearance rate for last year. See *composite index*. Baseline data is not a quota. Baseline data

is empirical and derived from actual past experience, usually based on data captured over a large period such quarterly, semi annually or annually. A quota is typically a predetermined target such as the number or proportion of arrests, summonses, field interrogations or other measurable output. See *quota* for a definition and prohibitions.

Benchmarking (also best practice benchmarking or process benchmarking)   A management process in which organizations evaluate various aspects of their processes in relation to best practice, usually within their own practice group. This permits organizations to develop plans on how to adopt such best practice, usually with the aim of increasing some aspect of performance. Benchmarking serves a reference point against which something can be measured or improved. See best practice.

Benefit   In an efficiency analysis, positive program outcomes, usually translated into monetary terms in cost-benefit analysis or compared with costs in cost-effectiveness analysis. Benefits may include both direct and indirect outcomes. See *Rossi, Lipsey and Freeman*, p.367.

Best Practice   A strategy, approach or process that, through experience and research, has been shown to deliver reliable and desired end outcomes and is accepted as superior to all other known methods. A best practice is considered a by-product of a successful end outcome and is often used in conjunction with benchmarking to improve effectiveness, efficiency and innovativeness. See benchmarking.

Bivariate Analysis   In statistics, the analysis of relationships between pairs of variables.

Boundering   During Compstat, a questioning technique used by the facilitator to prevent a participant from straying from the subject matter being discussed. See *Schroeder, Lombardo and Strollo*, (1995), p.133.

Budget Compliance   In management, the degree to which accountable personnel conform with or adapt their actions to the stated wishes, laws, rules or necessities established in the adopted financial plan.

Business Logic   In policing, the department's rules, policies and standard operating procedures that govern what will be done and the processes they adopt for getting things done.

Business Plan A written document used to communicate the agency's business, its objectives, strategies, and expected performance; comprehensive planning document that clearly describes where the agency is today, where it wants to go (goals) and how it is going to achieve its goals (performance objectives). The business plan outlines what, how and from where the resources needed to accomplish the goals will be acquired and utilized. See appendix 1 for a sample outline.

CAD System (Computer-Aided Dispatch System) A computer-driven system that assists emergency telecommunications operators and dispatch personnel in processing and prioritizing calls for emergency service by verifying address and location information, recommending units to respond, recording times, and printing and displaying information regarding the call.

Calls for Service (CFS) A telephonic request for emergency service. CFS are typically differentiated by: 1) the number of telephone calls received, and 2) the number of assignments dispatched. May be used a performance indicator for a PSAP.

Car Stop The act of demanding a motorist to stop their vehicle by a law enforcement officer. May be used a performance indicator for a patrol division and a traffic division.

Census Tract A small, relatively permanent statistical subdivision of a county established by the U.S. Census Bureau, which is designed to be homogenous with respect to population characteristics, economic status, and living conditions. Census tracts typically contain between 2,500 and 8,000 residents.

Central Data Collection The process of collecting data in a central repository within the agency.
CFS (Calls for Service) See *calls for service.*

Chart (also graph) A chart or graph is a type of information graphic that represents tabular numeric data. Charts are often used to make it easier to understand large quantities of data and the relationship between different parts of the data.

Citizen Complaint The act of accepting and investigating a grievance lodged against a law enforcement agency or a law enforcement officer by a member of the public. May be used a performance indicator for a department goal measuring reverence for law and authority.

Civilianization The extent to which the use of non-sworn personnel in a law enforcement agency is employed. May be used a budgeting performance indicator.

Clearance (also clearance rate)   A measure of crimes solved by the police. A crime is typically cleared by effecting an arrest or by exceptional means. An exceptional clearance occurs when the investigation has established an offender, there is sufficient information to support an arrest charge, and the location of the offender is known, but there are reasons outside police control that prevent arresting, charging and prosecuting the offender. Death of an offender is an example of an exceptional clearance. Clearance rate is calculated by dividing the number of investigation cleared by the number of investigations assigned, multiplied by 100 ($50_{cleared} \div 100_{assigned} = .5 \times 100 = 50\%_{clearance\ rate}$). May be used an investigative performance indicator for a detective bureau.

Communications Division   In a law enforcement agency, usually the primary answering point for telephone calls requesting emergency service and radio communication among officers in the field. See P.S.A.P.

Community Support   The level to which community members, elected officials, business owners and other stakeholders or constituent groups promote the interests or causes of the police department by arguing or voting in favor of policies, programs and other initiatives. May be used a performance indicator to measure police legitimacy.

Complement   The quantity or number required to make something complete; the quantity or number of something that is already complete.

Composite Index (also composite measure)   A measure that combines numerical information, such as the average, on more than one component variable to arrive at a measure of the same phenomenon. For example, the phenomenon "violent crime" may be expressed as an index of the combined average for murder, rape, robbery and aggravated assault (component variables). The phenomenon "property crime" may be expressed as an index of the combined average for burglary, larceny, auto theft, and arson. See *baseline*.

Compstat   Acronym for COMPuter STATistics or COMParative STATistics, a management technique developed by the New York City Police Department. Compstat is a dynamic managerial accountability process used by ranking police commanders and executives to manage crime, improve communication and improve resource management. The Compstat process employs various analysis tools to map crime incidents, detect patterns and hot spots, identify problems and affix accountability.

Compstat Book	The completed staff work of a crime analyst's effort that culminates in a collated, printed version of the previous Compstat period's activity.
Conceptualization	The process by which an abstract term or idea is defined so as to specify what is meant by the term. See also *operationalization*.
Confidence Level	In statistics, the upper limit of acceptability for the probability that a particular statistic, such as the t-statistic or the F-statistic would have occurred for some reason other than chance alone. By convention, the accepted degree of certainty that a statistical prediction is accurate is generally the 95% to 99% confidence level, expressed as .05 (95%) and .01 (99%). See *statistical significance*.
Consent Decree	A legally binding document, endorsed by a judge, which formalizes an out-of-court agreement between two parties and stipulates certain conditions that must be fulfilled. When signed a consent decree has the force of a court order. A consent decree is designed to cease or correct actions or practices that violate civil rights or constitutional safeguards or otherwise compel compliance with USDOJ-initiated regulatory enforcement action to resolve the issue.
Content Analysis (also textual analysis)	A set of procedures that uses carefully applied rules for collecting, organizing, analyzing and interpreting written and visual material such as magazines, public policies, television programs or advertisements, or photographs, by breaking them into meaningful units to draw inferences about the meaning or the characteristics of the material.
Content Validity	The ability of the items in a measuring instrument or test to adequately measure or represent the content of the property that the investigator wishes to measure.[141]
Correlation	A measure of the degree of fit (the coefficient indicating the relationship) between two sets of scores (variables). Correlation identifies the strength and direction of the relationship.
Correlation Coefficient (also Pearson Correlation Coefficient; symbolized by *r*)	A numerical measure of the strength of the relationship between two interval level variables. The *r* value identifies the strength and direction of the relationship, where +1 is a perfect positive relationship; 0 is no relationship; -1 is a perfect negative relationship.
Costs	In an efficiency analysis, the direct and indirect input or resources, to produce an intervention. See *Rossi, Lipsey and Freeman*, p.367.

Cost-Benefit Analysis (C.B.A) A type of efficiency assessment that "compares present values of all benefits less those of related costs when benefits can be valued in dollars the same way as costs." [142]

Cost-Effectiveness Analysis (C.E.A) A type of efficiency assessment that is "a criterion for comparing alternatives when benefits or outputs cannot be valued in dollars. This relates costs of programs to performance by measuring outcomes in non-monetary form. It is useful in comparing methods of attaining an explicit objective on the basis of least cost or greatest effectiveness for a given level of cost." [143]

Count In quantitative analysis, to indicate or name by units or groups so as to find the total number of units involved.

Covariance A measure of the relation between two variables; the tendency of two variables to exhibit similar variances, while not necessarily establishing a cause and effect relationship.

Crackdown Operation (also police crackdown) In policing, a sudden and dramatic increase in police officer presence, sanction, and threat of apprehension either for specific offenses or for all offenses in a specific place. See *Scott*, p.1. If the crackdown operation takes place in or near multi-family dwellings, then the crime prevention benefits can be sustained for longer periods if they are immediately followed by police contacts with landlords (Eck and Wartell, 1996). May be used a crime control performance indicator for various divisions.

Crime Map (also crime mapping) The process and result of using geographic information systems (GIS) to enable crime analysts to identify spatial and temporal distribution of crime; may culminate in something known as a "hot spot," which is a concentration of crime or criminals.

Critical Dimensions In performance measurement, the principle aspects of a goal that, if achieved, are intended to assure the goal is accomplished. Critical dimensions are often derived from a theory or from empirical observation. For example, it is believed that to control fear and crime (a goal), crime and criminal victimization must be reduced and calling offenders to account must be increased.

Cross Sectional Analysis (also cross sectional data) Data analysis method where the data are obtained at a single point in time. Contrast with time-series data and longitudinal data. See *Babbie*, p.96.

Cross tabulation (also cross tab, cross tab report or joint contingency)	A report, often presenting numerical data, that is formatted as a matrix in columns and rows that shows the joint distribution of two or more variables.
Cultural Deviation	Occurs when elements of the organization increasingly operate according to their own standards, with little regard for the larger organization and its rules. See *O'Hara*, p.19.
Cycle Time	The total elapsed time, usually measured in hours or fraction of hours, from the time a task or series of tasks is initiated to the time the task is completed. For example, the total time it takes to handle a single call for service from the time the call is received until an officer completes the assignment; the total time it takes to process a single prisoner from the time the prisoner enters the cell block until they are released from police custody. May be used a process indicator. See *throughput*.
Data	Information either numerical (quantitative) or alphabetic (qualitative) about the nature of phenomena derived from experience or observation.
Data Analysis	The process of systematically applying statistical and logical techniques to describe, summarize, and compare data. Processing information or data that has been gathered in order to draw inferences or conclusions.
Data Mining (also knowledge-discovery in databases-KDD)	The process of querying and analyzing extremely large, often ignored or undervalued, data that has been collected during the normal course of business to establish relationships and identify patterns that accurately predict behavior.
Data Set	A collection of individual datum that forms the basis for a study or analysis.
Decision Tree	A graphical representation of decisions and their possible consequences, including resource costs and risks, which are used to create a plan to reach a desired outcome.
Dependent Variable	In statistics, a variable presumed to be influenced by another variable; a variable presumed to result in some effect.
Deployment	The act of placing police personnel into the field especially based on pre-existing strategic plans.
Deployment Level (also manpower deployment)	The complement of police personnel in the field at a given time. May be used a performance indicator that measures equatability and workload equalization.

Descriptive Statistics	A branch of statistics that denotes any of the many techniques used to summarize a set of data; using the data on members of a set to describe the set.
Directed Citizen Contacts	The act of purposefully meeting with citizens in-person as an objective of a larger goal, such as improving police-community relations, reducing fear, establishing trust or exchanging information. May be used a performance indicator for a patrol division.
Directed Patrol	The act of assigning police officers to a specific area and freeing them from responding to calls for service in order for them to engage in proactive investigation and enforcement of suspicious activities. See McGarrell et. al., p.120. See also *Koper*, 1995. May be used a performance indicator for a patrol division.
Division of Labor	In policing, organizing the service delivery process into a series of functions with each worker focusing on a limited set of tasks, such as patrol, homicide investigation or forensics analysis. Division of labor permits each worker to practice and perfect a particular set of skills.
Dosage (also dosage level)	In policing, the process of increasing or decreasing the level of inputs during an intervention. For example, dosage may be the number of police officers and other resources committed to a program (input).
Ecological Fallacy	To draw inferences about the nature of individuals based solely upon aggregate statistics collected for the group to which those individuals belong. Ecological fallacy is a widely recognized error in the interpretation of statistical data.
Economic Model	In policing, a construct that represents budget processes by a set of work units and the quantitative relationships between the work units and the cost. See activity-base budgeting.
Economies of Scale	In policing, a condition where fewer inputs such as effort and time are needed to produce greater quantities of a single output due to process synergies that result in reduced per unit cost.
Economy	In the context of value, the management and regulation of resources (human, financial and in-kind contributions), expressed in monetary terms, that measures unit costs to deliver services.
Effective	Producing or capable of producing an intended overall result. See efficiency.

Effective Strength	The number of officers that are on duty at a given time.
Effective Tactics	In Compstat principle #2. To direct specific resources toward specific problems that deal with as much of the problem as possible.
Effectiveness	The ability to achieve stated goals or objectives, judged in terms of both output and impact.
Efficiency (also efficient)	The degree to which output is achieved in terms of input (resources allocated) as expressed by ratio; the quality of being efficient. Efficiency is a measure of performance insofar as management may set objectives and plan schedules and for which staff members may be held accountable through minimizing waste, expense, or unnecessary effort. Efficiency is the reciprocal of productivity. See example under Performance Indicator Classification System. Contrast with effective.
Efficiency Analysis (also efficiency assessment)	A series of different techniques that provide a frame of reference for relating costs to program results. See *Rossi, Lipsey and Freeman*, p.332. See *cost-benefit analysis* and *cost-effectiveness analysis*.
Empirical Data	Information or measurements derived from observations made in actual circumstances. For example, using actual data collected from a traffic survey, the computer-aided dispatch (CAD) system, the records management system (RMS) or some other source where the information was derived from actual observations not theory.
Employee Productivity (also productivity)	The relationship between production of an output and one, some, or all of the resource inputs used in accomplishing the assigned task. It is measured as a ratio of output per unit of input over time. It is a measure of efficiency and is usually considered as output per person-hour. [144]
Empowerment Grant	Funding, typically from the state or federal government, to help communities increase personal, community, interpersonal and political power to enable individuals or groups to improve their life circumstances.
End Outcome	An envisioned or desired state resulting from operationally defined goals and objectives, which usually culminates in measured performance. See goal.

Ex Ante Efficiency Analysis (also prospective efficiency analysis)

An efficiency analysis, either cost-benefit or cost-effectiveness analysis undertaken prior to program implementation, usually as part of program planning, to estimate net outcomes in relation to costs. See Rossi, Lipsey and Freeman, p.368.

Ex Post Efficiency Analysis (also retrospective analysis)

An efficiency analysis, either a cost-benefit or cost-effectiveness analysis undertaken after a program's outcomes are known. See Rossi, Lipsey and Freeman, p.368.

Exhaustive Measurement (also exclusive measurement)

In measurement, each individual, object, or attribute is assigned to a single category. Exhaustiveness can be handled by adding a final category such as "other" or "combined" to ensure all attributes appear in only one category; for example, all racial categories are covered by these five categories: black, white, Hispanic, Asian, "other." See Maxfield and Babbie, p.108.

Explanatory Research

Research that is designed to identify cause and effect. Explanatory research attempts to answer why something occurred. For example, why does city "A" have a crime rate higher than city "B" when both are similar in many respects? "Identifying variables that explain why some cities have higher crime rates than others involves explanation" See Babbie, p.85. If an agency executive wants to know why a civil disturbance erupted or why a significant proportion of suspects are charged with resisting arrest, then the investigation has an explanatory purpose

Exploratory Research

Research that is designed to investigate a topic on which little information exists. Exploratory research seeks patterns, ideas, or hypotheses about something rather than to test or confirm their existence. The aim is to gain more information before doing more thorough research or changing processes. An example is an inquiry into how citizens feel about the police after being serviced, including the citizens' expectations and level of satisfaction.

Extrapolation (also extrapolation analysis and trend extrapolation)

A measurement technique for forecasting some future state based on known facts and observations. The assumption is the variables will continue to behave in the future as they have in the past. Because extrapolation calculates the value of something outside the range of known values, its results may sometimes be invalid or subject to uncertainty depending on how things actually behave. See forecasting.

Face Validity	A form of content validity that addresses whether or not a measurement appears to be measuring something sensible, thus rendering it valid on its face.
FBI Part I Crimes	The 8 crimes specified under the FBI Uniform Crime Reporting program (UCR). The 8 offenses are: 1) murder and non-negligent manslaughter, 2) forcible rape, 3) robbery, 4) aggravated assault, 5) burglary, 6) larceny-theft, 7) motor vehicle theft, and 8) arson. May be used a crime control indicator. May be used a crime control indicator.
FBI UCR Program (also the UCR or UCR Program)	A voluntary city, county, state, tribal, and federal law enforcement program that provides a nationwide view of crime based on the submission of statistics by law enforcement agencies throughout the country. See www.fbi.gov.
Fear of Crime	"An emotional reaction characterized by a sense of danger and anxiety produced by the threat of physical harm... elicited by perceived cues in the environment that relate to some aspect of crime."[145] See Garafalo, 1981, p.840. Fear of crime is especially acute in the case of older people, although they comprise a group who are actually less likely to be victimized, as well as other vulnerable populations and is included in the wider concept of quality of life.
Field Interview (also field interrogation)	An encounter between a police officer and a citizen typically to confirm or dispel the officer's suspicions that criminal activity may be afoot by inquiring about the citizen's purpose and whether the citizen has any outstanding wants or warrants, and usually results in the officer documenting the encounter.
Fixed-Post Position (also steady post position)	Positions that necessitate staffing regardless of the volume of work expected or imposed.
Focus Group	A form of qualitative research in which a small group of stakeholders, typically between 8 and 15 people, assemble and participate in a guided open-ended discussion of a particular topic, often moderated by an agency representative, where participants are encouraged to offer their opinions, personal experiences, perceptions, and recommendations for resolving an issue or deciding on a course of action for a program or policy.

Forecast Period   In statistics, the time interval for which a forecast is developed; an upcoming time period of interest in which a forecast is to be made. A forecast period is typically weeks, months, quarters and years.

Forecasting (also to forecast)   A quantitative method to help calculate or predict future values from existing values, as in the amount of crime predicted for the ensuing year. An estimate or prediction of a future condition or outcome. See *extrapolation*.

FTE (abbreviation for full time equivalent)   A unit of the size of the staff body which considers both the number of staff and the fraction of full-time work status of each. For example, a staff member working full-time will register as 1 FTE, while a staff member working a fractional load of half-time will register as 0.5 FTE. One FTE equals one full-time position or two half-time positions and so forth. The FTE representation is used during the budget process and during staffing analysis.

General Deterrence   Crime prevention measure that seeks to prevent or inhibit criminal behavior by instilling fear in the general population through punishing offenders. General deterrence is a primary goal of criminal sentencing. See specific deterrence.

Goal   Broad statements intended to provide direction for change; a goal statement is used to describe desired future states or some intended change in the problem. See end outcome.

Graph   See chart.

Gridlock (also traffic deadlock)   A vehicular traffic condition resulting in an inability to move on a roadway system. The condition occurs when in a grid network where intersections are blocked, prohibiting vehicles from moving through the intersection, backing up to an upstream intersection. [146]

Hedging Actions   An organizational action to be taken in the current planning cycle and is intended to better prepare the organization for the potential failure of one of its load-bearing assumptions. See Dewar, p.123.

Hot Spot (also hot spot analysis)   In crime analysis, specific locations or small geographic areas that suffer a disproportionate amount of crime. Examples include specific addresses and neighborhoods.

Hypothesis   An educated guess about the relationship between two variables that seems valid in the face of the available information; a specific statement about the relationship between two variables that is testable.

Impact Evaluation (also impact assessment or outcome evaluation)	"An evaluative study that answers questions about program outcomes and impact on the social conditions it is intended to ameliorate." See Rossi, Lipsey and Freeman, p.427.
Implementation Failure	Occurs when a "program does not adequately perform the activities specified in the program design that are assumed to be necessary for bringing about the intended social improvement. It includes situations in which no service, not enough service, or the wrong service is delivered, or the service varies excessively across the target population." See Rossi, Lipsey and Freeman, p.427.
Incidence	The number of new cases of a condition during a defined time interval. Incidence is useful to police management because it is a measure of the risk of occurrence. The "incidence rate" is defined as the incidence divided by the sum of the different times each individual was at risk of the incident. For example, the incidence of resisting arrest is calculated like this:

$$\frac{\text{Number of new cases of resisting arrest in a specified time period}}{\text{Number of officers at risk of encountering resistance during that period}}$$

$(3_{\text{ new cases in 1 year}}) \div (37_{\text{ officers at risk of encountering resisting in 1 year}}) = .08 \times 100 = 8\%$

Resisting arrest has an 8% incidence rate. Contrast with prevalence.

Independent Variable	In statistics, a variable presumed to influence or precede another variable (usually the dependent variable); the variable believed to be the cause of something usually designated by the letter "x."
Indicators of Success (also success indicators)	The individual components of a strategic management model that, if carried out, are believed to create a positive impact on the agency or the community and which contribute to a specified goal.
In-kind Contribution	The value of non-cash contributions, including supplies, personnel, space, real property, equipment, and other expendable property in lieu of a direct cash contribution, which directly benefit and relate to a project or program.

Input (also input indicators)	The specific resources, including human and financial, that an organization must invest to produce the output necessary to achieve the desired end outcome.
Institutionalization	Occurs when an organization increasingly bases its approach to customers or clients on what best serves the comfort or preferences of the employees. See O'Hara, p.20.
Intelligence-Led Policing	An emerging policing philosophy that centers around collecting, analyzing and drawing conclusions from data in order to explain a criminal phenomenon and respond with preventive tactical plans and strategic resource plans. See Carter, 2005.
Intercept	In statistics, the value of the dependent variable (Y) when all independent variables (X) in the equation equal zero (0).
Intermediate Objective (also interim indicator or interim goal)	The process of defining and monitoring strategies and changes necessary to achieve the stated end outcome; assessing short-term progress toward the stated end outcome-interim progress.
Interval-Level Data	In statistics, data that is divided into ranges that represents quantities in terms of equal intervals but whose zero point is arbitrarily fixed.
Investigative Division	An organizational element of a police department whose primary function is to investigate specific crimes, such as homicide, sexual assault, burglary or robbery.
Kurtosis	A measure of the peakedness of a frequency distribution. A normal distribution has a kurtosis of 3. A negative value characterizes a relatively flat distribution, whereas a positive value characterizes a relatively peaked distribution. See Dretzke, p.75.
Law of Parsimony (also parsimonious)	The preference for the least complex explanation for an observation, which is driven by the theory that it is always advisable to make as few assumptions as possible while eliminating those that make no difference in the prediction. This means using the least number of independent variables to obtain the greatest explanatory power in the dependent variable.
Leadership Development	As a component of organizational development, the strategic investment in, and utilization of, human capital within an organization.

Learning Organization	An organization that is continually expanding its capacity to create its future (See Senge, 1994, p.vx, 14). An organization that actively monitors change in the environment, then adapts to and learns from that change typically by acquiring new KSA's (knowledge, skills, or abilities) and applying them to improve service quality.
Leave of Absence (with or without pay)	A period of absence from employment, with or without pay, authorized and approved by the employer.
Level of Effort	The amount of effort in terms of hours expended and number of personnel required to meet the actual or predicted workload. May be used a performance indicator for any division.
LexisNexis®	A premium service that permits subscribers access to information, services and solutions, including web-based research services and a wide range of professionals in the legal, risk management, corporate, government, law enforcement, accounting and academic markets. (See www.lexisnexis.com).
Light Duty	A temporary duty status designation whereby an employee is incapable of performing their assigned duties, whether from illness or injury, to the fullest extent. May be used as a service and accountability performance indicator.
Likert Scale	A multi-point measurement scale that measures the strength of a respondent's agreement with a clear statement, such as "strongly agree," "agree," "neither agree nor disagree," "disagree," and "strongly disagree." Named for Rensis Likert, who invented the scale in 1932.
Linear Regression Analysis (also linear regression)	In statistics, a method of estimating the conditional expected value of one variable (Y) given the values of some other variable or variables (X).
List Serv (also email list serv)	An Internet-based mailing list to disseminate newsworthy information to all those who subscribe. List serv includes the means to subscribe and unsubscribe and is usually offered at no cost. May be used as a performance indicator for a community affairs division.
Load-bearing Vulnerable Assumptions	In assumption-based planning, an assumption is load bearing if its failure would require significant changes in the organization's plans. See Dewar, p.66.

Logic Model	A systematic and visual way to present the perceived relationships among the resources you have to operate a program, the activities you plan to do, and the changes or results you hope to achieve.[147]
Longitudinal Data Analysis (also longitudinal study)	Data analysis of the same group over a period of time, generally used to monitor change, which requires measures during at least 3 points but preferably at least 5 points. See Shadish, Cook and Campbell, p.266. Contrast with cross sectional data analysis and time-series data analysis.
Long-Term Medical Disability	A period of infirmity that renders an employee incapable of working, for a period of more than two months. May be used as a service and accountability performance indicator.
Lord Kelvin	William Thomson, 1st Baron Kelvin (June 26, 1824-December 17, 1907), a mathematical physicist for whom the Kelvin temperature scale is named.
Maternity Leave	Leave granted to a female employee who is pregnant. The period of leave is variable depending upon individual conditions but usually consists of 30 days prior to birth and 90 days post parturition. May be used as a service and accountability performance indicator.
Maximum	The highest value in a data set.
Mean (arithmetic average)	The sum of a series of numbers divided by the number of entries in the series.
Measure of Central Tendency	In statistics, the degree to which the quantities of a variable converge. The most common measures of central tendency are mean, median and mode.
Measure of Dispersion	In statistics, a technique that describes the spread or variability in a distribution of scores.
Measurement	The act or process of assigning numbers to phenomena according to a rule; the determination of the size or magnitude of something.
Median	The middle number or item in a set of numbers or objects arranged from lowest to highest, or the mean of the two middle numbers when the set has two middle numbers. Median is the score that divides the distribution into halves; half of the scores are above the median and half are below it when the data are arranged in numerical order.

Micromanage	According to Webster's, to micromanage is "to manage with great excessive control or attention to details" (www. m-w.com). A more flexible definition may be the unnecessary interference by agency executives in the delegated responsibilities of various subordinate commanders, managers and professional staff.
Middle Managers	A group of employees who are typically responsible for executing and interpreting policies, and normally responsible for the operation of divisions. The rank of lieutenant or its equivalent in a police department is typically considered a middle manager.
Military Leave	Leave granted to an employee for a time period of time to serve in the Armed Forces of the United States on active duty.
Minimum	The lowest value in a data set.
Mobile Data Computer (M.D.C)	A vehicle-mounted device for two-way data communication, vehicle tracking and other communications systems.
Mode	The most frequently occurring value in a data set.
Motive	In a criminal act, the emotions or desires that impel a person to action.
Multiple R (also correlation coefficient)	See correlation coefficient.
Multiple Regression Analysis	In statistics, a prediction of the scores of a given dependent variable (Y) using the scores of a set of independent variables (X).
Mutually Exclusive Measurement	In measurement, an individual, object, or attribute must only be included in one category. Mutual exclusivity can be handled by restricting the attributes so no attribute can have more than one quality; for example, all persons must be classified as either male or female. See Maxfield and Babbie, p.109.
NCJ#	A document retrieval number assigned by the National Criminal Justice Reference Service (NCJRS) that is unique to each publication. The NCJ# is searchable from the NCJRS home page (www.ncjrs.org).

Negative Relationship	In statistics, a relationship between variables that move in opposite directions. A negative relationship means that as the predictor variable (X) increases there is a corresponding decrease in the dependent (Y) variable.
Neighborhood Conditions	The existing environment in a neighborhood characterized by the level of tranquility, cleanliness, and orderliness as perceived by the residents or as measured by workload. See note #37 for a list of conditions.
Net Annual Work Hours (N.A.W.H)	The number of hours staff members are actually available to work based on the contracted number of hours per year, minus the number of hours off per staff member per year.
Nominal Level Data (also name data)	In statistics, data that is described by the qualities of a category and is not ranked or ordered according to the values.
Normal Accident	Occurs when complex technological elements malfunction and human operators misjudge what's happening, responding with actions that can accelerate the deterioration of the situation. See O'Hara, p.18.
Objective	Explicit and measurable outcomes that consist of 4 components: 1) a time frame, 2) a target population, 3) a result and 4) a criterion.
Offender Profile	The pedigree information, lifestyle, habits and routine activities of a criminal offender.
Omnipresence (also police omnipresence)	In policing, the sense that the police are present in every place at the same time; a universal presence of sorts. Omnipresence is theoretically established through random patrol in marked police vehicles and may be augmented by patrolling with the overhead emergency lights activated.
Operationalization (also operationalize)	The process by which measurements are taken after concepts have been defined. Part of the process is how the data will be collected (i.e., surveys, official reports and documents–see conceptualization).
Operations Research (OR)	The use of mathematical models, statistics and data to aid in decision-making and to determine the most efficient way to do something. OR is often used to analyze complex real-world systems, typically with the goal of improving or optimizing performance.

Order of Operations (also precedence of operations)	In arithmetic and elementary algebra, a set of rules that determines the order for simplifying expressions when more than one operation is involved. The acronym P.E.M.D.A.S. is used to describe the order of operations: P = parentheses; E = exponents; M = multiplication; D = division; A = addition; S = subtraction.
Order of Precedence	The sequential hierarchy of nominal importance of employees in a police department. The rank structure in a police department denotes the order of precedence. See rank.
Ordinal Level Data (also ordered data)	In statistics, data that quantify differences by order such as "larger," "smaller," "higher," "lower," "more" or "less," not magnitude; the size of the interval is not specified. Ordinal level data points are labeled to provide information about the sequence of the items reported, but not the distance between the points within that sequence.
Organizational Capacity	The totality of an organization's resources including human, intellectual and financial means to achieve a specified goal.
Organizational Support	The extent to which an organization's incumbent employees promote the interests of, or concur with, the organization's policies, programs and other initiatives, often marked by their cumulative experience and institutional continuity. See Moore, (1995), p.51.
Outcome (also end outcome, effectiveness indicators or measures of effect)	A measure of the degree to which a service has achieved its goal, and as defined, met the needs of its recipients in terms of quantity and quality.
Outlier	In statistics, within a set of numerical data, any data point that is notably smaller or larger than other values. For example, in the data set {6, 5, 4, 3, 50, 2, 7, 7, 8, 6} the data point 50 is an outlier.
Output (also output indicators and measures of effort)	The direct products or services of personnel activities. Output typically measures the amount of something (e.g., the number of...; the percent of...; the ratio of...; the incidence of...).
Oversight Failure	Occurs when operational supervision and oversight staff fail to detect and/or address organizational conditions that depart significantly from the norm. See O'Hara, p.19.
Overtime	Work time in excess of a standard day or week that is typically compensated at a pay rate 1½ times the standard hourly pay rate.

Paradigm Blindness	A mode of thinking, often resulting from complacency, which impedes an organization's ability to see beyond its own perceptions of how things should be done. Paradigm blindness is reflected in the statement "the way we do it is the best because this is the way we've always done it."
Partnership	A relationship, which may be legally binding or informal, that is marked by close cooperation between parties who have specified joint rights and responsibilities.
Patrol Force	In a police department, the largest organizational element consisting primarily of uniformed sworn personnel whose primary responsibility is service delivery through field deployment.
Pattern Crime	A discernable set of 3 or more criminal acts that have similar traits or other observable characteristics. An **emerging trend** begins with 2 criminal acts that have similar traits or other observable characteristics.
P.E.M.D.A.S.	See order of operations.
Percentage	A method of expressing a proportion, a ratio or a fraction as a whole number, by using 100 as the denominator.
P.E.R.F (Police Executive Research Forum	A national membership organization of progressive police executives from the largest city, county and state law enforcement agencies dedicated to improving policing and advancing professionalism through research and involvement in public policy debate (See www.policeforum.org).
Performance Indicators	Methods of measuring how a police department or a workforce is performing through qualitative or quantitative measurements that demonstrate meaningful steps are being taken to achieve a stated goal.
Performance Management	The process of defining a mission and desired outcomes, setting performance standards, linking budget to performance, reporting results, and holding public officials accountable for results on a regular basis.
Performance Standard	A measurable number specifying the minimum acceptable outcome for an organizational element or practice, typically expressed as degree of excellence or level of requirement that meets or exceeds predefined specifications.

Personnel Availability	In a workload analysis, the difference between the maximum number of hours an employee could potentially work in a given year and the amount of time off the employee is granted (e.g., $1{,}534_{\text{personnel availability}} = 2{,}086_{\text{maximum work hours}} - 552_{\text{hours off}}$).
P.E.S.T Analysis	A technique for structuring an environmental analysis by identifying the Political, Economic, Social and Technological dimensions of the operating environment.
Plan of Action (also action plan)	A detailed written document describing the actions and steps necessary to implement a strategic plan, which may contain specific task assignments, responsibilities, milestones, time lines, resource allocations, data collection methodology, and evaluation criteria. See strategy.
Plausible Events	In assumption-based planning, events that are reasonably likely to occur within a given time period and whose occurrence would cause an assumption to fail. See Dewar, p.73.
Police Legitimacy	As an institution, the police department's need for public support, voluntary cooperation and compliance in order to be effective in their crime control role and to be perceived as fair and equitable in their treatment of members of the public; the social acceptance of the police department and its aims; perceived to conform with both the "spirit of the law" and the "letter of the law." Legitimacy is often "measured in terms of support, allegiance, institutional trust and confidence" (National Research Council, 1994:299).
Police Pursuit	"An active attempt by a law enforcement officer operating a motor vehicle and utilizing emergency warning lights and an audible device to apprehend one or more occupants of another moving vehicle when the officer reasonably believes that the driver of the fleeing vehicle is aware of the officer's attempt to stop the vehicle and is resisting apprehension by increasing vehicle speed, ignoring the officer or otherwise attempting to elude the officer." [148]
Positive Relationship	In statistics, as the predictor variable (X) increases there is a corresponding increase in the dependent variable (Y). An example of a positive relationship would be as the unemployment rate increases (predictor variable) there is a corresponding increase in the crime rate (dependent variable).
Predictor Variable	In a regression analysis, a variable that can be used to predict the value of another variable; commonly called independent variables and designated "x."

Prevalence	The number of new and pre-existing cases of a condition on a specific date. Prevalence is a function of both the incidence of a condition and existing cases of that same condition on a given date. For example, the prevalence of resisting arrest is calculated like this:

$$\frac{\text{Number of new cases + number of pre-existing cases during a specified time period}}{\text{Number of officers at risk of encountering resistance during that time}}$$

$(3_{\text{new cases in the current year}}) + (6_{\text{pre-existing cases from the previous year}}) = 9 \div 37 (_{\text{total officers at risk that year}}) = .24 \times 100 = 24\%$. Prevalence is a proportion that is typically expressed as a percentage. It is useful for police management because it is a measure of the commonality (frequency) of a particular condition.

Resisting arrest has a prevalence rate of 24% over the last 2 years (current year + previous year). Contrast with incidence.

Principal Modalities	In an activity-base budget, the major activities of an organizational element such as a bureau, division, section or unit that comprise the overall workload.
Prisoner Debriefing	In policing, the act of interviewing a person who is in custody for an unrelated charge, to uncover other crime and quality of issues and to promote police problem-solving.[149]
Process Evaluation	An evaluation that assesses the extent to which a program or process is operating as intended and identifies opportunities for streamlining or otherwise improving it. Process evaluations often begin with an analysis of how a program currently operates. Process evaluations may also assess the extent to which program activities conform to statutory and regulatory requirements, agency policies, program design or customer expectations.[150]
Production	In performance management, the three indicators that demonstrate economy, efficiency and productivity: 1) cost per unit (economy), 2) the cost per unit serviced (efficiency), and the number of units serviced per a defined metric of expenditures (productivity).
Productivity	As a measure of efficiency, expresses the ratio of output to input resources, usually per a defined metric. Productivity is the reciprocal of efficiency. See example under *Performance Indicator Classification System*.

Program	1) A system of projects or services intended to meet a public need; 2) in a police department, the individual organizational elements, usually depicted on the organizational chart as bureaus, divisions, sections, or units, that comprise the entire organization. Contrast with project.
Program Theory	A set of assumptions about the manner in which a program relates to the social benefits it is expected to produce and the strategy and tactics the program has adopted to achieve its goals and objectives. See Rossi, Lipsey and Freeman, p.432.
Project	A temporary endeavor undertaken to fill an unmet need through established goals and measurable objectives within defined constraints of time, resources and quality. A project is temporary since there is a definitive starting and ending date. Contrast with program.
P.S.A.P (public safety answering point)	The first point of reception for a 9-1-1 call. See communications division
Public Value	The sentiment expressed in public management that individual employees are free to pursue and propose new ideas about how to improve the workings of the agency in terms of efficiency or service delivery, in order to enrich citizen quality of life through lower crime rates or positive neighborhood conditions and by rewarding employee efforts toward that end. See Moore, 1995, p.52.
Qualitative Method	A method for exploring and answering analysts' questions that focus on how individuals and groups view and understand their world and construct meaning out of their experiences. It is typically narrative-oriented and relies on content analysis methods for selected levels of communication content. Qualitative methods are also laden with minute details and descriptions of social phenomena such as how humans interact with each other and with their environment and interpersonal relations.
Quantitative Method	A method for exploring and answering analysts' questions with numerical data and other data elements that are measurable. The results of quantitative research are generally counts, percentages, positive and negative data relationships, ratios, decimals or a series of numbers that are often presented in tables or charts.

Queue	In a public safety communications center, a stack of prioritized calls for service that are pending a police, fire or medical response via dispatch, often held in a computer-aided dispatch system.
Quota	"Any requirement, in writing or otherwise, regarding the number of arrests made or the number of citations issued within a defined period of time by a law enforcement officer, or regarding the proportion of the arrests made and citations issued by the law enforcement officer relative to the arrests made and citations issued by another law enforcement officer or group of officers." (NJS Title 40A: 40A:14-181.1 et. seq.) This practice is prohibited in New Jersey.
Radar Operations	In a police department, a proactive speed enforcement initiative designed to improve traffic safety through the use of radar to detect speed.
Raid (also police raid)	A police tactic encompassing a sudden, unannounced and overwhelming demonstration of force and authority typically exerted during the execution of an arrest or search warrant.
Random Error	In statistics, the component of total error which is due to chance alone.
Range	The difference between the largest and smallest value in a data set.
Rank (also rank structure, department hierarchy or hierarchical structure)	In a police department, a system for differentiating sworn officer positions through a series of successive promotions, typically achieved through an examination process, which results in career ascension marked by progressive increases in status, salary and responsibility. See order of precedence.
Rapid Deployment of Personnel and Resources	In Compstat principle #3. The act of gaining the upper hand on a crime or quality of life problem by setting a plan in motion rapidly and decisively, usually within 24 hours of development.
Rate	A ratio that expresses a relationship between two measurements with different units and is a fundamental descriptive statistic. Rates are useful for standardizing a metric for comparison purposes. See Maxfield and Babbie, 2001 p.387.
Ratio	A relationship between two quantities. Ratios are useful when, for example, you want to examine the relative amount of individual output to the whole division. The convention for expressing a ratio is the colon (:), which means "to" as in the ratio 2:1 (2 to 1).

Ratio Level Data (also interval/ratio level data)	In statistics, data that is represented in terms of equal distance between points and an absolute zero point. Age is an example of ratio level data.
Rave Party (also a free party)	Typically an all-night dance event where DJ's and other performers play fast-paced, repetitive electronic dance music accompanied by light shows. Problems related to rave parties include "assaults in and around bars, thefts of and from cars in parking facilities, disorderly youth in public places, graffiti, street-level drug dealing, clandestine drug labs, high-level drug trafficking in rave-related drugs, and use of illicit drugs in acquaintance rape." See Scott, p.3.
Recap (Recapitulation)	In Compstat, a concise summary of items designated for follow-up attention and which are reviewed during the next Compstat session; in a budget a concise summary of the individual organizational elements' budgets that comprise the total agency budget.
Recidivism (also repeat offending)	The continued, habitual or compulsive commission of law violating behavior that may be measured from different perspectives: 1) police perspective = rate of rearrest; 2) prosecutorial perspective = rate of reconviction; 3) corrections perspective = rate of reimprisonment.
Regression Analysis	A statistical method for determining the association between a dependent variable (Y) and one or more independent variables (X).
Relentless Follow-up and Assessment	In Compstat principle #4. The act of inspecting and reviewing the implementation and results of plans set in motion to ensure goals are achieved.
Relief Factor (also non-productive FTE, availability factor, and staff adjustment factor-SAF)	The number of full-time-equivalent (FTE) staff required to fill a single position that requires relief (i.e., a post or position that must be continuously covered 24 hours per day, 365 days per year).
Resource Diversion	Occurs when organizational resources end up being used for other than their intended purposes through illicit schemes or legal but exploitative manipulations by employee beneficiaries. See O'Hara, p.20.

Response Time	The total elapsed time, as measured from the time a call for service is entered into the CAD system until a police officer arrives on scene to service the request. Response time encompasses queue time and the travel time required to get to the scene. May be used as a performance indicator for the patrol division.
Result	A describable or measurable change in state that is derived from a series of steps intended to produce said state.
RMS (Records Management System)	A relational database designed to process, store and retrieve law enforcement records, such as incidents reports.
Road-Safety Checkpoints	At a designated location, police officers establish a presence to stop and inspect vehicles and drivers for sobriety, equipment violations, or other social utilitarian purposes. May be used as a performance indicator for the patrol division and the traffic division.
R.O.I (Return on Investment)	In policing, the ROI is the actual or perceived future value of a monetary expense or investment in a particular service that is delivered. For example, crime control ROI is a metric that attempts to determine what the community receives in return for the cost of the crime control program, usually in terms of fewer crime victims or fewer dollars lost to property damage.
R-squared (also multiple coefficient of determination)	Measures the "goodness of fit" of a regression line and describes the amount of variation in the dependent variable that is explained by the independent variable. The R-squared measure takes on a value from 0 to 1. See also adjusted R-squared.
Sample Variance	A measure of a random variable's statistical dispersion indicating how far from the expected value its values typically are.
Scattergram (also scatterplot)	A chart used in statistics that visually displays and compares two sets of related quantitative data with each point having a coordinate on a horizontal (X) and a vertical (Y) axis.
Scenario (also "what if" analysis)	A plausible description of how the future may develop based on a coherent and internally consistent set of assumptions about key relationships and driving forces (e.g., arrest rate, budget constraints, and unemployment). Note that scenarios are neither predictions nor forecasts.

| Scenario Learning | Using scenarios to augment understating, produce new decisions, reframe existing decisions and identify contingent decisions. See Dewar, p.233. |

Scofflaw A person who persistently ignores the law and does not answer court summonses, especially traffic court summonses, where fines accrue and where an arrest warrant may be in effect for the violator.

Season (also seasonality) The natural rise and fall of data over the course of a year and the patterns that generally appear as a result.

Self-Defense Measures The nature and extent to which citizens protect themselves and their possessions, such as carrying a weapon, installing a burglar alarm, erecting a fence, or buying a guard dog. May be used as a crime and fear control performance indicator.

Self-initiated Assignments Activities undertaken by a police officer without being directed to do so; proactive actions, as compared to reactive actions.

Service Demands The type and amount of police intervention needed as expressed by the request for such service from citizens.

Service-Time Threshold The upper limit of the total time a request for service is allotted. For example, the service-time threshold for a residential burglary report is 45 minutes; the service-time threshold for a stolen vehicle report is 25 minutes. May be used as a performance indicator for servicing calls or other requests for service.

Shaping Actions In assumption-based planning, an organizational action to be taken in the current planning cycle and intended to control the vulnerability of a load-bearing assumption; any action undertaken to shore-up uncertain assumptions to control the future as much as possible. See Dewar, p.233.

Sick Leave Authorized leave from duty granted to an employee to recover from sickness or injury. May be used as a service and accountability performance indicator.

Sign Post In assumption-based planning, warning signs that can be used to monitor those assumptions that are most likely to produce surprise. See Dewar, p.3.

Signing Language expressed through visible hand gestures; sign language.

Skewness   Skewness is a numerical index that represents the degree of asymmetry of a distribution around its mean. Positive skewness indicates a distribution with an asymmetric longer tail extending in the direction of more positive values. Negative skewness indicates a distribution with an asymmetric tail extending in the direction of more negative values. See Dretzke, p.75.

Slope   The ratio of change in the dependent variable (Y) compared to the change in the independent variable (X) when moving along the x-axis from one point to another.

Socio-demographic Variables (or factors)   Characteristics ascribed to people or places, such as income level, age, race, and sex.

Span of Control   An assumption that there is a limit to the number of subordinates a manger can effectively supervise, which subsumes the principle of delegation. Span of control describes the number of subordinates that report to each manager and is determined by a number of factors such as complexity of the work, degree of specialization required and individual competency. Current human resource theory fixes the manager/subordinate ratio at 3:7 with 5:1 established as optimum. See Hale, 1981:136.

Specific Deterrence   Crime prevention measure focused on instilling fear, through sufficiently severe punishments, in the specific individual being punished so that they refrain from future violation of the law. See general deterrence.

Spreadsheet   A table of numerical data in which columns and rows are related by formulae. MS Excel© is a spreadsheet application.

Staffing   An executive function of a police department that involves recruiting, training and assigning personnel to carry out the department's mission.

Standard Deviation   In statistics, a measure of variation based on squared deviations from the mean.

Standard Error   In statistics, the average amount by which an individual observation in a sample differs from the value predicted when using a particular statistical measure. In regression analysis the standard error is typically reported with the coefficient estimate. By social science convention, it is possible to say, with 95% confidence, that the true coefficient is within +/- 2 standard errors of the estimate.

Statistical Significance (also significance, alpha level or p-value)	In statistics, the probability that an event or difference occurred by chance alone. A result is statistically significant if it is unlikely to have occurred by chance. By convention, the alpha level is set at .05, or the 95% confidence level. Any result that achieves a reading of .05 or lower (.04, .03, .001), is considered statistically significant, meaning the result is unlikely to have occurred by chance alone. See confidence level.
Statistics	A mathematical science pertaining to collecting, analyzing, interpreting and presenting data.
Status Offense	Behavior by a minor that would not be criminal if committed by an adult (e.g., curfew violation, truancy, runaway), yet is defined as an offense when committed by a minor because of the person's "status" as a minor and which is generally adjudicated by a juvenile court. See Whitehead and Lab, p.3
Steady Post Position	See fixed post position.
Strategic Management	The managerial process of creating vision, identifying goals, setting objectives, developing a strategy around policies, allocating resources, implementing and executing the strategy for the overall direction of the entire organization. Strategic management is usually carried out at the agency's executive level.
Strategic Planning	In policing, a disciplined effort to produce fundamental decisions and actions that shape and guide what a police department is, what it does, and why it does it.
Strategy	The allocation of resources to a plan of action necessary for the organization to pursue and to gain a competitive or tactical advantage over others. See plan of action. See also tactics. See Michaelson, 2001.
Street Closure	A police problem-solving technique that entails permanently closing or vacating a public street or alley to control crime in residential or commercial areas. See Clarke, 2004. May be used as a crime and fear control performance indicator.
Structural Failure	Occurs when operations, procedures and processes that are functioning according to design, lead to failure. See O'Hara, p.18.
Success Indicator	In performance measurement, the part of a performance measure that defines the attribute or characteristic to be measured; a particular value or characteristic used to measure outcome or output.

Sum	The result of adding numbers.
Suppressible Incident	An incident is deemed suppressible if: 1) it occurred on-view, that is, where it occurred was visible from the street, or 2) it occurred as part of a pattern of recidivist behavior by an identified suspect. May be used as a crime and fear control performance indicator.
Suppression (also suppression hearing)	A hearing on a criminal defendant's motion to prohibit the prosecutor's use of evidence alleged to have been obtained in violation of the defendant's rights. May be used as a performance indicator to hold offenders accountable.
Survey	The systematic collection of data for the analysis of something.
S.W.O.T Analysis	A critical set of steps in a planning exercise used to perform internal and external assessments. S.W.O.T is an acronym for Strengths, Weaknesses, Opportunities, and Threats. Strengths and Weaknesses are internal to the organization; Opportunities and Threats originate from outside the organization. A S.W.O.T analysis helps organizations evaluate the environmental factors and internal situation facing a project. See Bryson 1995.
Table	A systematic arrangement of data usually in rows and columns for ready reference that helps convey raw or summarized data in a comprehensible format. Tables help the reader make sense of the information and help with interpretation.
Tactical Planner (planning)	A police department employee who is responsible for analyzing and identifying crime trends and patterns and making recommendations to command staff officers on deployment levels and anti-crime efforts.
Tactics	During the implementation of a plan of action, the employment of allotted resources to perform specific techniques or actions, which are used to achieve a planned strategy. Tactics are the contact actions for how the strategy is to be achieved. See strategy. See Michaelson, 2001.
Target	In performance measurement, the part of a performance measure that establishes the desired level to be reached in a defined time period, usually stated as an improvement over the baseline.
Target Population	The population, clients, or subjects intended to be identified and served by a project, program or other intervention.

Telephone Reporting Unit (T.R.U)	In a police department, an intra-division element, typically situated in the communications division, whose purpose is to resolve a request for service over the telephone thus avoiding the need to dispatch a police officer. TRU typically diverts incidents of a minor nature that do not necessitate a police officer come to the scene.
Temporizing	During a Compstat meeting, to draw out the discussion or negotiation with superfluous detail so as to gain time when a commander or other participant is questioned and does not know the answer to the question.
Throughput	The volume of output generated by a resource in a specific period of time; the amount passing through a system from input to output; the rate of production of a defined process over a specific period of time. Rates may be expressed in terms of units processed other meaningful measurements. For example the number of prisoners received and released per hour (or in a tour of duty); the number of calls for service received and disposed of per hour (or in a 24-hour period; or in one month).
Time Frame	A time period during which something occurs or is expected to occur.
Time Series (also time series data)	In statistics, a sequence of quantitative data points, measured at successive times and spaced apart at uniform time intervals. Contrast with cross-sectional data analysis and longitudinal data analysis.
Total Quality Management (T.Q.M)	A business improvement and management philosophy which involves an organization's entire workforce and emphasizes constant measures and statistical techniques to help improve and maintain output quality with an eye toward efficiency, effectiveness and adaptability of service delivery.
Traffic Calming	"The combination of primarily physical measures that reduce the negative effects of motor vehicle use, alter driver behavior, and improve conditions for non-motorized street users."[151] Typical traffic calming objectives include traffic circles, lane narrowing, speed tables, signage and lane markings.
Traffic Division	In a police department, an organizational element whose purpose is to enforce and investigate motor vehicle related laws.

Traffic Summons	In a police department, a legal document notifying a person that an action has been instituted against him or her and that he or she is required to answer it at the time and place named. Usually issued in response to an observed traffic violation. May be used as a performance indicator for the patrol division and traffic division.
Trend Line	In a chart, a line that depicts the statistical trend of a data series and shows the direction of change.
Triangulation	"The combination of methodologies in the study of the same phenomenon or construct; a method of establishing the accuracy of information by comparing three or more types of independent points of view on data sources (for example, interviews, observation, and documentation; different times) bearing on the same findings. Akin to corroboration and an essential methodological feature of case studies."[152] See composite index.
t-Statistic (also t-distribution or student's t-distribution)	In statistics, a probability distribution that arises in the problem of estimating the mean of a normally distributed population when the sample size is small.
Unexcused Absence (also away without leave - A.W.O.L)	To be absent from scheduled duty without authorization or permission.
Unfunded Mandate	A law that requires local or state agencies to provide a service or program but provides no money to carry out the law.
Unit	Basic work activities that imply demand.
Unit Cost	The monetary cost of delivering a single unit of service and includes the calculated costs for materials, equipment and salaries. See example under *Activity-Base Budgeting*.
Unit of Analysis	The basic observable construct being analyzed and for which data are collected. Units of analysis are virtually limitless; examples include individual people, families, cities, states, counties, countries, police precincts, census tracts.
Use of Force	As used by a law enforcement officer, the legitimate employment of constructive authority, physical contact or other coercive influence, whether lethal or less lethal, to ensure a non-compliant person refrains from doing something or submits to the officer's lawful authority. May be used as a performance indicator to measure reverence for law and authority.

Validity	The extent to which an empirical measure adequately reflects the real meaning of the concept under consideration. See Babbie, p.139. In statistics, a valid measure is one which is measuring what it is supposed to measure. Validity implies reliability (accuracy). A valid measure must be reliable, but a reliable measure need not be valid.[153]
Variable	In statistics, a concept specifying or implying more than one category to which phenomena may be assigned.
Vertical Patrol	In policing, the act of patrolling the interior of a building (such as a multiple occupancy building) on foot from top to bottom, or bottom to top, consisting of interior hallways, stairways, public areas and rooftops. May be used as a crime and fear control performance indicator.
Victimology	A qualitative process of determining why certain people are victims of crime and how their habits, routine activities and lifestyle may have precipitated their chance of becoming a victim.
Volume-based Position	In a workload analysis, the evaluation of a position based upon the amount of work that is expected to flow through the position.
Weighting (also prioritizing)	In a workload analysis, the aspect of assigning a numerical value, typically a percentage, as the upper limit for a specific task or category as it relates to distributing time.
Work Year	In a workload analysis the maximum number of hours in a year a single person can be expected to work.
Workflow Processing (also workflow)	The relationship among activities in a program, project or process from start to finish that shows how tasks are structured, who performs them, the order in which they are performed, their dependency on each other, how information flows to support the tasks and they are tracked. Often depicted graphically through a workflow diagram.
Workload	An expression of the total amount of work, identified by the number of work units, which is expected within a specified period of time. Estimates of expected workload for a specific activity are derived from a **workload analysis**.
Workload Analysis	The process of collecting and analyzing data on activities for the purpose of more efficient scheduling, deployment, and budgeting. See Hale, p.167.

X Variable (also independent variable) In statistics, the independent (X) variable; the variable that is believed to cause the dependent variable to change.

Y = a + bx + e The expression for a bivariate linear regression equation.

y = a + b₁x₁ + b₂x₂ + b₃x₃...+ e The expression for a multivariate linear regression equation.

Y Variable (also dependent variable) In statistics, the dependent (Y) variable; the variable that is believed to be affected by the independent variables.

Adler, F., Mueller, G.O. and Laufer, W. (2006). <u>Criminal Justice: An Introduction</u>. 4th ed. New York: McGraw-Hill

*Alpert, G.P. and Moore, M.H. (1994). *Measuring Police Performance in the New Paradigm of Policing.* In Geoffrey P. Alpert and Roger G. Dunham, 2001, <u>Critical Issues in Policing: Contemporary Readings</u>. 4th ed. Prospect Heights, Il: Waveland Press. Originally publication: U.S. Department of Justice, Bureau of Justice Statistics—Princeton University Study Group on Criminal Justice Performance Measures. *Performance Measures for the Criminal Justice System* 1994:108-141. Accessible at http://www.ojp.usdoj.gov/bjs/pub/pdf/pmcjs.pdf.

---Flynn, D. and A. Piquero (2001). *Effective Community Policing Performance Measures.* Justice Research and Policy, Vol. 3, No. 2:79-94.

Ammons, D.N. (1999). *A Proper Mentality for Benchmarking.* In Gerald J. Miller, W. Bartley Hildreth and Jack Rabin, *Performance Based Budgeting.* 2001. Boulder, CO: Westview Press. pp. 419-429.

Babbie, E. (2002). <u>The Basics of Social Research</u>. 2nd Ed. Belmont, Ca: Wadsworth.

*Bachman, R. and Paternoster, R. (2004) <u>Statistics for Criminology and Criminal Justice</u>. 2nd Ed. New York: McGraw Hill.

Bartol, K.M and David C. Martin. (1991). <u>Management</u>. New York: McGraw-Hill.

Bellair, P.E. (1997). *Social Interaction and Community Crime: Examining The Importance of Neighborhood Networks.* Criminology. Vol. 35. No. 4:677-701.

Bazemore, G., Stinchcomb, J.B. and Leip, L.A. (2004). *Scared Smart or Bored Straight? Testing Deterrence Logic in an Evaluation of Police-led Truancy Intervention.* Justice Quarterly, Vol. 21, No. 2:269-299.

*Behn, R.D. (2004). *Performance Leadership: 11 Better Practices That Can Ratchet Up Performance.* Managing for Performance and Results Series, IBM Center for Business of Government.

*Bennis, W. and Burt Nanus. (1997). <u>Leaders: Strategies for Taking Charge</u>. New York: Harper Collins.

Bok, D. (1997). *Measuring the Performance of Government.* In Nye, Jr, J.S., Zelikow, P.D. and King, D.C. (1997). <u>Why People Don't Trust Government</u>. Cambridge, Ma: Harvard University Press.

Bonasia, J. (2005). *As Crime Fighters Study Data, SPSS Steps In.* Investor's Business Daily, Internet and Technology. November 3rd.

Bradford, R. W., Duncan, P.J. and Tracy, B. (1999). Simplified Strategic Planning: A No-nonsense for Busy People Who Want Results Fast! New York: Chandler House Press.

Brandl, S.G. and Frank, J. (1994). *The Relationship Between Evidence, Detective Effort, and the Disposition of Burglary and Robbery Investigations*. American Journal of Police, Vol. XIII, No. 3:149-168. See also Eck, J. (1983). *Solving Crime: The Investigation of Burglary and Robbery*. Washington, D.C.: Police Executive Research Forum.

*Brantingham, P. J., and Brantingham, P. L. (1984). Patterns in Crime. New York: Macmillan.

---(Eds). (1991). Environmental Criminology. Prospect Heights, OH: Waveland.

*Bratton, W.J. with Peter Knobler. (1998). Turnaround: How America's Top Cop Reversed the Crime Epidemic. New York: Random House.

*Brizius, J. A., and Campbell, M. D. (1991). *Getting Results: A Guide for Government Accountability*. Washington, D.C.: Council of Governors Policy Advisors.

*Bryson, J.M.. (1995). Strategic Planning for Public and Non-Profit Organizations: A Guide to Strengthening and Sustaining Organizational Achievement. San Francisco: Jossey-Bass.

Cahn, M., and Tien, J.M. (1981). An Evaluation Report of an Alternative Approach in Police Response: The Wilmington Management of Demand Program. Cambridge, Ma: Public Systems Evaluation, Inc.

Carter, D.L (2005). *The Law Enforcement Intelligence Function*. FBI Law Enforcement Bulletin. June 2005:1-9; see also HMIC (Her Majesty's Inspectorate of Constabulary) (1997). *Policing with Intelligence*. Her Majesty's Inspectorate of Constabulary, London. In Ratcliffe, R.H. (2002). *Aoristic Signatures and the Spatio-Temporal Analysis of High Volume Crime Patterns*. Journal of Quantitative Criminology, Vol. 18, No. 1:23-43; Peterson, M. (2005). *Intelligence-Led Policing: The New Intelligence Architecture*. U.S. Department of Justice, Bureau of Justice Assistance. NCJ# 210681; Ratcliffe, J.H. (2003). *Intelligence Led Policing*. Trends and Issues in Crime and Criminal Justice, Paper 248, April 2003. Ratcliffe, J.H. (2002). *Intelligence-Led Policing and The Problems of Turning Rhetoric Into Practice*. Policing and Society, Volume 12 Issue 1: 53-66; Ratcliffe, J.H. (2000). Implementing and Integrating Crime Mapping Into a Police Intelligence Environment. International Journal of Police Science and Management, Volume 2 Issue 4: 313-323. Ratcliffe's publications are available in .pdf format from http://jratcliffe.net/papers/index.htm.

*Carter, L. and Wilson, M. (2006). *Measuring Professionalism of Police Officers*. The Police Chief, Vol. 73, No. 8 Alexandria, Va: IACP. Retrieved on August 30, 2006 from www.policechiefmagazine.org.

*Indicates author-recommended reading

*Clarke, R.C. (2004). *Closing Streets and Alleys to Reduce Crime: Should You Go Down This Road?* Washington, D.C: U.S. Department of Justice-COPS Office. Accessible at http://www.popcenter.org/Responses/response-closing_streets.htm.

---and Felson, M. (Eds.). (1993). *Routine Activity and Rational Choice: Advances in Criminological Theory* 5. New Brunswick, NJ: Transaction Books.

*---and Eck, J.E. (2005). Crime Analysis for Problem Solvers is 60 Small Steps. Washington, D.C: U.S. Department of Justice. Available at http://www.popcenter.org/

Coe, C. (1999). *Local Government Benchmarking: Lessons from Two Major Multigovernment Efforts.* Public Administration Review, 59(2):110-115

Cohen, M. and Miler, T. (1997). *The Cost of Mental Health Care for Victims of Crime.* Rev. In *Cost of Crime: A Review of the Research Studies.* Information Brief, Minnesota House of Representatives, August 1999. Retrieved on June 25, 2006 from http://www.house.leg.state.mn.us/hrd/pubs/costcrime.pdf

*Collier, P.M. (2006). *In Search of Purpose and Priorities: Police Performance Indicators in England and Wales.* Public Money and Management, Vol. 26:165-172.

*Collins, J. (2001). Good to Great. New York: Harper-Collins.

Collins, S. (1994). *Cost of Crime: $674 Billion.* U.S. News and World Report, January 17, 1994:40-41.

Commission on Accreditation for Law Enforcement Agencies-CALEA. (2001). Standards for Law Enforcement Agencies. 4th ed. Fairfax, VA: CALEA.

Cordner, G.W. (1981). *The Effects of Directed Patrol: A Natural Quasi-Experiment in Pontiac.* In J. Fyfe (ed.) Contemporary Issues in Law Enforcement. Beverly Hills, CA: Sage.

Cornish, D., and Clarke, R. V . (Eds.). (1986). The Reasoning Criminal. New York: Springer-Verlag.

Davis, K.C. (1974). *An Approach to Legal Control of the Police.* Texas Law Review, Vol. 52:703-725.

Decker, S.H. (2005). *Using Offender Interviews to Inform Problem Solving.* Washington, D.C: U.S. Department of Justice-COPS Office.

*Delorenzi, D., Shane, J.M. and Amendola, K.L. (September 2006). *The CompStat Process: Managing Performance on the Pathway to Leadership.* Police Chief, Vol. 79, No. 9. Alexandria, Va: IACP.

*Indicates author-recommended reading

DeMaio, C. (no date). *Strategic Management and Performance Measures for Law Enforcement: A Framework for Driving Change, Enhancing Public Trust and Improving Performance* . San Diego, Ca: The Performance Institute. (p.18). Unpublished document. Retrieved on April 24, 2006 from http://www.performanceweb.org/CENTERS/LE/Innovate/index.htm

*Dewar, J.A. (2002). Assumption-Based Planning: A Tool for Reducing Avoidable Surprises. New York: Cambridge University Press.

Dhiri, S. and Brand, S. (1999). *Analysis of Costs and Benefits: Guidance for Evaluators.* London: Home Office, Research, Development and Statistics Directorate

*Dretzke, B.J. (2004). Statistics with Microsoft Excel. 3rd ed. Upper Saddle River, NJ: Prentice-Hall.

Drucker, P.F. (1990). Managing the Nonprofit Organization: Principles and Practices. New York: Harper Perennial.

Eck, J.E., and Wartell, J. (1996). *Reducing Crime and Drug Dealing by Improving Place Management: A Randomized Experiment.* Washington, D.C: Police Executive Research Forum.

Fahey, L. and Randall, R.M. (1997). Learning from the Future: Competitive Foresight Scenarios. New York: John Wiley and Sons. In Dewar, J.A. (2002). Assumption-Based Planning: A Tool for Reducing Avoidable Surprises. New York: Cambridge University Press. p.132.

Federal Bureau of Investigation. (2004). Crime in the United States 2004: Uniform Crime Report. Washington, D.C.: U.S. Department of Justice.

---(2006). Preliminary Semiannual Uniform Crime Report. Washington, D.C.: U.S. Department of Justice.

Felson, M. (1987). *Routine Activities and Crime Prevention in the Developing Metropolis.* Criminology, Vol. 25, No. 4:911-931 for description of how "capable guardians" can prevent crime. See Mazerolle, L.G., Kadleck, C. and Roehl, J. (1998). *Controlling Drug and Disorder Problems: The Role of Place Managers.* Criminology, Vol. 36, No.2:371:403 for a description of how "place managers" can help control crime problems.

Fowler, F.J. (2002). Survey Research Methods. 3rd ed. Applied Social Research Methods, Vol. 1. Thousand Oaks, Ca: Sage.

Fridell, L., Lunney, R. Diamond, D. and Kubu, B. (2001). *Racially-biased Policing: A Principled Response*. Washington, D.C: Police Executive Research Forum.

*Indicates author-recommended reading

*Friedman, M. (2005). <u>Trying Hard is Not Good Enough: How to Produce Measurable Improvements for Customers and Communities</u>. Vancouver, B.C., Canada: Trafford Publishing.

*---(1997). A Guide to Developing and Using Performance Measures in Results-based Budgeting. Washington, D.C. The Finance Project. Available at http://www.finance project.org/Publications/measures.html.

Fyfe, J. (no date). *Good Policing*. In Geoffrey P. Alpert and Roger G. Dunham, 2001, <u>Critical Issues in Policing: Contemporary Readings</u>. 4th ed. Prospect Heights, Il: Waveland Press.

---(1983). *Police Personnel Practices, Baseline Data Reports*. Vol. 15, No. 1: Washington, D.C: International City Management Association.

---and Kane, R. (2006). Bad Cops: A Study of Career-ending Misconduct among New York City Police Officers. Washington, D.C: National Institute of Justice. NCJ# 215795.

Garofalo, J. (1981).*The Fear of Crime: Causes and Consequences*. The Journal of Criminal Law and Criminology, Vol. 72, No.2:839-857.

*Garry, E.M. (1997). *Performance Measures: What Works?* Fact Sheet #71. Washington, D.C.: Office of Juvenile Justice and Delinquency Prevention. Retrieved on June 12, 2005 from http://www.ncjrs.org/pdffiles/fs-9771.pdf.

Gay, W., Schell, T. and Schack, S. (1977). <u>Improving Patrol Productivity: Routine Patrol</u>. Volume 1. Washington, D.C.: NILECJ. In Michelle Sviridoff, 1982, *Calls for Service: Recent Research on Measuring and Managing the Demand,* New York: Vera Institute of Justice. Retrieved on May 28, 2006 from http://www.vera.org/publica tion_pdf/79_553.pdf.

*Geller, W.A. (1997). *Suppose We Were Really Serious About Police Departments Becoming "Learning Organizations"?* National Institute of Justice Journal, December:2-8.
---and Swanger, G. (1995). <u>Managing Innovation in Policing: The Untapped Potential of the Middle Manager</u>, Washington, D.C.: Police Executive Research Forum.

*George, D. and Mallery, P. (2006). <u>SPSS for Windows Step by Step: A Simple Guide and Reference</u>. 6th ed. New York: Pearson.

Glenn, R.W., Panitch, B.R., Barnes-Proby, D., Williams, E., Christian, J., Lewis, M.W., Gerwehr, S. and Brannan, D.W. (2003). <u>Training the 21st Century Police Officer: Redefining Police Professionalism for the Los Angeles Police Department</u>. Santa Monica, Ca. RAND. Accessible at www.rand.org.

Gorr, W. and Harries, R. (2003). *Introduction to Crime Forecasting.* International Journal of Forecasting, 19:551-555.

Governor's Center for Local Government Services. (1998). *Administering Police Services in Small Communities: A Manual for Local Government Officials.* 2nd ed. Harrisburg, PA: Department of Community and Economic Development.

Grabosky, P.N. (1988). *Efficiency and Effectiveness in Australian Policing.* No. 16, December. Canberra, Australia: Australian Institute of Criminology.

Greenberg, D.F., Kessler, R.C. and Loftin, C. (1983). *The Effect of Police Employment on Crime.* Criminology, Vol. 21, No. 3:375-394.

Greene, J.R. Tim S. Bynum and Gary W. Cordner. (1986). *Planning and the Play of Power: Resource Acquisition among Criminal Justice Agencies.* Journal of Criminal Justice, Vol. 14. pp.529.544.

Grizzle, G.A. (1985). *Performance Measures for Budget Justifications: Developing a Selection Strategy.* Public Productivity and Management Review, 9:328-341. In Miller, G., Hildreth, W.B. and Rabin, J. (2001). *Performance Based Budgeting.* Boulder, Co: Westview Press.

---(1987. *Linking Performance to Funding Decisions: What's the Budgeter's Role?.* Public Productivity and Management Review, 41 (Spring):33-44. In Miller, G., Hildreth, W.B. and Rabin, J. (2001). *Performance Based Budgeting.* Boulder, Co.: Westview Press.

*Giuliani, R. W. (2002). Leadership. New York: Talk Miramax Books-Hyperion.

--and Safir, H. (1998). *Compstat: Leadership in Action* New York: NYPD.

Gosselin, D.K. (2005). Heavy Hands: An Introduction to the Crimes of the Family. 3rd ed. Upper Saddle River, NJ: Prentice-Hall.

Hale, C.D. (1981). Police Patrol: Operations and Management. New York: John Wiley and Sons. See also http://www.911dispatch.com/shifts/ for additional information on shift configurations and relief factoring methodology.

Hatry, H.P., Blair, L.H., Fisk, D.M., Greiner, J.M., Hall, Jr. J.R., and Schaenman, P.S. (1992). How Effective are your Community Services? Procedures for Measuring their Quality. 2nd ed. Washington, D.C: Urban Institute and International City/County Management Association. In Edward R. Maguire, *Measuring the Performance of Law Enforcement Agencies,* Fairfax, Va: Commission on Accreditation for Law Enforcement Agencies, CALEA, pp.11-12.

*(1999). Performance Measurement: Getting Results. Washington, D.C.: Urban Institute Press. Retrieved on October 28, 2006 from http://www.urban.org/books/pm/chapter1.cfm.

*Indicates author-recommended reading

Headden, S. (1996, July 1). *Guns, Money, and Medicine*. U.S. News and World Report, Vol. 121, No. 1:31-40.

*Healey, Joseph F. (2002). Statistics: A Tool for Social Research. 6th ed. Belmont, Ca: Wadsworth.

*Henry, V.E (2002). The Compstat Paradigm: Management Accountability in Policing, Business and the Public Sector. New York: Looseleaf Law Publications. p.227.

*Hoover, L.T. (1995). Quantifying Quality in Policing. Washington D.C.: Police Executive Research Forum.

Horsch, K. (2006). Indicators: *Definition and Use in a Results-Based Accountability System*. Cambridge, Ma: Harvard Family Research Project. Retrieved on November 5, 2006 from http://www.gse.harvard.edu/hfrp/pubs/onlinepubs/rrb/indicators.html.

Huntington, S.P. (1957). The Soldier and the State: The Theory and Politics of Civil-Military Relations. New York: Vintage.

Iannone, N.F. (1987). Supervision of Police Personnel. 4th ed. Englewood Cliffs, NJ: Prentice-Hall.

Jacob, H. (1984). *Using Published Data: Errors and Remedies*. Sage University Paper 42. London: Sage Publications.

Jankofsky, D.P. (no date). *Developing and Using Performance Measures in Arizona State Government*. Managing for Results Strategic Planning Workshop State of Arizona. Unpublished PowerPoint presentation. Retrieved on April 24, 2006 from www.per formanceweb.org/images/media/david_revised.ppt (slide #12).

*Jones, T. (1998). *Developing Performance Standards*. Law and Order Magazine, July:109-112. Herndon Publishing.

Jurkanin, T.J., Hoover, L.T., Dowling, J.L. and Ahmed, J. (2001). Enduring, Surviving and Thriving as a Law Enforcement Executive. Springfield, Il: Charles C. Thomas.

*Kelling, G.L. (1995). *How to Run a Police Department*. City Journal. Vol. 5. No. 4. Autumn 1995.

*---and William H. Sousa, Jr. (2001). *Do Police Matter? An Analysis of the Impact of New York City's Police Reforms*. Civic Report #22. Retrieved on May 4, 2003, from http://www.manhattan-institute.org/html/cr_22.htm. 2003.New York: The Center for Civic Innovation at the Manhattan Institute.

---and Ronald Corbett. (2003). *This Works: Preventing and Reducing Crime*. Civic Bulletin, No. 32, March 2003. p.5.

Indicates author-recommended reading

---Pate, T., Dieckman, D. and Brown, C.F. (1974). *The Kansas City Preventive Patrol Experiment: A Technical Report.* Washington, D.C.: Police Foundation.

Kelly, A. (2001). *An Advocate's Guide to the Budget.* Trenton, NJ: New Jersey Policy Perspective.

*Kelly, J.M. and Swindell, D. (2002). *A Multiple–Indicator Approach to Municipal Service Evaluation: Correlating Performance Measurement and Citizen Satisfaction across Jurisdictions.* Public Administration Review. Vol. 62, no. 5:610-621.

Kelly, J.M. and Swindell, D. (2002b). *Service Quality Variation Across Urban Space: First Steps Toward a Model of Citizen Satisfaction.* Journal of Urban Affairs. Vol. 24:271. See also D. Rosenbaum et. al. (2005). *Attitudes Toward the Police: The Effects of Direct and Vicarious Experience.* Police Quarterly. Vol. 8, no.3:343-365; W.G. Skogan. (2005). *Citizen Satisfaction with Police Encounters.* Police Quarterly. Vol. 8, no.3:298-321; Wietzer, R. and Tuch, S.A. (2005). *Determinants of Public Satisfaction with the Police.* Police Quarterly. Vol. 8, no.3:279-297; Tyler, T.R. (2005). *Policing in Black and White: Ethnic Group Differences in Trust and Confidence in the Police.* Police Quarterly. Vol. 8, no.3:322-342.

Klinger, D.A. (1997). *Negotiating order in patrol work: An ecological theory of police response to deviance.* Criminology, Vol. 35, No. 2:277-306.

*Knoke, D., Bohrnstedt, G.W. and Mee, A.P. (2002). Statistics for Social Data Analysis. 4th ed. Belmont, Ca: Wadsworth.

*Koper, C.S. (1995). *Just Enough Police Presence: Reducing Crime and Disorderly Behavior by Optimizing Patrol Time in Hot Spots.* Justice Quarterly, Vol. 12, No. 4:649-672.

Kosslyn, S. (1994). Elements of Graph Design. New York: W.H. Freeman.

Kolesar, P.J., Rider, K.L., Crabill, T.B., Walker, W.E. (1975). *A Queuing-Linear Programming Approach to Scheduling Police Patrol Cars.* Operations Research, Vol. 23, No. 6:1045-1062.

Krueger, R. A. (1988). Focus Groups. Thousand Oaks, Ca: Sage.

Langworthy, R.H. (1999). *Measuring What Matters: Proceedings From the Policing Research Institute Meetings.* Washington, D.C: U.S. Department of Justice, COPS Office. NCJ# 170610. Retrieved on June 12, 2006 from http://www.ncjrs.gov/pdffiles1/nij/170610.pdf.

Latham, G.P. and Wexley, K.N. (1981). Increasing Productivity Through Performance Appraisal. Reading, Ma: Addison-Wesley Publishing Company.

Law Enforcement News. (1996). *Justice by the Numbers: A Statistical Profile of Criminal Justice in the United States, Vintage 1996.* New York: John Jay College of Criminal

*Indicates author-recommended reading

Justice/CUNY. Retrieved on June 25, 2006 from http://www.lib.jjay.cuny.edu/len/96/31dec/html/27.html

Leibert, D. R. and Miller, R. (2003). *Staffing Analysis Workbook for Jails.* 2nd ed. Washington, D.C.: U.S. Department of Justice, National Institute of Corrections. Retrieved on April 22, 2006, http://www.nicic.org/pubs/2001/016827.pdf.

Lerner, M. (2001). Math Smart: Getting a Grip on Basic Math. The Princeton Review. New York: Random House.

Linden, R.M. (2002).*Working Across Boundaries: Making Collaboration Work in Government and Nonprofit Organizations.* Jossey-Bass/John Wiley and Sons. Retrieved on June 1, 2003 from http://www.josseybass.com/WileyCDA/Section/id-10980.html. For more information see http://www.baltimorecity.gov/news/citistat/.

Lindquist, B.S., O'Connell, P. and List, F.A. (985). *Pompano Beach Police Perform Detective Bureau Manpower Assessment.* The Florida Police Chief, July:57:69.

Liska, A.E., Chamlin, M.B. and Reed, M.D. (1985). *Testing the Economic Production and Conflict Models of Crime Control.* Social Forces, Vol. 64:119-138.

Lucas, S.E. (1992). The Art of Public Speaking. New York: McGraw-Hill.

Lynn, Jr., L.E. (1980). Designing Public Policy. Santa Monica, Ca: Scott, Foresman.

Maddox, D. (1999). Budgeting for Not-for-Profit Organizations. New York: John Wiley and Sons.

Maguire, E.R. (2003). *Measuring the Performance of Law Enforcement Agencies.* CALEA Updates, Number 83 and 84. Fairfax, Va: Commission on Accreditation for Law Enforcement Agencies (CALEA). Accessible at http://www.calea.org/newweb/newsletter/Newletters.htm.

*---(2004. *Police Departments as Learning Laboratories.* Ideas in American Policing, No. 6. Washington, D.C: Police Foundation. Available at www.policefoundation.org.

Maltz, M.D. (1990). *Measuring the Effectiveness of Organized Crime Control Efforts.* Monograph 9. University of Illinois, Office of International Criminal Justice. p.39.

Maple, J. with Chris Mitchell. (1999). The Crime Fighter: Putting the Bad Guys Out of Business. New York: Doubleday

Marion, N.E. (1997). *Symbolic Policies in Clinton's Crime Control Agenda.* Buffalo Criminal Law Review. Vol. 1, No. 67:67-108.

Mastrofski, S.D. (1999). Policing for people. Ideas in American Policing. Washington, D.C: U.S. Department of Justice, Police Foundation, March. In Edward R. Maguire, *Measuring the Performance of Law Enforcement Agencies,* Fairfax, VA: Commission on Accreditation for Law Enforcement Agencies, CALEA, pp.11-12.

*Indicates author-recommended reading

*Mastrofski, S.D. (1999). Policing for people. Ideas in American Policing. Washington, D.C: U.S. Department of Justice, Police Foundation, March. In Edward R. Maguire, *Measuring the Performance of Law Enforcement Agencies*, Fairfax, Va: Commission on Accreditation for Law Enforcement Agencies, CALEA, pp.11-12. Available at www.policefoundation.org.

Maxfield, M.G. and Babbie, E. (2001). Research Methods for Criminal Justice and Criminology. 3rd ed. Belmont, Ca: Wadsworth.

Mazerolle, L.G. and Roehl, J. (1998). *Civil Remedies and Crime Prevention: An Introduction.* Crime Prevention Studies, Vol. 9:1-18. Available at http://www.popcenter.org/Library/CrimePrevention/Volume%2009/0b%20editor20introduction.pdf.

McManus, S.A. (1984). *Coping with Entrenchment: Why Local Governments Need to Restructure Their Budget Document Formats.* Public Budgeting and Finance, 4 (3):61-64. In Miller, G., Hildreth, W.B. and Rabin, J. (2001). *Performance Based Budgeting.* Boulder, Co.: Westview Press.

*McCue, C. (2003). *Data Mining and Crime Analysis in the Richmond Police Department.* SPSS Executive Report. Retrieved on May 17, 2006 from ftp://hqftp1.spss.com/pub/web/wp/DMWPEB-0203.pdf

*McDonald, P.P. (2002) Managing Police Operations: Implementing the New York Crime Control Model Using Compstat. Belmont, Ca: Wadsworth.

McGarrell, E.F., Chermak, A., Weiss, A. and Wilson, J. (2001). *Reducing Firearms Violence Through Directed Patrol.* Criminology and Public Policy, Vol. 1, No.1:119-148;

McGreevy, P. (2006, December, 20). Panel gives Bratton vote of confidence. Los Angeles Times. Retrieved on December 20, 2006 from http://www.latimes.com/news/local/la-me-`chief20dec20,1,7062859.story.

*Metzenbaum, S.H. (2006). *Performance Accountability: The Five Building Blocks and Six Essential Practices.* Managing for Performance and Results Series, IBM Center for Business of Government. Retrieved on June 14, 2006 from http://www.businessofgovernment.org/pdfs/MetzenbaumReport2.pdf

*Michaelson, G.A. (2001). The Art of War for Managers: 50 Strategic Rules. Avon, Ma: Adams Media Corporation.

*Miller, J.E. (2004). The Chicago Guide to Writing about Numbers: The Effective Presentation of Quantitative Information. Chicago: University of Chicago Press.

Miller, T.R., Cohen, M.A. and Weirsema, B. (1996). *Victim Costs and Consequences: A New Look.* Washington, D.C: National Institute of Justice. NCJ# 155282.

Millett, A.R. (1977). *Military Professionalism and Officership in America*, Mershon Center, Briefing Paper Number Two, Columbus, Ohio: The Ohio State University.

*Indicates author-recommended reading

Milligan, S.O. and Fridell, L. (April 2006). *Implementing an Agency-Level Performance Measurement System: A Guide for Law Enforcement Executives*. Final Report to the National Institute of Justice. Washington, D.C: U.S. Department of Justice.

Moore, M.H. (1980). *The Police and Weapons Offenses:* Annals of the American Academy Political and Social Science. 452:22-32.

    *--(1995). Creating Public Value: Strategic Management in Government. Cambridge, Ma: Harvard University Press.

*Moore, M. Thatcher, D., Dodge, A. and Moore, T. (2002). *Recognizing Value in Policing: The Challenge of Measuring Police Performance*. Washington, D.C.: Police Executive Research Forum. *See also M.H. Moore and Anthony Braga, 2003, *The "Bottom Line of Policing:" What Citizens Should Value (and Measure!) in Police Performance*. Washington, D.C.: Police Executive Research Forum.

Morenoff, J.D., Sampson, R.J. and Raudenbush, S.W. (2001). *Neighborhood Inequality, Collective Efficacy, and the Spatial Dynamics of Urban Violence*. Criminology, Vol. 39, No. 3:517-559

Morgan, D.L. (1993). Successful Focus Groups: Advance the State of the Art. Thousand Oaks, Ca: Sage.

*National Center for Public Productivity. (2006). *A Brief Guide For Performance Measurement In Local Government*. Newark, NJ: Rutgers University. Retrieved from http://www.andromeda.rutgers.edu/%7Encpp/cdgp/teaching/biref-manual.pdf on May 5, 2006.

National Oceanic and Atmospheric Administration. (2004). *Performance Measurement Guidelines*. Washington, D.C: NOAA Strategic Planning Office. Available at http://www.spo.noaa.gov/performance.htm.

National Research Council. (1996). Understanding Violence Against Women. Washington, D.C: National Academy of the Sciences.

    ---(2004). Fairness and Effectiveness in Policing: The Evidence. W. Skogan and K. Frydl (eds.). Washington, D.C: National Academy of the Sciences.

New York City Police Department. (1994). *The Compstat Process*. Unpublished document BM 754: NYPD.

*Norusis, M.J. (2000). SPSS 11.0 Guide to Data Analysis. Upper Saddle River, NJ: Prentice-Hall.

Nye, Jr, J.S., Zelikow, P.D. and King, D.C. (1997). Why People Don't Trust Government. Cambridge, Ma: Harvard University Press.

*Indicates author-recommended reading

*O'Connell, P.E. (2001). *Using Performance Data for Accountability: The New York City Police Department's CompStat Model of Police Management.* Managing for Results Series, August. The PricewaterhouseCoopers Endowment for The Business of Government. Retrieved from http://www.businessofgovernment.org/pdfs/Oconnell_Report.pdf on June 18, 2006.

*O'Hara, P. (2005). Why Law Enforcement Organizations Fail: Mapping the Organizational Fault Lines in Policing. Durham, NC: Carolina Academic Press.

*O'Neil, M.W., Needle, J.A. and Galvin, R.T. (1980). Appraising the Performance of Police Agencies: The PPPM (Police Program Performance Measures) System. Journal of Police Science and Administration, Vol. 8, No. 3:253-264. In Edward R. Maguire, *Measuring the Performance of Law Enforcement Agencies,* Fairfax, VA: Commission on Accreditation for Law Enforcement Agencies, CALEA, pp.11-12.

O'Shea, T.C. and Nicholls, K. (2002). *Crime Analysis in America.* Center for Public Policy, University of South Alabama for U.S. Department of Justice, COPS Office. Retrieved on April 27, 2006 from http://www.cops.usdoj.gov/mime/open.pdf? Item=790

Ostrom, E., Whitaker, G. and Parks, G. (1978). Policing: Is There a System? In J. May. and A. Wildavsky (eds.), *The Police Cycle,* New York: Russell Sage Foundation.

*Paik, L. (no date). *Surveying Communities: A Resource for Community Justice Planners.* Washington, D.C: U.S. Department of Justice, Bureau of Justice Assistance. NCJ# 197109. Accessible at http://www.ncjrs.gov/pdffiles1/bja/197109.pdf.

Paternoster, R. and Piquero, A.R. (1995). *Reconceptualizing Deterrence: An Empirical Test of Personal and Vicarious Experiences.* Journal of Research in Crime and Delinquency. 31:235-263.

Pease, K. (1998). Repeat victimization: Taking stock. Home Office Police Research Group, Crime Detection and Prevention Series Paper 90. London: Home Office.

---and Laycock, G. (1996). Revictimization: Reducing the heat on hot victims. Washington, D.C: National Institute of Justice, NCJ#162951.

Plateau/Knowledge Infusion. (February, 2006). *10 Steps to Getting Started with Performance Management.* Retrieved on May 11, 2006 from http://www.plateau.com/offers/10_Steps_Performance.htm.

Plunkett, W.R. (1994). Supervision: Diversity and Teams in the Workplace. Boston, Ma: Allyn Bacon.

*Police Executive Research Forum. (2002). *Police Department Budgeting: A Guide for Law Enforcement Chief Executives.* Washington, D.C.: PERF.

*---(2006). *A Gathering Storm: Violent Crime in America.* Chief Concerns. Washington, D.C: Police Executive Research Forum.

Indicates author-recommended reading

President's Commission on Law Enforcement and Administration of Justice, Task Force Report on Assessment. (1967). *Crime and its Impact: An Assessment*. Washington, D.C: U.S. Government Printing Office.

*Pryor, T. (2004). *What happened to ABB?* Integrated Cost Management Systems, Inc. Retrieved on December 23, 2004, from http://www.icms.net/news-18.htm.

Ratcliffe, J.H. (2002). *Aoristic Signatures and the Spatio-Temporal Analysis of High Volume Crime Patterns*. Journal of Quantitative Criminology, Vol. 18, No. 1: 23-43. See also Ratcliffe, J. H. (2000). *Aoristic Analysis: The Spatial Interpretation of Unspecific Temporal Events*. International Journal of Geographical Information Science 14(7): 669–679.

---(2003). *Intelligence-led Policing*. Trends and Issues in Criminal Justice. Paper 248, April. Canberra, Australia: Australian Institute of Criminology.

---(2004). *The Hot-Spot Matrix: A Framework for the Spatio-Temporal Targeting of Crime Reduction*. Publication pending *Police Practice and Research, vol. 5*; unpublished paper presented at the 11th International Symposium on Environmental Criminology and Crime Analysis/ECCA, June 20th, 2003., Cincinnati, OH. Retrieved on June 26, 2003 from http://www.jratcliffe.net/conf/Ratcliffe%20(2004)%20Hotspot %20matrix%20final%20draft.pdf. Several articles are available from Jerry Ratcliffe's home page; visit http://www.jratcliffe.net for details.

Raymond, B., Hickman, L.J., Miller, L. and Wong, J.S. (2005), *Police Personnel Challenges after September 11th: Anticipating Expanded Duties and a Changing Labor Pool,* Santa Monica, Ca: RAND Corporation.

Reiss, A.J. (1971). The Police and the Public. New Haven, Ct: Yale University Press.

Riley, S. L and Colby, Peter W. (1991). Practical Government Budgeting: A Workbook for Public Managers. Albany: State University of New York Press.

*Rossi, P.H., Lipsey, M.W. and Freeman, H.E. (2004). Evaluation: A Systematic Approach. 7th ed. London: Sage Publications.

Roth, J.A. and Ryan, J.A. (2000). *The COPS Program after 4 Years—National Evaluation*. Washington, D.C: U.S. Department of Justice, COPS Office. Research in Brief, NCJ#183644.

Rubin, I. S. (2000). *The Politics of Public Budgeting: Getting, and Spending, Borrowing and Balancing*. 4th ed. New York: Chatham House.

Sampson, R. and Cohen, J. (1988). *Deterrent Effects of the Police on Crime: A Replication and Theoretical Extension*. Law and Society Review, 22:163-191.

San Francisco Board of Supervisors. (2002). *Management Audit of the San Francisco Fire Department*. San Francisco, Ca: Board of Supervisors, Budget Analyst. Retrieved on January 2, 2005, from http://www.ci.sf.ca.us/site/budanalyst_page.asp? id=4860

Indicates author-recommended reading

Schneider, S. (2005). *Predicting Crime: The Review of Research*. School of Justice Studies Ryerson University, Department of Justice, Canada. Retrieved from http://www.justice.gc.ca/en/ps/rs/rep/2002/rr2002-7/rr2002-7.html on April 24, 2006.

Schroeder, D., Lombardo, F. and Strollo, J. (1995). Management and Supervision of Police Personnel. Binghamton, NY: Gould Publications.

*SEARCH, The National Consortium for Justice Information and Statistics. (2003). *Measuring the Success of Integrated Justice: A Practical Approach*. SEARCH Special Report, Issue 2 (September). Sacramento, Ca: SEARCH.

Senge, P.M. (1994). The Fifth Discipline: The Art and Practice of the Learning Organization. rev. ed., New York: Currency Doubleday. In William A. Geller, 1997, *Suppose We Were Really Serious About Police Departments Becoming "Learning Organizations"? National Institute of Justice Journal,* December 1997:2-8.

Scott, M.S. (2003). *The Benefits and Consequences of Police Crackdowns*. Problem Oriented Guides for Police, Response Guides Series, No.1. Washington, D.C.: U.S. Department of Justice, COPS Office. Available at www.popcenter.org.

---(2002). *Rave Parties*. Problem Oriented Guides for Police, Response Guides Series, No.14. Washington, D.C.: U.S. Department of Justice, COPS Office. Available at www.popcenter.org.

Shadish, W.R., Cook, T.D. and Campbell, D.T. (2002). *Experimental and Quasi-Experimental Designs for Causal Inference*. New York: Houghton-Mifflin.

Shane, J.M. (2004). *Differential Response: Neighborhood Social Disorganization and Police Response to Domestic Violence*. Unpublished Masters Thesis. Newark, NJ: Rutgers School of Criminal Justice.

Sherman, L.W. (1990). *Police Crackdowns: Initial and Residual Deterrence*. Crime and Justice, Vol. 12:1-48.

---and Berk, R.A. (1984). The Minneapolis Domestic Violence Experiment. *Police Foundation Reports*, 1. Washington D.C.: Police Foundation.

---and Rogan, D.P. (1995). *Deterrent Effects of Police Raids on Crack Houses: A Randomized Controlled Experiment*. Justice Quarterly, Vol. 12, No. 4:755-781.

---and Gottfredson, D.C., MacKenzie, D.L., Eck, J., Reuter, R. and Bushway, S.D. (1998). *Preventing Crime: What Works, What Doesn't, What's Promising*. NIJ Research in Brief, NCJ# 171676. Washington, D.C: U.S. Department of Justice.

---Shaw, J.W. and Rogan, D.P. (1995). *The Kansas City Gun Experiment*. Washington, D.C: National Institute of Justice, Research in Brief. NCJ# 150855.

*Indicates author-recommended reading

Skogan, W.G. (1990). Disorder and Decline: Crime and the Spiral of Decay in American Neighborhoods. New York: Free Press

---and Hartnett, S.M. (1997). Community Policing: Chicago Style. New York: Oxford University Press.

Skolnick, J.H. (1968). Justice Without Trial. New York: John Wiley and Sons.

*---(1999). *On Democratic Policing.* Ideas in American Policing. Washington, D.C: Police Foundation. Available at www.policefoundation.org.

Stafford, M.C. and Warr, M. (1993). *A Reconceptualization of General and Specific Deterrence.* Journal of Research in Crime and Delinquency. Vol. 30, No. 2:123-135.

Sullivan, G.J., Bellmio, P., Hubler, G., Somers, S. and Adkins, B. (2001). *Performance Audit of the Pierce County Sheriff's Department.* Carlsbad, Ca: Police Management Advisors.

Swanson, C.R. Chamelin, N.C. and Territo, L. (1996). Criminal Investigation. 6th ed. New York: McGraw-Hill.

Sweeney, T. (1982). *Managing Time–The Scarce Resource.* Law Enforcement News, (VII, 1) Jan. 11. p. 1, 8-11. In Michelle Sviridoff, 1982, *Calls for Service: Recent Research on Measuring and Managing the Demand,* New York: Vera Institute of Justice. Retrieved from http://www.vera.org/publication_pdf/79_553.pdf on May 28, 2006.

Szanton, P. (1981). Not Well Advised: The City as Client—An Illuminating Analysis of Urban Governments and Their Consultant. New York: Russell Sage Foundation and The Ford Foundation. W.A. Geller. (1997). *Suppose We Were Really Serious About Police Departments Becoming "Learning Organizations"?* National Institute of Justice Journal, December.

Tein, J.M. et al. (1977). *Evaluation Report of an Alternative Approach in Police Patrol: The Wilmington Split-Force Experiment.* Cambridge, Ma: Public System Evaluation, Inc. pp. vii-viii. In C.D. Hale, (1981), Police Patrol: Operations and Management. p122.

Thomas, R.C. (1984). *The Use of Workload Data in Reactive Patrol Allocation and Scheduling.* Police Studies: International Review and Police Development. 7:64-67.

Thompson, M. (1980). Benefit-Cost Analysis for Program Evaluation. Beverly Hills, Ca: Sage.

University of Pennsylvania Health System. (2006). *Stairway to Recovery: Economic Impact on Society.* Philadelphia, Pa: UPHS. Retrieved on June 25, 2006 from http://www.uphs.upenn.edu/addiction/berman/society/econ.html

U.S. General Accounting Office. (March 1998). *Measuring Performance and Demonstrating Results of Information Technology Investments,* Executive Guide, GAO/ AIMD-98-89.

*Indicates author-recommended reading

*---(1996). *Executive Guide: Effectively Implementing the Government Performance and Results Act.* GOA/GDD-96-118. Retrieved on November 9, 2006 from http://www.gao.gov/archive/1996/gg96118.pdf.

van der Heijden, K. (1996). Scenarios: The Art of Strategic Conversation. New York: John Wiley and Sons. In Dewar, J.A. (2002). Assumption-Based Planning: A Tool for Reducing Avoidable Surprises. New York: Cambridge University Press. p.132.

Walker, S. (1977). A Critical History of Police Reform. Lexington, Ky: Lexington Books.

Watson, S. (2000). Using Results to Improve the Lives of Children and Families: A Guide for Public-Private Child Care. Child Care Partnership Project. Harvard Family Research Project. Cambridge, Ma.

Webster, J.A. (1970). *Police Task and Time Study.* Journal of Criminal Law, Criminology and Police Science. Vol. 61, No. 1:94-100.

Weisburd, D, Mastrofski, S. D., Greenspan, R., and Willis, J. (2004). *The Growth of Compstat in American Policing.* Washington, D.C., Police Foundation Reports.

Weisel, D.L. (2005). *Analyzing Repeat Victimization.* Washington, D.C.: U.S. Department of Justice, COPS Office.

Welsh, W.N. and Harris, P.W. (2004). Criminal Justice Policy and Planning. 2nd ed. Anderson Publishing.

Whitehead, J.T. and Lab, S.P. (1999). Juvenile Justice: An Introduction. 3rd ed. Cincinnati, Oh: Anderson

Wildavsky, A. (1979). The Politics of the Budgetary Process. 3rd Ed. Boston, MA: Little Brown and Company, pp.63-126.

Willis, J.J., Mastrofski, S.D, Weisburd, D. and Greenspan, R. (2003). Compstat and Organizational Change in the Lowell Police Department: Challenges and Opportunities. Washington, D.C. Police Foundation. Available at www.policefoundation.org. See also Weisburd, D., Mastrofski, S.D., McNally, A. and Greenspan, R. (2001). Compstat and Organizational Change: Findings from a National Survey. Report submitted to the National Institute of Justice by the Police Foundation.

---Mastrofski, S.D, and Weisburd, D. (2003). Compstat in Practice: An In-Depth Analysis of Three Cities. Washington, D.C. Police Foundation. Available at www.policefoundation.org.

Wilson, J.Q., (1970). Varieties of Police Behavior. New York: Atheneum.

---and Boland, B. (1978). *The Effect of Police Crime.* Law and Society Review, 12:367-384.

Yates, B.T. (1996). Analyzing Costs, Procedures, Processes and Outcomes in Human Services: An Introduction. Thousand Oaks, Ca: Sage.

*Indicates author-recommended reading

Appendix 1

▶ **Sample Business Plan Outline**

A Google© search of the words "police business plan" returns 631 results, many of which contain replicable business plans. A variety of well-conceived business plans come from Australian, Canadian and European police agencies that have been publishing such plans for many years. Most of the plans are in .pdf format and can be easily downloaded. Before you embark on creating your agency's business plan, it will be worthwhile to review some existing plans for ideas and formatting styles. The contents of a business plan can also be used to formulate the department's annual report. Here are a few Internet sites to get started; the business plans also appear on the Resource CD, except for Strathclyde, United Kingdom Police Department, which was temporarily unavailable at time of publication. Check the web sites periodically for new plans and to get an international perspective on the trends in police performance:[154]

Tasmania, Australia Police Department
http://www.police.tas.gov.au/__data/assets/pdf_file/3475/DPPS-Business-Plan-05-06.pdf

Northwest Territory, Australia Police Department
http://www.nt.gov.au/pfes/documents/File/police/publications/strategic/2006-police-bus-plan.pdf

Victoria, Australia Police Department
http://www.police.vic.gov.au/content.asp?a=internetBridgingPage&Media_ID=646

Windsor, Ontario, Canada Police Department
http://www.police.windsor.on.ca/Business%20Plan_new/Business%20Plan%202002-2004.pdf

Kingston, Ontario, Canada Police Department
http://www.police.kingston.on.ca/Kingston%20Police%20Business%20Plan%202005-07.pdf

Barrie, Ontario, Canada Police Department
http://www.police.barrie.on.ca/pdfs/publications/BusinessPlan2004-2007.pdf

Durham Regional Police Service, Ontario, Canada
http://www.drps.ca/drps_business_plan/2005_2007_Busplan.pdf

York Regional Police, Ontario, Canada
http://www.police.york.on.ca/yrp%20bus%20plan.pdf

Ottawa, Canada Police Department
http://www.ottawapolice.ca/en/resources/publications/pdf/business
plan_2004-06.pdf

Strathclyde, United Kingdom Police Department
http://www.strathclyde.police.uk/index.asp?locID=347&docID=-1

Central Scotland, United Kingdom Police
http://www.centralscotland.police.uk/about/exec/docs/csp_busplan_
0506.pdf

1. Cover Page
2. Table of Contents
3. Executive Summary
4. City Profile
    4.1. Brief history
    4.2. Perennial problems
    4.3. Demographic and Economic indicators
        4.3.1. Population description
                4.3.1.1. Full-time residential
                4.3.1.2. Workforce-daytime
                4.3.1.3. Seasonal
                4.3.1.4. Tourist
        4.3.2. Median income
        4.3.3. Unemployment rate
        4.3.4. Racial demographics
        4.3.5. Age demographics
        4.3.6. Homeownership rate
5. Department Profile
    5.1. Legal authority (municipal law; charter)
    5.2. Brief history
    5.3. Location
    5.4. Services provided
    5.5. Management structure
        5.5.1. Command staff profile
        5.5.2. Organizational plan
        5.5.3. Rank structure
        5.5.4. Personnel complement

6. Marketing Plan
    6.1. Target population
    6.2. Methods of dissemination
        6.2.1. Public information office
        6.2.2. Public service announcements (PSA's)
        6.2.3. Recruiting campaign
        6.2.4. Internet web page
        6.2.5. Brochures, TV commercials, billboards, print media
        6.2.6. College career day
    6.3. Policing trends and best practices
        6.3.1. Programs
        6.3.2. Strategies
        6.3.3. Policies
        6.3.4. Equipment
        6.3.5. Information/Technology
        6.3.6. Privatization
        6.3.7. Civilianization
7. Operating Environment
    7.1. Performance Data
        7.1.1. Patrol Workload
            7.1.1.1. Calls for service
            7.1.1.2. Self-Initiated assignments
            7.1.1.3. Response time
        7.1.2. Investigative Workload
            7.1.2.1. Cases assigned
            7.1.2.2. Clearance rate
            7.1.2.3. Time to warrant
            7.1.2.4. Time to arrest
        7.1.3. Offender Accountability
            7.1.3.1. Arrests effected for:
                7.1.3.1.1. Pt I
                7.1.3.1.2. Pt II
                7.1.3.1.3. Pt III
            7.1.3.2. Conviction rate
            7.1.3.3. Forensic samples matched
            7.1.3.4. Local incarceration rate
        7.1.4. Traffic Management
            7.1.4.1. Summonses Issued
                7.1.4.1.1. Parking
                7.1.4.1.2. Moving
            7.1.4.2. Warnings Issued
            7.1.4.3. Traffic Calming Projects
            7.1.4.4. Reduced traffic collisions

7.1.4.4.1. Fatalities
7.1.4.4.2. Injuries and damage
7.1.4.4.3. Pedestrians struck
7.1.5. Field Interviews Conducted
7.1.6. Warrants Issued and Served
7.1.6.1. Arrest
7.1.6.2. Search
7.1.7. Crime Statistics
7.1.7.1. Pt I offenses
7.1.7.2. Pt II offenses
7.1.7.3. Pt III offenses
7.1.7.4. Crime rate per 100,000
7.1.7.5. Victimization rate per 100,000
7.1.8. Community Perception
7.1.8.1. Change in levels of fear
7.1.8.2. Change in self-defense measures (levels and types)
7.1.8.3. Partnerships created
7.1.8.4. Utilization of parks and other public spaces
7.1.8.5. Property values
7.1.8.6. Satisfaction with police services
7.1.8.7. Citizen perception of fairness
7.1.8.8. Satisfy customer demands/achieve legitimacy with those policed
7.1.9. Legal Legitimacy
7.1.9.1. Citizen complaints
7.1.9.2. Internal complaints
7.1.9.3. Settlements in liability suits
7.1.9.4. Police shootings
7.1.9.5. Police pursuits
7.1.9.6. Use of force
7.2. Staffing and Deployment
7.2.1. Officers per 100,000 people
7.2.2. Officers per square mile of coverage area
7.2.3. Meeting Minimum Staffing Requirements
7.2.4. Deployment efficiency/proportional staffing
7.3. Vehicle Assets
7.3.1. Total marked fleet
7.3.2. Total unmarked fleet
7.3.3. Total non-traditional fleet
7.3.4. Total motorcycles
7.3.5. All other vehicles
7.3.6. % of vehicle availability
7.4. Command Staff Profile

7.5. Management Process (Compstat)
7.6. Leadership Development Program
    7.6.1. FBI National Academy
    7.6.2. National Executive Institute
    7.6.3. West Point Leadership
    7.6.4. Northwestern School of Command and Staff
    7.6.5. Senior Management Institute for Police (PERF)
7.7. In-service training
8. Goals
  8.1. Controlling Fear and Crime
  8.2. Delivering Public Value through Budgeting Accountability
  8.3. Reverence for Law and Authority
  8.4. Satisfying Customers through Service and Accountability
  8.5. Building Organizational Support, Capacity and Value
    8.5.1. Reducing Normal Accidents [155]
    8.5.2. Reducing Structural Failure
    8.5.3. Reducing Oversight Failure
    8.5.4. Avoiding Cultural Deviation
    8.5.5. Avoiding Institutionalization
    8.5.6. Avoiding Resource Diversion
    8.5.7. Achieving National Accreditation (Commission on Accreditation for Law Enforcement Agencies-www.calea.org)
9. Comparison Data
  9.1. Week to week
  9.2. Month to month
  9.3. Quarter to quarter
  9.4. First six months to last six months
  9.5. Last 12 months
  9.6. Year to date
  9.7. Current year date to previous year's date
  9.8. Similar jurisdictions
    9.8.1. Neighboring city profiles
    9.8.2. National city profiles
  9.9. Privatization
10. Financial Posture
  10.1. Activity-base budget linking workload to costs and expected performance
  10.2. Three years of previous department annual budgets (line-item recap only)
  10.3. Grant funding
    10.3.1. Grants received
    10.3.2. Prospective grants
  10.4. Private funding

10.5. Fund-raising activities

10.6. Cost per citizen

10.7. Cost per call for service by type

10.8. Unfunded mandates or priorities

10.9. Budget compliance

10.10.   Overtime expenditures

10.11.   Ratio of civilianization

10.12.   Efficiency analysis of major programs

11.   Assumptions Upon which Future Projections are Based

11.1. Anticipate hiring personnel (attrition rate)

11.2. Anticipate promoting personnel (supervision ratio)

11.3. Prospective grant funds

11.4. S.W.O.T. analysis (Strengths, Weaknesses, Opportunities and Threats) [156]

11.5. P.E.S.T. analysis (Political, Economic, Social, Technological)

12.   Supporting Documents

12.1. Copy of CALEA accreditation

12.2. Copies of resumes of command staff

12.3. Copies of letters of reference/intent from partners and supporting organizations

▶ Endnotes

1   Visit www.campbellcollaboration.org for a collection of systematic reviews of high-quality research conducted worldwide on the effective methods to reduce crime and delinquency and improve the quality of justice. These studies will help criminal justice professionals make informed decisions about intervention strategies based on rigorous scientific evaluation.

2   For groundbreaking research on why many municipal agencies have difficulty effectively learning from their consultants, see Szanton 1981.

3   For a contemporary example of how county government measures and compares its police department's performance see the *Prince William (Va) County FY 2004 Service Efforts & Accomplishments Report*, retrieved on June 17, 2006 from http://www.pwcgov.org/docLibrary/PDF/003255.pdf.

4   Also refer to the International City/County Management Association's (ICMA) Center for Performance Management. The purpose of the center is to help local governments measure, compare, and improve municipal service delivery. The ICMA publishes an annual report entitled *Comparative Performance Measurement,* which provides comparative data on a variety of municipal and county services, including police. The report can be purchased on-line at http://bookstore.icma.org/. Cities and counties may elect to participate in the comparison program.

5   The concept of exit and voice are from Hirschman, Albert O. (1970). *Exit, Voice and Loyalty: Response to Decline in Firms, Organizations and States.* Cambridge, MA: Harvard University Press.

6   For a discussion of the factors associated with producing crime statistics in police departments see Dale K. Nesbary, 1998, *Handling Emergency Calls for Service: Organizational Production of Crime Statistics,* Policing: An International Journal of Police Strategies and Management, MCB University Press, pp. 576-599.

7   In business vernacular ideal firm size is, theoretically, the most competitive size for any company, in a given industry, at a given time, which should ideally correspond with the highest possible per-unit profit. A police department should not be overstaffed with personnel, particularly superior officers, if they can achieve the same results with fewer personnel while yielding the lowest per-unit cost. Retrieved from http://en.wikipedia.org/wiki/Ideal_firm_size on June 12, 2006.

8   For more information on incorporating an evaluation component into a grant application visit http://www.ojp.usdoj.gov/BJA/evaluation/evaluation-rfp.htm. Or, download Justice Research and Statistics Association. (2002). Incorporating Evaluation Into the Request for Proposal (RFP) Process. Washington, DC: Author.

9   SPSS Statistics in government white paper. Successful Program Implementation Through Statistics. p.2 Retrieved from LINK "ftp://hqftp1.spss.com/pub/web/wp/SWPGOV.pdf"ftp://hqftp1.spss.com/pub/web/wp/SWPGOV.pdf on May 17, 2006.

10 In most states a "school report card" can be obtained. This is an annual report prepared by the state department of education for all public schools in the state. The report card is used to increase school- and district-level accountability through performance monitoring. Check your local area for such a report.

11 For more on solving specific problems see www.popcenter.org. The POP Center is funded by the U.S. Department of Justice and publishes the Problem-Oriented Guides for Police Series. There are several problem-specific guides that can help police departments solve common crime and quality of life problems.

12 See for example DMG-Maximus. (1999). *Summary of Municipal Services Alternatives: Villages of Carthage and West, New York.* Framingham, Ma. Retrieved on May 3, 2006 from http://www.dos.state.ny.us/lgss/pdfs/carthage.pdf.

13 For an excellent source on linking input to output and implementing police activity measures see: Steering Committee for the Review of Commonwealth/State Service Provision (SCRCSSP), 1999, *Linking Inputs and Outputs: Activity Measurement by Police Services*, AusInfo, Canberra. Retrieved on June 23, 2006 from http://www.pc.gov.au/gsp/reports/research/policeservices/policeservices.pdf.

14 The recommendations for implementation parallel those developed by Jim Collins in his book *Good to Great*. The concepts emanate from the business sector; Collins recognized them as universal characteristics of highly successful companies. The Dallas Police Department (DPD) implemented these principles and was showcased on a PBS (WNET) television documentary in January 2007 about its successes:

1. The **right people** is, as Collins defines it, *"First Who...Then What"* implying the need to identify and place competent people first, *then* devise the plan;

2. The **right resources** is *"Technology Accelerators,"* which describes the need for "carefully selected" technology, *not* technology for technology's sake. Over reliance on and investing in technology to transform the agency's business model can cripple the agency. Use technology resources sparingly and wisely to accomplish the task at hand;

3. **Analyzing the right data** is *"Confront the Brutal Facts (Yet Never Lose Faith).* The right data may, and usually will, reveal startling evidence of under performance. This is okay. The agency cannot improve without first knowing just how poorly they are performing compared to some other standard, peer group or desired end state. The idea is to confront that which may have been buried under the carpet for many years, accept it and have the will to change it: a relentless pursuit for overachievement;

4. **Devolving decision-making and accountability to get things done** is the *"Culture of Discipline"* described by Collins. This is disciplined action (tactics) within the confines of a prepared plan (strategy). The freedom to execute plans, take risks and assume responsibility by adopting an entrepreneurial attitude is, as Collins says, "...the magical alchemy of great performance;"

5. **Building expertise by developing knowledge, skills and ability (KSA's)** is the *"Hedgehog Concept (Simplicity within the Three Circles)."* Collins describes this as "transcending the curse of competence." Crime control is the core business of policing and those who do it for a living are generally competent at it. But if the agency has not

adopted best-practices, continues to rely on outmoded processes, or suffers from paradigm blindness, then it will not form the basis for a widely admired, cosmopolitan and high performing police department. This comes only by continuously developing the employees' core competencies within the three-circle concept: 1. *"What can you be the best in the business at? 2. What drives your economic engine? and 3. What are you deeply passionate about"?* Egos, arrogance and rote procedure in police departments form the basis for complacency, inaction and stifled creativity...transcend it!

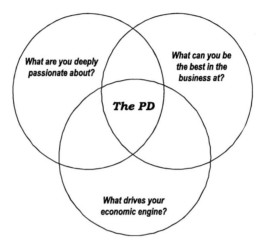

Visit www.jimcollins.com for diagnostic tools, commentary and more information on how to implement these principles. Also review *Good to Great and the Social Sectors: Why Business Thinking is Not the Answer*, a monograph to accompany *Good to Great* that is available from most retail booksellers (ISBN: 0977326403).

15   For convenient and easy mathematics refresher, refer to: Lerner, M. (2001). *Math Smart: Getting a Grip on Basic Math*. The Princeton Review. New York: Random House.

16   Retrieved from http://en.wikipedia.org/wiki/Statistics on March 5, 2006.

17   Retrieved from http://www.scotland.gov.uk/News/Releases/2006/05/18141635 on June 13, 2006. Another source for involving the community in police learning is Association of Police Authorities. (2004). *Involving Communities in Police Learning and Development: A Guide*. London: Association of Police Authorities. Retrieved on June 23, 2006 from http://www.apa.police.uk/NR/rdonlyres/3AB64E1C-5C90-4D30-9D8E-6A9A263FE7E4/0/INVCOMG.pdf.

18   Retrieved from http://www.managementhelp.org/perf_mng/terms.htm#anchor 1787027 on May 11, 2006. Material assembled by Dr. Carter McNamara.

19   Sullivan, Bellmio, Hubler, Somers, and Adkins (2001:25) point out that calculations such as one officer per 1,000 population do not account for segments of the population that are most reliant upon the police, including "the poor or vulnerable who generally have the greatest need for police services." Calculations such as officers per population are an indicator of budget priority, not actual need.

20 For how to design and administer community surveys see reference list Leslie Paik, Bureau of Justice Assistance.

21 This is modified from the National Oceanic and Atmospheric Administration's *Performance Measurement Guidelines*, (NOAA, 2004:6).

22 Modified From Ministry of Finance Public Management Department. (2006). *Handbook on Performance Management.*p.54. Helsinki, Finland: Ministry of Finance. Available at http://www.ministryoffinance.fi /publications.

23 Overall discipline is defined as the degree of orderliness present in an agency; it means the workforce is in voluntary compliance with the rules and regulations of the agency and works efficiently to achieve the goals of the organization. See Schroeder, Lombardo and Strollo, 1995, p.232.

24 This is modified from the National Oceanic and Atmospheric Administration's *Performance Measurement Guidelines*, (NOAA, 2004:6).

25 The data presented in Table 1 is not exhaustive or mutually exclusive; rather it is intended to serve as *guide* for a department annual report and to stimulate thought about creating performance measures. Creating performance measures in law enforcement agencies can be very complex and demanding. There is no single performance measure that provides a direct assessment of police performance. Rather, a series of measures for each end outcome that presumably measures the same thing, a process known as triangulation (see glossary), is generally more effective. Alternatively, a composite index (see glossary) can be created, which will help the agency account for the variability in the phenomenon under examination. Also refer to the work of Edward R. Maguire, Associate Professor, Administration of Justice Program, George Mason University, Fairfax, Va. who authored two articles for the Commission on Accreditation for Law Enforcement Agencies (CALEA). Both articles refer to measuring performance in law enforcement agencies, internally and externally, and some of the issues surrounding measurement. The articles can be accessed at http://www.calea.org/newweb/news letter/Newletters.htm, Number 83, September 2003; Number 84, February 2004. Visit http://www.business-ethics.com/whats_new/2002_100_best_corporate_citizens.html for an explanation of the dimensions used to evaluate corporate responsibility.

26 Retrieved from http://www.theacsi.org/government/govt-model.html on August 15, 2006. The ACSI government model uses the same concepts and measurements as the corporate model, except for pricing and repurchase, which substitutes outcomes. Here are the definitions upon which measurement is based:
"Customer Expectations
Expectations combine customers' experiences with a product or service and information about it via media, advertising, salespersons, and word-of-mouth from other customers. Customer expectations influence the evaluation of quality and forecast (from customers' pre-purchase perspective) how well the product or service will perform.
Perceived Quality

Perceived quality is measured through three questions: overall quality, reliability, and the extent to which a product or service meets the customer's needs. Across all companies and industries measured in the ACSI, perceived quality proves to have the greatest impact on customer satisfaction.

Perceived Value
Perceived value is measured through two questions: overall price given quality and overall quality given price. In the ACSI model, perceived value influences ACSI directly, and is affected by expectations and perceived quality. Although perceived value is of great importance for the (first) purchase decision, it usually has somewhat less impact on satisfaction and repeat purchase.

Customer Complaints
Customer complaint activity is measured as the percentage of respondents who reported a problem with the measured companies' product or service within a specified time frame. Satisfaction has an inverse relationship to customer complaints.

Customer Loyalty
Customer loyalty is measured through questions on the likelihood to purchase a company's products or services at various price points. Customer satisfaction has a positive effect on loyalty, but the magnitude of that effect varies greatly across companies and industries."
Retrieved from http://www.theacsi.org/model.htm on August 15, 2006.

27   For a practical example of the success in closing streets see James Lasley, (1998), *"Designing Out" Gang Homicides and Street Assaults*. Research in Brief, National Institute of Justice. Washington, D.C: U.S. Department of Justice. NCJ# 173398. Available at http://www.ncjrs.gov/pdffiles/173398.pdf.

28   Domestic violence is one crime that should receive special attention. Police agencies are well poised to intervene and prevent repeat victimization. For further reading on domestic violence see Gosselin, 2005; National Research Council, 1996; for general repeat victimization see Weisel, 2005, available at www.popcenter.org

29   An incident is deemed suppressible if it: 1) occurred on-view, that is, the location where it occurred was visible from the street, or 2) occurred as part of a pattern of recidivist behavior by an identified suspect. For example, if there is an active domestic violence investigation pending by the police department, and the suspect has been identified and the detectives fail to make an arrest or take some other enforcement action (e.g., serve a restraining order) and the suspect commits another domestic violence incident, then the second incident is deemed suppressible.

30   For an interesting use of civil enforcement see New York City Police Department, 1997, *The Cutting Edge of Policing: Civil Enforcement for the 21st Century*, New York: NYPD, Office of the Deputy Commissioner for Legal Matters. See also Mazerolle and Roehl, 1998 for theory and practice of civil remedies.

31   Expressed differently, this is the department's conviction rate. Conviction rate is measured by dividing the number of *offenders convicted* by the number of *offenders*, not by the number of crimes. This is because more than one offender

may be involved in one offense. For example, if 3 offenders commit 1 bank robbery, all 3 are subject to arrest, prosecution and conviction. If all 3 are convicted, then the conviction rate is 1, or 100% ($3\div3=1 \times 100=100\%$). It is not logical to say if 3 offenders (which represents 100% of the offenders) are convicted for 1 bank robbery, then the conviction rate is 33% ($1_{crime}\div3_{offenders}=.33 \times 100=33\%$)? If all 3 were convicted, then the only logical conclusion is that 100% of the offenders were held accountable. Similarly, if 9 gang members commit 3 aggravated assaults and 7 are convicted, then the conviction rate is 77% ($7\div9=.77 \times 100=77\%$).

32   NCIC = National Crime Information Center. NCIC is the United States' central database for tracking crime-related information. Maintained by the FBI's Criminal Justice Information Systems Division (CJIS), NCIC is interlinked with similar systems that each state maintains. Retrieved on June 24, 2006 from http://en.wikipedia.org/wiki/NCIC.

33   CODIS = Combined DNA Index System, available at http://www.fbi.gov/hq/lab/codis/index1.htm; NIBIN = National Integrated Ballistic Information Network, available at http://www.nibin.gov/.

34   The ratio of arrests to reported crimes is a measure of the "certainty of arrest," which is a good indicator of the likelihood that an offender will be held accountable. See Liska, Chamlin and Reed (1985:123).

35   For more about prisoner debriefings and offenders' interviews, see Decker, 2005.

36   For more about creating partnerships and sharing responsibility see:
1. Michael S. Scott and Herman Goldstein. (2005). *Shifting and Sharing Responsibility for Public Safety Problems*. Problem-Oriented Guides for Police, Problem-Solving Tools Series, No. 5.
2. Sharon Chamard. (2006). *Partnering with Businesses to Address Public Safety Problems*. Problem-Oriented Guides for Police, Problem-Solving Tools Series, No. 3.
Both documents available at www.popcenter.org.

37   Neighborhood conditions can be anything area residents perceive as disrupting their quality of life including crime and nuisance offenses. The two recognized conditions that contribute to fear and blight are social and physical disorder. Social disorder typically consists of: "1) drinking in public, 2) youth gangs, 3) illegal drug use in public, 4) drunk driving, 5) public drug sales, 6) vandalism, 7) public prostitution, 8) panhandling, 9) loitering, 10) truancy, 11) speeding vehicles, 12) domestic violence, 13) car theft, 14) homelessness, 15) groups of teens hanging out on corners or streets, 16) loud music/parties, 18) neighborhood fights, 19) racial prejudice/hate crimes, 20) disturbance in public place, 21) disturbance in licensed premises, 22) disturbance in private property, 23) civil dispute, and 24) other unlisted disorder/nuisance. Physical disorder typically consists of: 1) garbage/litter, 2) abandoned cars, 3) rundown buildings, 4) poor lighting, 5) overgrown shrubs, 6) empty lots 7) graffiti and 8) people not keeping up houses or apartments" (Milligan and Fridell, 2006:22-23). For a similar conceptualization of disorder conditions see Wesley G. Skogan, 1990, Disorder and Decline: Crime and the Spiral of Decay in American Neighborhoods. New York: Free Press.

38   "Professional Competence" should be defined as: "extending beyond the technical aspects of the work to encompass individual and institutional integrity" (Fridell, Lunney, Diamond, and Kubu, 2001:38). This can be measured in the following ways: 1) the ratio of sustained officer complaints:not sustained complaints; 2) the department's overall citizen satisfaction rating, via community survey; 3) number of personnel identified through an early warning system and counseled or retrained; 4) percent of personnel who receive "satisfactory" or "above average" ratings on performance evaluations; 5) percent and nature of personnel receiving commendations/awards; 6) number of years of consecutive department accreditation (CALEA); 7) percent of workforce satisfied with employment conditions and relationships at work, via a cultural diagnostic; and 8) the percent of the workforce in compliance with department policy (drug screening; integrity tests; bureau and division audits; failure to appear in court; resource diversion; cultural deviation; oversight failure). By measuring professional competence an agency is able to reduce, if not eliminate, institutionalization (see O'Hara, 2005:147-180).

The notion of professionalism has been researched for many years. Here are two conceptions:

Allen Millett (1977:2) defines a "profession" as consisting of the following six elements:

1.   "The occupation is a full-time and stable job, serving continuing societal needs;
2.   The occupation is regarded as a lifelong calling by the practitioners, who identify themselves personally with their job subculture;
3.   The occupation is organized to control performance standards and recruitment;
4.   The occupation requires formal, theoretical education;
5.   The occupation has a service orientation in which loyalty to standards of competence and loyalty to clients' needs are paramount;
6.   The occupation is granted a great deal of collective autonomy by the society it serves, presumably because the practitioners have proven their high ethical standards and trustworthiness."

Samuel P. Huntington (1957:8-10, 15) defines a "profession" within three broad categories: corporateness, responsibility and expertise.

"Corporateness
The members of a profession share a sense of organic unity and consciousness of themselves as a group apart from laymen. This collective sense has its origins in the lengthy discipline and training necessary for professional competence, the common bond of work, and the sharing of a unique social responsibility . . . . Entrance into this unit is restricted to those with the requisite education and training and is usually permitted only at the lowest level of professional competence.

Responsibility The professional man is a practicing expert, working in a social context, and performing a service, such as the promotion of health, education, or justice, which is essential to the functioning of society. The client of every profession is society, individually or collectively... Financial remuneration cannot be the primary aim of the professional man. . . . The profession [is] a moral unit positing certain values and ideals which guide its members in their dealings with laymen. This guide may be a set of unwritten norms transmitted through the professional educational system or it may be codified into written canons of professional ethics.

Expertise
The professional man is an expert with specialized knowledge and skill in a significant field of human endeavor. His expertise is acquired only by prolonged education and experience. It is the basis of objective standards of professional competence."

Excerpts from Millett and Huntington are derived from Glenn, Panitch, Barnes-Proby, Williams, Christian, Lewis, Gerwehr, and Brannan (2003). *Training the 21st Century Police Officer: Redefining Police Professionalism for the Los Angeles Police Department.* Santa Monica, CA: RAND. pp. 26-28.

39 **Northwestern Staff and Command** = Northwestern University Traffic Institute, Evanston, IL

40 See Richard C. Larson, Michael F. Cahn and Matrin C. Shell, 1993, *Improving the New York City Arrest-to-Arraignment System*, Interfaces, 23:1 January-February, pp.76-96, for discussion of queuing theory and how to reduce arrest processing cycle times. Available at http://iew3.technion.ac.il/serveng/Lectures/v23n1a5.pdf.

41 Visit www.calea.org for details on the national accreditation process.

42 "Unfounded" calls for service (CFS), or "radio runs" as they are also known, is an indicator of integrity. Police officers may dispose of a CFS as "unfounded" to avoid contacting a complainant and having to complete paperwork. By monitoring unfounded CFS police executives can uncover patterns where police officers may be intentionally reducing their workload by failing to provide service (Maxfield and Babbie, 2001:338).

43 For a discussion on shifting police personnel profiles see Raymond, Hickman, Miller, and Wong, 2005.

44 MDC = Mobile Data Computer, an in-car mounted computer used for communicating among other police vehicles and central communications. Hand Held Devices are any palm-sized electronic devices that can be carried by police officers while in the field and are used similarly to the MDC.

45 Retrieved from http://popcenter.org/about-keyelements.htm on May 14, 2006. Visit www.popcenter.org to learn more about problem-solving, problem specification and analysis and problem-oriented policing.

46 Problem analysis framework modified from an example provided by Dr. James O. Finkenauer, Rutgers University School of Criminal Justice, fall 2005.

47 The Prince William County (VA) Police Department uses a comprehensive strategic plan that is tied to performance measurement. See http://www.co.prince-william.va.us/default.aspx.

48   See Garry, 1997 for an example of the difference between quality (outcome) and quantity (output).

49   "A directed patrol is the act of assigning police officers to an identified area and freeing them from responding to calls for service in order for them to engage in proactive investigation and enforcement of suspicious activities." McGarrell, E.F., Chermak, A., Weiss, A. and Wilson, J. (2001). *Reducing Firearms Violence Through Directed Patrol.* Criminology and Public Policy, Vol. 1, No.1:119-148; see also Cordner, G.W. (1981). *The Effects of Directed Patrol: A Natural Quasi-Experiment in Pontiac.* In J. Fyfe (ed.) Contemporary Issues in Law Enforcement. Beverly Hills, Ca: Sage; Moore, M.H. (1980). *The Police and Weapons Offenses:* Annals of the American Academy Political and Social Science. 452:22-32; Koper, C.S. (1995). *Just Enough Police Presence: Reducing Crime and Disorderly Behavior by Optimizing Patrol Time in Hot Spots.* Justice Quarterly, Vol. 12, No. 4:649-672.

50

51   See for example U.S. Department of Justice, Bureau of Justice Assistance-Center for Program Evaluation. Various logic modeling resources are available, including:
1. McCawley, P. F. (n.d.) *The logic model for program planning and evaluation.*
2. Taylor-Powell, E., Jones, L., and Henert, E. (2002). *Enhancing program performance with logic models.*
3. Juvenile Justice Evaluation Center. (2003). JJEC logic model.

Retrieved from http://www.ojp.usdoj.gov/BJA/evaluation/guide/guide-references.htm on May 13, 2006.

52   See glossary for definitions of specific and general deterrence.

53   During the development of the Chicago Police Department's CAPS (Chicago Alternative Policing Strategy) program, the mayor questioned why the rank of captain was necessary. A management consulting firm recommended "compressing the rank structure," which was favored by the mayor since he believed "the work performed by most captains did not justify their lofty civil service status." The mayor once exclaimed "Captains! Nobody can tell me what they do!" See Skogan and Hartnett, 1997:34.

54   Refer to http://www.sba.gov/starting_business/planning/usingplan.html for business plan variations.

55   Visit www.fbi.gov/publications.htm to review the FBI's 2004-2009 strategic plan in .pdf format; visit http://lapdonline.org/search_results/content_basic_view/6561 to review the Los Angeles Police Department's State of the Department plan of action in .pdf format. Both retrieved on April 22, 2006.

56   An excellent source is the *Law Enforcement Tech Guide: How to Plan, Purchase and Manage Technology (successfully!) A Guide for Executives, Managers and Technologists. Washington, D.C:* U.S. Department of Justice, COPS Office. Accessible at http://www.cops.usdoj.gov/default.asp?Item=512. Also visit www.search.org for assistance in managing technology projects. See also U.S. Depart-

ment of Justice, COPS Office, 2003, *Policing Smarter Through IT: Learning from Chicago's Citizen and Law Enforcement Analysis Reporting (CLEAR) System.* Available at www.cops.usdoj.gov.

57   If your organization is planning to implement an information/technology project, then a good source for guidance is by Kelly J. Harris and William H. Romesburg, (2002), *Tech Guide: How to Plan, Purchase, and Manage Technology (Successfully!)*, A Guide for Executives, Managers and Technologists. Washington, D.C.: U.S. Department of Justice Cops Office. Can be ordered from www.cops.usdoj.gov or 1-800-421-6770. To maximize results from information/technology investments see U.S. General Accounting Office, March 1998, *Measuring Performance and Demonstrating Results of Information Technology Investments,* Executive Guide, GAO/AIMD-98-89.

58   Retrieved from http://www.ojp.usdoj.gov/bjs/dtd.htm on May 26, 2006.

59   Retrieved from http://www.ojp.usdoj.gov/bjs/ on May 26, 2006.

60   Retrieved from http://www.ojp.usdoj.gov/bjs/sourcebook.htm on May 26, 2006.

61   Retrieved from http://www.ncovr.heinz.cmu.edu////Docs/datacenter.htm on May 26, 2006.

62   Retrieved from http://en.wikipedia.org/wiki/Statistics on January 26, 2006.

63   Retrieved from http://zapatopi.net/kelvin/quotes/ on January 26, 2006.

64   For an on-line statistics resource visit http://www.davidmlane.com/hyperstat/index.html or http://www.statsoft.com/textbook/stathome.html.

65   Retrieved from http://en.wikipedia.org/wiki/Descriptive_statistics on January 26, 2006.

66   Retrieved from http://en.wikipedia.org/wiki/Percentages on March 15, 2006.

67   Benchmarking (also 'best practice benchmarking' or 'process benchmarking') is a process used in management and particularly strategic management, in which organizations evaluate various aspects of their processes in relation to best practice, usually within their own sector. This, then, allows organizations to develop plans on how to adopt such best practice, usually with the aim of increasing some aspect of performance. Benchmarking may be a one-off event, but is often treated as a continuous process in which organizations continually seek to challenge their practices. Benchmarking is a powerful management tool because it overcomes 'paradigm blindness.' Paradigm Blindness can be summed up as the mode of thinking, 'The way we do it is the best because this is the way we've always done it.' Benchmarking opens organizations to new methods, ideas and tools to improve their effectiveness. It helps crack through resistance to change by demonstrating other methods of solving problems than the one currently employed, and demonstrating that they work, because they are being used by others. The process of benchmarking may be:
   1. **Identify your problem areas and decide what process to benchmark–**

Because benchmarking can be applied to any business process or function, a range of research techniques may be required. They include: informal conversations with [citizens], or employees; exploratory research techniques such as focus groups; or in-depth surveys, questionnaires, reengineering analysis, process mapping, quality control variance reports, or financial ratio analysis.

2. **Study the process in your own organization**–Identify the time and resources involved in cycle times including the unit cost. Also, identify where in the process improvement can be made.

3. **Identify organizations that are leaders in these areas and who may serve as benchmarking partners**–Look for the very best in any industry and in any country. Consult [other police executives], [universities], trade associations, and magazines to determine which [agencies] are worthy of study." Retrieved on April 22, 2006 from http://en.wikipedia.org/wiki/Bench marking. See also Ammons, D.N. (1999). A Proper mentality for Benchmarking. Public Administration Review, 59: 105-109.

4. **Analyze the processes of benchmarking partners to identify differences that account for superior performance**–What is it that the benchmarking partners are doing differently that make them more efficient? What are the comparative costs for processing?

5. **Adapt and implement "best practices"**–Make the necessary organizational adjustments that account for the uniqueness of your organization and set an implementation schedule.

6. **Monitor and revise**–Intermediate objectives will serve as guideposts to ensure the process is meeting expectations. If not, then revise those portions of the process that are deficient.

68   Retrieved from http://en.wikipedia.org/wiki/Standard_deviation on April 22, 2006.

69   See Municipal Research and Services Center for Washington. Retrieved on May 9, 2006 from http://www.mrsc.org/subjects/pubsafe/le/le-ig.aspx.

70   Retrieved from http://en.wikipedia.org/wiki/Data_analysis on April 6, 2006.

71   Retrieved from http://www.b-eye-network.com/view/728 on April 6, 2006. Also retrieved on April 6, 2006, http://www.techweb.com/wire/showArticle.jhtml?article ID=173600535 regarding the products used by the Richmond, Va police department to forecast likely locations of crime. See also www.spss.com/success for more information on how Atlanta, Ga police department and Richmond, Va police department use statistical analysis to help manage the agency and create efficiency. Retrieved on May 17, 2006.

72   Retrieved from http://en.wikipedia.org/wiki/Chart#Common_charts on April 21, 2006.

73   Retrieved from http://en.wikipedia.org/wiki/Scattergram on April 21, 2006.

74   Retrieved from http://en.wikipedia.org/wiki/Crosstab on April 21, 2006.

75   Retrieved from http://en.wikipedia.org/wiki/Crosstab on May 3, 2006.

76   A good companion document that complements the methodology used here and highlights the necessity for conducting regular comprehensive management audits of police service demands and the impact to patrol, investigations and support services is by George J. Sullivan, Peter Bellmio, George Hubler, Scott Somers and Ben Adkins. (2001). *Performance Audit of the Pierce County Sheriff's Department.* Prepared for the Pierce County Performance Audit Committee, final report issued June 8, 2001. Carlsbad, Ca: Police Management Advisors. Available on-line at http://www.co.pierce.wa.us/xml/abtus/plans/perf-audit/reports/SHR-The%20 Report.pdf.

77   It is generally conceded that using per capita estimates is useful for projecting the anticipated workload for a growing community. If population estimates are expected to increase, then extrapolation analysis could be performed to estimate the future workload. The same is true for square mileage: if a community is expanding, then officers per square mile could be used to develop a staffing model that accounts for service area. As used here, complexity means the total amount of time and the number of officers required to handle the work.

78   The "effective strength" of the patrol force is how many officers are on duty at a given time. See Hale, p.167.

79   See http://www.911dispatch.com/shifts/ for additional information on shift configurations and relief factoring methodology.

80   See Lindquest, O'Connell and List (1985) for a variant of the detective workload analysis conducted here.

81   Numbers may not equal 100% due to rounding.

82   First publication: Shane, J.M. (2005). *Activity-base Budgeting*. FBI Law Enforcement Bulletin. Vol. 74, No. 6:11-23. (June). Washington, D.C: U.S. Department of Justice. Accessible at www.fbi.gov/publications.htm.

83   A zero-base budget (ZBB) begins by building a budget from scratch, identifying each activity or position that must be funded. In ABB we already know the activities and positions that must be funded. We are merely tying those positions to a specific level of effort. Essentially ZBB requires that a program be justified from the ground up each fiscal year. An easy starting point for a ZBB is to use the prior funding level for that program as the basis for further adjustments.

84   See, for example Kelly, A. (2001). *An Advocate's Guide to the Budget*. Trenton, NJ: New Jersey Policy Perspective.

85   2006 American Society of Criminology Conference. *Policing Urban America: Challenges and Successes*. Presidential Session #250. November 2, 2006. Los Angeles, Ca.

86   Both definitions from Merriam-Webster on-line retrieved on August 31, 2004 from http://m-w.com.

87 PERF. p.2. See also Aaron Wildavsky, *The Politics of the Budgetary Process*, 3rd Ed. (Boston, MA: Little Brown and Company, 1979), pp.63-126.

88 Any portion of an hour is calculated as such. For example, 20 minutes is captured as .33 hours; 47 minutes is captured as .783 hours.

89 In budgeting, "modalities" are the attributes (i.e., major activities) that are being examined. In this case the attributes are the types of calls for service.

90 These are three generally accepted management categories and they are not mutually exclusive.

91 Ammons, D.N. (1999). *A Proper Mentality for Benchmarking*. In Gerald J. Miller, W. Bartley Hildreth and Jack Rabin, *Performance Based Budgeting*. 2001. Boulder, CO: Westview Press. pp. 419-429. In public sector application the term "benchmarking" "features the identification of a point of reference for comparison or measurement purposes. With a benchmark, public officials can measure the performance gap between where they are and where they want to be, and can track their progress in closing the gap." See also Coe, C. (1999). *Local Government Benchmarking: Lessons from Two Major Multi-government Efforts*. Public Administration Review, 59(2):110-115 for some technical, political and practical problems associated with benchmarking.

92 Retrieved from ftp://hqftp1.spss.com/pub/web/wp/SWPGOV.pdf on May 17, 2006.

93 For more details on opportunity theory and prevention see Marcus Felson and Ronald v. Clarke *Opportunity Makes the Thief: Practical Theory for Crime Prevention*. 1998. Policing and Reducing Crime Unit, Home Office, London, UK. Retrieved from http://www.homeoffice.gov.uk/rds/prgpdfs/fprs98.pdf on May 17, 2006.

94 Visit www.spss.com/success for more information on how Atlanta, Ga. police department and Richmond, Va. police department use statistical analysis to help manage the agency and create efficiency. Retrieved on May 17, 2006.

95 Retrieved from http://en.wikipedia.org/wiki/Cross-sectional_data on April 11, 2006. See also Babbie, p.96 and Shadish, Cook and Campbell, p.267.

96 Visit www.spss.com to review products and services. If you are contemplating purchasing SPSS, then you will be interested in purchasing the base model. As of the writing of this book SPSS base model 14 is the latest version.

97 Retrieved from http://en.wikipedia.org/wiki/Linear_regression on April 23, 2006.

98 The formulas are already constructed on the accompanying CD. Open the regression workbook on the CD and select the worksheet named "regression crime data" to review the details.

99 This example must be interpreted with a bit of caution: Overtime hours do not reduce crime, police activity reduces crime! Simply because more overtime is appropriated it does not mean crime will go down. In theory as overtime hours

increase, crime should decrease, all else being equal. "All else being equal" means, theoretically, the police officers will continue with their current level of output.

100   Some analysts will set the significance level lower to .10 or 90%. This lower or less stringent level means you risk accepting that what you are seeing is true even though it is false. This is known as a "false positive." Conversely, an analyst might set the significance level higher to .01 or 99%. This is a higher or more stringent level and might cause you to reject a perfectly valid and true response. This is known as a "false negative." See Clarke and Eck, 2005, p.53.

101   In this example we examine the relative importance of police employment (number of police personnel) on the crime rate. We must be cautious about drawing inference *solely* from the number of police personnel employed by the department. At least some research suggests that the level of police employment does not necessarily affect the crime rate (see Greenberg, Kessler and Loftin, 1983:385). The researchers learned, in response to rising violent crime and property crime rates in the 1960's and 1970's, many police departments hired more officers. This seems like a plausible means for controlling crime (face validity). However, the research revealed that simply increasing the strength of the sworn force to address the violent and property crime rate was ineffective: "In neither cities nor suburbs did a marginal increase in police strength reduce reported violent crime or property crime. Although we argued that crime rates might be more responsive to police employment than to probability of arrest, and property crime more responsive than violent crimes, our findings do not confirm these predictions" (Greenberg, Kessler and Loftin, 1983:387). This is just one more reason to use the techniques described here to analyze the influence of police officers' output on the crime rate. A wise police executive will do well to analyze the influence of officers' output *and* the strength of the sworn force before suggesting to the elected governing body that he or she "needs" more officers to control crime. Advocating for more police officers is always a noble proposition but "throwing police officers at a problem" is hardly the answer to controlling crime.

102   This needs further qualification. The intercept 44350 is the raw number of Part I offenses in this example. To derive the crime rate, the total Part I offenses must be divided by the population. We are using a hypothetical population of 275,221. The predicted crime per 100,000 is 16114 ($16114 = 44350 \div 2.75221$).

103   The calculations can be found on the Resource CD in the regression workbook under the worksheet "Regression Crime Control Data." It must be noted that simply hiring more police officers will not reduce crime; rather the activities of the officers is paramount. At least one study found no relationship between the number of police officers and the violent or property crime rate. See Greenberg, Kessler and Loftin, 1983.

104   This is the essence of queuing theory. Although very complex and beyond the scope of this text, queuing theory is the mathematical study of waiting in line (queuing). Queuing theory is useful for analyzing response time and telephone waiting times. For example, in the patrol division queuing analysis examines the amount of time

someone will have to wait for police to respond. In the communications division queuing analysis examines telephone waiting time for incoming phone calls. Efficiency is gleaned by knowing whether is it more economical to add another police officer to the field to handle calls for service or to add another call taker to answer incoming calls or leave the situation as is. The implication of adding another server (i.e., an officer; a call taker) includes whether to hire a new employee or pay overtime. Queuing theory helps derive performance measures such as average waiting time in the queue (e.g., before a police officer is dispatched; before a call taker answers an incoming call), the expected number customers (citizens) waiting or receiving service and the probability of encountering the system in certain states, such as empty, full, having an available officer (or call taker) or having to wait a certain amount of time to be serviced. The simplest application of queuing is to set call-answer thresholds (e.g., no more than 10 seconds) and response time standards (e.g., no more than 3 minutes) then estimate what will be needed to achieve those service standards. Queuing theory is common in customer service industries, of which policing is a part. See Kolesar, Rider, Crabill and Walker (1975) for an example queuing theory and patrol-car scheduling in New York City.

105 Retrieved from http://en.wikipedia.org/wiki/Unit_of_analysis on April 10, 2006. See also Maxfield, M.G. and Babbie, E. (2001). *Research Methods for Criminal Justice and Criminology*. 3rd ed. Belmont, Ca: Wadsworth. pp.75-81; Shadish, W. R., Cook, T.D. and Campbell, D.T. (2002). *Experimental and Quasi-Experimental Designs for Generalized Causal Inference*. Boston, Ma: Houghton-Mifflin. p.13.

106 "The ecological fallacy is a widely recognized error in the interpretation of statistical data, whereby inferences about the nature of individuals are based solely upon aggregate statistics collected for the group to which those individuals belong" retrieved from http://en.wikipedia.org/wiki/Ecological_fallacy on April 10, 2006. See also Maxfield, M.G. and Babbie, E. (2001). *Research Methods for Criminal Justice and Criminology*. 3rd ed. Belmont, Ca: Wadsworth. pp.79-80.

107 Response time is but one performance indicator that may suffer from excessive absenteeism. The same formula can be applied to criminal investigations (e.g., # of days to case closure; # of days to secure a search/arrest warrant, and communications (e.g., # of seconds to answer an incoming 911 call; # of calls per hour answered by operators).

108 Retrieved from http://en.wikipedia.org/wiki/Qualitative_research on April 25, 2006.

109 The calculations for this example are not shown, but the data on the CD uses the forecast function, which is the subject of this section.

110 Two examples immediately come to mind. First, if a natural disaster such as hurricane Katrina, which struck the gulf coast of Louisiana in 2005, displaces a significant portion of the population, then quantitative predictions would have to be revised. In addition to the aggregate population change in New Orleans due to the hurricane, there are also drastic changes in the racial composition and employment status of the residents. Similarly, if a resort town or vacation

destination experiences an unusually high or low visitor rate, beyond what is typically experienced, then the quantitative predictions will have to be revised as well. This is why multiple regression analysis and qualitative analysis are essential tools for drawing inferences and making accurate predictions.

111   The data must be organized in a linear manner in the Excel© spreadsheet. This means the data that will be used for the forecast must be arranged in a single row or a single column. For example, if you wish to forecast crime for 24 months, then the data must be arranged in successive months from 1 to 24. Months 1 through 12 (Jan – Dec) represent the full year; month #13 starts the new year and is the successive (i.e., the linear) month in the data set.

112   You may derive an answer to your forecasting equation that appears like this: 39175.92. Don't worry, this is just the serial date. All you need to do is format the cell by selecting the **date** format m/dd/yyyy and Excel© will display the actual date, April 3, 2007.

113   First publication: Shane, J.M. (2004). *The Compstat Process*. FBI Law Enforcement Bulletin. Vol. 73, No. 4, 5 and 6 (April, May and June). Washington, D.C: U.S. Department of Justice. Accessible at www.fbi.gov/publications.htm.

114   Kelling, G. L. and William H. Sousa, Jr. (2001). The findings of this study concluded that: 1) "broken windows" policing is significantly and consistently linked to declines in violent crime; 2) Over 60,000 violent crimes were prevented in New York City from 1989 to 1998 because of "broken windows" policing; 3) Changes in the number of young men of high-school age were not associated with a decline in violent crime; 4) Decreasing use of crack-cocaine was also not associated with a decline in violence; 5) Other changes in police tactics and strategy may also be responsible for some of the City's drop in crime, and 6) As implemented by the NYPD, "broken windows" policing is not the rote and mindless "zero tolerance" approach that critics often contend it is. Case studies show that police vary their approach to quality-of-life crimes, from citation and arrest on one extreme to warnings and reminders on the other, depending on the circumstances of the offense. (p.1-2).

115   Compstat in known by many names throughout the policing industry. The New York City Police Department coined the term Compstat, which stands for COMPuter STATistics. Other terms include ComStat (Command Status in Newark), and FastTrack (formerly in Los Angles). For the challenges and opportunities arising from organizational change to support Compstat see Willis, Mastrofski, Weisburd, and Greenspan, 2003, and Willis, Mastrofski and Weisburd, 2003. Available at www.policefoundation.org.

116   Michael Hammer and James Champy (1993) define five ideals that characterize business re-engineering. An agency introducing Compstat will likely find these principles necessary to support the process:1) A focus on revolutionary, rather than evolutionary, approach—abandonment of "outdated" assumptions; 2) Dramatic Change–in the shape of the program, instead of less painful incremental improvements; 3) Radical Redesign–disregarding existing structures and inventing

new ways of accomplishing work; 4) Shift to process-oriented thinking–away from task based, and 5) Use of information/technology–as an enabler to allow organization to do work in a radically different way. In *Re-engineering the Corporation: A Manifesto for Business Revolution.* 1ˢᵗ ed. New York: Harper Business

117 Philadelphia Police Department. (2003). *The Compstat Process.* Retrieved on May 6, 2003, from http://www.ppdonline.org/ppd_compstat.htm.

118 McDonald, P.P. (2002) *Managing Police Operations: Implementing the New York Crime Control Model—Compstat.* p.8. See also John M. Bryson. (1995). *Strategic Planning for Public and Non-Profit Organizations: A Guide to Strengthening and Sustaining Organizational Achievement.* San Francisco: Jossey-Bass. p. 30; Bryson describes how to identify strategic issues, both internally and externally, that threaten the organization.

119 One of the most effective and efficient ways to determine what the strategic objectives should be is to undergo a simple environmental assessment (i.e., SWOT analysis: strengths, weaknesses, opportunities and threats). To learn about SWOT analysis see John M. Bryson. (1995). *Strategic Planning for Public and Non-Profit Organizations: A Guide to Strengthening and Sustaining Organizational Achievement.* San Francisco: Jossey-Bass; and Dr. Randy Garner. (2005, November). SWOT Tactics: Basics for Strategic Planning. FBI Law Enforcement Bulletin, Vol. 74, No. 11:17-19. Accessible at http://www.fbi.gov/publications/leb/leb.htm.

120 The definition of a particular crime differs between FBI-UCR and an individual state's criminal code. Most police departments investigate a crime based upon the state-provided definition offered in the criminal code. The FBI-UCR definition may differ significantly, therefore, for deployment and investigative purposes, the state's definition should supercede the administrative definition offered by UCR.

121 A wireless records management environment provides commanders access to current data that they would not be able to get from any other source. Real time data is dynamic information of events that concern the police; hard-copy Compstat reports are usually a week or more old, but, nonetheless, contain useful information for commanders. Used effectively, real time data enable commanders to become actively involved in their crime control efforts and to assume a leadership role while exploring trends and correlations, and identifying connections.

122 McDonald, P.P. (2002) *Managing Police Operations: Implementing the New York Crime Control Model—Compstat.* p.78-82.

123 Hale, C.D. (1981). *Police Patrol: Operations and Management.* New York: John Wiley and Sons. For further evaluation of the split-force patrol concept see James T. Nolan and Laurie Solomon. *An Alternative Approach in Police Patrol: The Wilmington Split-Force Experiment.* The Police Chief. 44 (November 1977), pp.58-64; James M. Tien et al. *An Evaluation Report of an Alternative Approach in Police Patrol: The Wilmington Split-Force Experiment.* Cambridge, Ma: Public System Evaluation, Inc.(1977).

124   The crime control officer (CCO) is a division/district-based position that monitors crime trends and patterns, on a daily basis. The CCO is responsible for advising the commander of conditions on a daily basis, capturing crime data, analyzing trends and patterns, and making recommendations on deployment strategies and tactics.

125   Some departments use a two week Compstat period with a one week overlap for all commands. The departments felt they were better able to gauge trends and emerging patterns than a one week analysis.

126   Paul and Patricia Brantingham have conducted work on the "geometry of crime" suggesting that ". . .each offender tends to be somewhat lazy, sticking close to known places and routes." In Marcus Felson, 1998, *Crime and Everyday Life*, 2nd ed. Thousand Oaks, Ca: Pine Forge Press-Sage Publications. p.58. See also P.J. Brantingham and P.L. Brantingham, 1991, *Environmental Criminology*. Prospect Heights, Il: Waveland; P.J. Brantingham and P.L. Brantingham, 1993, *Environment, Route and Situation: Toward a Pattern Theory of Crime*. In R.V. Clarke and M. Felson (Eds.), Routine Activity and Rational Choice: Advances in Criminological Theory, 5. New Brunswick, NJ: Transaction Books; P.J. Brantingham and P.L. Brantingham, 1995, *Criminality of Place: Crime Generators and Crime Attractors*. European Journal of Criminal Policy and Research, 3. p.5-26.

127   Ratcliffe, J.H. (2004). *The Hot-Spot Matrix: A framework for the spatio-temporal targeting of crime reduction*. Publication pending *Police Practice and Research, vol. 5*; unpublished paper presented at the 11th International Symposium on Environmental Criminology and Crime Analysis/ECCA, June 20th, 2003., Cincinnati, OH. Retrieved on June 26, 2003 from http://www.jratcliffe. net/conf/Ratcliffe%20(2004)%20Hotspot%20matrix%20final%20draft.pdf. Several articles are available from Jerry Ratcliffe's home page; visit http://www. jratcliffe.net for details.

128   "The Police Foundation is an independent and unique resource for policing. The Police Foundation acts as a catalyst for change and an advocate for new ideas, in restating and reminding ourselves about the fundamental purposes of policing, and in ensuring that an important link remains intact between the police and the public they serve." The Police Foundation can be reached at www.policefound ation.org. For additional crime mapping resources visit http://www.cslj.net/links/ CrimeMapping.htm.

129   To better manage spontaneous events, the Newark Police Department established a "24-hour rule." The "24-hour rule" states that a commander is not expected to answer for the 24-hour period immediately preceding Compstat. A shooting, for example, that occurred overnight, will not be part of the *regular* Compstat session; however, the commander must be able to answer basic questions about the incident, not the usual intimate details. When asked about an event within the last 24-hours, it is known as "breaking the 24-hour rule." If the Chief wishes to break the 24-hour rule, then it will usually come after the recap items. The rule exists so commanders are not surprised by questions that arise from a spontaneous event,

and because they have not had sufficient time before Compstat to explore the details.

130 There will generally be an overlap of data analysis with specialty commands (e.g., robbery, narcotics, homicide, auto crimes) who participate each week. The two-week interval gives commanders a better picture of trends and patterns than does just one week's worth of data.

131 Boundering is a questioning technique used by an interviewer to prevent an interviewee from straying from the subject matter being discussed. In Donald Schroeder, Frank Lombardo and Jerry Strollo. (1995). *Management and Supervision of Police Personnel.* Binghamton, NY: Gould Publications. p.133.

132 Philadelphia Police Department. (2003). *The Philadelphia Compstat Meetings.* Retrieved on May 6, 2003, from http://www.ppdonline.org/ppd_compstat.htm.

133 Linden, R.M. (2002).*Working Across Boundaries: Making Collaboration Work in Government and Nonprofit Organizations.* Jossey-Bass/John Wiley and Sons. Retrieved on June 1, 2003 from http://www.josseybass.com/WileyCDA/ Section/id-10980.html. For more information see http://www.baltimorecity. gov/news/citistat/.

134 Source: NYPD crime figures from the NYPD CompStat Unit for the week of April 21, 2003 through April 27, 2003; retrieved from http://www.nyc.gov/ html/nypd/pdf/chfdept/cscity.pdf, on May 6, 2003. Philadelphia, Baltimore and Newark crime figures retrieved from the FBI UCR from 1995 through 2001.

135 Definition verbatim from http://www.ojp.usdoj.gov/BJA/evaluation/glossary/ glossary_c.htm retrieved on May 25, 2006.

136 The dollar values for robbery, arson and burglary were derived from the 2004 FBI UCR, pp.34, 42, 47, 62. The dollar value for sexual assault was derived from Illinois Coalition Against Sexual Assault, "Economic Costs of Sexual Assault" in *By the Number: Sexual Violence Statistics* (April 2001), retrieved on May 25, 2006 from www.icasa.org/uploads/economic_costs.pdf. The dollar value for aggravated assault was derived from T.R. Miller and M.A. Cohen, 1997, *Costs of Gunshot and Cut/Stab Wounds in the United States, With Some Canadian Comparisons,* Accident Analysis Prevention, Vol. 29, No. 3:329-341, retrieved on May 25, 2006 from http://www.ncbi.nlm.nih.gov/entrez/query.fcgi?cmd=Retrieve &db=PubMed&list_uids=9183471&dopt=Abstract

137 Definition verbatim from http://www.ojp.usdoj.gov/BJA/evaluation/glossary/ glossary_c.htm retrieved on May 25, 2006.

138 Retrieved from http://www.fbi.gov/ucr/cius_04/offenses_reported/offense_tabula tions/table_01-01a.html on November 1, 2005. The murder and non-negligent homicides that occurred as a result of the events of September 11, 2001, are not included in the violent crime graph.

139   As of 2003 the U.S. led the world with a per capita incarceration of 686 per 100,000 (Adler, Mueller and Laufer, 2006:344). That figure rose about 7.5% to 737 per 100,000 U.S. residents by the end of 2005. "At year end 2005, 1 in every 136 U.S. residents was incarcerated in a State or Federal prison or a local jail" (Bureau of Justice Statistics, 2006:2; see NCJ# 215092)."Throwing cops" at a problem is akin to "generally applied intensive enforcement and arrest policies," which is one of the "five general types of strategies that have been prominent in the 'standard model of policing'…Despite the continued reliance of many police agencies on these standard practices, the [research] evidence…suggests that such approaches are generally not the most effective strategy for controlling crime and disorder or reducing fear of crime" (National Research Council, 2004:223-224). The five general types of strategies that comprise the standard model of police practices are:
1. "Increasing the size of the police agency
   2. Random patrol across all parts of the community
   3. Rapid response to calls for service
   4. Generally-applied follow-up investigations
   5. Generally applied intensive enforcement and arrest policies" (National Research Council, 2004:224).

140   Retrieved from http://www.nhtsa.gov/people/injury/enforce/aggressdrivers/aggen force/defined.html on May 17, 2006.

141   Definition verbatim from http://www.ojp.usdoj.gov/BJA/evaluation/glossary_c.htm retrieved on May 31, 2006.

142   Definition verbatim from http://www.ojp.usdoj.gov/BJA/evaluation/glossary_c.htm retrieved on May 25, 2006.

143   Definition verbatim from http://www.ojp.usdoj.gov/BJA/evaluation/glossary_c.htm retrieved on May 25, 2006.

144   Definition verbatim from U.S. Department of Justice, Bureau of Justice Assistance—Center for Program Evaluation. Retrieved from http://www.ojp.usdoj.gov/ BJA/evaluation/glossary/glossary_p.htm on My 8, 2006.

145   Definition verbatim from http://www.acjnet.org/docs/feardoj.html retrieved on May 21, 2006.

146   Retrieved from http://www.en.wilkipedia.org/wiki/Gridlock on May 17, 2006.

147   Definition verbatim from Centers for Disease Control, National Center For Chronic Disease Prevention and Health Promotion. Retrieved from http://www.nj. gov/tobacco/evaluation_manual/glossary.html on May 8, 2006.

148   Definition verbatim from http://www.nj.gov.lps/dcj/agguide/vehpurs_2001.pdf (p.4), retrieved on June 8, 2006.

149   For a related discussion see Scott H. Decker, 2005, *Using Offender Interviews to Inform Police Problem Solving,* Washington, D.C.: U.S. Department of Justice-COPS Office. Accessible at www.popcenter.org.

150 Verbatim from http://www.epa.gov/evaluate/glossary/p-esd.htm

151 Definition retrieved on May 20, 2006 verbatim from http://www.mydelraybeach. com/Delray/Departments/Environmental+Services/Quick+Links/Traffic+Calmin g.htm#002.

152 Definition verbatim from http://www.ojp.usdoj.gov/BJA/evaluation/glossary/ glossary_t.htm retrieved on May 22, 2006.

153 Definition verbatim from http://en.wikipedia.org/wiki/Validity_(statistics) retrieved on May 13, 2006.

154 The URL's were valid as of June 23, 2006. Several business plans are reprinted on the Resource CD for your convenience. All documents have been reprinted with permission from the respective agencies. All documents are owned and copyright protected by the respective agencies and may not be reproduced in any format or media without acquiring specific permission. The information is supplied without conferring any recommendation or endorsement of any product.

155 For a complete discussion and explanation of items 8.5.1 through 8.5.6 see Patrick O'Hara. (2005). *Why Law Enforcement Organizations Fail: Mapping the Organizational Fault Lines in Policing.* Durham, NC: Carolina Academic Press.

156 For more on SWOT and PEST analysis, see http://www.quickmba.com/stra tegy/pest/. For more on strategic planning see: Bradford, R.W., Duncan, P.J. and Tracy, B. (1999). *Simplified Strategic Planning: A No-nonsense Guide for Busy People Who Want Results Fast!* New York: Chandler House Press.